Archibald Forbes, Helmuth Moltke

The Franco-German War

of 1870-71

Archibald Forbes, Helmuth Moltke

The Franco-German War
of 1870-71

ISBN/EAN: 9783337845919

Printed in Europe, USA, Canada, Australia, Japan

Cover: Foto ©Andreas Hilbeck / pixelio.de

More available books at **www.hansebooks.com**

THE

FRANCO-GERMAN WAR

OF

1870-71

BY

FIELD-MARSHAL

COUNT HELMUTH VON MOLTKE

TRANSLATION REVISED BY

ARCHIBALD FORBES

WITH A MAP, NOTES, AND ORDERS OF BATTLE

LONDON

JAMES R. OSGOOD, McILVAINE & CO.

45, ALBEMARLE STREET, W.

1893

NOTE.

THE translation has been thoroughly revised for the sense as well as in regard to technical military terms and expressions. To the name of every German general officer mentioned in the text has been affixed, within brackets, his specific command, a liberty which the reader will perhaps not resent, since the interpolation is intended to facilitate his clearer understanding of a narrative condensed by the author with extreme severity.

In further aid of elucidation there has been occasionally inserted, also within brackets, a date, a figure, or a word.

A few footnotes will be found, which may perhaps be excused as not wholly irrelevant. In the Appendix have been inserted the " Orders of Battle " of both sides, as in the first period of the war.

A. F.

PREFACE.

FIELD-MARSHAL VON MOLTKE began this history of the War of 1870-1 in the spring of the year 1887, and during his residence at Creisau he worked at it for about three hours every morning. On his return to Berlin in the autumn of that year, the work was not quite finished, but he completed it by January, 1888, at Berlin, placed it in my hands, and never again alluded to the subject.

The origin of the book was as follows. I had several times entreated him, but in vain, to make use of his leisure hours at Creisau in noting down some of his rich store of reminiscences. He always objected, in the same words: "Everything official that I have had occasion to write, or that is worth remembering, is to be seen in the Archives of the Staff Corps. My personal experiences had better be buried with me." He had a dislike to memoirs in general, which he was at no pains to conceal, saying that they only served to gratify the writer's vanity, and often contributed to distort important historical events by the subjective views of an individual, and the intrusion of trivial details. It might easily happen that a particular character which in history stood forth in noble simplicity should be hideously disfigured by the narrative of some personal experiences, and the ideal halo which had surrounded it be destroyed. And highly characteristic of Moltke's magnanimity are the words he once uttered on such an occasion, and which I noted at the time: "Whatever is published in a military history is always dressed for effect: yet it is a duty of piety and patriotism never to impair the prestige which identifies the glory of our Army with personages of lofty position."

Not long after our arrival at Creisau, early in 1887, I repeated my suggestion. In reply to my request that he would write an account of the Campaign of 1870-1, he said: "You have the official history of the war. That contains everything. I admit," he added, "that it is too full of detail for the general type of readers, and far too technical. An abridgment must be made some day." I asked him whether he would allow me to lay the work on his table, and next morning he began the narrative contained in this volume, and comparing it as he went on with the official history, carried it through to the end.

His purpose was to give a concise account of the war. But, while keeping this in view, he involuntarily—as was unavoidable in his position—regarded the undertaking from his own standpoint as Chief of the General Staff, and marshalled results so as to agree as a whole with the plan of campaign which was known only to the higher military authorities. Thus this work, which was undertaken in all simplicity of purpose, as a popular history, is practically from beginning to end the expression of a private opinion of the war by the Field-Marshal himself.

The Appendix: "On a pretended Council of War in the Wars of William I. of Prussia," was written in 1881. In a book by Fedor von Koppen, "Männer und Thaten, vaterländische Balladen" (*Men and Deeds : Patriotic Songs*), which the poet presented to the Field-Marshal, there is a poem entitled, "*A German Council of War at Versailles*" (with a historical note appended), describing an incident which never occurred, and which, under the conditions by which the relations of the Chief of the Staff to his Majesty were regulated, never could have occurred. To preclude any such mistakes for the future, and to settle once and for all the truth as to the much-discussed question of the Council of War, the Field-Marshal wrote this paper, to which he added a description of his personal experi-

ence of the battle of Königgrätz.   It is this narrative
which, shortly after the writer's death, was published
in the *Allgemeine Zeitung* of Munich, in the somewhat
abridged and altered form in which the Field-Marshal
had placed it at the disposal of Professor von Treitscke,
the well-known historian.

COUNT HELMUTH VON MOLTKE,
Major and Adjutant to his
Imperial Majesty.

Berlin, June 25th, 1891.

CONTENTS.

PART I.

PART II.

CONTENTS.

APPENDIX.

THE FRANCO-GERMAN WAR.

PART I.

THE days are gone by when, for dynastical ends, small armies of professional soldiers went to war to conquer a city, or a province, and then sought winter quarters or made peace. The wars of the present day call whole nations to arms; there is scarcely a family that has not had to bewail lost ones. The entire financial resources of the State are appropriated to military purposes, and the seasons of the year have no influence on the unceasing progress of hostilities. As long as nations exist distinct one from the other there will be quarrels that can only be settled by force of arms; but, in the interests of humanity, it is to be hoped that wars will become the less frequent, as they become the more terrible.

Generally speaking, it is no longer the ambition of monarchs which endangers peace; but the impulses of a nation, its dissatisfaction with its internal conditions, the strife of parties and the intrigues of their leaders. A declaration of war, so serious in its consequences, is more easily carried by a large assembly, of which no one of the members bears the sole responsibility, than by a single individual, however lofty his position; and a peace-loving sovereign is less rare than a parliament composed of wise men. The great wars of recent times have been declared against the wish and will of the reigning powers. Now-a-days the Bourse possesses so great influence that it is able to have armies called into the field merely to protect its interests. Mexico

B

and Egypt have had European armies of occupation
inflicted upon them simply to satisfy the demands of
the *haute finance.* To-day the question is not so much
whether a nation is strong enough to make war, as
whether its Government is powerful enough to prevent
war. For example, united Germany has hitherto used
her strength only to maintain European peace ; while
the weakness of a neighbouring Government continues
to involve the gravest risk of war.

It was, indeed, from such a condition of relations
that the war of 1870-71 originated. A Napoleon on
the throne of France was bound to justify his preten-
sions by political and military successes. Only temporarily was the French nation contented by the victories
of its arms in remote fields of war ; the triumphs of
the Prussian armies excited jealousy, they were regarded
as arrogant, as a challenge ; and the French demanded
revenge for Sadowa. The liberal spirit of the epoch
set itself against the autocratic Government of the
Emperor ; he was forced to make concessions, his
internal authority was weakened, and one day the
nation was informed by its representatives that it
desired war with Germany.

PREPARATIONS FOR WAR.

The wars carried on by France beyond seas, essentially
on behalf of financial interests, had consumed immense
sums and had undermined the discipline of the army.
Her army was by no means in thorough preparedness
for a great war, but, in the temper of the nation, the
Spanish succession question furnished an opportune
pretext on which to go to war. The French Reserves
were called out on July 15th, and, as if the opportunity
for a rupture was on no account to be let slip, only

four days later the French declaration of war was presented at Berlin.

One Division of the French Army was ordered to
the Spanish frontier as a corps of observation; only
such troops as were absolutely necessary were left in
Algiers and in Civita Vecchia; Paris and Lyons were
sufficiently garrisoned. The entire remainder of the
army: 332 battalions, 220 squadrons, 924 guns, in all
about 300,000 men, formed the Army of the Rhine,
which, divided into eight Corps, was, at any rate in the
first instance, to be under the sole direction of a central
head. The Emperor himself was the fitting person to
undertake this weighty duty, pending whose arrival
Marshal Bazaine was to command the gathering forces.

It is very probable that the French reckoned on the
old dissensions of the German races. Not that they
dared to look forward to the South Germans as allies,
but they hoped to paralyze their offensive by an early
victory, perhaps even to win them over to their side.
It was true that Prussia by herself was still a mighty
antagonist, and that her armed forces were of superior
strength; but peradventure this advantage might be
counterbalanced by rapidity of action.

The French plan of campaign was indeed based on
the delivery of sudden unexpected attacks. The
powerful fleet of war-ships and transports was to be
utilized to land a considerable force in Northern
Prussia, which should there engage a part of the
Prussian troops, while the main body of the German
army, it was assumed, would await the first French
attack behind the strong defensive line of the Rhine.
A French force was to cross the Rhine promptly, at
and below Strasburg, thus avoiding the great German
fortresses; its function being, at the very outset of the
campaign, to cut off the South-German army charged
with the defence of the Black Forest, and prevent it
from effecting a junction with the North Germans.
In the execution of this plan it was imperative that the

main body of the French army should be massed in
Alsace. Railway accommodation, however, was so
inadequate that in the first instance it was only possible
to transport 100,000 men to Strasburg; 150,000 had to
leave the railway at Metz, and remain there till they
could be moved forward. Fifty thousand men in the
Châlons camp were intended to serve as supports, and
115 battalions were destined for field service as soon as
the National Guard should relieve them in the interior.
The various Corps were distributed as follows:—

Imperial Guard, General Bourbaki—Nancy.
Ist Corps, Marshal MacMahon—Strasburg.
IInd Corps, General Frossard—St. Avold.
IIIrd Corps, Marshal Bazaine—Metz.
IVth Corps, General Ladmirault—Thionville.
Vth Corps, General Failly—Bitsch.
VIth Corps, Marshal Canrobert—Châlons.
VIIth Corps, General Félix Douay—Belfort.

Thus while there were but two Corps in Alsace, there
were five on the Moselle; and, so early as the day of the
declaration of war, one of the latter, the IInd Corps,
had been pushed forward close to the German frontier,
about St. Avold and Forbach. General Frossard, its
commander, was, however, under strict injunctions to
commit himself to no serious undertaking.

The regiments had been hurried away from their
peace stations before the arrival of their complement of
men, and without waiting for their equipments. Meanwhile the called-out reservists accumulated in the
depôts, overflowed the railway stations and choked the
traffic. Their transmission to their destinations was at
a standstill, for it was often unknown at the depôts
where the regiments to which the reservists were to be
sent were for the time encamped. When at length
they joined they were destitute of the most necessary
articles of equipment. The Corps and Divisions lacked
trains, hospitals and nearly the whole of the *personnel*

of their administration. No magazines had been established in advance, and the troops were to depend on the stores in the fortresses. These were in a neglected state, for in the assured expectation that the armies would be almost immediately launched into the enemy's country they had received little attention. It was of a piece with this that the French Staff-officers had been provided with maps of Germany, but not of their own country. The Ministry of War in Paris was overwhelmed with claims, protestations, and expostulations, till finally it was left to the troops to help themselves as best they could. " *On se débrouillera,*" was the hope of the authorities.

When the Emperor arrived at Metz eight days after the declaration of war, the forces were not yet up to their strength, and even the precise whereabouts of whole bodies of troops was for the time unknown. He ordered the advance of the army, but his Marshals protested that its internal plight was so unsatisfactory as to make this impossible for the time. The general conviction was gradually impressing itself on the French, that instead of continuing to aim at invasion of the enemy's country, their exertions would have to be confined to the defence of their own territory. A strong German army was reported to be assembling between Mayence and Coblentz; and instead of reinforcements being sent forward from Metz to Strasburg, much heavier ones would have to be ordered from the Rhine to the Saar. The determination to invade South Germany was already abandoned; the fleet sailed, but without carrying a force to be landed on the north German coast.

Germany had been surprised by the declaration of war, but she was not unprepared. That was a possibility which had been foreseen.

After the withdrawal of Austria from the German connection, Prussia had taken upon itself the sole leadership, and had gradually formed closer relations with the South-German States. The idea of national

unification had been revived, and found an echo in the
patriotic sentiments of the entire people.

The mobilization machinery of the North-German
army had been elaborated from year to year, in accord
with the changing conditions, by the combined exertions
of the War Ministry and the General Staff. Every
branch of the administration throughout the country
had been kept informed of all it needed to know in this
relation. The Berlin authorities had also come to
a confidential understanding with the Chiefs of the
General Staffs of the South-German States on all
important points. The principle was established that
Prussian assistance was not to be reckoned on for the
defence of any particular point, such as the Black Forest;
and that South Germany would be best protected by an
offensive movement into Alsace from the middle Rhine,
to be effectively supported by a large army massed
there. That the Governments of Bavaria, Würtemberg,
Baden and Hesse, to all appearance uncovering their
own territories, were ready to place their contingents
under the command of King William, proved their
entire confidence in the Prussian leadership.

This understanding enabled the preparations which
it entailed to be proceeded with. The train and march
tables were worked out for each body of troops, with
the most minute directions as to the respective starting-
points, the day and hour of departure, the duration of
the journey, the refreshment stations, and points of
detrainment. In the locality of concentration cantonments were assigned to each Corps and Division, and
magazines were established with due regard to the most
convenient sites; and thus, when the stroke of war
inevitably impended, there was required only the Royal
signature to start the whole mighty movement in its
smooth, swift course. Nothing needed to be changed in
the directions originally given; it sufficed to follow the
plans previously thought out and prepared.

The aggregated mobile forces were formed into three

separate Armies, on the basis of an elaborate tabular statement drawn up by the Chief of the Prussian General Staff.

The Ist Army, under the command of General von Steinmetz, consisted of, in the first instance, only the VIIth and VIIIth Corps, with one Division of cavalry; 60,000 men all told. It was ordered to assemble at Wittlich and form the right wing.

The IInd Army, under the command of Prince Frederick Charles, consisted of the IIIrd, IVth, Xth, and Guard Corps, with two Divisions of cavalry. Assembling in the vicinity of Homburg and Neunkirchen, it was to form the centre, with a strength of 134,000 men.

The IIIrd Army, under the command of the Crown Prince of Prussia, consisted of the Vth and XIth Prussian, and the Ist and IInd Bavarian Corps, the Würtemberg and Baden Field Divisions, with one Division of cavalry. Its approximate strength was 130,000 men; it was to constitute the left wing, and to concentrate about Landau and Rastatt.

The IXth Corps, consisting of the 18th and the Hesse Divisions, was along with the XIIth Royal Saxon Corps to form a reserve of 60,000 men in front of Mayence, for the reinforcement of the IInd Army to a strength of 194,000 men.

The three Armies numbered together 384,000 men.

There still remained the Ist, IInd, and VIth Corps, numbering 100,000 men; but they were not at first included, as railway transport for them was not available for three weeks to come. The 17th Division and certain bodies of Landwehr troops were detailed to defend the coasts.

It is apparent that numerically the German armies were considerably superior to the French. Inclusive of the garrisons and reserves about one million of men and over 200,000 horses were on the ration list.

On the night of July 16th the Royal order for mobilization was issued, and when his Majesty

arrived in Mayence fourteen days later, he found
300,000 men assembled on the Rhine and beyond.

The plan of campaign submitted by the Chief of
the General Staff, and accepted by the King, proves
that officer to have had his eye fixed, from the first,
upon the capture of the enemy's capital, the possession of which is of more importance in France than in
other countries. On the way thither the hostile forces
were to be driven as persistently as possible back from
the fertile southern provinces into the more confined
background to the north. But beyond everything the
plan of campaign was based on the resolve to attack the
enemy at once, wherever found, and keep the German
forces always so compact that this could be done
with the advantage of superior numbers. The specific
dispositions for the accomplishment of those objects
were left to be adopted on the spot ; the advance to the
frontier was alone pre-arranged in every detail.

It is a delusion to imagine that a plan of campaign
can be laid down far ahead and fulfilled with exacti-
tude. The first collision with the enemy creates a new
situation in accordance with its result. Some things
intended will have become impracticable ; others, which
originally seemed impossible, become feasible. All
that the leader of an army can do is to form a correct
estimate of the circumstances, to decide for the best for
the moment, and carry out his purpose unflinchingly.

The advance of the French troops to the frontier,
while as yet imperfectly mobilized, which was an extremely hazardous measure in itself, was evidently with
the intent of utilizing the temporary advantage of
having a superior force at immediate disposition by
taking at unawares the German armies in the act of
developing their advance-movements. But, notwithstanding, the German commanders did not deviate
from their purpose of promptly effecting this first
advance in front of the Rhine. The railway transport
of the Corps of the IInd and IIIrd Armies, however,

ended at the Rhine; thence the troops marched on foot into the cantonments prepared on the left bank of the river. They moved in echelon, advancing only so many at a time as would make room for the body in rear, in the first instance to the line Bingen-Dürkheim-Landau. The farther advance towards the frontier was not to be undertaken until the Divisions and Corps were all assembled, and provided with the necessary trains; and then they were to march forward in a state of readiness to confront the enemy at any moment.

The massing of the Ist Army appeared to be less threatened, because its route was protected by neutral territory, and was covered by the garrisons of Trèves, Saarlouis and Saarbrücken, the German outposts on the Saar.

The Ist Army, 50,000 strong, was concentrated at Wadern, in the first days of August. The IInd Army, which meanwhile had been increased to a strength of 194,000 men, had pushed forward its cantonments to Alsenz-Günnstadt, at the farther base of the Haardt Mountains, a position which had been thoroughly inspected by an officer of the General Staff, and where the troops might confidently await an attack. The 5th and 6th cavalry Divisions were reconnoitring the country in front. The IIIrd Army was still assembling on both banks of the Rhine.

The French so far had made no serious attempt at Saarbrücken; Lieutenant-Colonel Pestel, with one battalion and three squadrons, was able successfully to withstand their petty attacks. It had meanwhile been observed that the hostile forces were moving farther to the right, towards Forbach and Bitsch. This seemed to indicate that the two French Corps known to be about Belfort and Strasburg, might purpose crossing the Rhine and marching through the Black Forest. It seemed therefore all the more important that the IIIrd Army should be set in motion as early as possible, for one

thing to protect the right bank of the Upper Rhine by
an advance on the left; for another, to cover the left
flank of the IInd Army during its advance.

A telegraphic order to that effect was despatched
on the evening of July 30th, but the Head-quarters of
the IIIrd Army wished to wait for the arrival of the
VIth Corps and of the trains.   Whereupon, regardless of this delay, the IInd Army was put in march
towards the Saar, where the French were beginning
to be active.

The time had gone by when they might have taken
advantage of their over-hasty mobilization ; the inefficient condition of the troops had paralyzed every
attempt at activity.   France had been long waiting
for the news of a victory, and something had to be done
to appease public impatience.   So, in order to do something, it was resolved (as is usual in such circumstances)
to undertake a reconnoissance in force, and, it may be
added, with the usual result.

On August 2nd three entire Army Corps were set
in motion against three battalions, four squadrons, and
one battery in Saarbrücken.   The Emperor himself and
the Prince Imperial shared in the enterprise.   The
IIIrd Corps advanced on Völklingen, the Vth through
Saargemünd, the IInd on Saarbrücken.

Saarbrücken was evacuated after a gallant defence
and repeated counter-strokes, but the French did not
press across the Saar ; convinced, possibly, that they had
wasted their strength in a stroke in the air, and had
nowhere gained any insight into the dispositions of the
enemy.

The French military chiefs now hesitated for a long
while between conflicting resolutions.   Orders were
given and recalled on the   strength of mere rumours.   The left wing was reinforced because 40,000
Prussians were supposed to have marched through
Trèves, the Guard received contradictory orders, and
the bare apparition of a small German force about

Lörrach in the Black Forest occasioned the order that the VIIth Corps must remain in Alsace. Thus the French forces were straggled over the wide area between the Nied and the Upper Rhine, while the Germans were advancing in compact masses towards the Saar.

This scattered state of their forces finally induced the French leaders to divide them into two separate Armies. Marshal MacMahon took command, but only provisionally, of the Ist, VIIth, and Vth Corps, of which the latter had therefore to draw in to him from Bitsch. The other Corps remained under Marshal Bazaine, with the exception of the Imperial Guard, the command of which the Emperor reserved to himself.

It had now become a pressing necessity to protect the left wing of the advancing IInd German Army against the French forces in Alsace, and the IIIrd Army was therefore ordered to cross the frontier on August 4th, without waiting any longer for its trains. The Ist Army, forming the right wing, was in complete readiness near Wadern and Losheim, three or four days' march nearer to the Saar than the IInd Army in the centre. It received the order to concentrate in the neighbourhood of Tholey and there halt for the present. For one thing, this army, the weakest of the three, could not be exposed single-handed to an encounter with the enemy's main force ; and for another, it was available to serve as an offensive flank in case the IInd Army should meet the enemy on emerging from the forest zone of the Palatinate.

In the execution of this order, the Ist Army had so extended its cantonments southward that they trenched on the line of march of the IInd Army, and it had to evacuate the quarters about Ottweiler in favour of the latter. This involved a difficulty, as all the villages to the north were full, and as room had also to be found for the Ist Corps, now advancing by Birkenfeld. General von Steinmetz therefore decided to march his whole

army in the direction of Saarlouis and Saarbrücken.
The IInd Army, on August 4th, stood assembled ready
for action, and received orders to deploy on the farther
side of the forest zone of Kaiserslautern.

COMBAT OF WEISSENBURG.

(August 4th.)

On this day the Corps of the IIIrd Army, consisting of 128 battalions, 102 squadrons, and 80 batteries,
which had been assembled in bivouac behind the Klings-
bach, crossed the French frontier, marching on a broad
front to reach the Lauter between Weissenburg and
Lauterburg.   This stream affords an exceptionally
strong defensive position, but on August 4th only one
weak Division and a cavalry brigade of the Ist French
Corps covered this point, the main body of that Corps
being still on the march towards the Palatinate.

Early in the morning the Bavarians forming the
right wing encountered a lively resistance before
the walls of Weissenburg, which were too strong to be
stormed.   But very soon after the two Prussian Corps
crossed the Lauter lower down.   General von Bose
led forward the XIth Corps (which he commanded)
with intent to turn the French right flank on the
Geisberg, while General von Kirchbach, with the Vth
Corps (which he commanded) advanced against the
enemy's front.   Thirty field-guns were meanwhile
massed against the railway station of Weissenburg.
It and subsequently the town were taken, after a bloody
struggle.

So early as ten o'clock General Douay had ordered a
retreat, which was seriously threatened by the movement against the Geisburg; and the château of that
name, a very defensible building, was most obstinately
defended to enable the French to retire.   The Grena-

diers of the King's Regiment No. 7 in vain assailed it by storm, suffering heavy loss; nor did its defenders surrender until, with the greatest difficulty, artillery had been dragged up on to the height.

The French Division, which had been attacked by three German Corps, effected a retreat after an obstinate struggle, though in great disorder, having suffered much loss. Its gallant Commander had been killed. The Germans had to bewail a proportionately considerable loss; their casualties were 91 officers and 1460 men. General von Kirchbach had been wounded while fighting in the foremost rank.

The 4th Division of cavalry had met with much delay in the course of a nineteen miles' march by the crossing of the columns of infantry. It did not reach the scene of combat, and all touch of the enemy, now retiring to the westward, was lost.

Uncertain as to the direction whence fresh hostile forces might be approaching, the IIIrd Army advanced on the 5th of August by diverging roads in the direction of Hagenau and Reichshofen; yet not so far apart but that it should be possible for the Corps to reconcentrate in one short march. The Crown Prince intended to allow his troops a rest on the following day, so as to have them fresh for a renewed attack as soon as the situation was made clear.

But already, that same evening, the Bavarians on the right flank and the Vth Corps in the front had a sharp encounter with the enemy, who showed behind the Sauer in considerable strength. It was to be assumed that Marshal MacMahon had brought up the VIIth Corps from Strasburg, but it remained a question whether he intended to join Marshal Bazaine by way of Bitsch, or whether, having secured his line of retreat thither, he meant to accept battle at Wörth. Yet again there was the possibility that he might himself initiate the offensive. The Crown Prince, to make sure in any case of a preponderance of force, determined

to concentrate his army in the neighbourhood of Sulz
on August 6th. The IInd Bavarian Corps received
separate instructions to watch the road from Bitsch with
one Division; the other Division was to strike the hostile
attack in flank on the western bank of the Sauer, in
the event of artillery fire about Wörth being heard.

Marshal MacMahon was endeavouring with all his
might to concentrate his three Corps, and he really had
the intention to make an immediate attack on his
invading foe. A Division of the VIIth Corps, which
had but just been sent to Mülhausen to strengthen the
defence of Alsace, was at once recalled to Hagenau,
and early on the 6th formed the right wing of the
strong position which the Ist Corps had taken up behind the Sauer, and in front of Fröschwiller, Elsasshausen, and Eberbach. On the left, Lespart's Division
of the Vth Corps was expected from Bitsch, of which
the other Divisions were only now on march from
Saargemünd by way of Rohrbach. Meanwhile Ducrot's
Division formed a refused flank on the French left.

Neither the German nor the French leaders expected
the collision before the following day, but when, as in
this case, the adversaries are in so close proximity, the
conflict may break out at any moment, even against
the wish of the higher commanders.

BATTLE OF WÖRTH.

(August 6th.)

After a good deal of skirmishing between the respective outposts during the night, the Commander of
the 20th German Brigade [1] thought it expedient to seize

---

[1] General Walther von Montbary. It is Molkte's custom throughout this work, except in regard to his prime aversion, Prince
Frederick Charles, to refrain from naming an officer whom by im-
plication he is censuring, but this is simply a *nuance*, since he
specifies the culprit's military position.

a passage over the Sauer, which flowed just in his front and constituted a serious obstacle. The bridge leading to Wörth had been destroyed, but the sharpshooters waded through the river, and at seven o'clock pressed into the town, which the French had left unoccupied.

Soon enough they realized that before them was a numerous enemy in a strong position.

The broad meadows of the Sauer all lie within effective range of the commanding slopes on the right bank; and the long-ranging chassepôt fire could not but tell heavily. On the French side of the river the terrain was dotted with vineyards and hop-gardens, which afforded great advantages for defensive purposes.

The combat which had begun at Wörth was broken off after lasting half an hour, but the artillery of both sides had taken part in it, and the sound of cannon-fire had been the signal prescribed to Hartmann's IInd Bavarian Corps, acting on which it now advanced from Langensulzbach, and was soon engaged in a brisk fight with the left flank of the French. The latter on their side had advanced on their right to the attack of Gunstett, where they came in contact with the advancing XIth Prussian Corps.

The din of battle, rolling from the north and south alike, was heard by the Vth Corps in its position opposite to Wörth; and it seemed imperative that it should engage with vigour the enemy's centre in order to hinder him from throwing himself with all his strength on one or other of the German flanks.

The artillery was brought up, and by ten o'clock 108 guns were in action on the eastern slope of the Sauer valley.

Some infantry detachments waded breast-high through the river, but this dashing attempt, undertaken in inadequate strength, miscarried, and it was only by strenuous efforts that a foothold was maintained on the other side.

The Crown Prince sent orders that nothing was to be undertaken that would bring on a battle on that day. But by this time the Vth Corps was so seriously engaged that the fight could not be broken off without obvious disadvantage. General von Kirchbach therefore determined to continue the contest on his own responsibility.

The frontal attack was an undertaking of great difficulty, and could scarcely succeed unless with the co-operation of another on the flank. But at this juncture the Bavarians, who, in position as they were on the right, could have afforded this co-operation, obeyed the breaking off command, which had also reached them in the course of the fighting, and withdrew to Langensulzbach. There was, however, the XIth Corps in position on the left, eager to strike in. It seized the Albrechts-häuser farm, and pressed forward into the Niederwald.

In front of Wörth the battle hung, consisting of a succession of attacks renewed again and again on either side; each assailant in turn getting worsted, in consequence of the nature of the country. By degrees, however, the collective battalions, and finally the artillery of the Vth Corps, were brought over to the west bank of the Sauer; while the XIth Corps had already won there a firm point of support for further advance.

Just then, near Morsbronn, notwithstanding the evident unfavourable nature of the ground, two Cuirassier and one Lancer regiments of Michel's brigade hurled themselves with reckless daring on a body of German infantry taken in the act of wheeling to the right. But the 32nd Regiment, far from seeking cover, received in open order the charging mass of over 1000 horse with a steady fire which did great execution. The Cuirassiers especially suffered immense loss. Only a few horsemen broke through the firing line and gained the open ground; many were taken prisoners in the village, the remainder rode

in wild gallop as far as Walburg. There they encountered the Prussian 13th Hussars, suffered further
loss, and disappeared from the field.

It is true that the infantry of the French right
wing succeeded in driving back the foremost detachments of the Germans about Albrechts-häuser farm,
but the further advance of the former was shattered by
the fire of newly-unmasked artillery.

When finally the last battalions had crossed the
Sauer, the XIth Corps made its way through the
Niederwald, fighting its way step by step. The
northern edge of the forest was reached by 2.30, and
there a junction was formed with the left flank of the
Vth Corps. The burning village of Elsasshausen was
carried by storm, and the little copse south of Fröschwiller was also won after a gallant defence.

Thus crowded together in a limited space, the French
army was in a situation of imminent danger. Its left
flank, it is true, still held out against the renewed attack
of the Bavarians, who had re-entered the action,
but its front and right flank were terribly hard
pressed, and even its retreat was seriously threatened.
Marshal MacMahon therefore tried to obtain a
breathing space by a heavy counter-stroke to the
south. The weak German detachments standing to
the east of Elsasshausen, thrown into confusion by
the vehement attack, were in part driven back into
the Niederwald, but were quickly rallied and brought
up again. Here the French cavalry strove once
more to change the fortunes of the day. Bonne-
main's Division, notwithstanding the unfavourable
nature of the ground, threw itself on the dishevelled
front of the enemy, suffered terrible losses, and was
shattered without having been able effectively to
charge home.

The Württembergers now came up from the south,
and the Bavarians from the north. General von Bose,
though twice wounded, led what of his troops he

C

could collect to the storm of the burning Fröschwiller, the enemy's last stronghold. The artillery moved up within case-shot range, and thus cleared the road for the infantry which was pushing forward from all sides. After maintaining to the utmost a resolute and gallant resistance until five o'clock, the French retreated in great disorder towards Reichshofen and Niederbronn.

At the Falkenstein stream, Lespart's Division, just arrived on the field, made a short stand, but these fresh troops offered only brief resistance, and were swept away in the general rout.

This victory of the IIIrd Army had been dearly paid for with the loss of 489 officers and 10,000 men. The loss on the French side is not exactly known, but of prisoners alone they left 200 officers and 9000 men, and in the German hands there remained 33 guns and 2000 horses.

The disintegration of the French army must have been so complete as to throw it altogether out of hand. Only one brigade of Lespart's Division took the road by Bitsch to join the French main army at St. Avold; all the rest of the army, following an infectious impulse, rolled unhaltingly in a south-western direction towards Saverne.

As in the Head-quarter of the IIIrd Army it had not been intended to fight on August 6th, the 4th Division of cavalry had not left its quarters in the rear, and was therefore not available to take up the pursuit; it did not reach Gunstett until nine o'clock in the evening. But, in order to be at hand at any rate for the next day, Prince Albert marched his command on during the night as far as Eberbach; after three hours' rest he started again, and after covering thirty-six miles,[1] came up in the evening with the rearguard of the enemy near Steinberg, at the foot of the Vosges. Without infantry it would have been impossible for the

---

[1] Throughout the miles are English miles.

Division to push farther, but the sight of it gave the enemy a fresh impulse of flight. The Ist Corps stampeded again in the night and reached Saarburg, where it joined the Vth Corps. Thus the French had a start of twenty-three and a half miles, and continued their retreat on Luneville, unmolested by the Germans.

BATTLE OF SPICHEREN.

(August 6th.)

Let us now turn to the events which occurred, on this same 6th of August, in another part of the theatre of war.

The IInd Army, its southern (left) flank covered by the IIIrd Army, had been moving to the westward, while the Corps it still lacked were being brought up by railway. Its leading Corps, having traversed unmolested the long defiles of the forest-belt of Kaiserslautern, reached on the 5th the line Neunkirchen—Zweibrücken. The cavalry, scouting into French territory, reported that the enemy was retreating. Everything seemed to indicate that the French would await the attack of the Germans in a strong defensive position. The nearest position of the kind that offered was that on the farther bank of the Moselle, of which Metz protected one flank, Thionville the other. It was decided that if the French were found in that position, the Ist Army should hold the enemy in front, while the IInd made a circuit south of Metz, and so the enemy be forced either to retire or to fight. In case of disaster the IInd Army was to fall back on the IIIrd, now advancing over the Vosges.

The protrusion to the south-westward[1] of the Ist Army towards the Saar, which had not been intended by the

---

[1] South-eastward.

supreme Command, had brought its left wing in upon the
line of march laid down for the IInd, and detachments of
the two armies had to cross each other at Saarbrücken
on the 6th.   Thus there was indeed no lack of strength
at that point; but as a battle on that day was neither
expected nor probable, the synchronous arrival of
troops had not been pre-arranged, and so detachments
could only come up by quite unprescribed routes and
arrive one after the other at different hours.

The 14th Division of the VIIth Corps was the first
to reach Saarbrücken, towards noon on the 6th.

General Frossard, considering his position there very
hazardous, had left the night before, without waiting
for permission, and had fallen back with the IInd Corps
on Spicheren, where it had entrenched itself.   The
IIIrd, IVth, and Vth Corps were behind, at distances of
from nine to nineteen miles, and the Imperial Guard
was about twenty-three miles rearward.   The Emperor,
therefore, had it in his power to collect five Corps for a
battle in the vicinity of Cocheren, or, on the other
hand, to support Frossard with at least four Divisions,
if that General were confident that his position was
strong enough to hold.

The range of heights which upheaves itself immediately behind Saarbrücken is capable of affording a
serious obstacle to a hostile passage of the Saar.   It
was known that the French had evacuated those
heights, but General von Kameke thought it prudent
to seize them at once, in order to secure the debouche
of the columns following him.   When, in the forenoon,
two squadrons of the 5th Cavalry Division showed
themselves on the drill-ground on the ridge above the
farther bank, they were greeted with a hot fire from
the Spicheren heights.   But as it seemed highly probable, from the previous behaviour of the French, that
the force seen there was only the rear-guard of the
retiring enemy, General von Kameke (commanding
14th Infantry Division) ordered an immediate attack,

since he had the promise of reinforcements. General von Zastrow (commanding VIIth Corps), as soon as he recognized that the 14th Division had involved itself in a serious engagement, allowed the 13th to go forward. General von Alvensleben (its commander) also ordered up to Saarbrücken all the available troops of the IIIrd Corps, and with equal promptitude General von Goeben (commanding VIIIth Corps) hurried thither the entire 16th Division. Generals von Döring (commanding 9th Infantry Brigade) and von Barnekow (commanding 16th Infantry Division), belonging respectively to these two Corps (IIIrd and VIIIth), had besides already struck forward from Tudweiler and Fischbach in the direction of the cannon-thunder, even before receiving orders to that effect.

The position occupied by the French was one of exceptional advantage. In the centre projected the Red Hill (der Rothe Berg), a precipitous and almost inaccessible cliff; and the steep slopes on either side were densely wooded. On the left the massive buildings of the Stiering-Wendel ironworks furnished a separate defensive position.

Had the strength of the enemy been fully known the attack would certainly have been delayed until the whole of the 14th Division had arrived. As a matter of fact, at the beginning of the fight, about noon, only von François' Brigade (27th) had come up, and this force, in the effort to facilitate an attack on the naturally strong position held by the enemy's front, assailed in the first instance both his flanks.

At first it succeeded in making progress. On the left the 39th Regiment drove the swarms of hostile skirmishers out of the wood of Gifert, but then became exposed to the bitter fire of a French battalion lining the farther side of a deep hollow. On the right flank its 3rd Battalion, together with the 74th Regiment, seized the wood of Stiering. But the enemy's superior strength soon displayed itself in violent counter-attacks,

and when Von Woyna's[1] Brigade (28th) reached the
field it had to furnish reinforcements to both flanks.
Thus, at an early stage, intermingling of battalions and
companies began, which increased with every subsequent rush, and made the control of the combat a
matter of extraordinary difficulty. Added to this was
the circumstance that three Commanding Generals in
succession came up to the scene of the conflict, and one
after the other took the chief control.

At about one o'clock, simultaneously with the
flanks, the Fusilier Battalion of the 74th Regiment
pushed forward in front, under a severe fire across
the open ground towards the Red Hill, and, under such
trivial cover as offered, established itself at the foot
of the cliff. When at about three o'clock the Prussian artillery compelled the foe to move his guns
farther up the hill, the Fusiliers, with General von
François at their head, began to climb the cliff. The
French Chasseurs, evidently taken by surprise, were
driven from the most advanced entrenchments with
clubbed rifles and at the point of the bayonet. The
9th company of the 39th Regiment followed close, and
the gallant General, charging farther forward along
with it, fell pierced by five bullets. Nothing daunted,
the small body of Fusiliers made good its grip of the
narrow spur of the cliff.

Nevertheless, a crisis was imminent. The 14th
Division was extended over a distance of about three
and a half miles, its left wing had been repulsed by
greatly superior forces in the wood of Gifert, its right
wing was hard pressed at Stiering. But now, at four
o'clock, the heads of the 5th and 16th Divisions simultaneously struck in, shortly after their batteries, which
had been sent on ahead, had come into action.

The left wing, strongly reinforced, now again pressed
forward. General von Barnekow[2] led trusty succours

---

[1] There were two Major-Generals of this name, both commanding
Brigades; one the 28th, VIIth Corps, the other 39th, Xth Corps.
[2] Commanding 16th Division, VIIIth Corps.

up on to the Red Hill, where the Fusiliers had almost entirely exhausted their ammunition, and drove the French out from all their entrenchments. As the result of a fierce struggle the Germans also succeeded in taking possession of the western part of the wood of Gifert. The right wing with sharp fighting had pressed on to Alt Stiering and was approaching the enemy's line of retreat, the Forbach highway. General Frossard had, however, recognized the danger threatened at this point, and reinforced his left wing to the strength of a Division and a half. This force advanced to the attack at five o'clock. On the German side there was no formed force to oppose to it, so all the previously gained advantages were lost.

If the 13th Division [1] had here struck in with a resolute attack, the battle would have ended. This Division after, indeed, a march of nearly nineteen miles had reached Puttlingen at one o'clock, where it was little more than four miles distant from Stiering. When the fighting about Saarbrücken was heard it is true that at four p.m. the advanced guard moved forward to Rossel. It would seem that the roar of the cannon was not audible in that wooded region; the impression was that the combat was over, and the Division bivouacked at Völkingen, which place had been previously named as the end of its march by the Corps Commander at a time when he was, of course, unable to foresee the change in the situation.

The French offensive movement had meanwhile been brought to a stand by the seven batteries in position on the Folster height; the infantry then succeeded in making fresh progress, under the personal leadership of General von Zastrow.

The nature of the ground entirely prohibited the twenty-nine squadrons of cavalry which had arrived from all directions and were drawn up out of the range of fire, from taking part in the action. The Hussars tried in vain to ride up the Red Hill, but in spite of

[1] Commanded by General Glümen.

incredible difficulties Major von Lyncker finally gained the summit with eight guns, amid the loud cheering of the hard-pressed infantry. The guns, as each one came up, at once came into action against three French batteries ; but quite half of the gunners were shot down by sheltered French tirailleurs, at a range of about 800 paces. A small strip of ground in front was indeed won, but the narrow space allowed of no deployment against the wide front of the enemy.

But effective assistance was coming from the right. General von Goeben had despatched all the battalions of the 16th Division not yet engaged, in the decisive direction toward Stiering. While one part of these troops made a frontal attack on the village, the rest climbed from the high-road up the defiles of the Spicheren woods, in a hand-to-hand encounter drove the French from the saddle leading to the Red Hill, and pushed them farther and farther back towards the Forbach height.

Even as late as seven o'clock on the French right wing Laveaucoupet's Division, supported by part of Bataille's, advanced to the attack and once more penetrated into the oft-contested Gifert wood, but the danger threatening the French left wing from the Spicheren wood paralyzed this effort. By nightfall the French were falling back over the whole plateau.

At nine o'clock, when their "Retreat" call was sounding from the heights, General von Schwerin (commanding 10th Infantry Brigade) made sure of night quarters by occupying Stiering, where resistance was only quelled, at many points, after a hand-to-hand fight. The advanced guard of the 13th Division advanced on Forbach, but did not occupy it, having allowed itself to be hoodwinked by some French Dragoons in possession.

Apart from this, General Frossard had abandoned the line of retreat by the so seriously threatened Forbach-St. Avold road, and fell back with all his three divisions on Oetingen. The darkness, and the impossibility of handling large bodies of cavalry in such a country, saved him from further pursuit.

General von Steinmetz ordered the re-organization of the dislocated bodies of troops that same night. Some of them had marched more than twenty-eight miles ; two batteries, arriving from Königsberg by rail, had immediately set out for the battle-field. But it remains that the Germans at no time of the day attained the numerical strength of the enemy in this engagement, which had been begun with insufficient forces. Only thirteen batteries could be brought into action in the limited space, and the cavalry remained excluded from all participation. It was only natural, under the circumstances, that the losses of the assailants were greater than those of the defence. The Prussians lost 4871, the French 4078 men. The fact was significant that a considerable number of unwounded French prisoners were taken in this early action.

In strong contrast to the comradeship and mutual helpfulness displayed by the Prussian Generals, and the eagerness of their troops to hurry into the fight, was the strange vacillation of the Divisions in General Frossard's rear ; of which three, indeed, were sent forward to his support, but only two came up, and that when the fight was already ended.

It has been vehemently asserted that the battle of Spicheren was fought in an ill-judged locality, and that it interfered with more important plans. It certainly had not been anticipated. But, generally speaking, a tactical victory rarely fails to fit in with a strategic design. Success in battle has always been thankfully accepted, and turned to account. By the battle of Spicheren the IInd French Corps was prevented from withdrawing unharmed ; touch of the enemy's main force was obtained, and to the supreme Direction of the armies was afforded a basis for further resolutions.

RIGHT WHEEL OF THE GERMAN ARMY.

Marshal MacMahon in his retreat had taken a
direction which entirely severed his touch with Marshal
Bazaine.

As he was not pursued, he could have used the Lune-
ville-Metz railway to effect his union with the French
main army; for up to the 9th it was still open. But
rumour had it that the Prussians had already appeared
in Pont à Mousson, and the state of his troops did not
permit him thus early to risk another engagement.

His Ist Corps, therefore, marched southwards on
Neufchâteau, whence Châlons could be reached by railway. The Vth Corps was being shifted to and fro by
contradictory orders from the Emperor's head-quarters.
First it was to proceed to Nancy, then to take an
opposite direction towards Langres. On arriving at
Charmes it was ordered to Toul, but from Chaumont it
was finally directed to proceed to Châlons. General
Trochu had there located the newly-formed XIIth
Corps, and behind this gathering point the VIIth Corps
also managed to get away from Alsace and reach Rheims
by rail by way of Bar sur Aube and Paris.

Thus by August 22nd a Reserve Army was formed,
consisting of four Corps and two Cavalry Divisions,
under the command of Marshal MacMahon, who, however, at a distance, as he was, of about 120 miles,
was unable to render timely assistance to Marshal
Bazaine, who stood directly in the line of the advancing
enemy.

When the news of the double disaster of August 6th
reached the Imperial Head-quarter, the first impression there was that it would be necessary to retreat
immediately on Châlons with Bazaine's army; and the
VIth Corps, a portion of which was already being
transported thence to Metz, was ordered to retrace its
steps. But this resolution was presently retracted.
The Emperor had not merely to consider the foreign

enemy, but public opinion within his own realm.   The sacrifice of entire provinces at the very beginning of a war which had been undertaken with such high anticipations, would have provoked the unbounded indignation of the French people.   There were still 200,000 men who could be brought together in front of the Moselle, supported by a large fortress, and though the enemy would still have the superiority in numbers, his army was holding a line nearly sixty miles long. It had yet to cross the Moselle, and this would necessitate a dislocation which might create a weakness at the critical moment.

In the IIIrd German Army the disorderly condition of the defeated enemy was not known, nor even the direction of his retreat.   It was expected that MacMahon's Army would be found rallied on the farther side of the Vosges for renewed resistance ; and as it was impossible to cross the mountains except in detached columns, the German advance was very cautious, and by short marches only.   Though the distance between Reichshofen and the Saar is not more than about twenty-eight miles in a straight line, that river was only reached in five days.   Nothing was seen of the enemy, except in the fortified places, small indeed, but too strong to be taken by storm, which command the highways in the mountains.   Bitsch had to be avoided by a fatiguing circuit, Lichtenberg was captured by surprise, Lützelstein had been abandoned by its garrison, the investment of Pfalzburg was handed over to the approaching VIth Corps, and Marsal capitulated after a short resistance.

The German left wing had no enemy before it, and could be brought into closer connection with the centre. To bring the three armies abreast of each other a wheel to the right was requisite.   The advance of the Ist and IInd Armies had, however, to be delayed, as the IIIrd did not reach the Saar until August 12th.   The whole movement was so arranged that the IIIrd Army was to

use the roads by Saarunion and Dieuze, and to southward ; the IInd those by St. Avold and Noményand to
southward ; the Ist those by Saarlouis and Les Etangs,
the last also taking the direction of Metz.

The cavalry Divisions which were reconnoitring far
to the front, reported the enemy as retreating all along
the line. They ranged close up to Metz, and across
the Moselle both above and below the place, forcing
the detachments of Canrobert's Corps, which had again
been ordered up from Châlons, to return thither. All
their information indicated that very large masses were
encamped in front of Metz. From this it might equally
be inferred that the enemy intended to retreat further,
or, with his whole force concentrated, to strike hard at
the right wing of the German Army, at the moment
when the impending crossing of the Moselle should
make its severance from the left wing unavoidable.

The chief Head-quarter restricted itself in ordinary
course to issuing general directions, the execution of
which was left in detail to the army commanders ; but
in this instance it was deemed necessary in the
momentary circumstances to regulate the movements of
each separate corps by specific orders. On August
11th the Head-quarter of his Majesty was therefore
transferred to St. Avold, in the front line, and midway
between the Ist and IInd Armies, so as, by being in
the immediate vicinity, to be able to exercise timely
authority to either hand. The three Corps of the Ist
Army advanced towards the German Nied on August
12th, only to find that the French had evacuated that
position. Three Corps of the IInd Army on the left of
the Ist also moved forward in prolongation of the same
front by Faulquemont and Morhange, while two others
followed.

On the next day the IInd Army reached the Seille,
without encountering the enemy, and occupied Pont à
Mousson with infantry.

The strangely inactive attitude of the French made
it seem quite probable that they might not make any

stand in front of Metz, a probability strengthened by the reports of the German cavalry, which was scouting as far as Toul and on to the Verdun road.   But there always loomed the possibility that the enemy would throw himself with 200 battalions on the Ist Army, now in his immediate front.   The two Corps forming the right wing of the IInd Army were, therefore ordered to halt for the present, a little to the south of Metz, ready to deliver a shattering blow on the flank of any such attack.   If the enemy preferred to assail these Corps, then would devolve on the Ist Army on its part the prompt assumption of the offensive.

Meanwhile the other Corps of the IInd Army were pursuing the march towards the Moselle farther to the southward ; if the enemy should attack them with superior forces after they had crossed the river, it would be possible for them, in case of need, to fall back on the IIIrd Army.

So much caution was not universally deemed essential ; it was argued that the French seemed already committed to full retreat, they ought not to be allowed to get away without punishment, and it followed that the German Army should strike without delay.   The French had, indeed, already committeed themselves to a further retreat ; but when in the after-noon (of the 14th) the VIIth Corps discerned their retro-grade movement, a fight began on the hither side of the Moselle, which, by the voluntary intervention of the nearest bodies of troops, developed into a battle in the course of the evening.

BATTLE OF COLOMBEY—NOUILLY.

(August 14th.)

The Commandant of Metz had declared his inability to hold that place for a fortnight, if left to his own resources ; but the chosen and intrenched position on the Nied, taken up to cover the fortress, had been found locally defective, and the French Head-quarter hoped to find a more favourable defensive position in the vicinity of Verdun.

Military necessity outweighed even a politic regard for public opinion, and the Emperor, although he had transferred the command-in-chief to Marshal Bazaine, still remained with the army, for it would have been impossible for him to return to Paris in existing circumstances.

Very early in the morning of the 14th August the multitudinous trains were being withdrawn through the city, and towards noon the IInd, IVth, and VIth Corps got in motion, while the IIIrd Corps remained in position behind the deep valley of the Colombey brook, to cover the retirement.

When, at four in the afternoon, the break-up of the enemy was perceived, General von der Goltz (commanding 26th Infantry Brigade) with the advanced guard of the VIIth Corps struck him in the act, and wrenched from him Colombey and the Château d'Aubigny on his right flank. But, at the first cannon sound, the French columns immediately turned about, fully equipped for fighting, and eager, after their many previous disasters, to break the spell by a desperate effort. Castagny's Division threw itself in greatly superior force upon the weak German detachment in the isolated position of Colombey, which held its own only by the utmost exertion.

Already the advanced guard of the Ist Army Corps was approaching by both the high-roads from Saarbrücken and Saarlouis; and its batteries having pushed on ahead, at once took part in the engagement. Passing through Lauvallier, the infantry followed close, climbed the eastern slope of the plateau of Bellecroix, and farther to the right drove the enemy out of the wood east of Mey. But the presence at this point of the main body of the French IIIrd Corps gave pause to the German offensive for the time.

The 13th, 1st, and 2nd Divisions had meanwhile followed their respective advanced guards, the two latter having been held in full readiness by General von Manteuffel ever since his outposts had reported that the enemy was moving. General von Zastrow, too, arrived on the field, and took over the command of the left wing. Soon sixty field-pieces were in action against the enemy. General von Osten-Sacken hurried forward the 25th Brigade through the hollow of Coincy, and climbed on to the edge of the upland. The clump of fir-trees on the road to Bellecroix was taken by storm, was surrounded on three sides, was lost again in a bloody conflict, and was once more recaptured. Soon afterwards two batteries succeeded in establishing themselves above Planchette, whose fire drove the French back as far as Borny; yet still the conflict raged on both sides with the utmost fury.

But now there threatened the German right the danger of being out-flanked. General Ladmirault, on learning that Grenier's Division had been driven out of Mey, immediately set out to its support with his other two Divisions, retook the village, and pressed farther forward by the Bouzonville road. General von Manteuffel had meanwhile given the necessary orders for holding, at all hazards, the deep-cut trough of the Vallières brook which covered the flank. The 1st Brigade was posted behind Noisseville as general reserve, the 4th, and part of the artillery of the Ist Corps, marched by the Bouzonville road to confront General Ladmirault near Poix, while the remaining batteries from the southern slopes to the eastward of Nouilly enfiladed his advance. On the left, Glümer's Division (13th) had all this time been holding its ground at Colombey, and now, at seven o'clock in the evening, Woyna's Brigade came to its assistance, and took possession of the copses westward of Colombey. A very welcome reinforcement now arrived from the IInd Army remaining halted on the Seille.

The 18th Infantry Division, after a heavy march, had bivouacked near Buchy in the afternoon, but when General von Wrangel (its commander) was informed that fighting was audible from the locality of the Ist Army, he promptly set his Division in motion in that direction. He drove the enemy out of Peltre, and then in conjunction with Woyna's Brigade occupied Grigy, somewhat in rear of the French position in front of Borny.

On the right wing of the fighting line, the 2nd Division had also pushed on towards Mey, by way of Nouilly and through the adjacent vineyards; and, as darkness was setting in, that village and the adjoining woods were wrenched from the enemy. The French had not advanced beyond Villers l'Orme, and they now withdrew all along their line from that village to Grigy. The Prussians, as they followed up after dark, were molested only by the fire of the heavy guns of the forts, more especially Fort St. Julien.

The engagement of August 14th cost them the heavy loss of 5000 men, inclusive of 200 officers; while the French lost only 3600 men, their IIIrd Corps being the heaviest sufferer. The vicinity of a great fortress of course prevented the reaping of the fruits of victory by an immediate pursuit. It was for the same reason that a battle on the part of the Ist Army on that day had not been included in the concerted plan of action, though the possibility of such an occurrence had been foreseen. Although it was true that but one Division of the IInd Army (the 18th) had been able to hasten to the aid of the Ist, and that after the late opening of the fight, its assault on the left [1] flank of the enemy had not failed of its effect.

The manner in which the battle originated rendered unity of direction impossible.

It was but the advanced-guards of four Divisions which were the troops principally engaged; and the

[1] Clearly should be "right."

daring attacks made on greatly superior hostile forces by small bodies unfollowed by immediate supports occasioned many critical moments, which might have been dangerous if the enemy had pushed forward more energetically in closely concentrated strength. But while, for instance, his IIIrd Corps received no support from the Imperial Guard standing close behind it, the contrast presented itself that on the Prussian side, in this as in the previous battles, there shone forth, along with their ready acceptance of personal responsibility, the eager mutual helpfulness of all the commanders within reach of the battle-field.

An essential share of the success of the day must be attributed to the artillery. Hurrying along in front, leaving the responsibility of covering it to the advanced guards which reached forward before the main bodies of the Divisions had time to come up, it drove the French completely out of their positions before Metz, and back under the guns of the defences of the place.

The protection so afforded to the enemy rendered it impossible that the victory of Colombey-Nouilly should yield any trophies, but the supreme Command was quite content with the results obtained. The retreat of the enemy had been arrested, and a day had been gained for the crossing of the Moselle by the IInd and IIIrd Armies.

August 15*th.*—In the early morning of the 15th the cavalry had ridden forward to the outworks of Metz, but found none of the enemy on this side of the fortress. A few shells scared away the Imperial Head-quarter from Longeville on the further side of the Moselle.

As King William was riding over to visit the Ist Army, immense clouds of dust were observed rising on the further side of the fortress; and it was no longer doubtful that the French had begun their retreat, and that the IInd Army was henceforth free to follow across the Moselle with all its Corps.

D

The Ist Corps of the Ist Army was necessarily left at
Courcelles, south of Metz, to protect the railway, the
other two were brought up left-ward towards the Seille ;
and they were also by-and-by to cross the Moselle higher
up, so as to avoid interference from the fortress.

The French had started again on the retreat interrupted on the previous day, but proceeded little more
than four miles [1] beyond Metz on August 15th. Their
cavalry only went somewhat farther ahead, by both the
roads to Verdun.

The IIIrd Corps of the German IInd Army crossed
the Moselle at Novéant, by the bridge which was found
intact, and by a flying pontoon bridge ; its artillery,
however, was forced to make a détour by Pont à Mousson.

It was not until late at night that the troops were
all across and in bivouac close to the left bank. One
Division of the Xth Corps remained at Pont à Mousson
and the other advanced to Thiaucourt. The cavalry
scouted farther forward towards the Metz-Verdun
road, and struck in on the French cavalry near Mars la
Tour. Several small engagements took place, but
when early in the afternoon twenty-four Prussian
squadrons had assembled, the French retired on Vionville. The Guard Corps and the IVth Corps crossed at
Dieulouard and Marbache, higher up the river.

The IIIrd Army advanced to the line Nancy-
Bayon. On this day an attempt to seize the fortress of
Thionville by surprise proved a failure.

BATTLE OF VIONVILLE—MARS LA TOUR.

(August 16th.)

In the Head-quarter of the IInd Army there was the
belief that serious fighting with the French was no

---

[1] On the night of 15th, four of Bazaine's five Corps (less one
Division) bivouacked at distances of from eight to ten miles westward
of Metz ; viz., from beyond Rezonville rearward to Gravelotte.

more to be anticipated on the Moselle, and therefore two Corps, the IIIrd and the Xth, were ordered to march on August 16th, northwards toward the road to Verdun by way of Gorze and Thiaucourt, while the other Corps were directed to advance by forced marches westwards towards the Meuse.

The French retreat from Metz was, however, not completely effected on this day. The trains blocked every road, and in the forenoon three Divisions still remained behind in the Moselle valley. The Emperor, however, escorted by two brigades of cavalry, had departed at an early hour by the road through Etain, which was still comparatively safe. As the right wing of the army could not yet follow, the prosecution of the retreat was postponed until the afternoon, and the left wing, which had already begun the march, was sent back again into its bivouacs. But so early as nine o'clock Prussian shells startled the troops from their rest.

Major Körber had advanced with four batteries close up to Vionville under cover of the cavalry, and the French troopers, surprised by their fire, fled in utter confusion through the camp of the infantry. The latter, however, briskly got under arms in good order, and the artillery opened a heavy fire. Destitute at first of infantry supports, the Prussian guns were withdrawn. Matters soon became serious.

General von Alvensleben, fearing lest he should fail to overtake the enemy, had started again with the IIIrd Corps after a short night's rest. The 6th Division marched on the left, by Onville; the 5th, on the right, followed the long forest valley on the way to Gorze. This valley so capable of defence was found unoccupied by the enemy, who indeed had taken very few precautions. The advanced-guard presently encountered Bergés' French Division on the open plateau south of Flavigny, and General von Stülpnagel (commanding 5th Infantry Division) soon discovered that he had before

him an enemy whom it would take all his strength to
beat.   At ten o'clock he began operations by sending
forward the 10th Brigade (commanded by General von
Schwerin) ; and opened fire with twenty-four guns.

Both sides now assumed the offensive. The Prussians, on the right, fought their way with varying
fortunes through the wood, often in hand-to-hand
encounter, and, towards eleven o'clock, succeeded in
reaching the spur of the wood of St. Arnould projecting
in the direction of Flavigny.   Their left wing, on the
contrary, was repulsed ; even the artillery was in
danger ; but the 52nd Regiment hurried forward and
re-established the fight at the cost of bloody sacrifices.
Its 1st Battalion lost every one of its officers, the
colours passed from hand to hand as its bearers were
successively shot down, and the commander of the 9th
Brigade, General von Döring, fell mortally wounded.
General von Stülpnagel rode up into the foremost line
of fire, inspiriting the men with brave words, while
General von Schwerin collected the remnants of troops
bereft of their leaders, and, reinforced by a detachment of the Xth Corps from Novéant, carried the height
in front of Flavigny, whence the French presently
retired.

On the assumption that the French were already pro-
secuting the retreat, the 6th Division had been ordered
forward towards Etain by way of Mars la Tour, to bar
the enemy also from the northern road to Verdun. When
it reached the height of Tronville, whence could be seen
how things really stood, the brigades wheeled to the
right in the direction of Vionville and Flavigny.   The
artillery going on in advance, formed a formidable line
of batteries, the fire of which prepared the way for a
farther advance, and by half-past eleven the 11th Brigade had taken possession of Vionville in spite of heavy
losses.   From thence, and from the south, in conjunction with the 10th Brigade, an attack was then directed
on Flavigny, which had been set on fire by shell-fire.

The different detachments were hereabouts very much mixed, but by skilfully taking advantage of every fold of the ground, the individual regimental officers succeeded in getting their men steadily forward, in spite of the heavy fire of the hostile infantry and artillery. Flavigny was taken by assault, and one cannon and a number of prisoners fell into the hands of the brave Brandenburgers.

Vionville, Flavigny and the northern end of the forest of St. Arnould constituted the points of support of the Prussian front now facing to the east; but this front was more than four miles long, and the whole infantry and artillery were engaged up to the hilt all in one line. The second line consisted only of the 5th and 6th Cavalry Divisions and half of the 37th Brigade near Tronville.

The position of the French was one of great advantage. Their left flank leaned on Metz, their right was protected by formidable batteries on the old Roman road and a strong force of cavalry; and so they could await with confidence a frontal attack on the part of a venturesome enemy.

The possibility of continuing the march to Verdun on this day, under the protection of a strong covering rearguard, was, no doubt, out of the question. Supposing the Marshal earnest above everything to effect his retreat, he could do so only by fighting hard for his right of way, and by so freeing himself from the enemy blocking his path.

It is not easy to discern, from a purely military standpoint, why this course was not resorted to. There was the full certainty that only part, and probably only a small part, of the German host could as yet have reached the left side of the Moselle, and when in the course of the day the Divisions detained about Metz arrived, the French had greatly the superiority in strength. But it seems that the Marshal's chief solicitude was lest he should be forced to relinquish his touch of Metz; and he gave almost his whole attention to his left wing. Constantly sending fresh reinforcements thither, he massed the whole Guard Corps and part of the VIth Corps opposite the Bois des Ognons, whence an attack was exceptionally improbable. One is tempted to assume that political reasons alone thus early actuated Bazaine in his resolve to cling to Metz.

Meanwhile the Prussians slowly but surely made their way beyond Flavigny and Vionville, and, assisted by a heavy fire from the artillery, compelled the right wing of the IInd French Corps to retire on Rezonville, a movement which became a flight when the French Generals Bataille and Valazé were killed.

To regain the lost ground the French Guard Cuirassier Regiment threw itself resolutely on the pursuers. But its attack was cut short by the rapid fire of two companies of the 52nd Regiment drawn up in line, which reserved their fire till the enemy were within 250 paces. The horsemen sweeping right and left rushed into the fire of more infantry behind; 243 horses strewed the field, and only the remnants of the regiment wheeled about in swift flight, pursued by two Hussar regiments which had dashed forward from Flavigny. A French battery in front of Rezonville had hardly time to discharge a few shots before it was surrounded. For want of teams the Prussians could not, indeed, carry off the captured guns; but the Commander-in-Chief of the French army, who had himself brought them up, was for several minutes in imminent danger of being taken prisoner.

The 6th Prussian Cavalry Division had also been ordered to the front. After passing through the line of artillery and deploying as well as the limited space permitted, it found itself face to face with fresh and completely formed troops. Marshal Bazaine had taken the precaution of substituting for the routed bodies of the IInd Corps the Guard Grenadier Division, which he had at last prevailed on himself to bring up from his unengaged left wing, but not without filling the vacancy by a Division of the IIIrd Corps. Thus the Prussian cavalry was received with such an overwhelming musketry and artillery fire that it halted, and deliberately retired, its retreat being covered by two squadrons of Uhlans, which time after time showed a front against the enemy. The cavalry had not actually engaged, but its advance had gained time and opportunity for the artillery to move further forward in one line from the spur of the wood to Flavigny.

It was now two o'clock. So far General von Alvensleben had deceived the enemy with regard to the slenderness of his force by acting incessantly on the offensive. But the battle was now at a standstill, the battalions were visibly thinned, their strength was sapped by four hours of hard fighting, and the ammunition of the infantry was almost exhausted. Not a battalion, not a battery remained in reserve behind the fighting line standing there in the fire. It was now required to conserve the success won with so much blood by acting thenceforth on the defensive.

The left wing was in especial danger, being under the fire of the powerful artillery deployed on the Roman road. Their greatly superior numbers enabled the French to extend farther and farther to the right, threatening thus completely to envelop the Prussian flank.

Marshal Canrobert, in the French centre, had discerned the right moment to press forward against Vionville with all his might. At this critical instant there was on the German side only a small detachment of the 5th Cavalry Division available to check this effort. Two brigades had necessarily been sent to strengthen the left flank, and of the 12th Brigade remaining in rear of Vionville two squadrons had been detached to the Tronville copses. The two regiments ordered to undertake the task of charging the advancing enemy—

the Magdeburg Cuirassiers and the Altmark Uhlans—were consequently each but three squadrons strong, in all 800 horses.

General von Bredow, commanding the 12th Cavalry Brigade, first traversed in column the shallow hollow sinking down from Vionville, then wheeled to the right and mounted the slope to the eastward, both his regiments on one front. Received immediately with heavy artillery and infantry fire, he threw himself on the hostile ranks. The first line is ridden over, the line of guns is broken through, gunners and teams are put to the sword. The second French line is powerless to resist this vigorous onslaught, and even the more distant batteries limbered up to drive away.

But the rapture of victory and the impetuosity of the charge carried the handful of troopers too far, and after a gallop of 3000 paces they found themselves surrounded by the French cavalry, which attacked them from all sides. There was no scope for a second charge, and so after several encounters with the French horse the brigade was forced to cut its way back through the French infantry, whose bullets accompanied it home. Only one-half of the command returned to Flavigny, where it was re-organized into two squadrons. The devoted self-sacrifice of the two heroic regiments effected the result, that the French entirely discontinued their attack on Vionville.

At three o'clock four of their Divisions advanced towards the Tronville copses. Barby's cavalry brigade (11th), watching the western verge, had to retire before the enemy's fire, and the German infantry occupying the wood also had to yield to a strength so superior; the batteries which were in action between Vionville and the copses were assailed in rear from the west through the glades of the copses, and were likewise forced to retire. But not until the lapse of an hour did the French succeed in overcoming the obstinate resistance of four staunch battalions.

At the subsequent roll-call near Tronville, it was

ascertained that the 24th Regiment had lost 1000 men and 52 officers, and that the 2nd Battalion of the 20th Regiment had lost all its officers.   The 37th demi-Brigade, which of its own accord had been fighting valiantly in support since noon, took possession of the village of Tronville and prepared it for an obstinate defence.

It was not till after three that the IIIrd Corps, which had been fighting for seven [1] hours almost single-handed, received effective assistance.

While the Xth Corps was on the march through Thiaucourt, its advanced guard heard cannon-fire from the direction of Vionville.   The Corps Commander, General von Voigts-Rhetz, immediately set out for the battle-field, and having personally ascertained how matters stood, he sent back the requisite orders to his approaching troops.

In this instance again it was the artillery which, hurrying on in advance, masterfully struck into the conflict.   Its fire, in conjunction with that of the promptly further advancing batteries of the IIIrd Corps, checked the French rush made on both sides of the Tronville copses simultaneously.   At half-past three the head of von Woyna's Brigade (39th) fell on, drove the enemy back into the wood, and finally, supported by Diringshofen's Brigade (40th), took possession of its northern outskirts.

The right wing of the IIIrd Corps had also received some reinforcement.

The 32nd Brigade of the VIIIth Corps, on being called upon to assist the 5th Division, fatigued though it was by a long march, immediately advanced from the Moselle by Arry.   The 11th Regiment joined it, and three batteries were sent ahead to commence operations ; this force emerged at five o'clock from the forest of St. Arnould.   It at once made an assault on the heights in front of Maison Blanche, but, though it

---

[1] Five; viz. from 10 a.m. to 3 p.m.

made three strenuous efforts in succession, failed to carry them, since Marshal Bazaine had greatly strengthened his position in front of Rezonville. Then the French, in their turn, took the offensive there ; but were equally unable to establish themselves firmly on the heights, swept as they were by the well-directed fire of the Prussian artillery; and they had to withdraw from the attempt. Petty struggles for this position were renewed later on both sides, but those spurts came to nothing because of the fire of the respective artillery ; and the fighting on the German right became in the main stationary.

That on the German left two French Divisions had retired before a few newly-arrived battalions, and had evacuated the Tronville copses, can only be explained by a report having reached Bazaine's head-quarters that the enemy was coming in upon his right flank in the vicinity of Hannonville.

The enemy referred to was Wedell's Brigade (38th), which, while on the march in the direction of Etain according to its original orders, had received counter-instructions while halted at St. Hilaire at noon, to hurry to the field of battle. General von Schwartz-koppen (commanding 19th Infantry Division) decided to march by the highway to Mars la Tour, in the hope of falling on the enemy either in flank or in rear. But the French meanwhile had extended their reinforced right wing to the sunken valley west of Bruville, where three Divisions of their cavalry were massed in position.

Thus when General von Wedell advanced to the attack on both sides of Tronville, which the French themselves had fired, his brigade—only five battalions strong—found itself in face of the long deployed front of the 4th French Corps. The two Westphalian regiments advanced steadily under the storm of shell and mitrailleuse fire till they suddenly reached the edge of a deep ravine hitherto unseen. This, however, they soon traversed, and were climbing the farther ascent, when they were met by a murderous shower

of bullets from the French infantry which hemmed
them in closely on every side. After almost every
one of the commanders and regimental officers had
fallen, the wreck of the battalions fell back into the
ravine ; 300 men were taken prisoners, having no
strength left to ascend the steep southern rise after
the fatigue of a twenty-eight miles march.` The re-
mainder rallied at Tronville under the shot-torn colours
which Colonel von Cranach, the only officer who still had
a horse under him, had brought back in his own hand.
Seventy-two officers and 2542 men were missing
out of 95 officers and 4546 men—more than half.
The French followed up their success, but were checked
on the right by the headlong charge of the 1st Guard
Dragoons, which cost that regiment 250 horses and nearly
all its officers ; and on the left by the 4th squadron of the
2nd Guard Dragoons, which attacked three times its
strength of Chasseurs d'Afrique.

But there now imminently threatened the charge of
a great mass of French cavalry, which disclosed itself
on the open plateau of Ville sur Yron.   This consisted
of Legrand's Division and de France's Guard Brigade in
four compact echelons, overlapping each other to the
right.   On the German side, all the still disposable
cavalry joined Barby's brigade, and the body thus made
up, consisting only of sixteen squadrons, was formed for
action in two lines west of Mars la Tour.   Farther in
advance stood the 13th Dragoons, halted to receive the
Guard-squadron on its return from its recent charge.
The 13th galloped forward to meet the charge of
Montaigu's Hussar Brigade, which constituted the first
line of the French cavalry mass, and which broke
through the (over-wide) intervals of the Prussian
squadrons.   But General von Barby promptly appeared
with the other regiments on the upland of Ville sur
Yron, where at a quarter to seven the cavalry masses
came into collision.

A mighty cloud of dust concealed the varying phases
of the hand-to-hand encounter of 5000 horsemen which

gradually declared itself in favour of the Prussians. General Montaigu, severely wounded, was taken prisoner, and General Legrand fell while leading his Dragoons to the assistance of the Hussars.

De France's Brigade allowed the enemy to approach within 150 paces, and then its Lancer regiment rushed impetuously upon the Hanoverian Uhlans; but the latter outflanked it, and received unexpected assistance from the 5th squadron of the 2nd Guard Dragoons, which, returning from a reconnaissance, plunged forward over fences and ditches and fell upon the enemy in flank, while the Westphalian Cuirassiers at the same time broke his front. The Chasseurs d'Afrique strove in vain to hinder the enveloping tactics of the Hanoverian Dragoons; the clouds of dust drifted farther and farther northward, and the whole mass of French horse drew away towards the wooded slopes of Bruville, behind which there were still five regiments of Clérembault's Cavalry Division. Clérembault permitted one of his brigades to cross the valley, but the fleeing Hussars and some misunderstood signals threw it into confusion. It was borne back, and not until the French infantry confronted the Prussian pursuers in the covering valley did the latter desist from the pursuit.

The Prussian regiments quietly re-formed and then withdrew at a walk to Mars la Tour, followed at a great distance by part of Clérembault's Division.

This, the greatest cavalry combat of the war, had the effect of making the French right wing give up all further attempts to act on the offensive. The Germans mourned the loss of many superior officers, who always, at the head of their men, had set them a glorious example.

Prince Frederick Charles had hastened to the field of battle. The day was nearly at an end, darkness approaching, and the battle won. The Prussians in the evening stood on the ground which in the morning had been occupied by the French. Though General von Alvensleben had in the first instance been under the

impression that he would have only the French rear-
guard to deal with, he did not hesitate for a moment to
become the assailant when he found the entire French
Army before him. With his single Corps he maintained the fight till the afternoon, and drove back the
enemy from Flavigny to Rezonville, a distance of more
than two miles. This was one of the most brilliant
achievements of all the war.

Thanks to the valuable assistance of the Xth Corps it
was possible to carry on the battle through the afternoon on the defensive, but only by most resolute
counter-attacks by the cavalry, and by the unflinching
tenacity of the artillery.

It was clearly most unadvisable to challenge by renewed attacks an enemy who still outnumbered the
Germans; which action, since no further reinforcements
could be hoped for, could not but jeopardize the success
so dearly bought. The troops were exhausted, most
of their ammunition was spent, the horses had been
under the saddle for fifteen hours without fodder; some
of the batteries could only move at a walk, and the
nearest Army Corps on the left bank of the Moselle,
the XIIth,[1] was distant more than a day's march.

Notwithstanding all these considerations, an order
from Prince Frederick Charles's Head-quarter issued
at seven o'clock, commanded a renewed and general
attack on the enemy's positions. The Xth Corps was
quite incapable of answering this demand; and only
part of the artillery went forward on the right followed
by some infantry. The batteries indeed reached the
much-disputed plateau south of Rezonville, but only
to be exposed on two sides to the fire of infantry

[1] The Hessian Division of the IXth Corps was on the left bank,
much nearer the field than the XIIth—so near indeed that portions
of it were actually engaged; and its other Division crossed the river
in the night. The *Staff History* assigns the proximity of the IXth
Corps as a leading reason for the action of Prince Frederick Charles
which Moltke denounces. Both the VIIth and VIIIth Corps (the
latter of which had a brigade engaged in the battle) were more
immediately available than the distant XIIth.

and artillery. Fifty-four guns of the French Guard
alone, in position on the farther side of the valley, were
taking them in flank. The Prussian batteries were
compelled to retreat to their previous position, but
two brigades of the 6th Cavalry Division still pressed
forward. Scarcely able to discern in the increasing
darkness where lay their proper line of attack, they
came under very sharp infantry fire, and withdrew with
great loss.

Fighting did not entirely cease until ten o'clock. On
either side 16,000 men had fallen. On either side pursuit was out of the question. The Germans reaped the
fruits of this victory solely in its results. The troops,
worn out by a twelve hours' struggle, bivouacked on
the victorious but bloody field, immediately opposite
the French position.

Those Corps of the IInd Army which had not taken
part in the battle, were on that day on march towards
the Meuse. The advanced guard of the IVth Corps on
the left wing was heading towards Toul. This fortress,
commanding a railway-line of importance to the further
progress of the German Army, was reported to be but
feebly held, and it was resolved to attempt its capture
by a *coup de main*. But the bombardment of it by
field-artillery proved quite ineffective. Bastions of
masonry and wide wet ditches made a storm impossible. An attempt to batter down the gates by shot
and thus gain an entrance proved a failure. Finally
the undertaking was given up, and not without some
loss on the part of the Germans.

At the Royal Head-quarter in Pont à Mousson it
had become known by about noon on the 16th that the
IIIrd Corps was engaged in serious conflict, and that
the Xth and IXth were hastening up to its support.
The far-reaching consequences of this information were
recognized at once.

The French were arrested in their withdrawal from
Metz, but it was to be presumed as a certainty that

they would again make strenuous efforts to force open their interrupted line of retreat. The XIIth Corps was therefore ordered to set out for Mars la Tour as early as three o'clock next morning; the VIIth and VIIIth Corps to stand in readiness at Corny and Arry. The bridging operations were to be pushed with the utmost vigour during the night. The Head-quarter of the IInd Army sent from Gorze the order to the Guard Corps to make a forced march to Mars la Tour, and there take up a position on the left of the XIIth Corps. The execution of these orders was facilitated by the foresight of the Commanders, who had in the course of the day received news of the battle which was being fought. Prince George of Saxony at once placed his Division on the march to Thiaucourt, and the Prince of Würtemberg assembled the Infantry of the Guard in its cantonments farther northward in readiness for an early march.

August 17th.—On this morning, at sunrise, the French outposts were observed still occupying the sweep of front from Bruville to Rezonville. Behind them were noticed a stir and much noise of signalling, which might be the indications equally of an attack or of a retirement.

The King arrived from Pont à Mousson at Flavigny as early as six o'clock. The reports sent in to head-quarters until noon by the reconnoitring cavalry were somewhat contradictory; they left it uncertain whether the French were concentrating towards Metz, or were pursuing their retreat by the two still open roads through Etain and Briey. Preparations for the offensive were nowhere observed. By one o'clock, after a skirmish on the way, the head of the VIIth Corps had reached the northern skirt of the Bois des Ognons, over against which the French subsequently abandoned Gravelotte. The VIIIth Corps stood ready at Gorze, the IXth, IIIrd, and Xth remained in their positions, the XIIth and the Guard Corps were on the march. Seven Corps and three

Cavalry Divisions could be counted on for the following day ; for to-day all attacks were forbidden.

In making the dispositions for the impending battle of August 18th, two possible contingencies were foreseen and had to be provided for. To meet both the left wing was to be sent forward in a northerly direction through Doncourt towards the nearest of the routes still open for the retreat of the French. If the enemy were already retiring, he was to be at once attacked and detained while the right wing was hurrying up in support.

In case the enemy should be remaining about Metz, the German left wing was to swing eastwards and outflank his farthest north position, while the right was to hold his left closely engaged until this movement was accomplished. The battle, under these circumstances, probably could not be decided until late in the day, owing to the wide-sweeping movement of a portion of the army. A peculiar feature of the situation was that both parties had to fight with inverted front, and sacrifice for the time their respective lines of communication. The consequences of victory or defeat would thus be greatly enhanced or aggravated, but the French had the advantage of having as their base a large place of arms with its resources.

A decision having been arrived at, by two o'clock orders were published at Flavigny for an advance by echelons from the left wing. The guidance of individual Corps during the battle was to turn on the reports which should be brought in. The King then returned to Pont à Mousson.

As early as nine o'clock in the morning the Saxon Cavalry Division had reached the Etain road to the west of Conflans, and had reported no enemy visible except a few stragglers. Still, this only proved that on the 17th the French had not yet taken up their retreat.

In rear of its cavalry the XIIth Corps arrived

during the day in the vicinity of Mars la Tour and Puxieux, and left of it the Guard bivouacked in the evening at Hannonville sur Yron, in accordance with order. The IInd Corps, which ever since it left the railway had followed close on the IInd Army, reached Pont a Mousson, and was ordered to march forward by Buxières at four next morning.

BATTLE OF GRAVELOTTE—ST. PRIVAT.

(August 18th.)

Marshal Bazaine had not thought it advisable to prosecute the march to Verdun now that the Germans were so close on the flank of such a movement. He preferred to concentrate his forces near Metz, in a position which he rightly considered as almost impregnable.

Such an one was afforded him by the range of heights stretching along the western verge of the valley of Chatel. Their face looking toward the enemy sloped away like a glacis, while the short and steep decline in the rear afforded cover for the reserves. Along the flat crown of the heights from Roncourt to Rozerieulles, a distance of about seven miles, were posted the VIth, IVth, IIIrd, and IInd Corps in succession from the north; for which distance there were available from eight to ten men to the pace (Schritt). A brigade of the Vth Corps stood near Ste. Ruffine in the valley of the Moselle; the cavalry was in rear of both flanks. In front of the IInd and IIIrd Corps shelter-trenches had been thrown up, battery emplacements and covered ways of communication constructed, and the farmsteads lying out to the front converted into little forts. To approach this (left) wing from the west it was necessary to cross the deep ravine of the Mance. The VIth Corps on the other hand was wholly without

E

an engineer park; and it is indicative of the general
ill-equipment of the French that, for the transport of
the wounded to the rear, in spite of the enormous
trains, provision waggons had to be unloaded and their
contents burnt.   This Corps was therefore unable to
construct fortified flank defences toward the forest of
Jaumont, such as would have given to the right wing
the character of formidable strength.   This would un-
doubtedly have been the place for the Guard, but in
his apprehension of an attack from the south the
Marshal held that Corps in reserve at Plappeville.

The King returned to Flavigny at six o'clock on the
morning of the 18th.   All commanding officers were instructed to send their reports thither, and officers of the
General Staff belonging to the Royal Head-quarter
were besides sent out in different directions to report
information as to the progress of the engagement.

The following were the initial dispositions.   The
VIIth Army Corps, which was to form the pivot for
the eventual wheel to the right, occupied the Bois de
Vaux and Bois des Ognons; the VIIIth, which the
King had reserved at his own disposition, stood halted
near Rezonville ready to march to the north or to the
east, as might be required.   The IXth Corps, on its
left, advanced towards St. Marcel, while the IIIrd and
Xth followed in second line.   The Guard and XIIth
Corps moved in a northerly direction.

In consequence of the Head-quarter of the IInd
Army having ordered the XIIth Corps, although it
stood on the right,[1] to form the extreme left, a serious
delay occurred from the crossing of the respective lines
of march.   The Saxon troops had not entirely passed
through Mars-la-Tour until nine o'clock, and till then
the Guard Corps could not follow.

---

[1] The XIIth Corps never stood on the right.   It occupied its
assigned position on the extreme left, and the delay arose from the
Guard Corps having occupied a position other than that designed for
it, and having been allowed to remain there.

Meanwhile the advanced guard of the XIIth Corps had already reached Jarny, and pursued its march as far as Briey without encountering the enemy.

Before information to this effect came in, the conviction had been reached in the Royal Head-quarter that at all events the main forces of the enemy still remained before Metz ; there was, however, a difference of opinion as to the extension of the French front, which it was assumed did not reach beyond Montigny. The Head-quarter of the IInd Army was therefore instructed not to extend further northward, but to attack the enemy's right wing with the IXth Corps, and push in the direction of Batilly with the Guard and the XIIth Corps. The Ist Army was not to begin its frontal attack until the IInd should be ready to co-operate.

In obedience to those instructions Prince Frederick Charles ordered the IXth Corps to march towards Verneville, and, in case the French right wing should be found there, to begin the action by promptly bringing a large force of artillery into action. The Guard was to continue its advance by way of Doncourt to support the IXth as soon as possible. The XIIth was to remain at Jarny for the present.

A little later fresh reports came in, which indicated that the IXth Corps, should it proceed in the manner ordered, would not strike the enemy on his flank, but full on his front. The Prince, in the discretion of his high position, therefore determined that the Corps should postpone its attack till the Guard Corps should have been brought to bear upon Amanvillers. At the same time the XIIth Corps was to push on to Ste. Marie aux Chênes.

But while these orders were being expedited, there was heard from Verneville at twelve o'clock the roar of the first cannon shots.

The two Corps of the left wing had, moreover, of their own accord, taken an easterly direction, and the IIIrd Corps moved up in rear of the IXth to the Caulre farm.

General von Manstein, the commander of the IXth Corps, had observed from Verneville a French camp at Amanvillers, which apparently lay in negligent repose. From his standpoint it could not be discerned that to his left about St. Privat great masses of troops were in position. Thinking that in this camp he had the enemy's right wing before him, he determined to act on his original orders and at once take the foe by surprise. Eight of his batteries at once opened fire.

But the French troops showed great alacrity in moving up into their prepared positions. The isolated initiative of the single Corps naturally drew upon it not only the fire of the troops opposite to it, but also that of the hostile Corps to right and left.

In the effort to find a location affording something of shelter, the Prussian batteries had taken position in a fold of the slope looking towards Amanvillers, and facing to the south-east, where, however, they were exposed from the north, on the flank and even in the rear, to the fire of the enemy's artillery, as well as to the massed fire of his infantry.

To meet this, it was necessary to send forward the infantry battalions nearest at hand. They took possession of the eastern point of the Bois de la Cusse on the left, and on the right seized the farmhouses of L'Envie and Chantrenne, and forced their way into the Bois des Genivaux. Thus the front of the 18th Division in action extended along a distance of 4000 paces.

It had to endure very heavy loss from the circumstance that the French with their long-range Chassepôt rifles could afford to keep out of the effective range of the needle-gun; the artillery suffered exceptionally severely. One of the batteries had already lost forty-five gunners when the enemy's sharpshooters swarmed forward on it. Infantry protection was not available at the moment, and two guns were lost. By two o'clock the batteries still remaining in position were almost unserviceable, and no relief arrived till the

Hessian Division reached Habonville, and brought up on the left of the distressed batteries, five batteries on either side of the railway, which diverted on themselves to a considerable extent the concentrated fire of the enemy. The batteries of the 18th Division, which had suffered most, could now be withdrawn in succession, but even in the act of retreat they had to drive off the pursuers by grapeshot.

The artillery of the IIIrd Corps and the Guard also came to the aid of the IXth, and those of the damaged guns of the last, which were still at all fit for service, were at once brought up again into the fighting line. Thus there was formed in front of Verneville and as far as St. Ail an artillery front of 130 pieces, whose fire now opposed the enemy's artillery with conspicuous success. Now that the IIIrd Corps was approaching Verneville and the 3rd Guard Brigade had reached Habonville, it was no longer to be apprehended that the French would succeed in piercing this line.

The main body of the Guard Corps reached St. Ail so early as two o'clock. General von Pape (commanding 1st Guard Division) at once recognized that by wheeling to the east he would not only not strike the enemy on that right flank of his which had to be turned, but would expose his own left flank to the hostile force occupying Ste. Marie aux Chênes. This town-like village, in itself extremely strong, and also strongly flanked by the main stronghold of the enemy's right, it was necessary to gain before making any further advance; but, in obedience to superior orders, the General had to await the co-operation of the Saxon Corps.

The foremost troops of this Corps had already reached the vicinity of Batilly, but it was still distant from Ste. Marie more than two miles, so that its batteries could not be pushed forward into position west of that place until three o'clock. But as the Guard had sent most of its own artillery to the support of the IXth Corps the Saxon batteries were of essential service. Ten batteries now directed their fire upon Ste. Marie, and by the time its effect was discernible, the 47th Brigade of the XIIth Corps came up. At half-past three the Prussian and Saxon battalions hurled themselves on the town from the south, the west, and the north, with loud hurrahs and without returning the fire of the enemy. The French were driven from it with the loss of several hundred men taken prisoners.

The Saxons eagerly followed up, and north of Ste. Marie there ensued a lively infantry fight, which masked the fire of the artillery. The brigade having obeyed the order to retire, the batteries immediately re-opened fire, and the repeated efforts of the French to recover the lost position were frustrated.

Soon afterwards the IXth Corps succeeded in storming and firmly holding the farm of Champenois, but all further attempts by isolated battalions or companies to force their way forward against the broad and compact front of the French were then manifestly futile. Thus, towards five o'clock, the infantry fire altogether died out, and the artillery fired only an occasional shot. The exhaustion of both sides caused for the time an almost total suspension of hostilities in this part of the field.

The Royal Head-quarter had firmly maintained the resolution, that the Ist Army should not commit itself to a serious offensive until the IInd had grappled with the enemy. But when the day was half-spent and when about noon heavy firing was heard from Vionville,[1] it was to be assumed that the moment for action had arrived; still, for the present, permission was only given to the Ist Army to engage in the artillery preparation.

Sixteen batteries of the VIIth and VIIIth Corps accordingly drew up right and left of Gravelotte on the highway passing through that village. Their fire

---

[1] Vionville in text seems a slip of the pen for Verneville.

was ineffective, because they were too far distant from the enemy; and furthermore they suffered from the fire of the French tirailleurs nestling in the opposite woods. It became necessary to drive those out, and thus there occurred here a premature infantry fight. The French were cleared out from the eastern declivity of the Mance ravine, and the artillery line, now increased to twenty batteries, was able to advance closer up to the western brink and now direct the strength of its fire against the main position of the enemy.

But the battalions of the 29th Brigade pushed the attack further. They pressed on leftward into the southern section of the Bois des Genivaux, but were unable to obtain touch of the IXth Corps in possession of the northern portion of the forest, since the French firmly held the intervening ground. On the right sundry detachments took possession of the quarries and gravel-pits near St. Hubert.

The artillery meanwhile had gained the mastery over that of the enemy, several of whose batteries were silenced, and others prevented from coming into position. The French fire was in part directed on the farm-steading of St. Hubert, to the vicinity of which portions of the 30th Brigade had spurted forward. These formidable premises close under the face of the enemy's main position, and in spite of a very heavy fire therefrom, were stormed at three o'clock. The 31st Brigade also now promptly crossed the ravine, but a further advance against the farms of Moscou and Leipzig, over a bare stretch of ground encompassed by the enemy on its wooded edges, did not succeed, and resulted only in heavy loss. On the extreme right, the 26th Brigade had taken possession of Jussy, thus securing the connection of the German army towards Metz, but found it impossible to cross the deep valley of Rozerieulles.

Everywhere the advanced positions of the French had been driven in, the farms in their front were blazing, their artillery appeared to be crushed, and, as the situation was viewed from Gravelotte, there needed nothing but to follow up the success. General von Steinmetz therefore, at four o'clock, ordered a renewed attack with fresh forces.

While the VIIth Corps occupied the border of the woodland, four batteries, backed by the 1st Cavalry Division, moved at a trot through the ravine, about 1500 paces across, which lies east of Gravelotte. But as soon as the head of the deep column came in sight of the enemy he redoubled his rifle and artillery fire, which had till now been kept under. One battery lost in a twinkling the men serving four of its guns, and it was only by an extreme effort that it was withdrawn to the border of the wood; another never succeeded in deploying. On the other hand, Hasse's battery remained in action, in spite of the loss of seventy-five horses, and Gnügge's battery stood fast near St. Hubert, regardless of the return fire from the quarries.

The foremost regiment of cavalry bent to the right at a gallop on leaving the hollow way, and advanced towards Point du Jour, but the enemy, being completely under cover, offered no mark for an attack. Clearly there was no field here for the utilization of this arm, so the regiments withdrew across the Mance ravine under a heavy fire from all sides.

The result of the ill-success of this attempt was that swarms of French tirailleurs now poured down from Point du Jour, and drove the Prussian detachments still remaining on the bare plateau backward to the skirts of the wood. Chassepôt bullets even reached the position of the Royal Commander-in-Chief and his personal staff, and Prince Adalbert's horse was shot under him.

Fresh forces pushed forward and drove the enemy back into his main position. St. Hubert remained in German possession, though the gunners of the battery in post there were equal to the service of but one gun.

But all partial attempts to advance over the exposed plateau proved a failure; and here also at about five o'clock in the afternoon there occurred a lull in the fighting, during which the weary troops on both sides reorganized themselves and took breath.

About this time King William and his staff rode forward to the swell south of Malmaison. But from there nothing could be discerned of the situation of the left flank of the army, at a distance as it was of more than four miles. The French artillery had almost entirely ceased along the whole front from La Folie to Point du Jour; but to the northward the thunder of the cannon fire roared louder than ever. It was six o'clock, the day was nearly at an end, and it was imperative that the decisive result should be precipitated. The King therefore ordered the Ist Army to make a renewed advance in support of which he placed the IInd Corps, just arrived after a long march, at the disposal of General von Steinmetz.

The battalions of the VIIth Corps which were still serviceable, except five which remained in reserve, were again sent across the Mance ravine, and in support of them the battalions holding the Bois de Vaux advanced in the direction of Point du Jour and the quarries.

The IInd Corps of the French Army thus assailed was now reinforced by the Guard Voltigeur Division. All the reserves were hurried up into the foremost line. The artillery burst into redoubled fire, and a crushing musketry fire was concentrated on the advancing enemy. Then the French themselves took the offensive with a huge swarm of tirailleurs, which hurled backward upon the wood-fringes the small leaderless bodies to German troops that had been lying in the shallow folds of the plateau.

There, however, the sally found its limit; and there still remained at disposition a fresh Army Corps in full strength.

The IInd Corps, the last to come up by rail into the

theatre of war, had hitherto followed in the wake of the army by forced marches, and had not been able to take part in any engagement. It had started from Pont à Mousson at 2 a.m. and, taking the road by Buxières and Rezonville, arrived south of Gravelotte towards evening. The Pomeranians expressed their eager desire to get at the enemy before the day should end.

It would have been more proper if the Chief of the General Staff of the Army, who was personally on the spot at the time, had not permitted this movement at so late an hour of the evening. A body of troops, still completely intact, might have been of great value the next day; but it could hardly be expected on this evening to effect a decisive reversal of the situation.

Hurrying through Gravelotte, the foremost battalions of the IInd Corps pushed forward to the quarries, and up to within a few hundred paces of Point du Jour; but those following soon found themselves involved in the throng of the broken detachments remaining under fire south of St. Hubert, and the further advance towards Moscou was arrested. In the growing darkness friend became indistinguishable from foe, and the firing had to be broken off. Not, however, until ten o'clock did it entirely cease.

It was, to be sure, an advantage that the fresh troops of the IInd Corps were available to hold the foremost fighting-line for the night, behind which the intermixed detachments of the VIIth and VIIIth Corps were enabled to reorganize themselves.

The whole course of the struggle had conclusively proved that the French left flank, almost impregnable as it was by nature and art, could not be forced even by the most devoted bravery and the greatest sacrifices. Both sides were now facing each other in threatening proximity, and both in attitude to renew the battle on the following morning. The result of the day turned on the events evolving themselves on the opposite flank.

The Prince of Würtemberg,[1] then in St. Ail, had judged at a quarter-past five that the moment was come for an attack on the French right wing; but that wing extended considerably further north than the front of the Guard Corps reached; further, indeed, than the French Commander-in-Chief himself was aware. The Saxons had, indeed, participated in the seizure of Ste. Marie aux Chênes, but after that event the Crown Prince[2] deemed it necessary to assemble his Corps in front of the Bois d'Aubouć, before proceeding to attack the enemy in flank. One of his brigades had to come up from Jarny, another from Ste. Marie; and, since the Corps had been delayed in getting away from Mars la Tour, its direct attack could not be expected at the earliest for an hour to come.

The 4th Infantry Brigade of the Guard Corps, in accordance with orders received, proceeded in the prescribed direction of Jerusalem, immediately south of St. Privat. As soon as General von Manstein observed this movement, he ordered the 3rd Guard Brigade, which had been placed at his orders, immediately to advance from Habonville direct upon Amanvillers. Between and abreast of these two brigades marched Hessian battalions. It was not till half-an-hour later that the 1st Guard Division leftward of the 2nd moved forward from Ste. Marie against St. Privat. This combined offensive movement was directed against the broad front of the French VIth and IVth Corps. Their respective strongholds of St. Privat and Amanvillers had as yet hardly felt the fire of the German batteries, which had hitherto found enough to do in combating the enemy's artillery outside the villages.

In front of the French main position on the crown of the height had been prepared on the slope behind the hedges and low walls, which rose terrace-wise backward, tier on tier of shelter trenches. Behind these defences

---

[1] Commanding the Guard Corps.
[2] Of Saxony, commanding XIIth Corps.

towered the village named St. Privat, castle-like with its massive houses, which were garrisoned to the very roofs. The bare slope stretching in its front was thus exposed to an overwhelming storm of projectiles.

The losses of the Guard Corps marching forward to attack a front so formidable were simply enormous. In the course of half an hour five battalions lost all, the others the greater part of their officers, especially those of the higher grades. Thousands of dead and wounded marked the track of the battalions pressing valiantly forward in spite of their cruel losses. The ranks as fast as they were thinned constantly closed up again, and their cohesion was not lost even under the leadership of young lieutenants and ensigns. As they drew nearer to the enemy the needle-gun came into full utility. The French were driven from all their foremost positions, in which, for the most part, they did not await the final struggle. By a quarter-past six the battalions had advanced to within 600 to 800 paces of Amanvillers and St. Privat. The troops, weary from the strained exertion, halted under the steeper slopes offering some, though small, protection, and in the shelter trenches abandoned by the enemy. Only four battalions now remained in reserve at Ste. Marie, behind the line which now extended to a length of 4000 paces. Every charge of the French cavalry and of de Cissey's Division had been steadily repelled with the aid of twelve batteries of the Guard Corps which had hastened up; but detachments commingled under stress of untold losses, had to show a resolute front against two French Corps in close proximity for more than half-an-hour, before relief came to them.

It was nearly seven o'clock when on the left of the Guard, two brigades of Saxon infantry reached the scene of strife; the other two were still assembling in the forest of Auboué; their artillery, however, had for a considerable time been maintaining a lively fire on Roncourt.

When Bazaine received word that the Germans were stretching out in constantly increasing extension with intent to outflank his right, he at three p.m. ordered Picard's Guard Grenadier Division posted at Plappeville, to march towards the threatened flank. Though the distance to be covered was little more than four miles, this all-important reinforcement, having diverged to rightward from the direct road through the woodland, had not yet arrived; and Marshal Canrobert, who was fending off with all his might the converging masses of Prussian assailants, decided to concentrate his troops more closely about the strong position of St. Privat. The retreat from Roncourt would be adequately covered by a small rearguard, since the border of the Bois de Jaumont was being held.

Thus it happened that the Saxons did not find the strong resistance at Roncourt which they had expected, and after a slight skirmish entered the village together with the companies of the extreme left of the Guard; a body of Saxon infantry had previously been diverted to the right from the road to Roncourt and marched direct on St. Privat to the support of the Guard.

The fire of twenty-four batteries of the two German Corps wrought awful havoc there. Many houses were set on fire, or crumbled under the concentrated crash of the shells. But the French were determined to hold to the last extremity this point, decisive as it was of the fate of the day. The batteries of their right flank were hurried into position between St. Privat and the Bois de Jaumont, whence their fire would enfilade the further advance of the Saxons on the former place. Other batteries went southward to confront the Prussians, and the simultaneous final rush of the German battalions was met by a rattling fire from the French riflemen under cover in their lines of shelter trenches.

All those obstacles were gradually overcome in the course of the assault, although again with heavy loss; some detachments halting occasionally for a moment to

pour in a volley, others again never firing a shot. By
sundown the attack had swept up to within 300
paces of St. Privat. Some detachments of the Xth
Corps, which had reached St. Ail, closed up, and now
the final onset was made from every side at once.
The French still defended the burning houses and the
church with great obstinacy, till, finding themselves
completely surrounded, they surrendered at about
eight o'clock. More than 2000 men were here taken
prisoners, and the wounded were rescued from the
burning houses.

The defeated troops of the VIth French Corps hur-
riedly retired into the valley of the Moselle, their retreat
covered by the brigade holding the Bois de Jaumont
and by the cavalry. Only then did the Guard Grenadier Division make its first appearance, and the Reserve
Artillery of the French Army deployed east of Amanvillers. The German batteries at once took up the
fight, which lasted till late in the night, and in the
course of which Amanvillers was burned.

In that quarter the retirement of the IVth French
Corps had also already commenced, masked, however, by
repeated heavy attacks to the front. In the course of
these there occurred a hand-to-hand encounter with the
charging battalions of the right wing of the Guard and
the left of the IXth Corps. Amanvillers, however,
remained in the hands of the French for the night.
Not until three o'clock on the morning of the 19th
did the IIIrd French Corps evacuate its position about
Moscou ; and the IInd Corps held its ground until five
o'clock, engaged in constant sharp frays with the outposts of the Pomeranians, who on its withdrawal took
possession of the plateaus of Moscou and Point du
Jour.

The results attained on the 18th of August had been
made possible only by the battles of the 14th and 16th.

The French estimate their losses at 13,000 men. In
October 173,000 were still in Metz, consequently it is
certain that the enemy had at disposition in the battle

of the 18th of August more than 180,000 men. The exact strength of the seven [1] German Corps on that day amounted to 178,818 men. Thus with the forces on either side of approximately equal strength, the French had been driven out of a position of almost unrivalled natural advantage.

Naturally the loss of the assailants was much heavier than that of the defence; it amounted to 20,584 men, among them 899 officers.

Whereas by the war-establishment the average is one officer to every forty men, in this battle one officer fell to every twenty-three men; glorious testimony to the example set by their leaders to their brave men, but also a loss which could not be restored during the course of the war. Altogether the six battles fought in the first fourteen days of August had cost the German army 50,000 men.[2] It was naturally impossible immediately to call out at home a sufficient levy in substitution for the losses; but reinforcements drawn from the time-expired cadres were already bespoken.

First of all that same evening the earliest instalment of the trains and the Field-Hospitals had to be brought up from the right bank of the Moselle; and the ammunition had to be replenished throughout. In Rezonville, thronged as it was with the wounded, it was with difficulty that a little garret for the King and

---

[1] These figures represent only the infantry of the eight (not seven) Corps engaged; they do not include the cavalry, 24,584; the artillery, at least as strong; nor the officerhood of the two armies, numbering several thousands. Inclusive of those items the German host "employed" in the battle of Gravelotte—St. Privat numbered, in round figures, 232,000 combatants. Accepting Moltke's own estimate of ten defenders per "Schrith" of front, there works out a total of 133,000 men, as the strength of the French army "employed" in the battle.

[2] During the first fourteen days of August, the German troops were in conflict with the enemy on five occasions: viz. Saarbrücken, 2nd, loss 79, Weissenburg, 4th, loss 1551; Wörth, 6th, loss 10,642; Spicheren, 6th, loss 4871; Borny, 14th, loss 5000. Total losses during the fourteen days, 22,143.

shelter for his General Staff were found. Its members were engrossed throughout the night in preparing the dispositions which the new phase of the situation created by the victory rendered immediately necessary. This exertion enabled all those orders to be laid before his Majesty for approval on the morning of the 19th.

NEW DISTRIBUTION OF THE ARMY.

The siege of Metz had formed no part of the original plan of campaign ; it had been intended to do no more than merely to maintain an observation on the place when the main army should have passed it on the advance towards Paris; and a Reserve Division, consisting of eighteen battalions, sixteen squadrons, and thirty-six guns, detailed for that duty, was now near at hand.

Under the altered conditions, however, the regular investment of Metz was now necessary, and this involved a radical alteration of the existing arrangements throughout the whole army.

A separate army under the command of Prince Frederick Charles, consisting of the Ist, VIIth, and VIIIth Corps of the former Ist Army, the IInd, IIIrd, IXth, and Xth Corps of the IInd Army, the Reserve Division and the 1st and 3rd Cavalry Divisions, in all 150,000 men, was assigned to the duty of investing Metz.

The Guard, IVth, and XIIth Corps and the 5th and 6th Cavalry Divisions were formed into a separate army under the command of the Crown Prince of Saxony ; it was styled "The Army of the Meuse" and was 138,000 strong.[1] This and the IIIrd Army, which

[1] These figures are erroneous. It is manifest that three Corps and two Cavalry Divisions, most of which had been materially weakened by casualties, could not furnish a strength of 138,000 men ; nor could

numbered 223,000 men, were directed to advance against the new French army forming at Châlons.

Certainly the army investing Metz was left weaker than the blockaded enemy. It was to be expected that the latter would renew his efforts to break out to the westward. Prince Frederick Charles' main forces were therefore to remain on the left bank of the Moselle.

All these orders received the approval of the King, and were dispatched to the commanding officers by eleven o'clock on the morning of the 19th.

In accordance with the orders of Prince Frederick Charles, the Xth Corps occupied the woodland districts of the lower Moselle as far as St. Privat, while the IInd held the high ridge from that point to Moscou. To the right of the IInd, the VIIIth and VIIth Corps followed on, the latter positioned on both sides of the Upper Moselle. The Ist Corps occupied the Pouilly upland to left and right of the Seille, specially charged to protect the great magazines which were being established at Remilly and Pont à Mousson. The 3rd Reserve Division moved to the vicinity of Retonfay, north-east of Metz. The IXth and IIIrd Corps cantoned at St. Marie and Verneville as reserve. All the troops immediately set about the construction of earthworks, and of bridges over the Moselle above and below the fortress.

Of the Corps now belonging to the Army of the Meuse, the XIIth assembled at Conflans and the Guards at Mars la Tour; the IVth Corps, which had not been ordered to Metz, had already reached Commercy.

The IIIrd Army, after crossing the Vosges range, and having left a Bavarian brigade blockading Toul, was

the IIIrd Army, originally 130,000 strong, swelled by one Corps and diminished by battle losses of 12,000, approximate a strength of 223,000. As a matter of fact, on August 22nd, the Meuse Army was 86,275 strong, and the IIIrd Army 137,622; the two armies together had a total strength, in round numbers, of 224,000 men.

F

pressing forward in three columns. Its foremost Corps had already reached the Meuse, but were obliged to halt there for two days, so as to cross the river approximately abreast of the Meuse army. Its cavalry meanwhile patrolled three marches ahead as far as Châlons and Vitry, where, for the first time since Wörth, it regained touch of the enemy. The French encountered were only guarding posts on the Marne railway-line, which retired when the traffic thereon ceased.

The Army of Châlons.

Meanwhile at Châlons there had been formed a French army of 166 battalions, 100 squadrons, and 380 guns, consisting of the Ist, Vth, VIIth, and XIIth Corps.

Of the last the Division which had been left behind on the Spanish frontier formed the nucleus, to which was added a body of very superior troops, consisting of four regiments of marines; later the two cavalry divisions also joined. General Trochu, who had been made Governor of Paris, had taken back with him thither eighteen battalions of Gardes-Mobiles, they having already given such proofs of insubordination that it was thought unsafe to confront them with the enemy.

The Emperor had arrived in Châlons and had placed Marshal MacMahon in command of the newly-formed army. In the French Head-quarter it was not unnaturally assumed that Marshal Bazaine was in retreat from Metz. By an advance of the Army of Châlons merely to Verdun the armies could form a junction with each other in the course of a few days, and so a fighting force be formed which might make head against the hitherto victorious enemy. On the other hand, MacMahon had to concern himself with the duty of

covering Paris, and that capital, no less than his own
right flank, was threatened by the appearance of the
Crown Prince of Prussia's army on the Meuse.

For the attainment of a decision between advancing
and retiring, it was beyond everything necessary to
know the direction which Marshal Bazaine might have
taken.

On the 18th tidings had come from him, that he had
maintained his position in a battle about Rezonville,
but that his troops had to be supplied with ammunition and supplies before they could renew the march.
From this it seemed only too probable that the communications of the Army of the Rhine were already
threatened; and MacMahon determined to march on
Rheims, whence he could either reach Paris, though by
a somewhat circuitous route, or move in the direction
of the other army.

But when it became known that the Crown Prince
of Prussia's army had not even been near Metz, and
that Prussian cavalry had already appeared before
Vitry, the Marshal could not deceive himself as to the
danger involved in the latter alternative. With sound
judgment, therefore, he stood out against the order of
the Empress and the Ministry to undertake that enterprise; he determined against it, and announced his
resolution to march to Paris. Under its walls he could
accept a battle with advantage, since the fortifications,
even in the event of defeat, assured a safe retreat and
precluded pursuit.

Further reports from Metz did not afford a clear
insight into the situation there. Also on the 18th,
" the army had held its position," the narrative ran—
only the right wing had changed front. " The troops
required two or three days' rest," but the Marshal
" counted still on being able to move out in a northerly
direction," and fight his way to Châlons by the Montmédy—Ste. Menehould route, if this road was not
strongly held by the enemy. In that case, he would

march on Sedan, and even by Mézières, in order to
reach Châlons.

Bazaine might already have committed himself
to the movement thus indicated, and therefore Marshal MacMahon, who was not the man to leave
his fellow-soldier in the lurch, instead of marching
on Paris, set forth on the 23rd in the direction of
Stenay.

The suddenness of this decision caused all the preparations for the undertaking to be left unexecuted
At the end of the first day's march the troops reached
the Suippe late in the evening in pouring rain. They
lacked every necessary, and two Corps remained
entirely without food. The Marshal was therefore
forced to move his army further northward to . Rethel
where large magazines of provisions had been established, and where the railway facilitated the bringing
up of stores. Even on the third day's march the army
had made little progress eastward. The left wing
remained at Rethel, the right reached the Aisne, near
Vouziers. On August 26th the main army was still
standing between Attigny and Le Chêne on the
Ardennes canal, while the VIIth Corps and a regiment of Hussars lay in front of Vouziers for the
protection of the right flank.

While the French army was thus marching eastward
by a wide détour, the German forces, which had been put
in motion at the same time, were for their part marching
due westward.

According to orders issued from the supreme Head
quarter at Pont à Mousson, the advance on the enemy
supposed to be at Châlons, was to be effected in such
manner that the IIIrd Army, marching on the left of
the Army of the Meuse, should have the start by a
day's march, so that the enemy, wherever he might
stand halted, could be struck simultaneously in front and
on his right flank, and thus forced away northward from
the direction of Paris. The two armies were to converge

as they advanced, and to reach the line of Ste. Mene-hould—Vitry on the 26th,

On the first day's march, the armies still on a front some fifty-six miles long, the Meuse was reached ; on the second day, the 24th, they advanced to the line St. Dizier—Bar le Duc—Verdun. The attempts to take the latter place and Toul in the by-going proved unsuccessful.

So early as on that day the 4th Cavalry Division, which had pushed far ahead, sent in important news. The Rhenish dragoons had found Châlons and the camp at Mourmelon deserted, and notwithstanding the destruction effected, there still remained in the latter considerable booty. An intercepted letter written by a French officer, which intimated that the relief of Metz was in prospect, and another which stated that Marshal MacMahon was at Rheims with 150,000 men and was fortifying his position there, were corroborated by the Paris newspapers.

On the 25th the Army of the Meuse formed a line from Sommeille to Dombasle, while the heads of columns of the IIIrd Army were already executing the march prescribed for the following day, on the Ste. Menehould—Vitry road. The small fortress of Vitry, a few hours after a battalion of Mobiles had left the place, surrendered to the 4th Cavalry Division. On its march to Ste. Menehould, thence to be forwarded by train to Paris, this battalion, 1000 strong, fell into the hands of the 6th Cavalry Division as it was moving on Dampierre, and was carried away captive.

The 5th Cavalry Division reached Ste. Menehould, and the 12th followed on the same road as far as Clermont, patrolling the country up to Varennes, within nine miles of the French outposts at Grand Pré, but without learning anything as to the whereabouts of the French army.

The scouting service to any great distance on the right of the army was hindered by the vicinity of the forest of Argonnes, which it was difficult for the cavalry to penetrate without the assistance of infantry. The inhabitants of the country began to show themselves extremely hostile. The Government had provided them with arms, and organized a general rising. The Germans, who hitherto had made war on the Emperor alone, were now forced to use their arms against the population. The franc-tireurs, though not affecting operations on a large scale, were a source of much annoyance to the smaller undertakings, and as it naturally embittered the soldiers to realize that they were no longer safe either by day or night, the character of the war became more stern, and the sufferings of the country were increased.

A Paris telegram, sent by way of London, reached this day (25th) the Royal Head-quarter at Bar le Duc. It stated that MacMahon was at Rheims, and sought to effect a junction with Bazaine.

It is always a serious matter to exchange, without the most pressing necessity, a once-settled and well-devised plan for a new and unprepared scheme. It would have been unwise and unskilful hastily to alter the whole direction of the advance because of rumours and information which might later probably turn out to be unfounded. Endless difficulties must result from such a course ; the arrangements for bringing up baggage and reinforcements would have to be cancelled, and aimless marches might impair the confidence of the troops in their commanders.

The orders for the following day, issued at eleven o'clock in the morning, prescribed therefore for both armies merely a slight alteration of direction ; Rheims instead of Châlons was indicated as the objective. The cavalry of the right wing, however, was explicitly ordered to advance to Buzancy and Vouziers, where a thorough insight into the situation could not but be obtained.

In war it is for the most part with probabilities only

that the strategist can reckon ; and the probability, as a rule, is that the enemy will do the right thing. Such a course could not be anticipated as that the French army would uncover Paris and march along the Belgian frontier to Metz. Such a move seemed strange, and in deed somewhat venturesome ; but nevertheless it was possible. The chief of the General Staff, therefore, that same day worked out a tabular detail of marches, upon which the three Corps of the Army of the Meuse, together with the two Bavarian Corps which were nearest that army, could be brought together in the vicinity of Dam-villers, on the right bank of the Meuse, in three not over-severe marches.

These forces, with the two Corps standing in reserve at Metz, which could be brought up, would constitute a force of 150,000 men, which might give battle in the specified vicinity, or compel the enemy to do so on the march to Longuyon. Without employing this reserve, there was every prospect that the advance of the French could be brought to a halt on this side the Meuse, and then another Corps of the IIIrd Army could be brought up.

This march-table was soon to be brought into service. Fresh news arrived in the course of the same afternoon. The newspapers revealed the secret by publishing vehement speeches delivered in the National Assembly to the effect " that the French general who should leave his comrade in the lurch, deserved the execration of the country." It would be a disgrace, it was protested, to the French nation if the brave Bazaine were left un-succoured : from all this, and considering the effect of such phrases on the French, it was to be expected that military considerations would give way to political. A telegram from London, quoting the Paris *Temps*, stated that MacMahon had suddenly resolved to hasten to the assistance of Bazaine, though the abandonment of the road to Paris endangered the safety of France.

The King, before night, approved of the march to the right, and the orders were dispatched that night direct to the respective Army Corps on the march.

On the 26th his Majesty moved his head-quarter to Clermont. The Crown Prince of Saxony had set out for Varennes early in the morning with the XIIth Corps, and had ordered the Guards to Dombasle, the IVth Corps to Fleury.

The cavalry, sent forward in every direction, found that the enemy had evacuated the region of the Suippe valley and had not yet entered that of the Meuse; that Buzancy and Grand Pré were in occupation of the French, and that a large encampment of their VIIth Corps had been specifically perceived on the height of Vouziers. The apparition of a few handsful of cavalry, despatched thither on observation duty, occasioned an almost unaccountable excitement. General Douay, quartered at Vouziers, received the most exaggerated reports, and must have thought that a general attack by the German army was imminent. The VIIth Corps was kept under arms the entire night in pouring rain, and the Marshal resolved to advance towards Vouziers and Buzancy with all his forces on the following morning. Thus the march to the east received a check as early as the 27th, but the untruthfulness of the reports very soon became sufficiently apparent.

If the German chiefs were deeply interested in gaining an insight into the enemy's movements, so on the French side this requisite was certainly urgent in no less imperative degree. With judicious disposal of their cavalry on the right flank, a surprise like that above mentioned would have been impossible, but the 1st French Cavalry Division was placed on the left flank, where there was no danger whatever, and the 2nd was rearmost of everything. It seemed as though in the French army less attention was paid to the repulse of an attack than to the evasion of one, and to the unobserved attainment of Montmédy, the point of rendezvous with the other army. When the movement of the Germans from southward could no longer be doubted, it would certainly have been best for the French to take the vigorous offensive in that direction with intent· to defeat them, or at least to sweep them out of the vicinity of their own line of march. If they had failed in this they would, at any rate, have readily learnt that their undertaking was impracticable, and that its further prosecution must certainly result in a catastrophe. It must, however, be admitted that the German cavalry formed an almost impenetrable screen. The Marshal could not know that his enemy was echeloned from Vitry to Varennes, a distance of more than thirty-seven miles, and was not at all in form to attack him just then in serious earnest.

August 27th.—The Marshal had cleared up his misconception, and on the 27th he continued his march, at least with part of his troops. The VIIth and Vth Corps covered the movement at Vouziers and Buzancy, the XIIth advanced to Le Chêne, and the 1st Cavalry Division to Beaumont, probably to ascertain the whereabouts of Marshal Bazaine. The Ist Corps and the 2nd Cavalry Division remained behind on the Aisne.

The Saxon Corps, the furthest forward of the German Army, had received direct orders to march to Dun on the 27th, and secure on the right bank the passages over the Meuse, as far as Stenay. It reached Stenay at three o'clock in the afternoon, and threw forward a post on the left bank.

The cavalry clung closely to the enemy and followed his movements, often engaging in petty skirmishes. The departure of the Vth French Corps from Buzancy in the direction of Le Chêne was at once detected, as also was the march to Beaumont; and the Saxon Cavalry Division pushed forward that evening to

Nouart. The Bavarian Corps reached the Clermont—Verdun road, the 5th Ste. Menehould ; the other Corps of the IIIrd Army were hurrying by forced marches in a northerly direction.

The prospect now seemed certain that the enemy would be overtaken on the left bank of the Meuse. Word was sent to the blockading army before Metz that the two Corps asked for were no longer required, but they had already set out.

The latest dispositions made by Marshal MacMahon clearly betokened a last effort on his part to persevere in the original direction. He was echeloned along the northernmost of the roads by which he could reach Metz, but had left a strong reserve on the Aisne on which he might fall back. When he now learnt that nothing had been seen of the Army of the Rhine at Montmedy, but that it actually was still at Metz, he resolved on retreating, and, after giving orders to that effect for the following morning, reported his intention to Paris.

From thence during the night came the most strenuous remonstrances. The Minister of War telegraphed, "If you leave Bazaine in the lurch, the revolution will break out," and the Council of Ministers issued a peremptory order to relieve Metz. The troops in front of the Marshal, it was urged, were nothing more than part of the army investing Metz ; he had the start of the Crown Prince of Prussia by several days' march ; and General Vinoy had already left Paris for Rheims with the newly-formed XIIIth Corps as a reinforcement to him.

The Marshal silenced his military convictions and issued new orders. But the troops had started in advance of the promulgation of them. The change of route gave rise to much confusion ; the roads were bad, and quarters for the night were not reached until darkness had long set in ; the men were weary, wet to the skin, and depressed in spirits.

August 28th.—Little more than nine miles' distance eastward was attained. The XIIth Corps reached La

Besace, the Ist was on the march to Le Chêne, the VIIth was halted at Boult aux Bois because of a false report that two Prussian Corps were occupying Buzancy, further ahead. On the strength of this report the Vth Corps moved toward that town by way of Bar, but went on to Bois des Dames in the afternoon. Neither of these movements was interfered with. The German cavalry had strict orders, while watching the French as closely as possible, not in any way to check or press them, and the Saxon cavalry evacuated Nouart on the approach of the enemy. The Germans had to await the coming up of the IIIrd Army, the rearmost Corps of which, the VIth, had only just reached Ste. Menehould.

August 29th.—For this day also a non-offensive attitude was prescribed, and the bringing on of decisive operations was postponed until the 30th.

The Marshal in his head-quarter at Stonne had been informed that the Germans occupied Dun, and that the bridges over the Meuse had been destroyed. He had no pontoon-train, and could cross the river only lower down, at Mouzon and Villers. His XIIth Corps and 1st Cavalry Division passed over to the right bank unhindered at these points; the Ist Corps and the 2nd Cavalry Division proceeded to Raucourt. The VIIth Corps, delayed on march by petty skirmishes on its right flank, did not reach its destination at La Besace, but went into bivouac at Oches. The Vth Corps was to have moved to Beaumont, but the staff officer carrying the order fell into the hands of the Prussian cavalry together with his escort. General de Failly therefore marched upon Stenay, according to his original instructions.

Up to this time, apart from the cavalry, the Saxon Corps alone had been in contact with the enemy, but the Guard now came up to Buzancy in parallel line, while the Saxon Corps crossed over to the left bank of the Meuse at Dun. Its advanced guard at once took possession of the wooded spur to the north-east of Nouart, drove out the French cavalry, and pressed ahead to Champy, where it encountered a strong force in Lespart's Division. The purpose of the reconnaissance having been attained, the advanced guard was called in. The French Division, in consequence of fresh orders received from the Marshal, withdrew simultaneously in a northerly direction.

On the German side four Corps of the IIIrd Army were now within nine miles rearward of the Army of the Meuse. The 5th Cavalry Division stood at Attigny on the enemy's line of communication; the 6th was hanging on the heels of the French columns of march, and, among other things, had taken Boncq with a dismounted party. The Royal Head-quarter was now advanced to Grand Pré, and, as the result of the various reports which had poured in, the resolution was taken to attack the enemy on the following day, before he should cross the Meuse. The Army of the Meuse was to march towards Beaumont, the IIIrd Army to move forward between that place and Le Chêne. To bring both armies to a parallel front, the right wing was not to move until ten o'clock, while the left[1] was to start before six o'clock. Only the trains absolutely requisite for the battle were to follow.

BATTLE OF BEAUMONT.

(August 30th.)

On the 30th of August, at ten o'clock, the King set out for Sommauthe by way of Buzancy. Both the Bavarian Corps were on the march thither, the Vth

---

[1] The Army of the Meuse constituted the right wing; the IIIrd Army, the left.

Corps advanced in the centre towards Oches, the XIth, together with the Würtemberg Division, was heading for Le Chêne, the VIth for Vouziers. The IVth Corps on the right was advancing by Belval, the XIIth reached to the Meuse, while the Guard Corps followed in rear as a reserve.

Marshal MacMahon had issued orders for the attainment of the object that his entire army should on this day cross to the right bank of the Meuse; only the baggage trains and sick were to remain behind.

His Ist Corps and the 2nd Cavalry Division had left Raucourt so early as seven; they crossed the river at Remilly, light bridges having been thrown over for the infantry. The VIIth Corps at Oches had struck camp still earlier at four o'clock, but as it took with it in the march all its waggons, even the empty ones, the trains formed a column more than nine miles in length, and seven of its battalions were forced to march alongside the road in the capacity of baggage guard; so that the brigade bringing up the rear was unable to start until ten o'clock. This long procession soon came into contact with the Prussian cavalry, was fired upon by artillery, and compelled to arrest its march. Not till one o'clock could the movement on La Besace be resumed, and then, as heavy firing was heard from Beaumont, General Douay conceived it right to abandon the road to Mouzon and take that to Remilly.

To the Vth Corps had been precautionally assigned the duty of covering the march of the other two. The troops had reached the vicinity of Beaumont only at 4 a.m., and were thoroughly exhausted by fighting and the night-march. General de Failly therefore determined to halt his Corps for cooking and rest before pursuing the march. Precautionary measures seem to have been altogether neglected, though it must have been known that the enemy was now close at hand. While at half-past one the officers and men were engaged in their meal, Prussian shells suddenly burst among these heedless groups.

The two Corps of the German right wing had to move through a wooded tract in four wholly independent columns, by ways sodden with rain. The Crown Prince of Saxony therefore ordered that no single column should attempt to enter on an attack before the neighbouring one was ready to co-operate.

The IVth Corps had started very early, and after a short rest had pursued its march at ten o'clock. When at noon the head of the 8th Division emerged from the forest, it discerned from its elevated position the enemy's camp about 800 paces distant, in the condition as described. General Schöler (commanding the Division) held that the opportunity of so complete a surprise was not to be let pass; the proximity of his force could not long remain undetected by the enemy. He announced it by his cannon-fire.

The Division soon recognized that it had drawn upon itself an enemy of immensely superior strength. The French rapidly got under arms, and dense swarms of riflemen hurried to the front, whose long-range Chassepôts inflicted great losses, especially upon the artillerymen. The main body of the 8th Division had meanwhile come up to the assistance of its advanced guard, and ere long the 7th Division appeared on the right. The French assailed it too with great impetuosity, and could only be repulsed at the bayonet-point. Presently, however, the foremost battalions of both Divisions made their way into the French camp in front of Beaumont, into the town itself, and finally into a second camp located northward of it. Seven guns, of which the teams were missing, and which continued firing up to the last moment, a number of gunners, waggons and horses, fell into the hands of the assailants.

Whilst now, about two o'clock, a pause occurred in the infantry fight, fourteen batteries of the IVth

Corps engaged in a contest with the French artillery deployed on the stretch of heights north of Beaumont. The German artillery mass was presently strengthened by the Saxon artillery on the right, and by the Bavarian batteries on the left. This formidable and commanding artillery line, constantly advancing in echelon, promptly squandered the mitrailleuses, and at three o'clock the remaining French batteries also were silenced.

The IInd Bavarian Corps, on the left of the Prussian IVth, was advancing on La Thibaudine, when it was quite unexpectedly attacked from the west by a strong force of the enemy.

These troops were Conseil Dumesnil's Division of the VIIth French Corps, which was continuing in march to Mouzon in error, acting on its original orders. Completely surprised as it was, and attacked in front and flank, the Division gave up all hope of cutting its way through, and at about four o'clock beat a hasty retreat northwards, leaving two guns behind.

The Bavarians had in the meantime taken possession of the farm of Thibaudine, and the Prussians that of Harnoterie. The wooded hills prevented a clear view of the surrounding country ; the enemy had completely disappeared.

General de Failly was making strenuous efforts to collect his scattered forces in front of Mouzon, under cover of a rear-guard halted at La Sartelle ; and General Lebrun had left behind on the left side of the Meuse an infantry and a cavalry brigade and three batteries belonging to the XIIth Corps, to render him assistance.

At five o'clock the 8th Division, headed by the 13th Brigade, was pushing toilsomely through the dense forest of Givodeau, on its way to operate against this new defensive position. On emerging from the wood the battalions, which had fallen into some confusion, were received by a brisk fire at short range. The repeated efforts of the riflemen to advance were unsuccessful, and the dense underwood hindered the clubbed mass behind them from forming. By the time the Saxon Corps had succeeded with extreme difficulty in extricating itself from the forest and swamps of the Wamme stream, and had reached Létanne, the impracticability of further progress in the Meuse valley became apparent, since numerous French batteries, in unassailable positions on the opposite side of the river, commanded all the low ground. The Corps therefore ascended the plateau, moved in its turn through the Givodeau woods, and debouching thence swelled the strength of the forces assembled on the northern border, where, however, their development on a broader front was impossible. So about six o'clock the infantry engagement came to a stand for a time in this quarter.

On the left the 14th Brigade had come up into line with the 13th, and this body (the 7th Division) was followed by the 8th Division in two columns.

The 93rd Regiment had carried the height to the north-east of Yoncq, and advanced in pursuit of the enemy as far as to the foot of Mont de Brune. Four mitrailleuses and eight guns, some of them with their entire teams, fell thus into the hands of the Anhalters.

When, at half-past five, the artillery had come up into position, and at the same time the 27th Regiment was approaching, General Zychlinski (commanding 14th Brigade) advanced to the enveloping attack.

The French occupied in strength the summit of the entirely isolated hill; their batteries faced to eastward against the Bois de Givodeau, whence an assault threatened; but they swiftly changed front to the south and directed a heavy fire on the 93rd and the 2nd Battalion of the 27th, as they charged up on this face while the Fusilier battalion was at the same time pressing forward from the west. Regardless of their losses, the assailants eagerly scaled the ascent, the brigade and regimental commanders at their head. Six French guns were seized while in action, in spite of a brave resistance by the gunners and covering troops, and the enemy was pursued as far as the Roman road. Here four more guns, completely horsed, which had been abandoned by the artillerymen, fell into the hands of the conquerors.

The three battalions[1] hurried on towards Mouzon, without waiting for the support of the[2] 14th Brigade following in rear, but they suddenly found themselves threatened by a cavalry-charge.

Marshal MacMahon had recognized the fact that the only thing left him now to do was to effect as orderly an evacuation as possible of the left bank of the Meuse; the reinforcements sent across from the right had already been recalled. The 5th Cuirassier Regiment alone still remained. When, a little to the north of the Faubourg de Mouzon, it was reached by the fire of the advancing Prussians, the French regiment hurled itself upon the enemy with a noble contempt for death.

The shock struck the 10th Company of the 27th Regiment. The soldiers, without closing their ranks, waited for the word of command of their leader, Captain Helmuth, and then fired a volley at close range, which struck down eleven officers and 100 men, the brave commander of the band of horsemen falling fifteen paces in front of his men. The survivors rushed back towards the Meuse, and, as all the bridges had been removed, they strove to gain the other side by swimming.

Considerable masses of the enemy were still in front of Mouzon, and upon these the batteries of the IVth Corps, as one after another they came into action, directed their fire. Two Bavarian batteries brought under their fire the bridge at Villers, lower down the river, and prevented it from being used. Then the suburb was carried after a fierce encounter, and here too the bridge across the Meuse was taken and held. The enemy, deprived of every way of retreat, received

[1] Of 27th and 93rd Regiments.   [2] Read in " rest of the."

G

with a hot fire the 8th Division emerging from the valley
of the Yoncq, but was gradually driven back towards
the river. The French troops in front of the Bois de
Givodeau were also in a hopeless plight; they were
assailed by the 7th Division and XIIth Corps, and
were dispersed after an obstinate struggle. By night-
fall the French had ceased their resistance on the hither
side of the Meuse. Many lagging stragglers were taken
prisoners, others hid themselves in the copses and farmhouses, or tried to escape by swimming the river.

In this battle, as in the preceding ones, the attack
suffered far heavier loss than the defence. The Army
of the Meuse lost 3500 combatants, the preponderating
loss falling on the IVth Corps. The French estimated
their loss at 1800 ; but in the course of the day and on
the following morning, 3000 prisoners, mostly unwounded, fell into the hands of the victors, with 51
guns, 33 ammunition and many other waggons, and a
military chest containing 150,000 francs. And, what
was of supreme importance, by the result of this battle
the French army had been driven into an extremely
unfavourable position.

While the IVth Corps had been chiefly sustaining the
day's battle, the Saxon Cavalry had pushed forward
on the right bank of the Meuse, and had reconnoitred
towards Mouzon and Carignan. The Guard Corps
reached Beaumont, and General von der Tann with the
1st Bavarian Corps was at Raucourt, having marched
by way of La Besace with some slight skirmishing on
the way. The IInd Bavarian Corps was assembled at
Sommauthe, the Vth Corps had reached Stonne, the
XIth, La Besace. Thus seven Corps now stood in
close concentration between the Meuse and the Bar.

The King rode back to Buzancy after the battle, as
all the villages in the vicinity of the battle-field were
crowded with the wounded. Here, as previously at
Clermont, was felt the great inconvenience of inadequate lodging for hundreds of illustrious guests and

their suites, when, for once in a way for military reasons, head-quarters were established in a small village, instead of in a large town. Shelter for those officers whose duty it was to prepare the necessary orders for the morrow was only found late at night, and with considerable difficulty.

These orders instructed that on the 31st two Corps of the Army of the Meuse should cross over to the right bank of the river, to prevent the possibility of further progress of the French to Metz by way of Montmédy. Two Corps of the army besieging Metz were besides already posted in that direction about Etain and Briey. The IIIrd Army was to continue its movement in the northward direction.

As the situation had now developed itself, it already seemed within sight that the Army of Châlons might be compelled to cross over into neutral territory, and the Belgian Government was therefore asked through diplomatic channels to concern itself with its disarmament in that event. The German troops had orders at once to cross the Belgian frontier, should the enemy not lay down his arms there.

While the Vth French Corps was still fighting about Beaumont, and when the rest of the army had crossed the Meuse, General MacMahon had ordered the concentration of his army on Sedan. He did not intend to offer battle there, but it was indispensable to give his troops a short rest, and provide them with food and ammunition. He then meant to continue the retreat by way of Mézières, which General Vinoy was just then approaching with the newly-formed XIIIth Corps. The Ist Corps, which had arrived at Carignan early in the afternoon, detached two of its divisions to Douzy in the evening to check any further advance of the Germans.

Though any pursuit immediately after the battle of Beaumont was prevented by the intervening river, the retreat of the French soon assumed the ominous character of a rout. The troops were utterly worn out

by their exertions by day and night, in continuous
rain and with but scanty supplies of food. The marching to and fro, to no visible purpose, had undermined
their confidence in their leaders, and a series of luckless fights had shaken their self-reliance. Thousands of
fugitives, crying for bread, crowded round the waggons
as they struggled forward to reach the little fortress
which had so unexpectedly become the central rallying
point of a great army.

The Emperor Napoleon arrived at Sedan from
Carignan late in the evening of the 30th; the VIIth
Corps reached Floing during the night, but the XIIth
Corps did not arrive at Bazeilles until the following
morning. The Vth Corps mustered at the eastern
suburb of Sedan in a fearfully shattered state, followed
in the afternoon of the 31st by the Ist, which, after
many rear-guard actions with the German cavalry,
took up a position behind the Givonne valley. To
pursue the march to Mézières on that day was not to
be thought of. The XIIth Corps had that same
evening to show a front at Bazeilles, where the thunder
of their cannon already heralded the arrival of the
Germans. The destruction of the bridges there and at
Donchery was ordered, but the order remained unexecuted, owing to the worn-out condition of the men.

August 31st.—Of the army of the Meuse the Guard
and 12th Cavalry Divisions had crossed the Meuse
at Pouilly, and by a pontoon bridge at Létanne,
and swept the country between the Meuse and the
Chiers. Following close upon the rear of the French
and harassing them in skirmishes till they reached
their new position, they brought in as prisoners
numbers of stragglers. The Guard Corps then crossed
the Chiers at Carignan and halted at Sachy; the XIIth
pushed on to about Douzy on the Meuse,[1] while its
advanced guard thrust ahead on the further side (of
the Chiers) as far as Francheval. The IVth Corps
remained at Mouzon.

[1] Douzy is on the north bank of the Chiers.

The 4th Cavalry Division of the IIIrd Army reconnoitred in the direction of Sedan, drove back the French outposts from Wadelincourt and Frenois, and, moving from the latter place, seized the railroad under the fire of hostile artillery. The 6th Cavalry Division on the left flank proceeded on the way to Mézières as far as Poix.

When the Ist Bavarian Corps reached Remilly before noon, it came under heavy fire from the opposite side of the river, and at once brought up its batteries in position on the hither slope of the valley of the Meuse. A sharp cannonade ensued, by the end of which sixty Bavarian guns were engaged. It was only now that the French attempted to blow up the railway bridge south of Bazeilles, but the vigorous fire of the 4th Jäger Battalion drove off the enemy with his engineers, the Jägers threw the powder-barrels into the river, and at midday crossed the bridge. The battalion entered Bazeilles in the face of a storm of bullets, and occupied the northern fringe of the straggling place. Thus the XIIth French Corps was forced to move up into a position between Balan and Moncelle, where, having been reinforced by batteries belonging to the Ist Corps, it had to encounter, and that with considerable waste of power, the daring little band of Germans.

General von der Tann [1] did not however hold it advisable to commit himself on that day to a serious conflict on the further side of the Meuse with a closely compacted enemy, while his own Corps was still unconcentrated ; and, since the weak detachment in Bazeilles had no hope of being reinforced, it withdrew therefrom at about half-past three without being pursued.

Meanwhile two pontoon bridges had been laid at Allicourt, without molestation from the French. These and the railway bridge were barricaded for the night, while eighty-four guns further secured them from being crossed. The Ist Bavarian Corps went into bivouac at Angecourt, the IInd at Hancourt.

---

[1] Commanding 1st Bavarian Corps.

To the left of the Bavarians the XIth Corps marched towards Donchery, followed by the Vth. The advanced guard found the place unoccupied, and extended itself on the further side of the river. By three o'clock two other bridges were completed close below Donchery, whilst the railway bridge above the place, also found unguarded, was destroyed.

On the extreme left the Würtemberg and the 6th Cavalry Divisions came in contact with the XIIIth French Corps, which had just arrived at Mézières.

The King removed his head-quarters to Vendresse.

In spite of a succession of occasionally very severe marches in bad weather, and of being in regard to supplies chiefly beholden to requisitioning, the Army of the Meuse advancing on the east, and the IIIrd Army on the south, were now directly in face of the concentrated French Army. Marshal MacMahon could scarcely have realized that the only chance of safety for his army, or even for part of it, lay in the immediate prosecution of his retreat on the 1st of September. It is true that the Crown Prince of Prussia, in possession as he was of every passage over the Meuse, would have promptly taken that movement in flank in the narrow space, little more than four miles wide, which was bounded on the north by the frontier. That nevertheless the attempt was not risked was only to be explained by the actual condition of the exhausted troops; for on this day the French Army was not yet capable of undertaking a disciplined march involving fighting; it could only fight where it stood.

On the German side it was still expected that the Marshal would strike for Mézières. The Army of the Meuse was ordered to attack the enemy's positions with the object of detaining him in them; the IIIrd Army, leaving only one Corps on the left bank, was to press forward on the right side of the river.

The French position about Sedan was covered to rearward by the fortress. The Meuse and the valleys of the Givonne and the Floing brooks offered formidable obstructions, but it was imperative that those outmost lines should be obstinately held. The Calvary height of Illy was a very important point, strengthened as it was by the Bois de Garenne in its rear, whence a high ridge stretching to Bazeilles afforded much cover in its numerous dips and shoulders. In the event of a retreat into neutral territory in the last extremity, the road thereto lay through Illy. Bazeilles, on the other hand, locally a very strong point of support to the Givonne front, constituted an acute salient, which, after the loss of the bridges across the Meuse, was open to attack on two sides.

BATTLE OF SEDAN.

(September 1st.)

In order, in co-operation with the Army of the Meuse, to hold fast the enemy in his position, General von der Tann sent his Ist Brigade over the pontoon-bridges against Bazeilles so early as four o'clock in a thick morning mist. The troops attacked the place, but now found the streets barricaded, and were fired on from every house. The leading company pressed on as far as to the northern egress, suffering great losses, but the others, while engaged in arduous street-fighting, were driven out of the western part of Bazeilles by the arrival of the 2nd Brigade of the French XIIth Corps. They however kept possession of the buildings at the southern end, and from thence issued to repeated assaults. As fresh troops were constantly coming up on both sides, the French being reinforced to the extent even of a brigade of the Ist and one of the Vth Corps, the murderous combat long swayed to and fro; in particular the struggle for the possession of the Villa

Beurmann, situated in front of the exit, and commanding the main street throughout its whole length, lasted
for a stricken hour. The inhabitants took an active
part in the fighting, and so they inevitably drew fire
upon themselves.

The fire of the strong array of guns drawn up on the
left slope of the valley of the Meuse naturally could not
be directed on the surging strife in Bazeilles, which
was now blazing in several places, but at eight o'clock,
on the arrival of the 8th Prussian Division at Remilly,
General von der Tann threw his last brigades into the
fight. The walled park of the château of Monvillers
was stormed and an entrance won into the Villa Beurmann. The artillery crossed the bridges at about nine
o'clock, and the 8th Division was requested to support
the combat in which the right wing of the Bavarians was
also engaged southward of Bazeilles about Moncelle.[1]

In this direction Prince George of Saxony[2] had so
early as five o'clock despatched an advanced guard of
seven battalions from Douzy. They drove the French
from Moncelle, pressed ahead to Platinerie and the
bridge there, and, in spite of the enemy's heavy fire,
took possession of the houses bordering the further
side of the Givonne brook, which they immediately
occupied for defensive purposes. Communication with
the Bavarians was now established, and the battery of
the advanced guard moved up quickly into action on
the eastern slope ; but a further infantry support could
not at first be afforded to this bold advance.

Marshal MacMahon had been struck by a splinter
from a shell near Moncelle at 6 a.m. He had named
General Ducrot as his successor in the chief command,
passing over two senior Corps commanders. Apprized
of this promotion at seven o'clock, that General issued
the necessary orders for the prompt assemblage of the
army at Illy, in preparation for an immediate retreat

---

[1] Moncelle is northward of Bazeilles.

[2] Now commanding XIIth Corps, since his elder brother's appoint-
ment to command of the Army of the Meuse.

on Mézières. He had already despatched Lartigue's Division of his own Corps to safeguard the crossing of the Givonne ravine at Daigny; the Divisions of Lacretelle and Bassoigne were ordered to take the offensive against the Saxons and Bavarians, to gain time for the withdrawal of the rest of the troops. The divisions forming the second line were to start immediately in a northerly direction.

But the Minister of War had appointed General de Wimpffen, recently returned from Algiers, to the command of the Vth Corps in room of General de Failly, and had at the same time given him a commission empowering him to assume the command of the Army in case of the disability of the Marshal.

General de Wimpffen knew the army of the Crown Prince to be in the neighbourhood of Donchery. He regarded the retreat to Mézières as utterly impracticable, and was bent on the diametrically opposite course of breaking out to Carignan, not doubting that he could drive aside the Bavarians and Saxons, and so succeed in effecting a junction with Marshal Bazaine. When he heard of the orders just issued by General Ducrot, and at the same time observed that an assault on Moncelle seemed to be taking an auspicious course, he produced—to his ruin—the authoritative commission which had been bestowed on him.

General Ducrot submitted without any remonstrance ; he might probably not have been averse to be relieved of so heavy a responsibility. The Divisions of the second line which were in the act of starting immediately were recalled ; and the further advance of the weak Bavarian and Saxon detachments was soon hard pressed by the impact of the first stroke of the enemy rushing on to the attack.

By seven in the morning, while one regiment of the Saxon advanced guard had gone in upon Moncelle, the other on its right had to concern itself with the threatening advance of Lartigue's Division. With that body it soon became engaged in a heavy fire-fight.

The regiment had laid down its packs on the march, and had omitted to take out the cartridges carried in them. Thus it soon ran short of ammunition, and the repeated and violent onslaughts of the Zouaves, directed principally against its unprotected right flank, had to be repulsed with the bayonet.

On the left in this quarter a strong artillery line had gradually been formed, which by half-past eight o'clock amounted to twelve batteries. But Lacretelle's Division was now approaching by the Givonne bottom, and dense swarms of tirailleurs forced the German batteries to retire at about nine o'clock. The guns, withdrawn into a position at a somewhat greater distance, drove back with their fire the enemy in the hollow, and presently returned to the position previously occupied.

The 4th Bavarian Brigade had meanwhile pushed forward into Moncelle, and the 46th Saxon Brigade also came up, so that it was possible to check the trifling progress made by Bassoigne's Division.

On the right flank of the Saxons, which had been hard pressed, much-needed supports now arrived from the 24th Division, and at once took the offensive. The French were driven back upon Daigny, with the loss of five guns. Then in conjunction with the Bavarians, who were pushing on through the valley to the northward, the village of Daigny, the bridge and the farmstead of La Rapaille were carried after a bitter fight.

About ten o'clock the Guard Corps reached the upper Givonne. Having started in the night, the Corps was marching in two columns, when cannon thunder from Bazeilles heard afar off caused the troops to quicken their pace. In order to render assistance by the shortest road, the left column would have had to traverse two deep ravines and the pathless wood of Chevallier, so it took the longer route by Villers Cernay, which place the head of the right column passed in ample time to take part with the Saxons in the contest with Lartigue's Division, and to capture two of its guns.

The Divisions ordered back by General Ducrot had already resumed their former positions on the western slopes, and fourteen batteries of the Guard Corps now opened fire upon them from the east.

At the same hour (ten o'clock) the 7th .Division of the IVth Corps had arrived near Lamécourt, and the 8th near Remilly, both places rearward of Bazeilles ; the head of the latter had reached the Remilly railway station.

The first attempt of the French to break out eastward to Carignan proved a failure, and their retreat westward to Mézières was also already cut off, for the Vth and XIth Corps of the IIIrd Army, together with the Würtemberg Division, had been detailed to move northward to the road leading to that place. These troops had started early in the night, and at six a.m. had crossed the Meuse at Donchery, and by the three pontoon bridges further down the river. The advanced patrols found the Mézières road quite clear of the enemy, and the heavy cannonade heard from the direction of Bazeilles made it appear probable that the French had accepted battle in their position at Sedan. The Crown Prince, therefore, ordered the two Corps, which already had reached the upland of Vrigne, to swing to their right and advance on St. Menges ; the Würtembergers were to remain behind to watch Mézières. General von Kirchbach then indicated Fleigneux to his advanced guard as the objective of the further movement, which had for its purpose the barring of the escape of the French into Belgium, and the establishment of a junction with the right wing of the Army of the Meuse.

The narrow pass about 2000 paces long between the heights and the river traversed by the road to St. Albert, was neither held nor watched by the French. It was not till the advanced guard reached St. Menges that it encountered a French detachment, which soon withdrew. The German advance then deployed against Illy. Two companies moved to the right and took possession of Floing, where they maintained themselves for the next two hours without assistance against repeated attacks.

The earliest arriving Prussian batteries had to exert themselves to the utmost to maintain themselves against the much superior strength of French artillery in action about Illy. At first they had for their only escort some cavalry and a few companies of infantry, and as these bodies debouched from the defile of St. Albert, they found themselves an enticing object of attack to Margueritte's Cavalry Division halted on the aforesaid plateau of Illy. It was at nine o'clock that General Galliffet rode down to the attack at the head of three regiments of Chasseurs d'Afrique and two squadrons of Lancers formed in three lines. The first fury of the charge fell upon two companies of the 87th Regiment, which met it with a hail of bullets at sixty yards range. The first line charged some horse-lengths further forward, then wheeled outward to both flanks, and came under the fire of the supporting troops occupying the broom copses. The Prussian batteries, too, showered their shell fire into the throng of French horsemen, who finally went about in confusion, and, having suffered great losses, sought refuge in the Bois de Garenne.

At ten o'clock, the same hour at which the assaults of the French on Bazeilles and about Daigny were being repulsed, fourteen batteries of the XIth Corps were already in action on and near the ridge south-east of St.-Menges; to swell which mass presently came up those of the Vth Corps. Powerful infantry columns were in march upon Fleigneux, and thus the ring surrounding Sedan was already at this hour nearly closed. The one Bavarian Corps and the artillery reserves on the left bank of the Meuse were considered strong enough to repel any attempt of the French to break through in that direction; five Corps were on the right bank, ready for a concentric attack.

The Bavarians and Saxons, reinforced by the head of the IVth Corps, issued from the burning Bazeilles and from Moncelle, and, in spite of a stubborn resistance, drove the detachments of the French XIIth Corps in position eastward of Balan back upon Fond de Givonne.

Once in possession of the southern spur of the ridge sloping down from Illy, and while awaiting the renewed attacks of the French, the extreme urgency was realized of reassembling the different Corps and of re-forming the troops, which had fallen into great confusion.

As soon as this was done, the 5th Bavarian Brigade advanced on Balan. The troops found but a feeble resistance in the village itself; but it was only after a hard fight that they succeeded in occupying the park of the château situated at its extreme end. From thence, soon after midday, the foremost battalion extended close up to the walls of the fortress, and exchanged shots with the garrison. There now ensued a stationary musketry fight with the enemy once again firmly posted about Fond de Givonne. At one o'clock the French, having evidently been reinforced, took the offensive, after a preparatory cannonade and mitrailleuse fire. The 5th Bavarian Brigade was driven back for some considerable distance, but presently, supported by the 6th, regained its old position after an hour's hard fighting.

Meanwhile the Saxon Corps had extended itself in the northern part of the valley against Givonne. There also the foremost detachments of the Guard Corps were already established, as well as in Haybés. The Prussian artillery forced the French batteries to change their positions more than once, and had already caused several of them to go out of action. To gain breathing space here, the French repeatedly tried to send forward large bodies of tirailleurs, and ten guns were brought up into the still occupied Givonne, but these were taken before they could unlimber. The Prussian shells also fell with some effect among the French troops massed in the Bois de Garenne, though fired from a long distance.

After the Franctireurs de Paris had been driven out of Chapelle, the Guard-cavalry dashed through Givonne and up the valley, and at noon the Hussars had succeeded in establishing direct contact with the left flank of the IIIrd Army.

The 41st Brigade of that army had left Fleigneux and was descending the upper valley of the Givonne, and the retreat of the French from Illy in a southern direction had already begun. The 87th Regiment seized eight guns which were in action, and captured thirty baggage waggons with their teams, as well as hundreds of cavalry horses wandering riderless. The cavalry of the advanced guard of the Vth Corps also made prisoners of General Brahaut and his staff, besides a great number of dispersed infantrymen and 150 draught-horses, together with forty ammunition and baggage waggons.

In the direction of Floing there was also an attempt on the part of the French to break through; but the originally very weak infantry posts at that point had gradually been strengthened, and the French were driven from the locality as quickly as they had entered. And now twenty-six batteries of the Army of the Meuse[1] crossed their fire with that of the Guard batteries, in position on the eastern slope of the Givonne valley. The effect was overwhelming. The French batteries were shattered and many ammunition waggons exploded.

General de Wimpffen at first took the advance of the Germans from the north for nothing more than a demonstration, but toward midday became completely

---

[1] Sense and accuracy alike indicate that "Army of the Meuse" in text should be "Third Army," *vide* Staff History, part I. 2nd vol. pp. 361, 367, and 370.—Clarke's authorized Trs.

convinced that it was a real attack. He therefore ordered that the two Divisions of the Ist Corps halted in second line behind the Givonne front, should now return to the Illy height in support of General Douay. On rejoining the XIIth Corps he found it in full retreat on Sedan, and now urgently requested General Douay to despatch assistance in the direction of, Bazeilles. Maussion's Brigade did actually go thither, followed by Dumont's Division, which latter was relieved in the foremost line by Conseil Dumesnil's Division. All this marching and counter-marching was executed in the space south of the Bois de Garenne dominated by the cross fire of the German artillery. The recoil of the cavalry heightened the confusion, and several battalions drew back into the insecure protection of the forest. General Douay, it is true, reinforced by portions of the Vth Corps, retook the Calvary (of Illy), but was forced to abandon it by two o'clock; and the forest (of Garenne) behind it was then shelled by sixty guns of the Guard artillery.

Liébert's Division alone had up to now maintained its very strong position on the heights north of Casal. The amassing at Floing of a sufficient strength from the German Vth and XIth Corps could only be effected very gradually. After one o'clock, however, detachments began to climb the steep hill immediately in its front, while others went round to the south towards Gaulier and Casal, and yet others came down from Fleigneux. The complete intermixture of the troops prevented any unity of command; and a bloody contest was carried on for a long time with varying fortunes. The French Division, attacked on both flanks and also heavily shelled, at last had its power of resistance undermined; and the reserves of the VIIth Corps having already been called off to other parts of the battle-field, the French cavalry once more devotedly struck in to maintain the fight.

General Margueritte, with five regiments of light horse, and two of Lancers, charged to the rescue out of the Bois de Garenne. Almost at the outset he fell severely wounded, and General Galliffet took his place. The advance was over very treacherous ground, and even before the actual charge was delivered the cohesion of the ranks was broken by the heavy flanking fire of the Prussian batteries. Still, with thinned ranks but with unflinching resolution, the individual squadrons charged on the troops of the 43rd Infantry Brigade, partly lying in cover, partly standing out on the bare slope in swarms and groups ; and also on the reinforcements hurrying from Fleigneux. The first line of the former was pierced at several points, and a band of these brave troopers dashed from Casal through the intervals between eight guns blazing into them with case-shot, but the companies beyond stopped their further progress. Cuirassiers issuing from Gaulier fell on the hostile rear, but encountering the Prussian Hussars in the Meuse valley, galloped off northward. Other detachments cut their way through the infantry as far as the narrow pass of St. Albert, where they were met by the battalions debouching therefrom. Others again entered Floing only to succumb to the 5th Jägers, who had to form front back to back. These attacks were repeated by the French again and again in the shape of detached fights, and the murderous turmoil lasted for half an hour with steadily diminishing fortune for the French. The volleys of the German infantry delivered steadily at a short range strewed the whole field with dead and wounded horsemen. Many fell into the quarries or down the steep declivities, a few may have escaped by swimming the Meuse ; and scarcely more than half of these brave troops returned to the protection of the forest.

But this magnificent sacrifice and glorious effort of the French cavalry could not change the fate of the day. The Prussian infantry had lost but little in the cut-and-thrust encounters, and at once resumed the attack against Liébert's Division. But in this onslaught they sustained heavy losses ; for instance, all three battalions of the 6th Regiment had to be commanded by lieutenants. But when Casal had been stormed, the French, after a spirited resistance, withdrew at about three o'clock to their last refuge in the Bois de Garenne.

When between one and two o'clock the fighting in Bazeilles had at first taken a favourable turn, General de Wimpffen reverted to his original plan of driving from the village the Bavarians, now exhausted by a long struggle, and of breaking a way through to Carignan with the Ist, Vth, and XIIth Corps; while the VIIth Corps was to cover the rear of this movement. But the orders issued to that effect in part never reached the Corps; in part did so so late that circumstances forbade their being carried out.

In consequence of previously mentioned orders, besides Bassoigne's Division, the Divisions of Goze and Grandchamp were still available. Now, at about three in the afternoon, the two last-named advanced from Fond de Givonne, over the ridge to the eastward, and the 23rd Saxon Division, which was marching up the valley on the left bank of the Givonne, found itself suddenly attacked by closed battalions accompanied by batteries. With the support of the left wing of the Guard Corps and of the artillery fire from the eastern slope, it soon succeeded in repulsing the hostile masses, and indeed drove them across the valley back to Fond de Givonne. The energy of the French appeared to be by this time exhausted, for they allowed themselves to be taken prisoners by hundreds. As soon as a firm footing had been gained on the heights west of the Givonne, the German artillery established itself there, and by three o'clock an artillery line of twenty-one batteries stretching from Bazeilles to Haybés was in action.

The Bois de Garenne, in which many broken bands of all Corps and of all arms were straggling in search of refuge, still remained to be gained. After a short

H

cannonade the 1st Guard-Division climbed the
heights from Givonne, and were joined by Saxon
battalions, the left wing of the IIIrd army at the
same time coming on from Illy. A wild turmoil
ensued, in which isolated bands offered violent resistance, while others surrendered by thousands; nor was
it until five o'clock that the Germans had complete
possession of the forest.

Meanwhile long columns of French could be seen
pouring down on Sedan from the surrounding heights.
Disordered bodies of troops huddled closer and closer
in and up to the fortress, and shells from the German
batteries on both sides of the Meuse were constantly
exploding in the midst of the chaos. Pillars of fire were
soon rising from the city, and the Bavarian riflemen,
who had pushed forward through Torcy, were preparing
to climb the palisades at the gate when, at about half-
past four, the white flags were visible on the towers.

The Emperor Napoleon had declined to follow
General de Wimpffen in his attempt to break through
the German lines; he had, on the contrary, ordered
him to enter into negotiations with the enemy. In
consequence of the renewal of the order to that effect
the French suddenly ceased firing.

General Reille now made his appearance in the
presence of the King, who had watched the action
since early morning from the hill south of Frénois.
He was the bearer of an autograph letter from the
Emperor, whose presence in Sedan was till then unknown. He placed his sword in the hand of the
King, but as this was clearly only an act of personal
surrender, the answer stipulated that an officer should
be commissioned with full powers to treat with General
von Moltke as to the surrender of the French Army.

This painful duty was imposed on General de
Wimpffen, who was in no way responsible for the
desperate straits into which the French army had been
brought.

The negotiations were held at Donchery in the night between the 1st and 2nd September. On the part of the Germans it had to be insisted on that they durst not forego the advantages gained over so powerful an enemy as France. Since the French had regarded the victory of German arms over other nationalities in the light of an offence to France, any untimely generosity might cause them to forget their own defeat. The only course to pursue was to insist upon the disarmament and captivity of their entire army, with the exception that the officers were to be free on parole.

General de Wimpffen declared it impossible to accept conditions so hard, the negotiations were broken off, and the French officers returned to Sedan at one o'clock on the morning of the 2nd. Before their departure they were given to understand that unless the offered terms were accepted by nine o'clock that morning the artillery would reopen fire.

The capitulation was signed by General de Wimpffen on the morning of the 2nd, further resistance being obviously impossible.

Marshal MacMahon was very fortunate in having been disabled so early in the battle, else on him would have inevitably devolved the duty of signing the capitulation; and though he had only carried out the orders forced upon him by the Paris authorities, he could hardly have sat in judgment, as he afterwards did, on the comrade he had failed to relieve.

It is difficult to understand why we Germans celebrate the 2nd of September—a day on which nothing memorable happened, but what was the inevitable result of the previous day's work; the day on which the army really crowned itself with glory was the 1st of September.

The splendid victory of that day had cost the Germans 460 officers and 8500 men. The French losses were far greater; they amounted to 17,000 men, and were chiefly

wrought because of the full development of the fire
of the German artillery.

During the battle there
   were taken prisoners   21,000
By the Capitulation   83,000
_____

A total of 104,000 sent into captivity.

The prisoners for the present were assembled on the
peninsula of Iges formed by the Meuse. As supplies
for them were entirely lacking, the Commandant of
Mézières permitted the unrestricted transport of provisions by the railway as far as Donchery. Two Army
Corps were assigned to the duty of guarding and
escorting the convoys of prisoners, who were sent off in
successive bodies 2000 strong by two roads, one to
Etain, and the other by Clermont to Pont à Mousson,
where the prisoners were taken over by the army
investing Metz, and forwarded to various parts of
Germany.

On Belgian territory 3000 men had been disarmed.

The spoils of war taken at Sedan consisted of three
standards, 419 field-pieces, 139 fortress guns, 66,000
rifles, over 1000 waggons, and 6000 serviceable
horses.

With the entire nullification of this army fell the
Empire in France.

PART II.

WHILE one half of the German Army was thus engaged in a victorious advance, the other half remained stationary before Metz.

The foremost line of outposts of the investment embraced a circuit of more than twenty-eight miles. An attempt of the concentrated forces of the enemy to break through would have met at the beginning of the blockade with but slight opposition. It was therefore extremely urgent that the several posts should be strengthened by fortifications. These works, the clearing of the neighbouring battle-fields, the close watch kept over every movement of the enemy, the construction of a telegraph-line connecting the quarters of the several Staffs, and finally the erection of a sufficiency of shelter, kept the troops and their leaders amply occupied. Besides the care of the wounded, provision had to be made for the sick, whose number was daily increased by the unusually severe weather and lack of shelter. The provisioning of the troops was, however, facilitated by their stationary attitude, and in addition there now flowed in upon them from their homes a copious supply of love-gifts.

The first days of the investment went by without any attempts to break out on the part of the French. They too were busy reorganizing, collecting ammunition and supplies.

On the 20th of August Marshal Bazaine had written to Châlons: "I will give due notice of my march if, taking everything into consideration, I can undertake any such attempt." On the 23rd he reported to the Emperor : " If the news of the extensive reductions in the besieging army is confirmed, I shall set out on the march, and that by way of the northern fortresses, in order to risk nothing."

SORTIE FROM METZ.

(August 26th.)

On the 26th of August, when the Army of Châlons was still nearly seventy miles distant from the Ardennes Canal, and its advance on Metz was as yet not generally known, Marshal Bazaine collected his main forces on the right bank of the Moselle.

This movement had not escaped the notice of the German posts of observation, and the field-telegraph at once disseminated the information.

To support the 3rd Reserve Division at Malroy, ten battalions of the Xth Corps crossed from the left bank of the Moselle to Argancy on the right bank. The 25th Division held itself in readiness at the bridge of Hauconcourt, and the Ist Corps closed up towards Servigny. In the event of the success of a breach towards the north, the IIIrd, IVth, and part of the IXth Corps were available to intercept the enemy's march about Thionville.

The crossing from the island of Chambière by the field-bridges which had been built, seriously delayed the French advance ; the IIIrd, IInd, IVth, and VIth Corps, however, by about noon stood closely concentrated between Mey and Grimont. Advanced detachments had already at several points driven in the

German posts south-east of Metz, but instead of now entering upon a general attack, Marshal Bazaine summoned all his Corps Commanders to a conference at Grimont. The Commandant of Metz then made it known that the artillery ammunition in hand would suffice for only one battle, that when it was exhausted the army would find itself defenceless in midst of the German hosts; the fortress, he continued, was not defensible in its present state, and could not stand a siege if the army were to be withdrawn from the place. All those things might certainly have been seen into during the stay in Metz; and much more did they behove to have been known before the army should cut loose. It was particularly enforced, "That the preservation of the Army was the best service that could be rendered to the country, more especially if negotiations for peace should be entered into." The generals present all spoke against the prosecution of the proposed movement; and the Commander-in-Chief, who had refrained from expressing any opinion in the matter, gave the order to retire at four o'clock.

The whole affair of the 26th of August can only be regarded in the light of a parade manœuvre. Bazaine reported to the Minister of War that the scarcity of artillery ammunition made it "impossible" to break through the hostile lines, unless an offensive operation from the outside "should force the enemy to raise the investment." Information as to the "temper of the people" was earnestly requested.

There is no doubt that Bazaine was influenced, not wholly by military, but also by political considerations; still it may be asked whether he could have acted differently in the prevailing confusion of France. From the correspondence referred to, and his behaviour in the battles before Metz, his reluctance to quit the place was evident. Under its walls he could maintain a considerable army in unimpaired condition till the given moment. At the head of the only French army

not yet shattered,[1] he might find himself in a position
of greater power than any other man in the country.
This army must, of course, first be freed from the
bonds which now confined it. Even if it should succeed in forcibly breaking out it would be greatly
weakened ; and it was not inconceivable that the
Marshal, as the strongest power in the land, might be
able to offer a price which should induce the enemy to
grant him a passage. Then when at length the time
for making peace should come, the Germans would no
doubt ask : " Who in France is the authority with whom
we can negotiate now that the Empire is overthrown,
and who is strong enough to give a guarantee that the
obligations which he will have undertaken shall be performed ? " That the Marshal, if his plans had come
to fulfilment, would have acted otherwise than in the
interest of France is neither proved nor to be assumed.

But presently a number of men combined in Paris,
who, without consulting the nation, constituted themselves the Government of the country, and took the
direction of its affairs into their own hands. In opposition to this party, Marshal Bazaine, with his army at
his back, could well come forward as a rival or a foe ;
nay, and—this was his crime in the eyes of the Paris
Government—he might restore the authority of the
Emperor to whom he had sworn allegiance. Whether
he might not thus have spared his country longer
misery and greater sacrifices may be left undecided.
But that he was subsequently charged with treason
obviously arose, no doubt, from the national vanity of
the French, which demanded a " Traitor " as a scapegoat
for the national humiliation.

Soon after this demonstration, for it was nothing
more, of the besieged army, the investing forces were,
in fact, reduced by the despatch, on the 29th, in accordance with orders from the supreme Headquarter,

---

[1] The Army of Châlons was still unimpaired on August 26th.

of the IInd and IIIrd Corps to Briey and Conflans, there to remain. To be sure, from those positions it was in their power to attack either of the French Marshals, as might prove requisite ; while the XIIIth Corps, newly formed of the 17th Division, hitherto retained to defend the coast, and from the Landwehr, was already within a short distance of Metz.

Meanwhile Marshal Bazaine might have realized that he must abandon his delusion as to a release by means of negotiations ; and he now firmly resolved to cut his way out by dint of force. The troops were served out with three days' provisions, and the intendance was furnished with a supply of " iron rations " from the magazines of the fortress. That the attempt should again be made on the right bank of the Moselle was only to be expected ; since by far the larger portion of the enemy's forces stood entrenched on the left bank. It would have been very difficult to traverse that hilly region, intersected by deep ravines ; and finally the army of the Crown Prince on the march to Paris would have had to be encountered. East of Metz, on the other hand, there afforded ample space for the full development of the French forces. By bending of the south the open country was to be reached, offering no effective intercepting position to the enemy, whose line of investment was weakest in that direction. The march to the north and along the Belgian frontier entailed more danger and greater obstacles, yet the Marshal had explicitly indicated this particular road as that by which he intended to move. The Army of Châlons was also marching in that direction; its approach was already reported ; and on the 31st of August, on which day, in fact, Marshal MacMahon's forces reached Stenay[1] in such disastrous circumstances, Bazaine's army also issued from Metz.

---

[1] "Stenay," probably a slip of the pen for "Sedan," where MacMahon's army was gathered on August 31st. It never reached Stenay.

BATTLE OF NOISSEVILLE.

(August 31st.)

Of the French Corps then located on the right bank of the Moselle,[1] the IIIrd was to cover on the right flank the advance of the others; one Division was ordered to move early in a south-easterly direction with intent to mislead the enemy, its other three Divisions to take position threatening Noisseville. Three pontoon bridges were constructed for the crossing of the rest of the army, and accesses to the heights in front of St. Julien were prepared. The passage of the IVth and VIth Corps was to begin at six o'clock, and they were to take a position which, linking on its right with the IIIrd Corps, should extend from the village of Mey by Grimont to the Moselle; the IInd Corps and the Guard were to follow and form a second line. With the passage of the artillery reserve and the cavalry it was expected that the crossing of the Moselle should be finished by ten o'clock; the trains were halted on the Isle of Chambière. Thus it was intended that by noon five Corps should be ready for the assault of the section of the line of investment from Retonfay (on the French right) to Argancy (on the left), a distance of about seven miles, which space had for its defenders only two German Divisions.

So early as seven o'clock Montaudon's Division issued from Fort Queuleu, and heading eastward drove the opposing outposts back on Aubigny. But this demonstration did not in the least deceive the Germans. The stir in the French camp had been observed quite early, and when the mist cleared off and great masses of French troops were seen in front of Fort St. Julien, an attempt to break through to the north was anticipated with certainty, and the necessary dispositions were immediately undertaken to foil the effort.

[1] The IInd and IIIrd Army.

The 28th Brigade of the VIIth Corps was dispatched to protect Courcelles, so that thus the 3rd Brigade of the Ist Corps could be brought nearer to Servigny. The troops of the Xth Corps which could be spared from their own section of the line of defence on the left bank were again set in motion to cross to the right, and the IXth Corps was held in readiness in anticipation of its having eventually to follow. The IIIrd Corps and the Ist Cavalry Division were recalled from Briey and directed to the plateau of Privat; the IInd was to stand ready to move off.

The attempt of the French to break out proved on this day even less successful than on the 26th; the IVth and VIth Corps crossed each other at the bridges, and they only reached their rendezvous position at one o'clock, though it was little more than three miles further; they then abandoned the intention of an immediate assault, and set about cooking. A few skirmishes on the east of Aubigny and on the north towards Rupigny came to nothing. The Imperial Guard did not come up till three o'clock, the artillery and cavalry were still behind.

As entire quiescence now supervened, the Germans came to the conclusion that the attack must be intended for the following day. To save the strength of the troops, part of the reinforcements ordered up had already been sent back, when, at about four o'clock, the French suddenly opened a heavy artillery fire.

The Marshal had again summoned his commanders to assemble at Grimont, this time to inform them of his dispositions for the attack. It was evident that the French could not advance towards the north until they had gained elbow-room by means of an offensive movement in the eastern direction, and had secured their right flank. For even if they succeeded in breaking through the Malroy-Charly line, they could get no further so long as the Germans were at Servigny and swept with their fire the plain as far as the Moselle, a space not more than 5000 paces broad. The Marshal could not in any case reckon on carrying through his Artillery Reserve, which did not reach the battle-field until six o'clock, and the extrication of the baggage trains which had been left behind on the Isle of Chambière was clearly impossible. The Cavalry Corps was still defiling, and could not come up until nine o'clock in the evening.

This unsatisfactory aspect of affairs was in complete accord with the character of the dispositions of the French commanders.

Marshal Le Bœuf received orders to advance with the IInd and IIIrd Corps on both sides of the valley of St. Barbe, and outflank from the south the 1st Prussian Division at Servigny, while the IVth Corps assailed it in front. The VIth Corps had the task of thrusting forward against the Reserve Division at Charly-Malroy. Marshal Canrobert was to command the two latter Corps, and the Guard was to be held back as reserve.

Thus General von Manteuffel had at first to confront with a small force a greatly superior enemy. This opposition might be undertaken either in the St. Barbe position, to outflank which was by no means easy, or on the line of Servigny—Poix—Failly, which, though more exposed, afforded much greater scope for the use of artillery. The latter position was chosen on the advice of General von Bergmann commanding the artillery, and the Landwehr Brigade was ordered into it from Antilly, where its place was taken by the 25th Division. Ten batteries were advanced to a distance of 1000 paces in front of the line of villages held by the infantry. Their fire proved so superior to that of the enemy, that the hostile batteries were soon silenced. The attack on Rupigny by the French IVth Corps, supported on the flank though it was by three batteries, remained stationary for a considerable time, and as the Prussians had not yet been driven back on St. Barbe, the VIth French Corps meanwhile could not enter upon any serious attack on the Reserve Division at Malroy-Charly. For the same reason Marshal Canrobert received the order for the present only to send a detachment of his force to the attack of the village of Failly, the northern point of support of the Servigny position.

Tixier's Division therefore moved out at 7.30 in the evening from Villers L'Orme, but met with a most obstinate resistance at Failly. Though attacked on two sides, pelted by a storm of projectiles, and, as regarded a part of them, engaged in hand-to-hand fighting, the East Prussians stoutly held possession of their ground till the Landwehr Brigade came to their assistance from Vremy.

Up till now the situation southward of Servigny had worn a more favourable aspect for the French than in this northern re-entering angle between two hostile positions; their IInd and IIIrd Corps in the former quarter had only the 3rd Brigade of the Ist Prussian Corps to deal with in front of Retonfay. Montaudon's and Metman's Divisions moved down by way of Nouilly into the valley of the Vallières brook; Clinchant's Brigade stormed the brewery in the face of strong resistance, and by seven o'clock the defenders of Noisseville were forced to evacuate the place. Montoy and Flanville were also taken possession of by the French, and further south the outposts of the German 4th Brigade were thrown back through Coincy and Château Aubigny. The batteries of the 1st Division, after enduring for a long time the fire of strong swarms of tirailleurs from the deep hollow south of them, were forced about seven o'clock to retire in echelon to the infantry position on the Poix—Servigny line, fending off for a time the pursuing enemy with case-shot.

But to this position the Prussians now held on staunchly, although completely out-flanked on their left. Potier's Brigade ascended the northern slope of the Vallières valley, but found it impossible to reach

Servigny. A moment later Cissey's Brigade rushed forward from the west, and seized the graveyard outside the village. The French IVth Corps struck at the centre of the Prussian position, but without success. Its effort to penetrate between Poix and Servigny was frustrated by the offensive stroke delivered by the battalions of the 2nd Brigade constituting the last reserve—a counter attack in which all the troops at hand at once joined. With drums beating they hurled themselves on the French, swept them out of the grave-yard, and drove them back down the slope.

In support of the fierce fight here, the 3rd Brigade about half-past eight marched on Noisseville, whence it promptly expelled the small detachment found in possession, but subsequently yielded to superior numbers, and withdrew to St. Marais.

The din of strife had now fallen silent at all points, and the fight seemed to be ended. The infantry of the 1st Division were moving into the villages, and the artillery was going into bivouac, when suddenly at nine o'clock a great mass of French infantry advanced in the darkness to an attack on Servigny. This proved to be Aymard's Division; it entered the village without firing a shot, surprised the garrison, and drove it out after a fierce hand-to-hand fight. This episode remained unnoticed for a long time, even by the nearest troops; but these then rushed to arms, and pouring in from all sides, drove the French back beyond the grave-yard, which thenceforth remained in German possession.

It was now ten o'clock at night. The 1st Division had kept its ground against an enemy of superior strength; but the French had penetrated into the unoccupied gap between the 3rd and 4th Brigades, and were a standing menace to the German flank at Servigny from their position at Noisseville.

September 1st.—The 18th Division, by a night-march, crossed from the left to the right bank of the Moselle at four o'clock in the morning, and reinforced with a brigade both flanks of the line Malroy—Charly—Bois de Failly. The 25th Division was now able to fall back from Antilly to St. Barbe, where, with the 6th Landwehr Brigade, it formed a reserve for the Poix—Servigny position.

On the morning of the 1st of September a thick mist still shrouded the plain when all the troops stood to arms.

Marshal Bazaine now again indicated to his generals the seizure of St. Barbe as the prime objective, since that alone could render possible the march to the north ; and he added, " In the event of failure, we shall maintain our positions." This expression could only indicate the intention, in the event specified, of remaining under shelter of the cannon of Metz, and evinced but little confidence in the success of the enterprise now engaged in.[1]

So early as five o'clock the 3rd Brigade had deployed on the Saarlouis road to prevent the further progress of the enemy on the left flank of the 1st Division. It swept the slopes in the direction of Montoy with the fire of twenty guns, and when Noisseville had been well plied for a considerable time by the fire of the artillery of the 2nd Brigade, about seven o'clock the 43rd Regiment carried the village by storm. A fierce fight ensued in and about the houses : two French brigades struck into the combat, and after a long whirl of fighting the German regiment was driven out again. Battalions of the 3rd Brigade came up just as the fight was over, but the attack was not renewed.

Now that the direction of the French effort to break out was no longer doubtful, the 28th Brigade had started from Courcelles at six in the morning to rein-

---

[1] The wording of Bazaine's order dispenses with any speculation on this point. He wrote, " In the event of failure, we shall maintain our positions, strengthen ourselves therein, *and retire in the evening under Forts St. Julien and Queuleu.*"

force the Ist Corps. Its two batteries silenced those of
the French at Montoy, and then directed their fire on
Flanville. The enemy soon began to abandon the
burning village, which, at nine o'clock, the Rhine-
landers entered from the south and the East Prussians
from the north. Marshal Le Bœuf again sent forward Bastoul's Division on Montoy, but the extremely
effective fire of the Prussian artillery compelled it to
turn back.

The 3rd Brigade had meanwhile taken up a position
on the upland of Retonfay, where it was now joined by
the 28th. The 3rd Cavalry Division was reinforced by
the Hessian Horse Brigade, and these troops with the
artillery mass made up presently to 114 guns, formed
a rampart against any further progress of the IInd and
IIIrd French Corps.

The fighting had now died out on the right wing
of the French army; but the IVth Corps had been
enjoined to await the direct advance of the troops of that
wing before renewing its attack on the artillery-front
and village entrenchments of the line from Servigny to
Poix, whose strength had been proved on the previous
day. But towards eleven o'clock, after Noisseville
had been heavily bombarded, the 3rd Prussian Brigade,
supported by the Landwehr, advanced southward of the
position, pushed its attack against that point, and
compelled the French to withdraw from the burning
village.

Marshal Canrobert, on the northern front of the
sortie, had brought up his batteries at Chieulles by
half-past eight, and their fire, seconded by that of the
artillery of the fortress, caused a temporary evacuation
of Rupigny; but the village was soon reoccupied.
Tixier's Division had made two fruitless attempts to
seize Failly, and now, on the other hand, the 36th
Brigade of the 18th Division came up, and taking the
offensive in conjunction with the Reserve Division, at
ten o'clock drove the French back over the Chieulles

stream. They made still another onslaught on Failly, but the flanking fire made this also a failure.

Marshal Le Bœuf, though he still had more than two Divisions to oppose it, held himself obliged to retreat on account of the approach of the Prussian 3rd Brigade on his right flank; and in consequence of the receipt of this intelligence, Marshal Bazaine, at mid-day ordered the fighting to be broken off at all other points.

The Army of the Rhine which issued from Metz on August 31st, with a strength of 137,000 men,[1] had been successfully opposed by no more than 36,000 Prussians. In this battle for the first time in the war the French were the assailants, the Germans had the rôle of the defence. That the Germans lost 3400 men against the loss of 3000 by the French, must be attributed to the higher properties of the infantry weapon of the latter. But the superiority of the Prussian artillery was decisively proved, and this it was which rendered possible General von Manteuffel's unshaken resistance.

The VIIth Corps remained on the right bank of the Norelle, where the line of investment was now further strengthened by the arrival of the XIIIth Corps under the command of the Grand Duke of Mecklenburg. On the left bank the IInd and IIIrd Corps were now able to return to their respective previous positions. On the same day and at about the same hour when the destruction of one French army was completed at Sedan, the other was returning to an apparently more and more hopeless detention in Metz. Thus the issue of the war was already beyond doubt after a campaign of but two months' duration; though the war itself was far from being ended.

[1] The estimate of the total strength of the Army of the Rhine on the 22nd August is given at 137,728 men in the German Staff History. It deducts for garrison and normal outpost-duty details amounting to over 17,000 men; and reckons the marching out strength for the battle of 31st August—1st September at "about 120,000 men."

I

CHANGE OF GOVERNMENT IN PARIS.

When, in the night of the 4th of September, the
news of the disaster of Sedan and the Emperor's
surrender became known in Paris, the Legislative Body
met in a rapidly successive series of sittings for the purpose of selecting an Administrative Committee. The
mob cut those deliberations short by forcing its way
into the Chamber and proclaiming the Republic there
and at the Hôtel de Ville, amidst the acclamations of
the people. Though the troops were under arms in
their barracks, the Government till now in power
offered no resistance; the Empress left Paris; General
Trochu and several members of the Minority in the
Chamber combined to form a Government, which they
styled "The Government of National Defence and
War." "War to the bitter end" was its motto, and
the entire nation was to be called to arms. Not an inch
of territory, not a stone of the fortresses was to be
yielded up to the enemy.

Such a Government, devoid of any legitimate founda-
tion, necessarily thirsted for results, and could be little
disposed to allow the war to end in peace.

Notwithstanding all the early reverses of the war,
France was too rich in resources to find herself as yet
by any means defenceless. General Vinoy was still in
the field. All the scattered Corps, the Marine troops
and the Gendarmerie could gather to him. There was,
too, the "Territorial Militia," numbering 468,000 men,
an institution which the country owed to Marshal Niel,
whose far-seeing work of reorganization had been cut
short only too soon. Further, there was available
to be called up the falling-due contingent of 100,000
conscripts, as well as the National Guard. It followed that France was thus able to put into the field
a million of men, without reckoning Franctireurs and
Volunteer Corps. The reserve store of 2000 guns and
400,000 Chassepôts assured the means of armament,

and the workshops of neutral England were ready and willing to fulfil commissions. Such resources for war, backed by the active patriotism of the nation, could maintain a prolonged resistance if a master will should inspire it with energy.

And such a will was disclosed in the person of Gambetta.

Minister of War, he had at the same time, by the French system of government, the direction of military operations, and certainly he was not the man to loosen his grasp of the chief command. For in a Republic, a victorious general at the head of the Army would at once have become Dictator in his stead. M. de Freycinet, another civilian, served under Gambetta as a sort of Chief of the General Staff, and the energetic, but dilettante, commandership exercised by these gentlemen cost France very dear. Gambetta's rare energy and unrelenting determination availed, indeed, to induce the entire population to take up arms, but not to direct these hasty levies with comprehensive unity of purpose. Without giving them time to be trained into fitness for the field, with ruthless severity he despatched them into the field in utter inefficiency as they were called out, to attempt the execution of ill-digested plans against an enemy on whose firm solidity all their courage and devotion was inevitably wrecked. He prolonged the struggle at the cost of heavy sacrifices on both sides, without turning the balance in favour of France.

In any event the German chiefs had still great difficulties to overcome.

The battles already won had cost heavy losses; in officers especially the losses were irreparable. Half the army was detained before Metz and Strasburg. The transport and guarding of already more than 200,000 prisoners required the services of a large part of the new levies being formed at home. The numerous fortresses had not indeed hindered the invasion of the

German army, but they had to be invested or kept under observation to secure the rearward communications, and to safeguard the forwarding and victualling of troops; and each further advance into the enemy's country involved increased drafts of armed men. After the battle of Sedan only 150,000 men were available for further operations in the field. There could be no doubt that the new objective must be Paris, as the seat of the new Government and the centre of gravity, so to speak, of the whole country. On the very day of the capitulation of Sedan, all the dispositions were made for the renewal of the advance.

To spare the troops, the movement was to be carried out on a very broad front, which involved no risk, for of the French Corps, the XIIIth alone could possibly cause any detention. And, indeed, only Blanchard's Division of that Corps was now at Mézières; its other two Divisions had but just begun their march when they received orders to halt preparatory to returning (to Paris).

Retreat of General Vinoy.

General Vinoy's most urgent anxiety was—very rightly—to reach Paris with the least possible loss. This was not very easy to accomplish, since the VIth Prussian Corps, which had taken no part in the battle of Sedan, was at Attigny in such a position that as a matter of distance, as far as to Laon, it could reach any point of any line of the enemy's retreat before, or as soon as the latter. General von Tümpling, commanding that Corps, had already taken possession of Rethel with the 12th Division by the evening of September 1st, thus closing the high-road to Paris. Only extraordinary forced marching and a succession of fortunate circumstances could save from destruction Blanchard's Division, which had already wasted its ammunition in small conflicts.

General Vinoy supplied the troops with several days' rations, enjoined the strictest discipline on the march, and during the night between 1st and 2nd September set out on the road to Rethel, where he expected to find Exéa's Division; which, however, availing itself of the section of railway still undestroyed, had already gone back to Soissons.

It was still early morning (of 2nd) when the French column of march came in contact with the 5th and presently with the 6th Prussian Cavalry Divisions, without, however, being seriously attacked. It was not till about ten o'clock, and within about seven miles of Rethel, that the French general learnt that place was in hostile possession, whereupon he decided on turning westward to Novion Porcien. He sent his rear-guard against the enemy's horse-artillery, but seeing hardly anything but cavalry in its front, it soon resumed the march. At about four in the afternoon the Division reached Novion, where it went into bivouac.

General von Hoffmann (commanding the 12th Prussian Division) had taken up a position at Rethel, and was awaiting the enemy, of whose approach he had been warned. Having ridden out in person, he became aware of Vinoy's deviation from the Rethel road, and at four in the afternoon marched to Ecly, where he arrived late in the evening. Part of his troops scouted forward toward Château Porcien.

General Vinoy, on learning that this road, too, was closed to him, quited his bivouac again at half-past one on the morning (of 3rd), leaving his fires burning, and set out on a second night-march in pouring rain and total darkness.

At first he took a northerly direction, to reach Laon at worst by the byways. By tracks fathomless in mud, and with frequent alarms, but without being reached

by the enemy, he trudged into Château Porcien at
half-past seven on the morning of the 3rd, and there
halted for a couple of hours.   The trend of the roads
now compelled him again to take a southerly direction,
and when the head of his column reached Séraincourt,
the sound of firing told him that his rear had been
attacked by the Germans.

The Prussian cavalry had, early the same morning,
discovered the French departure, but this important
information found General von Hoffmann no longer in
Ecly.   He had already started thence to search for the
enemy at Novion-Porcien, where he might well be
expected to be after his first night-march, but at half-
past nine the Prussian general found the place empty.
Thus, that morning, the German and French Divisions
had marched past each other in different directions at
a distance apart of little more than four miles.   The
thick weather had prevented them seeing each other.
General Vinoy this day reached Montcornet, in what
plight may be imagined.   The 12th Division continued
its pursuit in the westerly direction, but came up
only with the rear stragglers of the fast-retreating
enemy, and took up alarm-quarters in Chaumont
Porcien.

This march of the enemy ought not indeed to have
remained unobserved and unchecked under the eye of
two Cavalry Divisions, but it has to be said that these
were called off at an unfortunate moment.

It was, in fact, in consequence of a report that the
French forces were assembled at Rheims, that the
Headquarter of the IIIrd Army had ordered the
immediate return of the VIth Corps and the two Divi-
sions of cavalry.   These at once relinquished the
pursuit, and General von Tümpling ordered his two
Infantry Divisions to march at once on Rheims.   The
11th, which had been holding Rethel, set out forthwith.
General von Hoffmann, on the contrary, followed up the
French, on his own responsibility, as far as was possible

without cavalry to overtake them.   Not till the following day did the 12th Division reach the Suippe.

September 4th.—General Vinoy made his way northward again, by way of Marle, where he received the news of the Emperor's surrender and of the outbreak of the revolution in Paris.   His presence there was now of the greatest importance, and on the 13th. he reached the French capital with the two other divisions of his Corps from Laon and Soissons.

THE MARCH ON PARIS

OF THE IIIRD ARMY AND THE ARMY OF THE MEUSE.

During these occurrences the German armies, on the 4th September, had begun their advance on Paris. The first thing to be done was to disentangle the mass of troops assembled in the cramped space around Sedan. The IIIrd Army, of which the XIth and the Ist Bavarian Corps were still remaining there, had to make two long marches forward in order that the Army of the Meuse should regain its line of supply (Etappen-line).

The news of a great assemblage of French troops at Rheims soon proved to be unfounded.   Early on the 4th, detachments of Prussian horse entered the hostile and excited city, the 11th Division arrived that afternoon, and on the following day the German King's head-quarters were established in the old city where the French Kings had been wont to be crowned.

On the 10th of September the IIIrd Army had reached the line Dormans—Sezanne, and the VIth Corps had pushed forward to Château Thierry.   The Army of the Meuse, after the failure of a coup-de-main on Montmédy, was advancing between Rheims and Laon.

Cavalry sent far in advance covered this march executed on a front so exceptionally broad. The scouts everywhere found the inhabitants in a very hostile temper; the franctireurs attacked with great recklessness, and had to be driven out of several villages by dismounted troopers. The roads were in many places wrecked by the tearing up of the stone pavement, and the bridges were blown up.

On the approach of the 6th Cavalry Division Laon had capitulated. Small detachments of troops of the line were taken prisoners, 25 guns, 100 stores of arms and ammunition were seized as prizes, and 2000 Gardes-Mobiles were dismissed to their homes on parole to take no further part in the war. While friends and foes were assembled in large numbers in the courtyard of the citadel, the powder-magazine blew up, having probably been intentionally fired, and did great damage both there and in the town. The Prussians had fifteen officers and ninety-nine men killed and wounded; among the wounded were the Division-Commander and his general-staff officer. The French lost 300 men; the commandant of the fortress was mortally wounded.

On the 16th the Army of the Meuse was between Nanteuil and Lizy-on-Ourcq; the 5th Cavalry Division had advanced to Dammartin; the 6th to beyond Beaumont, sending patrols up to before St. Denis. The IIIrd Army was spread over the area from Meaux to Compte Robert. Strong military bridges had been thrown over the Marne at Trilport and Lagny to replace the permanent ones which had been blown up, and on the 17th the Vth Corps reached the Upper Seine.

To secure the draw-bridges at Villeneuve St. Georges, the 17th Brigade pushed on down the right bank of the Seine towards Paris, and at Mont Mesly it encountered Exéa's Division, which had been sent out by General Vinoy to bring in or destroy stores of supplies. The

fight which ensued ended in the French being driven
back under shelter of Fort Charenton.

The IInd Bavarian Corps also reached the Seine on
this day and bridged the river at Corbeil. The 2nd
Cavalry Division was in observation in front of Saclay,
towards Paris. The Royal head-quarter moved to
Meaux by way of Château Thierry. The, complete
investment of the French capital was now imminent.

The works constructed under Louis Philippe effectually protected the city from being taken by storm.
The artillery armament of the place consisted of over
2627 pieces, including 200 of the largest calibres of naval
ordnance. There were 500 rounds for each gun, and
in addition a reserve of three million kilogrammes of
powder. As concerned the active strength of the
garrison, besides the XIIIth Corps which had returned
from Mézières, a new Corps, the XIVth, had been
raised in Paris itself. These 50,000 troops of the line,
14,000 highly efficient and staunch marines and sailors,
and about 8000 gensd'armes, customs officers, and
forest-guards, formed the core of the defence. There
were besides 115,000 Gardes-Mobiles, who had been
drawn in from outside at an earlier date. The National
Guard was formed into 130 battalions, which, however,
being defective in equipment and poorly disciplined,
could be employed only in the defence of the inner
circle of fortifications. The volunteers, though
numerous, proved for the most part useless.

In all the besieged force was over 300,000 strong,
thus it was far more than double the strength of the
besiegers as yet on the spot, of whom there were at
the outside only about 60,000 men available, with 5000
cavalry and 124 field-batteries. On the Seine the
defence had five floating batteries and nine section-built
gun-boats originally intended for the Rhine ; on the
railways were some guns mounted on armour-plated
trucks.

Great difficulties necessarily attended the victualling

of two million human beings for a long period ; however, the authorities had succeeded in gathering into Paris 3000 oxen, 6000 swine, and 180,000 sheep, with considerable stores of other provisions, so that perfect confidence was justifiable, that Paris could hold out for six weeks at least.

Orders issued from the head-quarter at Meaux charged the Army of the Meuse with the investment of the capital on the right bank of the Seine and Marne,[1] and the IIIrd Army with the section on the left bank of both rivers. As a general rule the troops were to remain beyond range of the fire of the fortress, but, short of that, were to keep as close as possible so as to curtail the circuit of environment. The close connection of the two armies was to be secured above Paris by several bridges across both the rivers, and below the city, by the cavalry occupying Poissy. To the IIIrd Army was to belong the duty of reconnoitring in the direction of Orleans. In case of any attempt to relieve the capital it was to allow the relieving force to approach within a short distance, and then, leaving the investment to be maintained by weak details, to strike the enemy with its main body.

Without relief from outside, a close passive blockade must inevitably result in the capitulation of Paris, though probably not for some weeks or even months. As an ultimate compulsory measure there remained recourse to a bombardment.

At the time when Paris was fortified it was not foreseen that improvements in the artillery arm would double or treble the range of fire. The exterior forts, especially on the south, were at so short a distance from the enceinte that the city could easily be reached by the fire of heavy batteries.

The Germans have been blamed for not having had recourse at an earlier date to this expedient of bom-

---

[1] Viz., from the Marne above Paris in a wide half-circle to the Seine below it. The rayon of the Army of the Meuse subsequently extended to the right bank of the Seine above Paris.

bardment; but this criticism indicates an inadequate appreciation of the difficulties which stood in the way of its earlier execution.

It may safely be accepted that the attack of a large fortified place in the heart of an enemy's country is simply impossible so long as the invader is not master of the railways or waterways leading to it, by which may be brought up in full quantity the requisite material. The conveyance of this by the ordinary highways, even for a short distance, is in itself a herculean undertaking. Up to this time the German army had the control of only one railway in French territory, and this was fully occupied in the maintenance of supplies for the armies in the field: in bringing up reinforcements and equipment; in conveying rearward wounded, sick and prisoners. But even this much of railway service ended at Toul; and the attempt to turn that fortress by laying a temporary section of line found insurmountable difficulties in the nature of the ground. Further forward there interposed itself a scarcely inferior obstacle in the complete destruction of the Nanteuil tunnel, to repair which would probably require weeks.

Even then, for the further transport from Nanteuil up to the Paris front of 300 heavy guns with 500 rounds for each gun, there were requisite 4500 four-wheeled waggons, such as were not in use in the country, and 10,000 horses. Thus a bombardment was, in the earlier period, not to be thought of, and in any case the object of it would not be to destroy Paris, but merely to exert a final pressure on the inhabitants; and this influence would be more effectual when a long blockade had shaken the resolution of the besieged than it was likely to be at the beginning of the investment.

September 18*th.*—Corresponding directions communicated to the respective army commands, ordered the resumption of the march on the enemy's capital.

On the 18th the Army of the Meuse, swinging leftward, had the XIIth Corps at Claye, the Guard Corps at Mitry, and the IVth Corps at Dammartin, one march from Paris.

All the villages in front of St. Denis were occupied by the French. It seemed as if the investment on the north front of Paris would be resisted, and the Crown Prince of Saxony took measures for next day to follow up and support the IVth Corps, which led the advance. The 5th and 6th Cavalry Divisions, hastening on to Pontoise, were given two companies of Jägers and a pontoon train, and after a bridge had been laid they crossed the Oise.

The Vth Corps of the IIIrd Army passed over the Seine at Villeneuve-St.-Georges and advanced to Palaiseau and the Upper Bièvre. The advanced guard came into collision with Bernis' French Cavalry Brigade. The 47th Regiment at once proceeded to the attack, and stormed the walled farmsteads of Dame Rose and Trivaux. But on the southern skirt of the forest of Meudon the whole of the French XIVth Corps was drawn up; on its left stood a Division of the XIIIth Corps. The regiment retired on Petit Bicêtre without being followed, and there took up a defensive position.

The IInd Bavarian Corps marched from Corbeil by Longjumeau on a parallel front with the Vth Corps, and on the right the VIth occupied both banks of the Seine. These Corps, too, had several brushes with the enemy.

The Würtemberg Division at Lagny and Gournay was to cross the Marne forthwith, and so establish communication between the two armies.

INVESTMENT OF PARIS.

(September 19th.)

On the 19th September the IVth Corps met with no opposition in its advance to St. Brice; it drove detachments of the enemy from the neighbouring villages back under cover of the heavy guns of St. Denis, and pushed forward towards the Lower Seine. The Guard Corps followed it as far as Dugny, and lined the Morée brook, which was dammed up at its mouth, and afforded useful cover for the line of investment along a considerable distance. Further to the left the XIIth Corps took up a position extending to the Marne, and on the left bank of that river the Würtemberg Division advanced to Champigny.

On this day the Vth Corps of the IIIrd Army marched on Versailles in two colunms. The 47th Regiment had again the duty of covering the march along the hostile front. The French evidently were anxious to remain masters of the important heights in front of the fortifications of Paris, and in the early morning two divisions of their XIVth Corps marched out of the neighbouring forest of Meudon against Petit Bicêtre and Villacoublay. Supported by a numerous artillery, which set on fire the farm-buildings of Petit Bicêtre, they drove back the German outposts; but reinforcements from the Vth Corps presently came up to Villacoublay, and to Abbaye aux Bois from the IInd Bavarian Corps.

The left brigade of the latter had crossed the columns marching on Versailles in the valley of the Bièvre; but the sound of fighting from the field of strife induced General von Dietl[1] to advance with his detachments as they came up singly, on both sides of the high-road to Bicêtre. A conjunct assault with the Prussians still fighting in the Bois de Garenne, was successful in repulsing the French at Pavé blanc. Meanwhile the enemy by half-past eight had formed an artillery front of fifty guns, and three regiments of march advanced to renew the attack on Petit Bicêtre and the Bois de Garenne. They were received with a destructive musketry fire, and not even General

[1] Commanding 1st Bavarian Infantry Brigade.

Ducrot's personal influence could persuade the troops, who were young recruits, to go forward. The Zouaves posted about the farm of Trivaux were finally thrown into such confusion by some shells falling among them that they hurried back to Paris in headlong flight.

General Ducrot had to abandon his attempt. His Divisions retired in evident disorder on Clamart and Fontenay, under cover of the artillery and of the cavalry, which had resolutely endured the hostile fire; pursued at their heels by the German troops. The Bavarians stormed Pavé blanc under a heavy cannon fire; the Prussians retook Dame Rose after a trivial skirmish, and pushed on past the farm of Trivaux into the forest of Meudon. The French still held the heights of Plessis-Piquet, which were to them of vast importance and very easy of defence, as well as the redoubt at Moulin de la Tour, where nine field-batteries at once came into action, the fire from which commanded the whole of the western field of operations.

The main body of the Bavarian Corps had meanwhile moved southward, and during its advance on Fontenay aux Roses, about nine o'clock, it came under a hot fire from the height, as well as a flanking fire from a redoubt near Hautes Bruyères. Being informed of the situation at the scene of conflict on the plateau of Bicêtre, General von Hartmann (the Corps Commander) at once sent thither an artillery reinforcement, and ordered the 5th Brigade to attempt a junction to his left by way of Malabry. As soon as this brigade had deployed under a hot Chassepôt and artillery fire between Pavé blanc and Malabry, General von Walther (commanding 3rd Bavarian Division) passed to the attack of Plessis-Piquet. The artillery advanced to a short distance on the hither side of the park wall, and then the infantry broke out from the wood of Verrières, and, after a brief but sharp struggle, took possession of the mill lying to the southward. After half an hour's artillery preparation, the Bavarians advanced on Hachette by rushes, and broke into the park of Plessis. The French kept up a hot fire from the redoubt of Moulin de la Tour on the localities wrenched from them, by which the Bavarian field batteries suffered severely; but they still effectively supported the further advance of the infantry, who now got close in under the earthworks. However, the defenders were already on the point of retiring, and when about three o'clock one Bavarian company entered, it found the place deserted and the guns left in position.

Caussade's Division had left Clamart and was on the way to Paris; Maussion's had abandoned the heights of Bagneux on the pretence of having received mistaken orders, and Hughes' Division was with difficulty brought to a halt under cover of Fort Montrouge.

The Bavarian Corps now took up the position it had won on the plateau of Bicêtre to the right of the Vth Corps. The fight had cost the former 265 men and the latter 178; the French lost 661 killed and above 300 prisoners.

The condition in which the French XIVth Corps returned to Paris caused such dismay that General Trochu found himself obliged to withdraw a Division of the XIIIth from Vincennes for the defence of the enceinte.

It was subsequently argued that it would have been possible to capture one of the forts on this day by forcing an entrance along with the fugitive enemy, with the result of materially shortening the siege. But the forts did not need to open their gates to shelter fugitives, to whom those of the capital stood open. The escalade of masonry escarpments eighteen feet high can never be successful without much preparation. Ventures of this character are rarely ordered by superior authority; but can be attempted only in a propitious moment by those on the spot. In this case probable failure would have endangered the important success of the day.

The Vth Corps had meanwhile proceeded on its march to Versailles; a few National Guards, who had collected at the entrance to the town, were driven off or disarmed by the German Hussars. The 9th Division held the eastern exits of the town, the 10th encamped at Rocquencourt, and strong outposts were pushed out on the Bougival—Sèvres line. The 18th Brigade, which remained at Villacoubay to support the Bavarians in case of need, did not reach Versailles until the evening.

The 3rd Bavarian Division remained on the heights in front of Plessis Piquet, its outposts confronting the forest of Meudon, where the French were still in possession of the château; and the pioneers at once altered the redoubt of La Tour du Moulin so as to front north. The 12th Division was encamped at Fontenay and rearward as far as Châtenay.

The main body of the VIth Corps had taken position at Orly, its outposts extending from Choisy le Roi past Thiais to Chevilly. Maud'huy's Division attempted to drive in the outpost line at the last-named village, but without success. A brigade of the same Corps at Limeil, on the right bank of the Seine, was engaged in skirmishing with the French at Créteil. Within touch, further to the right, the Würtemberg Division held the (left) bank of the Marne from Ormesson to Noisy le Grand, behind which latter place the pontoon bridge near Gournay assured communication with the Saxon Corps.

Thus on the 19th of September the investment of Paris was complete on all sides. Six Army Corps stood in a deployment some fifty miles in circumference immediately in front of the enemy's capital, in some places actually within range of his guns, its rear guarded by a large force of cavalry.

FIRST NEGOTIATIONS FOR PEACE.

In full expectation of a battle to the north of Paris, the King had ridden out to join the Guard Corps, and in the evening his head-quarters were moved to Ferrières.

Here thus early Monsieur Jules Favre made his appearance to negotiate for peace on the basis of "not one foot of soil." He believed that after all their victories and losses, the Germans would come to terms on payment of a sum of money. It was self-evident that such a proposal could not be taken into consideration, and only the eventuality of granting an armistice was seriously discussed.

It was in the political interest of Germany as well, to afford the French nation the possibility of establishing by its own free and regular election a government which should have full right to conclude a peace creditable to the people ; for the self-constituted de facto Government ruling in Paris was the offspring of a revolution, and might at any moment be removed by a counter-revolution.

From a military point of view it was true that any pause in the active operations was a disadvantage. It would afford the enemy time to push forward his preparations, and by raising for a time the investment of Paris would give the capital the opportunity to reprovision itself at discretion.

The armistice could, therefore, only be granted in consideration of a corresponding equivalent.

To secure the subsistence of the respective German armies, Strasburg and Toul, which now intercepted the railway communication, must be given over. The siege of Metz was to be maintained ; but with regard to Paris, either the blockade was to continue; or, if it were raised, one of the forts commanding the capital was to be occupied by the Germans. The Chamber of Deputies was to be allowed to meet at Tours in full freedom.

These conditions, especially the surrender of the fortified places, were absolutely rejected on the French side, and the negotiations were broken off. Eight days later Toul and Strasburg were in the hands of the Germans.

REDUCTION OF TOUL.

(September 23rd.)

As soon as the German coast seemed no longer threatened by the danger of a landing of French troops, the 17th Division, which had been left behind there, was ordered to join the army in France. It arrived before Toul on September 12th.

This place, in itself exempt from capture by storm but commanded by neighbouring heights, had till now been invested by Étappen troops of the IIIrd Army, and shelled by the guns taken at Marsal and with field-guns, but without any particular effect. The infantry on the other hand had established a footing behind the railway embankment and in the suburbs close up to the foot of the glacis, so that sorties by the garrison were rendered almost impossible. In view of these circumstances half the Division was presently sent to Châlons, where sixteen battalions and fifteen squadrons barely sufficed to deal with the extremely hostile attitude of the people, hold the Etappen-lines and safeguard the communication with Germany. Thus only seven battalions, four squadrons, and four field-batteries remained before Toul.

On the 18th there arrived from Nancy by railway ten 15 cm. and sixteen 12 cm. siege guns. The intention was to attack the western face, which was enfiladed from Mont St. Michel, and then to breach the south-west bastion ; but first an (unsuccessful) attempt was made to reduce the place by the shorter process of subjecting it to a bombardment with field artillery.

On the night of the 22nd battery-emplacements for the siege artillery were constructed by the infantry ; three on Mont St. Michel, seven on the heights on the left bank of the Moselle, and one on the right bank. Next morning sixty-two guns opened fire, and at half-past three in the afternoon the white flag was hoisted on the Cathedral.

The handing over of the place followed the same day (23rd), on the conditions as had been granted at Sedan. A hundred and nine officers were released on parole, 2240 rank and file were taken prisoners. Six companies took possession the same evening of the city, which on the whole had suffered little.

Twenty-one heavy guns, about 3000 stand of arms, and large stores of provisions and forage were the prizes of success.

REDUCTION OF STRASBURG.

(September 28th.)

Immediately after the victory of Wörth, the re-duction of Strasburg became a primary object. This strong fortified position, bridge-head as it was com-manding the Rhine, was a standing menace to Southern Germany.

When Marshal MacMahon evacuated Alsace, only three battalions of the line were left with the com-mandant of Strasburg. But with stragglers from the various regiments engaged at Wörth, with sundry fourth battalions and reserve detachments, and finally with Mobiles and National Guards, the strength of the garrison had increased to 23,000 men. There was a complete absence of engineer troops, but 130 marines formed an excellent nucleus; the armament of the fortress was also ample.

So early as on the 11th August the Baden Division had been detailed to observe Strasburg. Notwithstanding the smallness of its force the Division had advanced unchecked by the enemy on the Ruprechtsau as far as the Rhine-and-Ill Canal; had occupied the village of Schiltigheim, almost within rifle-shot of the fortifications: and, having promptly prepared it for defence, pushed forward into the suburb of König-shofen.

In the course of eight days there arrived, under the command of General von Werder, the Guard Landwehr and 1st Reserve Divisions, and one cavalry brigade, in all 46 battalions, 24 squadrons, and 18 field-batteries; as well as a siege-train of 200 rifled cannon and 88 mortars, with 6000 foot artillerymen and ten companies of fortress-pioneers; a total strength of 40,000 men.

The unloading of the guns brought from Magdeburg, Coblentz, and Wesel was begun on August 18th at the railway station of Vendenheim, by a detachment of the Railway Battalion.

The engineer-depôt was established at Hausberge, a wagon-park at Lampertsheim, and provision made for permanent magazines. A complete blockade was established, and the field-telegraph kept up communication between all the posts.

To attain the desired end with the least possible delay, an attempt was made, contrary to the advice of General of Engineers Schultz, though with the sanction of the supreme Head-quarter, to force the town to surrender by stress of a bombardment. The request that the women and children should be allowed to withdraw was necessarily refused.

The erection of the batteries for the bombardment in the dark, wet nights was attended with great difficulties. Meanwhile only the field-guns could fire on the city; but the batteries whose armament of heavy guns was complete opened fire on the night of the 24th—25th; and soon a great fire was raging. Kehl, on the right bank of the river, was also set on fire by the shell-fire.

The Bishop of Strasburg came out to the outposts at Schiltigheim to entreat forbearance for the citizens. Much as damage to this German city was to be regretted, since the Prelate was not empowered to negotiate the bombardment was continued through the night of the 25th, when it reached its height. But the headquarter staff at Mundolsheim became convinced that this mode of attack would not accomplish the desired object, and that the more deliberate course of a regular siege would have to be resorted to. General von Mertens was placed in charge of the engineer operations, General Decker was given the direction of the artillery.

During the night of the 29th—30th August the first parallel was opened very close to the glacis, and soon was prolonged from the Rhine and Marne canal, through the churchyard of St. Helena, to the Jewish cemetery at Königshofen.

The number of batteries on the left bank of the Rhine was soon increased to 21, on the right bank to 4; so that 124 guns of the heaviest calibre were ready in protected positions to begin the contest with the guns of the fortress. The further offensive operations were directed against bastions Nos. 11 and 12 on the north-west salient of the fortress. In the night of September 1st—2nd the second parallel was completed, but not without opposition. A strong sortie of fourteen companies of the garrison made at daybreak (of 2nd) upon the island of Waken, and in front of Kronenburg and Königshofen, was repulsed.

The fortress then opened a heavy fire, pouring such a storm of projectiles on the siege-works that they had to be abandoned, till at about nine o'clock the artillery of the attack had silenced the guns of the fortress. A second sortie followed on the 3rd September, which was not repulsed before it had reached the second parallel.

A short truce was granted at the request of the commandant, to allow of the burial of the dead lying in front of the works. And on this day a grand salvo announced to the besieged the victory of Sedan.

Incessant rain had filled the trenches of the second parallel, 2400 paces in length, ankle-deep with water, and it was not till the 9th that they were completely repaired. Five batteries were moved forward from the first parallel, as special batteries were required to crush the fire of lunette No. 44, which took in flank all the approaches. These soon silenced its guns, and the lunette was abandoned by the garrison.

There were now 96 rifled cannon pieces and 38 mortars in full fire at very short range. Each gun was authorized to fire twenty rounds a day and ten shrapnel each night. The large Finkmatt Barracks were destroyed by fire, and the Stone Gate was so much injured that it had to be buttressed with sandbags. The garrison withdrew the guns behind the parapet, and only fired their mortars. However, in order to push forward the siege-works, sap-rollers had to be brought into use.

When it was discovered that mining galleries were being driven in front of lunette No. 53, Captain Ledebour let himself down by a rope into the ditches, and with the help of his pioneers removed the charges of powder.

During the night of the 13th—14th, the crest of the glacis in front of both the lunettes Nos. 52 and 53 was reached. The crowning was then begun by means of the double traverse sap, and was finished in four days.

The attack henceforth was exclusively directed against bastion No. 11.

To run off the water from the ditches of the fortress it was necessary to destroy the sluices by the Jews' Gate. These were invisible from any part of the field of attack, and the desired result could only be very incompletely obtained by artillery fire at a distance of more than a mile. Detachments of the 34th Fusilier Regiment, therefore, on the 15th, marched on the sluices under a heavy rifle fire from the besieged, and destroyed the dam.

The island of Sporen was at this time taken possession of by the Baden corps.

When the mortar-batteries had for the most part been moved up into the second parallel, the gun-batteries were also advanced nearer, and the wall-piece detachments did such execution by their accurate practice that the defenders never more dared to show themselves by day.

The retaining wall of lunette No. 53 could only be reached by indirect fire; but 1000 shells made a breach, and on the 19th September two mines were fired, which blew up the counterscarp and brought it down to the level of the water of the ditch. The pioneers immediately set about laying a dam of fascines across the ditch. A party sent over in a boat found the work abandoned. The gorge was closed under heavy rifle fire from the ramparts of the main fortress, and the parapet reversed so as to face the place.

The next lunette to the left, No. 52, was merely an earthwork, and the attack had already been pushed forward as far as the edge of the ditch, but earth screens had first to be thrown up and covered in with railway iron, as a protection against the heavy fire of shell from bastion No. 12. The construction of a dam of fascines or earth, more than sixty paces across, and with the ditch full of water almost fathom deep, would have taken a long time; so it was decided to make a cask bridge of beer-barrels, of which a quantity had been found in Schiltigheim. This work was begun at dusk on the 21st, under no better protection than a screen of boards to prevent observation, and it was finished by ten o'clock. Here again the defenders had not waited for the escalade, and this lunette, too, was immediately prepared for being held. Both lunettes were now furnished with batteries of mortars and guns to silence the fire from the ravelines and counter-guards of the front of attack, against which five dismounted and counter-batteries were also directed.

During the night of the 22nd—23rd the Germans advanced from lunette No. 52, partly by flying sap and partly by the deep sap, and there followed the crowning of the glacis in the front of counter-guard No. 51. A breaching fire was immediately opened against the east face of bastion No. 11, and the west face of bastion No. 12. The splinters of stone compelled the defenders to abandon the counter-guards. The scarp of bastion No. 11 fell on the 24th, after a shell-fire of 600 rounds. The bringing down of the earthwork angle which remained standing, was postponed till the beginning of the assault.

It was more difficult to breach bastion No. 12, because of the limited opportunity for observing the effect of the fire. It was not till the 26th that a breach thirty-six feet wide was made, after firing 467 long shells. And even then, for the actual assault to succeed, the deep wet ditch at the foot of the bastion had to be crossed.

News of the fall of the Empire had indeed reached Strasburg, but General Uhrich would not listen to the prayers of the citizens that he would put an end to their sufferings. The Republic was proclaimed.

The siege had lasted thirty days, but the place was still well supplied with food and stores; the garrison was not materially weakened by the loss of 2500 men, but its heterogeneous elements prevented its effective employment in large bodies outside the walls. From the first the small blockading force had been allowed to approach close to the works; and the moment when the artillery of a fortress always has the advantage over the attack had been little utilized.

The German artillery had proved much the stronger, both as regards material and in its advantageous employment. Under its powerful protection the work of the pioneers and infantry was carried on with equal courage and caution, never swerving from the object in view. The storming of the main walls was now to be imminently expected, and no relief from outside could be hoped for.

On the afternoon of September 27th, the white flag was seen flying from the Cathedral tower; firing ceased and the sapper-works were stopped.

In Königshofen at two in the following morning the capitulation was settled, on the Sedan conditions. Five hundred officers and 17,000 men were made prisoners, but the former were free to go on their parole. The National Guards and franctireurs were dismissed to their homes, after laying down their arms and pledging themselves to fight no more. All the cash remaining in the state bank, 1200 guns, 200,000 small arms and considerable stores proved a valuable prize of war.

At eight o'clock in the morning of the 28th, companies of Prussian and Baden troops took over the National, Fischer, and Austerlitz gates. The French garrison marched out at the National Gate, General Uhrich at their head. At first the march was conducted in good order, but before long numbers of drunken men broke the ranks and refused to obey, or threw down their arms. The prisoners were taken in the first instance to Rastatt, under the escort of two battalions and two squadrons.

The old city of the German Reich, which had been seized by France in time of peace nearly two centuries earlier, was now restored by German valour to the German fatherland.

The siege had cost the Germans 39 officers and 894 men. The city unhappily could not have been spared great suffering. Four hundred and fifty houses were utterly destroyed, 10,000 inhabitants were roofless, nearly 2000 were killed or wounded. The museum and picture gallery, the town hall and theatre, the new church, the gymnasium, the Commandant's residence, and alas! the public library of 200,000 volumes had fallen a prey to the flames.

The noble Cathedral showed many marks of shot, and the citadel was a heap of ruins. Under the wreck of the assailed works in the western front lay buried burst cannon.

The fall of Toul and of Strasburg produced a not unimportant change in the military situation. Considerable forces were now free for other services, and the railway transport could be brought up nearer to the armies. The material no longer required at Strasburg could not indeed be at once employed for the artillery offensive against Paris; it needed considerable re-equipment, and was to do duty meanwhile in the reduction of several smaller places. The newly-opened railway line was made use of to bring up the Guard Landwehr Division to the army investing Paris. A new Army Corps, the XIVth, was created of the Baden Division, a combined brigade consisting of the 30th and 34th Prussian regiments, and one cavalry brigade; which, under the command of General von Werder, marched on the Upper Seine. The 1st Reserve Division remained behind as the garrison of Strasburg.

OPERATIONS ROUND PARIS TO 15TH OCTOBER.

The Government in the now closely-blockaded capital, could not make its behests heard and obeyed throughout France. It therefore decided on sending a delegation of two of its members out into the provinces, their seat of direction to be at Tours. They could quit Paris only in a balloon. One of these delegates was Gambetta, whose restless energy soon made itself conspicuously felt, and lasted during the continuance of the war. Monsieur Thiers, meanwhile, had been visiting the European courts on the errand of inducing them to interpose their good offices in favour of France.

After the mishap of September 19th the feeling in Paris was against any great offensive demonstrations for the present; but the troops of the line still remained outside the walls under protection of the outlying forts. The Divisions of the XIIIth Corps were encamped on the south front and on the plateau of Vincennes; the XIVth was at Boulogne, Neuilly and Clichy behind the loops of the Seine, with Mont Valérien in its front, which was held by two line-battalions, after the flight, on the 20th, of the Gardes-Mobiles from that impregnable stronghold, in great disorder back into Paris. The defence of the northern front of the city remained entrusted to the Gardes-Mobiles.

On the German side the positions of the Army of the Meuse, which were to be occupied and defended to the uttermost, extended from Chatou along the Seine to the heights of Montmorency, and onward along the Morée and the skirts of the forest of Bondy as far as the Marne. In close touch with the flank of the Army of the Meuse at the Marne, the lines of the Würtemberg Division carried on the investment from Noisy le Grand across the Joinville peninsula to Ormesson. The XIth Corps arriving from Sedan on the 23rd filled up the interval from Ormesson to Villeneuve St. Georges, and the 1st Bavarian Corps occupied Longjumeau as a protection against attempts from the direction of Orleans. The VIth Corps could now be entirely transferred to the left bank of the Seine, where the line of defence extended along the wooded heights south of Paris to Bougival.

The Head-quarter of the King and that of the IIIrd Army were at Versailles, that of the Army of the Meuse was transferred to Vert-Galant. Numerous bridges facilitated the inter-communication of the various portions of the forces, telegraphs and signal-lights insured their rapid concentration, and every movement of the French was watched from eligible posts of observation.

There was no lack of accommodation for the troops, for every village was deserted; but this made the difficulty of obtaining supplies all the greater. The fugitive inhabitants had driven off their cattle and destroyed their stores; there remained only the apparently inexhaustible wine-cellars. For the first few days all the food needed had to be drawn from the Commissariat trains, but ere long the cavalry succeeded in obtaining considerable supplies. High prices and good discipline secured a market. Only the troops in advanced positions had to bivouac or build huts, many within range of the hostile artillery, some even within rifle-shot of the enemy. Near St. Cloud, for instance, no one could show himself without becoming a mark for the chassepôts from behind the shutters of the houses opposite. The outposts here could only be relieved at night, and sometimes had to remain on duty two or three days at a time. The advanced positions of the Bavarians at Moulin la Tour were also much exposed, and the visits of superior officers to them always drew a sharp cannonade. Le Bourget, standing as it did in advance of the line of inundation, was especially liable to a surprise. That village had been seized on 20th (Sept.) by a battalion of the Guard Corps, at whose approach

400 Gardes-Mobiles had fled, leaving their baggage. Only one company occupied this post, on account of the heavy fire of the adjacent forts.

Some petty sorties from St. Denis met with no success ; but an attempt by detachments of the VIth Corps to occupy the village of Villejuif and the redoubt of Hautes Bruyères proved unsuccessful. They forced their way in several times, but always had to retire under the fire of the neighbouring forts of Bicêtre and Ivry, and because of the superior strength of Maud'huy's Division. The French afterwards armed the redoubts with heavy guns.

September 30*th*. —Early on this day a cannonade of an hour and a half's duration from the southern forts and batteries announced a sortie in that direction. By six o'clock two brigades of the XIIIth French Corps deployed against Thiais and Choisy le Roi. Strong swarms of tirailleurs drove in the outposts of the VIth Corps, and forced the field-guns in position between those two villages to retire ; but then the fire of the infantry garrisons checked any further attack on the part of the French. Further to the west a third brigade got into Chevilly and seized a factory on the road to Belle Epine ; but its determined attack failed to obtain possession of the whole village. The 11th Division was alarmed in its rearward quarters, and hurried forward to the support of the 12th. The factory was recovered from the French, and the Prussian batteries now opened fire, and worked such havoc among the enemy as he retired on Saussaye, that, shunning the attack of the infantry, he fled in great disorder to Hautes Bruyères and Villejuif, A brigade which had forced its way into L'Hay was in the same way driven back, leaving 120 prisoners for the most part unwounded. In the farmstead at the north entrance of Chevilly, however, the French still held their ground with great obstinacy. Not till they were completely surrounded, and had made an ineffectual attempt to force a passage, did surrender those brave defenders, who numbered about 100.

The whole series of attacks was entirely defeated by about nine o'clock, and General Vinoy vainly endeavoured to incite the diminished battalions at Hautes Bruyères to renew the struggle.

These few morning hours had cost the VIth Corps 28 officers and 413 men ; and the French many more.

Two simultaneous feint-attacks on Sèvres and on Mesly on the right bank of the Seine, came to nothing. The German outposts, at first driven in, re-occupied their ground by about nine o'clock.

After thus failing to gain space towards the southward by this sortie, the besieged proceeded to assure themselves of the ground already in their possession by the construction of entrenchments. They fortified Villejuif and extended their lines from Hautes Bruyères past Arcueil to the Mill of Pichon, so that there the Bavarian outposts had to be drawn in nearer to Bourg-la-Reine.

Otherwise, throughout the first half of the month of October the garrison of Paris restricted itself for the most part to daily cannonades. Guns of the heaviest calibre were directed on the most petty objects. It was sheer waste of ammunition, just as though the aim was to get rid of the stores on hand. If one of the gigantic long shells happened to fall on an outpost, the destruction was of course terrible ; but on the whole they did little execution.

Apart from the noise of the cannonade to which one soon became accustomed, in Versailles, whence none of the residents had fled, it might have been thought a time of profound peace. The admirable discipline of the German troops allowed the townsfolk to pursue their business undisturbed ; the hosts were well paid for the billeting imposed on them, and the country people could cultivate their fields and gardens in peace. At St. Cloud every room was kept in the same order as when the Imperial family had left it, till the shells from Mont Valérien reduced that delightful palace with all its treasures of art to a heap of charred ruins. It was the French fire, too, which wrecked the Château of Meudon, the porcelain factory of Sèvres, and whole villages in the nearer environs. And it was also the French themselves who, without any necessity, felled half the Bois de Boulogne.

The investment line was considerably strengthened on the 10th and 16th of October, when the 17th Division arriving from Toul relieved the 21st at Bonneuil, and the latter took up a position between the Bavarians and the Vth Corps, in the Meudon—Sèvres tract; and when the Guard Landwehr Division came up and occupied St. Germain.

These movements were observed from Paris, and to clear up the situation, General Vinoy advanced at nine o'clock on 13th October with about 26,000 men and 80 guns, against the position held by the IInd Bavarian Corps.

Four battalions of Gardes-Mobiles, protected by the fire of the nearest forts and of field batteries, advanced to the attack of Bagneux, and forced their way over the entrenchments wrecked by artillery fire, into the heart of the place, whence the defenders retired to Fontenay, when at eleven o'clock the French 10th Regiment of the line had also come up. Reinforced by a fresh battalion, and supported by an effective flanking fire from Châtillon, the Bavarians now made so firm a stand that the enemy could make no further progress, but began to put Bagneux in a state of defence. Meanwhile the 4th Bavarian Division had stood to arms, and by about 1.30 General von Bothmer (its commander) moved it up from Sceaux and from Fontenay, and proceeded to surround Bagneux. The barricades erected by the enemy were carried, who however still offered an obstinate resistance in the northern part of the village.

A French battalion had also made its way into Châtillon, but the Bavarian battalion in occupation there held its own until assistance came, and the enemy was driven out of the place after a sharp conflict.

A third brigade seized Clamart, which at that time was not yet included in the German intrenched lines; but it failed to climb the ascent to Moulin de la Tour, although the defenders on the plateau above were exposed to the fire of the forts.

General Vinoy had convinced himself that forces which were a match for him confronted him at every point, and at three o'clock he decided to break off the fight. The French bodies of troops gradually disappeared behind the forts, and had all vanished by dusk. The Bavarians returned to their former fore-post positions, and the garrison of Bagneux was increased to two battalions.

All France had meanwhile been arming with eager haste. Armies of considerable strength were being massed at Rouen and Evreux, at Besançon, and especially behind the Loire, of very various composition no doubt, and above all lacking in professional officers to drill and discipline them. Great battles were therefore in the first instance to be avoided; the enemy was to be constantly harassed by small engagements. Thus, towards the end of September, General Delarue advanced from Evreux with his "Eclaireurs de la Seine" up to the vicinity of St. Germain. But the 5th Cavalry Division, supported by two Bavarian battalions, drove these bands back to Dreux behind the Eure. The woods in front of the 6th Cavalry Division were also full of hostile parties, who were, however, swept out without much difficulty beyond Rambouillet to Epernon.

Matters looked more serious to the south of Paris, in front of the 4th Cavalry Division, which was in observation towards the Loire.

The newly-formed French XVth Corps had assembled at Orleans in three Divisions with a strength of 60,000 men, and it occupied the whole forest-belt on the right bank of the river. To counteract the danger threatening the investment from that direction, the 1st Bavarian Corps and the 22nd Division of the XIth had been put in march on Arpajon and Montcléry as soon as they were freed from duty at Sedan; and on the 6th of October they were placed, with the 2nd Cavalry Division, under the command of General von der Tann.

ACTION OF ARTENAY.

(October 10th.)

When General von der Tann received instructions to take the offensive against Orleans, he marched on the 9th of October to the vicinity of St. Péravy without meeting any serious opposition, and on the 10th advanced on Artenay. The 4th Cavalry Division covered the right flank; the 2nd remained near Pithiviers, where the enemy had collected in great force.

General La Motterouge on the same day also moved out on Artenay with the XVth French Corps, having the wood in his rear occupied by Gardes-Mobiles; and so the advanced guards of both sides met at a short distance to the north of the common objective.

While the Bavarian light horse on the right were driving the French cavalry before them, the infantry deployed across the road near to Dambron. The 22nd Division marched forward on Dambron with both Cavalry Divisions on its flanks. Under the fire of the Bavarian batteries, the French had gone

L

about to Artenay, where the Germans were ready to receive them. Attacked in front and threatened by bodies of horse, at about two o'clock, leaving their tents standing, they began a retreat which soon degenerated into flight. The cavalry seized four field-guns and took above 250 prisoners. Six hundred more, who had reached Croix Briquet, surrendered there to the Bavarian infantry on the arrival of the latter.

The German troops had made a long march; General von der Tann therefore allowed them rest for the day in and around Artenay, and only the advanced guard went on to Chevilly, to pursue the march to Orleans next day.

ENGAGEMENT AT ORLEANS.

(October 11th.)

On this day, the 22nd Division, for the time only 6000 strong, moved to the right flank of the advance, and drove the French out of several villages partly prepared for defence; it was not till about ten o'clock that it met with serious opposition from an intrenched position at Ormes.

The French Commander after the disaster at Artenay had decided on a retreat behind the Loire, to cover which he had halted about 15,000 men on the right bank of the river, in a position which possessed many essentials towards a good defence.

General von Wittich (commanding 22nd Division) first sent the 44th Brigade against this position at Ormes, and opened fire from seven batteries. The troops of his left wing, supported by the Bavarian right, made their way but slowly over the plain east of the enemy's position, and various enclosures and buildings had to be stormed and taken as they advanced. This threatening attitude of the German right, however, shook the firmness of the defence, and, after some hours' hard fighting, the French began to retreat. No sooner was this observed by the Germans than two batteries were brought up to within 800 paces, and the 83rd Regiment stormed the entrenchments at two in the afternoon, but with heavy loss. Detachments of the 43rd Brigade had meanwhile reached the road in rear of Ormes, and took 800 prisoners. But the villages, gardens and vineyards which line the road to Orleans for more than four miles on either side, were serious obstacles to the advance of the Germans in close formation, and the Division did not arrive at Petit St. Jean till three o'clock, of which the nearest buildings were forcibly taken possession of.

The Bavarian Corps, which had also met with a stout resistance at Saran, pushed forward to Bel Air, but with great loss, especially in the artillery. Here the nature of the ground did not allow of the deployment of the guns, a further attack came to a standstill, and at half-past four the French were still stoutly holding their own at Les Aides, till the advance of the 4th Bavarian Brigade to Murlins threatened their line of retreat. They made a renewed stand behind the railway embankment, 1000 paces in front of the town, and the railway-station and gas-works had also to be taken by assault.

It was already five o'clock when General von der Tann led his reserve, the 1st Bavarian Brigade, to the decisive assault of Grand Ormes. The 32nd Prussian Regiment crossed the embankment on the left flank of the French, who now retired into the suburb of St. Jean. The 1st Bavarian Regiment, hurrying in their rear, was received with a hot fire at the gate of the city; but with its officers marching at its head it reached the market-place about seven o'clock.

The French hurried across the bridge over the Loire,

while the 43rd Prussian and 1st Bavarian Brigades
seized the principal buildings and the passages across
the river; but as darkness fell they desisted from
further advance and bivouacked on the open places
of the city.

The day had cost the Germans a loss of 900 men, the
3rd Bavarian Brigade having suffered most severely.
But their hard-won victory promptly dispelled the disquietude of the investing armies caused by the threatening attitude of the French; and 5000 rifles, ten
locomotives and sixty railway-carriages were welcome
prizes.

The French rear-guard had lost in detached combats
and retreats alone 1800 prisoners; but it had covered
the retreat of the main body of the Army of the South
for a whole day against superior forces, with praise-
worthy determination.   In the open field, where skilful
handling of masses is possible, it would soon have been
defeated; but in street-fighting unflinching personal
courage is all that is needed in the defender, and the
latest recruits of the newly created French levies did
not lack that attribute.

On the following day the 1st Bavarian Division
took possession of the suburb of St. Marceau, on the
further side of the Loire, and advanced to the Loiret.
The 2nd Cavalry Division scouted through the Sologne,
the 4th on the right bank ranged to the westward.

The French XVth Corps had continued its retreat to
Salbris and Pierrefitte, behind the Sauldre.

It was certainly to be wished that its pursuit could
have been followed up to Vierzon and Tours, so that
the vast arsenals at the first-named town might have
been destroyed, and the Government Delegation driven
away from the other.   But it must not be forgotten
that though the French forces had been discomfited at
Artenay, favoured by the nature of the locality they
had escaped utter defeat by retreat.   General von der
Tann was disproportionately weak in the infantry arm,

and hostile masses were disclosing themselves on all sides. A new French Army Corps, the XVIth, appeared at Blois, below Orleans, and at Gien, above that city; the German cavalry met with resistance in the forest of Marchénoir and before Châteaudun; and everywhere the inhabitants and volunteers appeared so full of confidence that the proximity of reinforcements was to be presumed.

So it behoved the Germans to restrict themselves to the occupation of Orleans and the line of the Loire; and for this purpose the Bavarian Corps, with the 2nd Cavalry Division, seemed a sufficient force. The 22nd Infantry and 4th Cavalry Divisions were recalled to the IIIrd Army; on their return march they were charged to disperse the volunteers who had made their appearance at Châteaudun and Chartres.

General von der Tann had the bridges over the Loiret and the Loire prepared for destruction, an Etappen-line was established to Longjumeau, and the Bavarian Railway Detachment set to work to restore the line to Villeneuve.

REDUCTION OF SOISSONS.

(October 15th.)

Soissons still hindered the further utilization of the railway, which had been re-opened at the time of the fall of Toul as far as Rheims. This fortress had been bombarded by field artillery without success when the Army of the Meuse passed by it on the march to Paris, and since then it had only been kept under observation until on October 6th eight Landwehr battalions, four squadrons, two batteries, two companies of pioneers, and four of fortress artillery made good the investment.

Soissons, with its walls about 26 feet high, had complete immunity from escalade, and the damming of the Crise brook made it unassailable on the south. The south-west front, on the other hand, had only a dry ditch, with no counterscarp of masonry; here, too, the town was commanded by Mont Marion, rising to a height of 300 feet at a distance of little more than a mile. Against this face of the fortress, therefore, the artillery attack was directed at short range, when on the 11th October there arrived from Toul 26 Prussian siege-guns with 170 rounds for each, and 10 French mortars. The Grand Duke of Mecklenburg took over the command.

In a clear moonlight night the artillery with the help of the infantry was brought up on to the heights of Ste. Géneviève; the construction of the batteries about Belleu and in Mont Marion was completed and the arming of them effected. At six in the morning of 12th October they opened fire simultaneously.

The besieged answered with great spirit but with small results, and the accurate fire of the Prussian artillery soon subdued that of the enemy in the particular front.

A narrow breach was visible by next day, and the fire from the fortress was evidently much enfeebled; but the commandant decidedly rejected the demand that he should capitulate. On the 14th he increased the number of guns on his south front, so that the batteries on Ste. Geneviève had an arduous struggle. The French also laboured hard along the front of the attack to restore the severely damaged works, brought more guns up to the ramparts, and closed the breach by retrenchment.

But on the 15th these repairs were soon demolished again by the artillery of the attack, and a breach was made 40 paces wide and amply spread with earth. As the fortress still kept up a brisk fire, it was determined to bring up the field-batteries within 900 paces. But at eight in the evening, when this operation was just begun, the commandant opened negotiations and surrendered the place on the Sedan terms. The garrison marched out next morning, for the most part drunk. A thousand Gardes-Mobiles were dismissed on parole, 3800 regulars were made prisoners.

The attack had cost 120 men; 128 guns and 8000 small arms became prize of war, besides vast stores of provisions.

STORMING OF CHÂTEAUDUN.

(October 18th.)

In obedience to instructions, General von Wittich marched on Châteaudun with the 22nd Division on the afternoon of the 18th. The French troops of the line had already been ordered to retire on Blois, but about 1800 National Guards and volunteers still remained, prepared under cover of barricades and walls to receive the enemy. The infantry attack was also made more difficult by the nature of the ground, and four batteries had to keep up a hot fire for a long time.

It was not till dusk that a general assault was had recourse to. Inside the town the enemy made a desperate resistance. House after house had to be won, the fighting lasted until late into the night, and a large part of the place was set on fire. The volunteers finally escaped, leaving 150 prisoners and abandoning the inhabitants to their fate; and these, though they had taken part in the struggle, were let off with a fine.

At noon on the 21st the Division arrived in front of Chartres, where 10,000 French were said to have assembled. The marine infantry and Gardes-Mobiles advanced to the attack, but were repulsed by the fire of seven batteries. The General commanding the Division had deployed both his brigades southward of the city, and with the assistance of his cavalry, which had been joined by the 6th (Cavalry) Division, completely surrounded it. The fate of Châteaudun had been a warning to the municipal authorities, and at three o'clock an agreement was come to by which the troops were to be withdrawn, the National Guards to lay down their arms, and the gates to be thrown open.

General Wittich's orders were to remain at Chartres for the present, while the 6th Cavalry Division was to occupy Maintenon, and so cover the investing army to the west.

Not less fervid was the rush to arms in the north, in Picardy and Normandy. The Saxon Cavalry Division, supported by detachments of the Army of the Meuse, had in the early part of October driven the franc-tireurs and Gardes-Mobiles beyond the Oise and the Epte on Amiens, taking some hundreds of prisoners. But fresh swarms were constantly coming on, and had to be attacked at Breteuil, Montdidier, and Etrêpagny, so that no less than eleven battalions, twenty-four squadrons, and four batteries, were by degrees employed in this direction for the protection of the besieging force. But by the end of the month the French forces were so systematically organized and in so great strength, that for the time the Germans had to confine themselves to holding on the defensive the line of the Epte.

To the south-east also, in the forest-land of Fontaine-bleau, hostilities were prosecuted by the volunteers, particularly against requisition-parties of cavalry; and from Nangis obstruction was threatened to the transport of the siege-guns. A small force of Würtemberg troops seized Montereau, which, though barricaded, was not defended; the inhabitants gave up their arms, and the detachment marched on Nogent. This town was held by a large body of Gardes-Mobiles. After breaching the walls of the churchyard, the Würtembergers, in the face of a hot fire, made their way into the place. The French still offered a stout resistance in its interior, but finally retired on Troyes, leaving 600 dead and wounded. The small flying column rejoined its Division, having traversed over 126 miles in six days.

Sortie against Malmaison.

(October 21st.)

The French capital had now been invested for more than four weeks, and it seemed not impossible, because of the long continuance of inactivity, that it might be brought to surrender by famine. All the sorties hitherto attempted had only had for their object to drive the enemy from the closest vicinity; a new effort was to aim at greater results. The project was to cross the Seine below Paris at Bezons and Carrières, and to make a simultaneous attack on the positions of the IVth Prussian Corps on the heights of Argenteuil from the south, and from St.-Denis from the east. A march on Rouen by Pontoise was to follow, into a district not yet altogether exhausted of resources. The Army of the Loire was also to proceed thither by railway by way of Le Mans, and so there would be massed in that region an army of 250,000 men.

The Prussian Vth Corps, it was true, stood right on the flank of such an advance across the Seine; its outposts had several times been seen in Rueil. As a preliminary step, General Ducrot undertook to force back this body with 10,000 men and 120 field-guns. Then an intrenched line from Valérien to Carrières would close the peninsula against interference from the southward.

Perhaps, in the face of much-dreaded "public opinion" and the growing restlessness of political parties in Paris, it was more the urgency to be doing something than any serious hope of success which gave rise to such far-reaching schemes. Considerable difficulties had to be met in attacking the enemy's lines, and greater must inevitably arise if the attack should succeed. It was vain to think of bringing through the miles-long trains which are indispensable for victualling an army. Serious embarrassment would ensue when the troops had consumed the three days' rations they would carry with them. To live on the country the army must disperse itself; but with the enemy at its heels close concentration was indispensable. And, in any case, it is hard to see what would have been gained by withdrawing from Paris the forces which had been assembled for the defence of the capital. Success could only have been hoped for if an army from without had been so near as to be able immediately to give the hand to the troops marching out.

However, on the 21st of October, after Mont Valérien had all the morning kept up a seemingly ineffective fire, General Ducrot advanced at about one o'clock to attack the position of the Prussian 19th Brigade whose supports held the line Bougival — Jonchère — Fohlenkoppel. Fourteen French field-batteries deployed on either side of Rueil and about the southern base of Valérien; the infantry advanced in five columns behind this artillery front.

On the German side only two batteries could at first engage in the unequal duel, and one of these near the Villa Metternich had very soon to retire. The French guns advanced rightward to within 1400 paces of Bougival, and at three o'clock four companies of Zouaves rushed out of Rueil. Being received with a hot fire, they wheeled into the park of Malmaison, and without opposition seized the Château of Buzanval and the eastern slope of the deep-cut ravine of Cucufa. And here one of their batteries was brought up into the fighting-line to support them.

While the main body of the 9th Division advanced from Versailles on Vaucresson, the 10th deployed against the ravine and at Villa Metternich. The infantry fire lasted for a full hour, and wrought the French much loss. When at about four o'clock they seemed sufficiently shaken, and a reinforcement of the Guard Landwehr had come up from St. Germain on the left, the German left wing advanced from Bougival and over the height of Jonchère, forced its way into Malmaison in spite of violent opposition, and followed the retreating Zouaves as far as Rueil. The right wing at the same time having turned the head of the Cucufa ravine, charged against its eastern slope, drove out the enemy, seized the battery of two guns, and occupied the Château of Buzanval.

The French now retired on all sides, firing ceased by six o'clock, and the 10th Division, which had repulsed the enemy's assaults single-handed, re-established its previous fore-post line.

The struggle had cost the Germans 400 men. The French, on the other hand, had in this luckless enterprise left 500 dead and wounded, and 120 prisoners.

Soon after this affair the French began to throw up entrenchments within 800 paces of the line of the Guard Corps; and in the early morning of the 28th, General Bellemare, under cover of the darkness, advanced on Le Bourget with a force of several battalions.

The German company in occupation there, taken completely by surprise, could only retire before such overwhelming numbers, to Pont Iblon and Blanc Mesnil. The French promptly barricaded themselves in the place and prepared it for an obstinate defence. A German battalion made a vain attempt that evening to drive them out; it was repulsed with heavy loss. Equally unsuccessful next day was the fire of thirty field-guns directed against the place from Pont Iblon. Then, however, the Crown Prince of Saxony issued imperative orders to the Guard Corps to recapture Le Bourget without delay.

STORMING OF LE BOURGET.

(October 30th.)

Accordingly on October 30th, nine battalions of the 2nd Guard-Division and five batteries, under the command of Lieutenant-General von Budritzki,[1] were assembled at Dugny, Pont Iblon and Blanc Mesnil for a concentric attack on Le Bourget. The artillery in action along the bank of the Morée inundation opened the attack at about eight in the morning, and then the infantry went forward. The terrain was perfectly open, and the advance was under fire, not merely from Le Bourget, but also from the heavy guns of the forts. Nevertheless the Grenadier Battalion of the Queen Elizabeth Regiment, at the head of the central column, at nine o'clock made a successful assault, charging over the barricade at the northern end of the village, and entering it through a breach in the wall promptly made by the pioneers. The Emperor Francis Grenadier Regiment advanced against its western face and took possession of the park. A fierce street-fight ensued on a further advance into the village, in the course of which there fell the commanders of both regiments, Colonels von Zaluskowski and Count Waldersee. The walled farmsteads left of the main street, were stormed one after another in spite of a determined defence ; the windows of the church, high up in the walls as they were, were broken in and scaled, and a hand-to-hand fight raged furiously inside the sacred building. The Guard Rifle-Battalion forced its way into the glass-works.

---

[1] Commanding 2nd Guard-Division.

At half-past nine the French attempted to bring up into Le Bourget reinforcements from Aubervillers and Drancy; but the left German column had meanwhile seized the railway-embankment, placed a detachment of the Emperor Alexander Regiment to hold it, and was forcing its way into the southern quarter of the village. Two batteries had taken up position on the Mollette brook, and their fire drove back the enemy and even compelled him to evacuate Drancy.

At ten o'clock the French still held the buildings on the north side of the Mollette. These were now assailed from the south. The 4th Company of the Emperor Alexander Regiment crossed the stream and forced its way through a breach made by the sappers into the farmstead in which the enemy's main force was gathered. The defenders had to be quelled with the bayonet and with clubbed arms, and here the French Colonel de Baroche met his death.

Although by this time—eleven o'clock—all the three attacking columns had struck hands in the heart of Le Bourget, the enemy continued the struggle in detached houses and gardens with embittered desperation till the afternoon, while all the forts on the north front of Paris overwhelmed the place with shell-fire. It was not till half-past one that the troops of the attack could withdraw by companies to their respective quarters. Two battalions remained to garrison Le Bourget.

The desperate resistance of the French showed how important they considered their retention of this post. Its success had cost the 2nd (Guard) Division 500 men. The enemy's loss is not known, but 1200 prisoners were taken. This new disaster added to the dissatisfaction of the inhabitants of Paris. The revolutionary factions, which at all times lurk in the French capital, came ominously to the front.

Highly-coloured reports could no longer conceal utter lack of results; the authority of the Government was steadily on the wane. It was accused of in-

capacity, nay, of treason. Noisy mobs clamoured for
arms, and even a part of the National Guard took part
in the tumult. The Hôtel de Ville was surrounded by
a throng shouting "Vive la Commune!" and though
other troops dispersed these gatherings, the ringleaders,
though well known, went unpunished.

On the 31st of October uproarious masses again
paraded the streets. As General Trochu had forbidden the sentries at the Hôtel de Ville to use their
arms, the rebels forced their way in. The Ministers
were their prisoners till the evening, when some battalions which remained staunch liberated them.

Monsieur Thiers, who had returned from his fruitless
tour among the European Courts, thought the time
had come for re-opening negotiations with Versailles.
On the part of the Germans there was still the readiness
to grant an armistice, but it was naturally impossible
to accede to the condition demanded by the French, that
the city should be re-provisioned, and so hostilities had
to take their course.

At this time, towards the end of October, the situation on the Moselle had assumed an aspect which
essentially modified that of the whole war.

*　　　*　　　*　　　* [1]

By the exchange of German prisoners for French
who had fought at Sedan, details of the disaster which
had befallen France in that battle were currently
known in Metz. But Marshal Bazaine declared that
the Army of the Rhine would continue to defend
the country against the invaders, and maintain
public order against the evil passions of disloyal men
—a resolution which certainly could be interpreted
in more ways than one. It would have been
eminently satisfactory to the Germans, politically
speaking, if there had been in France an available

---

[1] In text there is at this point no Section-Headline, although the
subject changes; but the succeeding pages till commencement of
new Section are headed: "Die Lage vor Metz im October." This
heading is followed in translation.

power, apart from the pretentious but feeble Government in Paris, with which to come to an understanding as regarded the termination of the war. Permission was therefore given for the admission to Metz of a person representing himself to have a commission from the exiled Imperial family. As he was unable to authenticate himself in this capacity to the satisfaction of Marshal Bazaine, General Bourbaki was allowed to pass through the German lines that he might betake himself to London, where, however, the Empress Eugénie declined all intervention in the already so disastrous affairs of France. The General then placed his services at the disposal of the National Defence Government at Tours.

Meanwhile the army which had been beleagured in Metz since the day of Noisseville maintained a waiting attitude. The necessary supplies for 70,000 inhabitants, including the country-folk who had taken refuge in the city, had originally been enough to last three months and a half, those for the regular garrison were calculated for about five months; but for the Army of the Rhine there was sustenance in store for only forty-one days, and there was forage for only twenty-five.

Certainly it was possible to supplement the supplies for the troops by purchase from the abundant stores of the citizens; but ere long smaller rations of bread were served out and horses were being slaughtered to furnish animal food, so that most of the cavalry regiments were reduced to two squadrons.

On the German side, the service of supplying 197,326 men and 33,136 horses was one of great difficulty. The outbreak of cattle-plague in Germany restricted the importation of live beasts to those purchased in Holland and Belgium. The meat rations had to be supplemented by tinned provisions; and increased rations of oats had to take the place of hay and straw.

The losses of the army had hitherto been made good from the reserves, but the transport of the prisoners from

Sedan alone required the services of fourteen battalions of the force blockading Metz. Thus it had not yet been possible to provide sufficient shelter for the troops near the wide extension of the entrenched line. Raw, rainy weather had come on early in the season, and a fourth part of the men were still roofless ; so that by degrees the sick in hospital reached the alarming number of 40,000.

Although fifty heavy guns had been brought up from Germany, they were useless for the bombardment of Metz, since in consequence of the superior calibre of the fortress artillery they could only be fired at night, and with frequent change of position. There was nothing for it but to hope for the best, and have patience.

For four weeks already had the besieged been consuming their stores. To replenish those in some degree, and at the same time to revive the spirit of the troops by active measures, the Marshal decided on fetching in all the provisions to be found in the villages inside the line of the German investment, under cover of a sortie.

At noon on September 22nd Fort St. Julien opened a heavy fire on the outposts of the 1st Corps. Strong bodies of infantry then advanced on the villages to the eastward, drove in the picquets of the enemy, and returned to Metz with the stores which had been seized. But a similar attempt made next afternoon on the villages to the north was less successful. Most of the waggons had to return empty, under the fire of the Prussian batteries quickly brought up into position. Finally, on the 27th, a sortie for the same purpose was made to the southward, which led to a series of small conflicts and the capture in Peltre of a German company, which was surrounded by a much stronger force. A simultaneous sally on the left bank of the Moselle was baffled by the fire of the alert artillery of the besieging force.

Thionville, on the north of Metz, had hitherto only been kept under observation by a small force, which could not hinder the garrison from scouring the country as far as the neighbouring frontier, taking many prisoners, seizing fifty waggon-loads of supplies, and even diverting into the fortress a whole train of provision-trucks while passing by the now restored railway from Luxemburg.

In point of fact, the Army of the Rhine would have found in Thionville an important rallying-point at the end of its first day's march, if the blockade of Metz could have been broken through. Prince Frederick Charles, realizing this, took care to strengthen the investing lines to the north, on the right bank of the Moselle. On October 1st the Xth Corps took up the position hitherto held by the Reserve Division Kummer, which was transferred to the left bank of the river. The Ist, VIIth, and VIIIth Corps closed up to the right, and the IInd occupied the space between the Seille and the Moselle ; the troops before Thionville were also reinforced.

The Marshal had really once more determined to break out to the northward, and that on both banks of the river. New bridges were constructed behind St. Julien and from the island of Chambière, the nearest German outposts on the north and west of Metz were pushed back by a series of daily skirmishes. Under cover of the fire of the forts the French established themselves firmly in Lessy and Ladonchamps. The troops to be left in Metz were expressly selected ; the others tested as to their marching powers. Light-signals were arranged with Thionville, and all preparations made for a sortie on the 7th.

Then the French commander suddenly changed his mind, and the proposed enterprise collapsed into a foraging expedition.

For this, indeed, large forces were set in motion ; the Guard Voltigeur Division, the VIth Corps, and

M

the IVth in the forest of Woippy. The movement was also to be supported by the IIIrd Corps on the right bank of the river.

Four hundred waggons were in readiness to carry off the stores from the large farms lying north of Ladonchamps.

SORTIE FROM METZ AGAINST BELLEVUE.

(October 7th.)

Although the start from Woippy planned for eleven o'clock, was not effected till one, the Landwehr companies on outpost duty were driven in by superior numbers, and as they defended their positions till their ammunition was exhausted, they also lost a considerable number of prisoners. But the artillery of the Landwehr Division prevented the removal of the stores; the 5th Division advancing from Norroy struck the left flank of the French attack and drove the enemy back on Bellevue, where a stationary fight developed itself.

The French IIIrd Corps advanced on the right bank of the Moselle against Malroy and Noisseville. Here, too, the outpost line fell back; but behind it stood the Xth and Ist Corps, ready for action. The respective Corps commanders at once perceived that this attack was only a feint. Although threatened himself, General von Voigts-Rhetz sent his 38th Brigade across the Moselle at Argancy by half-past two to assist the Landwehr Division, and when General von Manteuffel forwarded him supports to Charly, the 37th Brigade followed.

No sooner had the first reinforcements arrived than General von Kummer on his side took the offensive, recaptured the farmsteads from the enemy after a sharp struggle just as the latter were about to retire, and then, supported on the right by part of the 5th Division, moved on Bellevue at about six in the evening. Ladonchamps, however, still remained in the hands of the French. Late in the evening the 19th and Reserve Divisions advanced on this place. The premises of the château, which were surrounded by a moat, were carefully intrenched and strongly defended by infantry and guns. The darkness precluded effective artillery action, and the attack failed; but all the other points previously held by the Germans were reoccupied.

The day had cost the Prussians 1700 killed and wounded, besides 500 reported missing. The French loss was given out to be no more than 1193.

This attempt on the part of the French might be regarded as tentative, and preliminary only to a real effort to break through; perhaps it was so intended. The German troops therefore remained in the positions they had occupied at the close of the fighting, in expectation of renewed hostilities on the morrow.

The forts in fact opened a heavy fire on the farm-buildings early on the 8th, while the German batteries directed their fire on Ladonchamps. Strong columns also advanced along the right bank of the Moselle, but nowhere attempted a serious attack. The Prussian troops therefore presently retired to their quarters.

The artillery duel was carried on for the next few days, but with diminished energy. Constant rain made all field operations very difficult, and increased the sufferings of the men on both sides. In Metz the lack of victuals was becoming very painfully felt. So early as on the 8th the commandant had announced that his stores would not last longer than for twelve days. A council of war, held on the 10th, was, however, of opinion that the greatest service the Army of the Rhine could do to France was to hold out as

M 2

long as possible, since it thus continued to detain a hostile army under the walls of Metz.

The Marshal now sent General Boyer to negotiate at Versailles, but his instructions were to demand a free exit for the army and explicitly to refuse the terms of the Sedan capitulation.

The state of affairs in Metz was perfectly well known to the Germans. The number of men who were taken willing prisoners while digging potatoes increased every day. They reported that disturbances had broken out in the city, in which even part of the soldiers had taken part, and that the commander-in-chief had been compelled to proclaim the Republic. And since the Empress had declared that she would never give her consent to any diminution of French territory, no further political negotiations were possible with the chiefs of the Army of the Rhine.

On the 20th the distribution of stores came to an end within the fortress, and the troops thenceforth for the most part subsisted on horseflesh. The original stock of 20,000 horses was reduced by a thousand a day. The want of bread and salt was severely felt, and the soaked, deep ground made living in camp almost unendurable.

After the failure of the negotiations at Versailles, the imperative necessity of entering into negotiations with the Headquarter of the besieging army was recognized by a council of war held on the 24th.

The first interview had no result, as the Marshal still stipulated for free egress on condition of withdrawing to Algiers, or the alternative of an armistice with the reprovisioning of Metz. On the German side the surrender of the fortress and the march out of the garrison as prisoners of war were insisted on, and on these conditions the capitulation was signed on the evening of the 27th of October.

CAPITULATION OF METZ.

(October 27th.)[1]

On the morning of the 29th[1] Prussian flags were hoisted on the great outworks of Metz. At one o'clock the French garrison marched out by six roads in perfect silence and correct military formation.[2] At each specified position a Prussian Army Corps stood to receive the prisoners, who were immediately placed in bivouacs previously prepared, and supplied with food. The officers were allowed to keep their swords and to return to Metz.; provisions were immediately sent in.

Marshal Bazaine set out for Cassel.

In the course of the day the 26th Brigade occupied Metz. The city had suffered no injury, but the state of the camps showed what the troops had suffered during the siege of seventy-two days.

The Germans during that time had lost 240 officers and 5500 men in killed and wounded.

Six thousand French officers and 167,000 men were taken prisoners, beside 20,000 sick who could not be at once removed, about 200,000 in all.[3] Fifty-six Imperial eagles, 622 field and 876 fortress guns, 72 mitrailleuses and 260,000 rifles fell into the hands of the Germans.

The prisoners were transported by way of Trèves and Saarbrücken, escorted by Landwehr battalions, and as these would have also to guard them when in Germany, their return to field service was not to be reckoned on.

---

[1] The Protocol embodying the terms of capitulation was signed on the evening of the 27th; its provisions came into effect at and after 10 a.m. of the 29th.

[2] On the contrary, there were much drunkenness and disorder.

[3] The 20,000 sick were included in the total of 173,000 officers and men surrendered.

NEW DISTRIBUTION OF THE ARMY.

The capitulation of Metz, which Prince Frederick Charles had brought about under such serious difficulties, materially improved the prospects of the war for Germany.

At the Royal Headquarter at Versailles, even before the catastrophe but in confident anticipation of it, decisions had been arrived at as to the respective destinations of the forces it would release for service, and communicated in advance to the superior Commanders.

The Ist, VIIth and VIIIth Corps, with the 3rd Cavalry Division, were thenceforth to constitute the Ist Army, under the command of General von Manteuffel. Its orders were to advance into the Compiegne region and cover the investment of Paris on the north. But apart from these orders it had various other duties to fulfil; it was to occupy Metz and lay siege to Thionville and Montmédy.

The IInd, IIIrd, IXth and Xth Corps, with the 1st Cavalry Division, were to constitute the IInd Army under the command of Prince Frederick Charles, which was ordered to advance on the Middle Loire.

OPERATIONS OF THE XIVTH CORPS IN THE SOUTH-EAST.

(October.)

Since the fall of Strasburg the newly-formed XIVth Corps had been employed in safe-guarding the communications between the German armies standing fast respectively before Metz and before Paris. General von Werder had no great battle to look forward to, but a succession of small engagements. To prepare his four infantry brigades for independent action under such circumstances, he detailed artillery and cavalry to each. In this formation the Corps crossed the Vosges by the two roads through Schirmeck and Barr, driving swarms of hostile Franctireurs out of the narrow passes without material delay. But on emerging from the mountains it at once met with serious opposition.

The French General Cambriels had been at Epinal with about 30,000 men ever since the beginning of October, and under cover of this force numerous battalions of National Guards and Gardes-Mobiles had been formed in the south of France.

On the 6th, General von Degenfeld[1] with the advanced guard of the Baden force approached St. Dié, marching on both banks of the Meurthe. The weak column was beset on all sides by far superior forces, yet after repeated attacks it succeeded in taking the villages which the enemy had been holding.

The struggle, which lasted seven hours, ended with the eccentric retreat of the enemy to Rambervillers and Bruyères. It had cost the Germans 400 and the French 1400 men. The Baden force bivouacked on the field, and presently found that the French had evacuated St. Dié. General Cambriels had, in fact, collected all his available forces in intrenched positions about Bruyéres. The Baden Brigade advanced on these on the 11th, drove the Gardes-Mobiles and volunteers from the outlying villages, climbed the heights on both sides of the town, and forced its way into it with inconsiderable loss. The enemy retired to the southward on Rémiremont.

From the small resistance hitherto made by the French, though so far superior in numbers, General von Werder assumed that they would hardly make a stand before reaching Besançon, so he immediately

[1] Commanding 2nd Baden Brigade.

countermanded further pursuit, though somewhat early in the day, and concentrated his forces on Epinal, which place was taken possession of by the Germans after insignificant fighting. From thence an etappen-route and telegraph-line were opened to Luneville and Nancy, magazines were formed, and the trains, which were following the Corps from Saverne by Blamont to Baccarat, were brought up. The railway along the Moselle remained, however, useless for a long time, in consequence of injury done to it by the enemy.

General von Werder was now anxious, in accordance with his instructions of September 30th, to march on the Upper Seine by Neufchâteau, but a telegram from the supreme Headquarter directed him in the first instance to complete the rout of the enemy in his vicinity under General Cambriels.

The Corps accordingly put itself in motion forth-with through Conflans and Luxeuil on Vesoul, and information was received that the enemy had in fact halted at the Ognon, taken up quarters there, and received reinforcements. General von Werder deter-mined to attack at once. He ordered that the passages over the river should be secured on the 22nd; further decisions were postponed till reports should be brought in. The 1st Baden Brigade came up on the right by nine o'clock, reaching Marnay and Pin without having encountered the French; it secured the bridges there, and then halted to await further orders. On the left flank the franctireurs were driven out of the woods by the 3rd Brigade, which also stormed Perrouse, and at about half-past two seized the bridge over the Ognon at Voray. In the centre the head of the advanced guard of the 2nd Brigade entered Etuz after a slight skirmish, but had to withdraw at eleven o'clock to the northern bank, before the enemy's flank attack from out the woods. Afterwards, when the main force came up and the artillery opened fire, the place was taken for the second time at one o'clock.

But a prolonged fire-fight ensued, the French making an obstinate stand in front of the passage over the river at Cussey. Orders had already been sent to the 1st Brigade to move up on the southern bank from Pin on the enemy's flank and rear. But it could not reach the ground until six o'clock, when the battle was over. When two batteries had made good the possession of the bridge over the Ognon under a heavy fire, the enemy hastily retired, pursued by the Badeners; he was again driven out of his rearward positions, but when night fell he still remained in possession of several points in front of Besançon.

The Germans had lost 120 men, the French 150 and 200 prisoners. In opposition to Gambetta, who was himself in Besançon, General Cambriels obstinately resisted every order to renew the advance, and would only consent to maintain his strong position under the walls of the fortress.

Parties sent out to reconnoitre on the right reported the presence of French forces at Dôle and Auxonne, the advance-guard probably of an "Army of the Vosges" under Garibaldi, which was assembling on the Doubs. General von Werder disregarded it, and on the 26th moved his Corps to Dampierre and Gray. Beyond the Saône all the roads were broken up, the woods choked with abatis, and the whole population in arms. But the franctireurs and Gardes-Mobiles were dispersed without difficulty, and a column marching without any precautions was driven back on the Vingeanne brook, where 15 officers and 430 men laid down their arms.

From further reports and the information of the prisoners it was known that Dijon was strongly garrisoned. In expectation, therefore, of an attack from that side, the XIVth Corps was assembled behind the Vingeanne, whence early on October 30th General von Beyer [1] marched on Dijon with the 1st and 3rd Brigades.

[1] Commanding Baden Division.

Filled with apprehension by recent events, the National Guards in Dijon had already laid down their arms, the Gardes-Mobiles and the line troops of the garrison had retreated southwards; but the inhabitants were assured that the forces would be brought back to defend them. About 8000 men were available, but they insisted on their commander pledging himself to fight only outside the city.

The advanced posts on the Tille were driven in by the Baden advanced guard; the village of St. Apollinaire and the neighbouring heights were taken with a rush at noon, in spite of a hot fire. Meanwhile the main body had come up, and at three o'clock six German batteries opened fire. The vineyards and numerous farmsteads in the neighbourhood of Dijon, and especially the strongly barricaded park south of the city, gave the defence a great advantage. Nevertheless, the Baden infantry continued its steady advance and closed in on the northern and eastern suburbs by a wide encircling movement.

Here a fierce combat ensued, in which the inhabitants took part. House after house had to be stormed, but the attack came to a stand at the deep-cut bed of the Suzon brook, which borders the city on the east. It was four o'clock, and the impending struggle could not be ended before dark. General von Beyer therefore broke off the fight; the battalions were withdrawn and retired to quarters in the adjacent villages; only the artillery still kept up its fire.

The Germans had lost about 150 and the French 100 men; but of the latter 200 were taken prisoners.

In the course of the night a deputation came out to beg that the town might be spared; its members undertook to furnish supplies for 20,000 men, and to guarantee the good behaviour of the inhabitants. The Baden troops took possession of Dijon on the 31st.

Meanwhile fresh instructions had reached General von Werder. They prescribed that he was to protect the left flank of the IInd Army advancing to the Loire and at the same time to cover Alsace and the troops besieging Belfort, where two reserve Divisions had now arrived. It was intended that the XIVth Corps, while retaining its hold on Dijon, should also move to Vesoul and hold in check from there the gathering of hostile troops round Besançon and at Langres. Some offensive movement on Châlons[1] and Dôle was also insisted on.

General von Werder's position was more difficult than was recognized at Versailles. At Besançon alone there were 45,000 French troops, under the command of a new leader, General Crouzat. Garibaldi had collected 12,000 between Dôle and Auxonne; lower down the Saône valley a new Corps was being formed of 18,000 men, and 12,000 National Guards and Gardes-Mobiles threatened from Langres the flank of the isolated German Corps. But the French, instead of attacking this slender force with overwhelming numbers —spread out as it was over a distance of fifty-six miles from Lure to Dijon and Gray—were haunted by the apprehension that the Germans, reinforced from Metz, might be intending an attack on Lyons. General Crouzat, leaving a strong garrison in Besançon, consequently marched to Chagny, where up to November 12th he was reinforced from the south to a strength of 50,000 men. The Garibaldian volunteers moved up to Autun to protect Bourges.

General von Werder meanwhile had occupied Vesoul, and had the south face of the city put in a state of defence.

The only event of importance during the course of October which remains to be mentioned was the action taken against the French forts lying rearward of the German armies.

At the beginning of the month the newly constituted 4th Reserve Division, of fifteen battalions, eight squad-

[1] Châlons-sur-Saône.

rons, thirty-six guns, and a company of fortress-pioneers, had assembled in Baden, and crossed the Rhine at Neuenburg. The vicinity was first cleared of franctireurs, Mulhausen was occupied, and, by the express desire of its municipal authorities, the excited artisan inhabitants were disarmed. General von Schmeling (commanding the Division) was instructed to besiege Neu-Breisach and Schlettstadt, and at once set about the investment of each of these places with a brigade. On October 7th the East Prussian Landwehr invested Breisach, and the field-batteries shelled the place, but without effect. The other brigade, having been forced to detach considerably, reached Schlettstadt very weak, but was reinforced by Etappen troops to such extent that the place was invested with 8 battalions, 2 squadrons, and 2 batteries. At the same time 12 companies of fortress-artillery and 4 companies of pioneers arrived from Strasburg with the necessary siege material, and an artillery park of fifty-six heavy guns was established at St. Pilt; the engineer park was located at Kinzheim.

REDUCTION OF SCHLETTSTADT.

(October 24th.)

At the beginning of the blockade, inundations and marsh-land rendered Schlettstadt, a fortified town of 10,000 inhabitants, unapproachable on the east and south, and partly on the north. The place itself, perfectly safe from storm, with high walls and a wet ditch, was armed with 120 guns, but garrisoned with only 2000 men, for the most part Gardes-Mobiles. There was a deficiency of safe casemates, and on the west front vineyards and hedgerows favoured the near approach of assaults, while the railway embankment was a ready-made protecting wall for the construction of the first parallel. To divert the attention of the besieged from this front of attack, a battery was constructed on the 20th at the Kappel Mill on the southeast, from which fire was opened on the barracks and magazine in the town, and on the sluice which maintained the inundation. By the evening of the 21st, the infantry posts had advanced to within 400 paces of the glacis, and the construction of the first parallel was proceeded with that night, immediately behind the railway, as well as of emplacements for six batteries within 1230 feet from the ramparts. The garrison fired in the dark on the entire field of attack, but almost without effect. By the morning the trenches were two feet wide and three and a half feet deep, and 20 heavy guns and 8 mortars were ready to open fire. A hot artillery duel now began with the fortress, which replied very steadily. The battery at the mill subjected the west front to a telling reverse fire, and several guns and embrasures were severely damaged. The town was fired at several points, and the defenders' fire gradually ceased. During the night, which was very stormy, the batteries of the attack kept up their fire, the parallel was widened and two new batteries were begun.

At daybreak of the 24th the white flag was seen flying, and a capitulation was forthwith signed, by which Schlettstadt surrendered with its garrison and war-material. The commandant begged the Germans to take possession at once, as the greatest disorder reigned within the town. The public buildings were being plundered by the mob and the drunken soldiery, and a powder-magazine was actually on fire. The German battalions promptly restored order, extinguished the flames, and took away the prisoners. Seven thousand stand of arms fell into German hands, besides the fortress artillery and a large quantity of stores. The siege had cost the victors only twenty men. Schlettstadt was occupied by Etappen troops, and the battalions released from duty there marched into southern Alsace, three of them going to strengthen the siege of Breisach, which was now being proceeded with.

REDUCTION OF BREISACH.

(November 10th.)

This fortress, lying in the plain and of very symmetrical shape, was proof against a coup-de-main because of its ditches, which were dry indeed, but faced with solid masonry. The garrison of over 5000 men had well-protected quarters in the bomb-proof casemates of the ravelins. Fort Mortier, standing near the Rhine, and constructed for independent defence, effectually commanded the ground over which the intended attack must be made on the north-west front of the fortress. Therefore 12 heavy guns were brought up from Rastatt to Alt Breisach, where the right bank of the Rhine commands the fort at effective range.

It was not till near the end of October that the siege-guns arrived before New Breisach from Schlettstadt, and when the infantry had closed up and all preparations were complete, fire from 24 heavy guns was opened on the fortress on November 2nd from Wolfganzen, Biesheim and Alt Breisach.

By three o'clock a large part of the town was on fire, and detachments of infantry were skirmishing with the French posts at the foot of the glacis. Fort Mortier had suffered exceptionally severely. Nevertheless, an attempt to storm it was repulsed, but at six o'clock it capitulated, an utter ruin. Only one gun remained in serviceable condition. Two new mortar batteries were erected to shell the main fortress, the defence became perceptibly more feeble, and on November 10th Breisach surrendered on the same terms as Schlettstadt, but the garrison was allowed to march out with the honours of war. The fortifications were almost uninjured, but the town was for the most part burnt down or severely damaged. The success had cost the Germans only 70 men; 108 guns, 6000 small arms and large quantities of stores fell into their hands.

While these strongholds in Alsace-Lorraine were thus being reduced, Verdun still intercepted the line of railway which formed the shortest line of communication with Germany.

TAKING OF VERDUN.

(November 9th.)

This place, too, was made quite storm-free by high walls and deep wet ditches; but, on the other hand, it was surrounded by a ring of heights whence it could be seen into, and at the foot of these heights villages and vineyards favoured an approach to within a short distance of the outworks.

The fortress was armed with 140 guns and abundantly victualled, and the garrison, which had been supplemented by escaped prisoners, was 6000 strong. A bombardment by field-artillery had already proved perfectly ineffectual. For a long time Verdun was only under observation, at first by cavalry, and afterwards by a small mixed force. At the end of September the 65th Regiment and twelve companies of Landwehr assembled under General von Gayl before the east face of the place. It was not till October 9th that two companies of fortress-artillery brought up some French heavy guns from Toul and Sedan. The infantry now advanced to within a few hundred paces of the west and north fronts and there established itself. Under this cover the construction of the batteries was begun on the evening of October 12th.

The heavy ground after the rain, and the rocky subsoil very thinly covered, made the work uncommonly difficult, yet by next morning fifty-two guns were able to open fire. But the fortress replied with such effect that before noon two batteries on the Côte de Hayvaux on the westward were reduced to inaction.

In the course of this three days' artillery engagement, 15 German guns were placed out of action, the artillery lost 60 men and the infantry 40. The disabled guns on the walls of the enemy were constantly replaced by fresh ones.

The garrison, which was far stronger than the besiegers, now assumed the offensive. During the stormy night of the 19th—20th, the picquets on the Hayvaux were overpowered, and the guns in the battery there were spiked. On the 28th a sortie in greater force was made. The French climbed up Mont St. Michel, lying northward of Verdun, and destroyed the breast-works and bomb-proofs of the batteries, from which, however, the guns had been withdrawn. Another body pushed up the Hayvaux, and as the soaked state of the ground prevented the guns from being withdrawn, they were totally disabled. The villages in the neighbourhood were also occupied by the French.

It was now evident that the means hitherto brought to bear on the reduction of Verdun were quite inadequate.   But after the fall of Metz the Ist Army was able to send up reinforcements.   At the end of the month 5 battalions and 2 companies of pioneers and several of artillery arrived, and also a quantity of German material.

The siege park now numbered 102 guns with abundant ammunition, and preparations were at once made for a regular attack.

But for this the garrison did not wait.   After an armistice had been granted, the place capitulated on November 8th, in virtue of which the garrison, with exception of the local National Guards, became prisoners of war.   The officers were dismissed on parole with their swords and personal property, and it was agreed that the war-material in store should be given back on the conclusion of peace.

ADVANCE OF IST AND IIND ARMIES UP TO MID NOVEMBER.

The Ist Army having in addition undertaken the siege of Mézières, the 1st Infantry Division moved on that place, and the 3rd Brigade, sent forward by railway to Soissons, on November 15th set about the siege of the small fortress of La Fère.   The rest of the Ist Corps reached Rethel on the same day, the VIIIth Rheims, and the 3rd Cavalry Division Tagnon, between the two places named.   The VIIth Corps was still fully engaged in guarding the prisoners and in besieging Thionville and Montmédy.

Of the IInd Army the IXth Corps and 1st Cavalry Division reached Troyes on the 10th, the IIIrd Vendeuvre, the Xth Neufchâteau and Chaumont.   The important railway connections there and at Bologne

N

were occupied, and the injury done to the line to Blesme was repaired, so as to open up a new line of communication. The health of the German forces had been materially improved by short marches along good roads and by abundant supplies; but a telegram from Versailles now ordered an accelerated advance.

The Government in Paris being powerless, the Delegation at Tours was displaying increased activity. Gambetta, as Minister both of War and of the Interior, was exercising the power almost of a Dictator, and the fiery energy of this remarkable man had achieved the feat of placing 600,000 armed men and 1400 guns in the field in the course of a few weeks.

In the Arrondissements the National Guards were formed into companies and battalions; then in each Department these were consolidated into brigades; and finally the brigades were incorporated along with the nearest troops of the line and Gardes-Mobiles into the larger Army-Corps.

Thus, in the course of October, under cover of the troops of General D'Aurelle de Paladines which had re-crossed the Loire, a new XVIIth Corps was made up at Blois, another, the XVIIIth, at Gien, and a third, under Admiral Jaures, at Nogent le Rotrou. A large force was in Picardy under General Bourbaki, another at Rouen under Briand, and a third on the left bank of the Seine under Fiéreck.

The detachments of the army investing Paris, which were pushed forward to the south, west, and north, already met in all directions strong forces of the enemy, which they indeed repulsed in many small encounters, but could not follow up to the places of their origin. For such purposes the arrival of the army released from the siege of Metz was needed, and this was not to be looked for before some time in November, while now in October there was threatened a general advance of the French forces on Paris.

Having regard to the inferior strength of General

von Tann's Division holding Orleans, at a French council of war held at Tours it was decided to recover that important place. The attack was to be delivered chiefly from the west. The French XVth Corps—two Infantry Divisions and one of Cavalry—therefore assembled at Mer on the northern bank of the Lower Loire, and the main body of the XVIth behind the forest of Marchénoir. The remaining portions of both Corps were to co-operate on the Upper Loire by way of Gien. Any further advance was not projected, at any rate for the present; on the contrary, General d'Aurelle's instructions were to form an intrenched camp about Orleans for 200,000 men.

General von Tann's reconnoitring parties to the westward everywhere met hostile detachments, which were indeed driven back by restraining skirmishes into the forest of Marchénoir without much difficulty, but which betrayed the vicinity of large forces of the enemy. On the whole an attack from the south-west on the investing army before Paris seemed the likeliest event, since this would threaten both the German Head-quarter in Versailles and the siege-park at Villacoublay; while the German reinforcements from the eastward would have the furthest distance to reach the quarter indicated.

The French forces to the west of Orleans were already extended over a wide stretch of country from Beaugency to Châteaudun. The volunteers grew bolder every day, and the people more hostile.

At last, in quest of some more accurate information, Count Stolberg (commanding 2nd Cavalry Division) on November 7th made a reconnaissance in force. Three regiments of the 2nd Cavalry Division, two batteries, and some companies of Bavarian Infantry advanced by Ouzouer and drove the enemy out of Marolles, but they found the skirts of the forest strongly held.

General Chanzy had brought up all his immediately available troops to St. Laurent des Bois. A sharp fire-

fight ensued, lasting about half an hour, which caused
severe losses in the Bavarian infantry; and then, as
the great superiority of the French was evident, the
engagement was broken off.

As a matter of fact, both the French Corps were
already in full march on Orleans. Reaching the forest
on the 8th, they occupied it firmly, their right wing at
Messas and Meung, their left at Ouzouer. The XVth
Corps was next to move to the right to the Mauve and
the XVIth to the left on Coulmiers. The heads of
those Corps showed themselves at Bardon and Charson-
ville respectively. Both the French Cavalry Divisions
were directed northward on Prénouvellon to turn the
right wing of the Bavarians with a force of ten regiments, six batteries, and numerous volunteer bands,
and thus to cut off their retreat on Paris.

To counteract this attempt the Bavarian Cuirassier
Brigade started for St. Péravy, the 2nd Cavalry Division for Baccon, and, further south, the 2nd Bavarian
Infantry Division advancing from Orleans held the
country about Huisseau and St. Ay.

But an attack was also threatening the German rear
from the considerable force at Gien. General von der
Tann realized that it was now the last moment when
he could hope to extricate himself from so hazardous a
position; and that same evening he issued the necessary
orders. However desirable it was to keep possession
of Orleans, he could not accept battle in so thickly
wooded country, where the action of his relatively strong
artillery and cavalry would be seriously impeded, and
where indeed he might be entirely hemmed in. The
General, however, determined to strike at the most
immediately threatening hostile force in the open
country about Coulmiers, where he would at the same
time be nearer to the 22nd Division at Chartres, on
which he could call for support.

General von Wittich had already asked and obtained
permission to fall back on Orleans, but on the 9th

he had only reached Voves, with his cavalry at Or-gères; thus he could not take any direct part in that day's fighting.

The IInd Army was in full march from Metz, but on this day its head had but just arrived at Troyes.

ENGAGEMENT AT COULMIERS.

(November 9th.)

Left thus to its own resources, the Ist Bavarian Corps moved out in the night, and on the morning of the 9th stood concentrated on the skirts of the forest between Château Montpipeau and Rosières, with the village of Coulmiers in its front. The Bavarian Cuirassiers on the right wing protected the line of retreat by St. Sigismond; the 2nd Cavalry Division was distributed by brigades along the whole front, with detachments well in advance and infantry posts ready in support. Only a small detachment remained in Orleans after the bridge over the Loiret had been destroyed, to protect the numerous sick and wounded in the field hospitals, and occupy the city at any rate till the result of the fight was decided.

The first reports brought in that morning were of the advance of a strong hostile column from Cravant on Fontaines and Le Bardon. This was Rébillard's Brigade, which, as it seemed, aimed at turning the Bavarian left flank and marching direct on Orleans. To oppose it on the bank of the Mauve, General von der Tann at about nine o'clock sent the 3rd Brigade in a southerly direction to Préfort, a little over two miles distant, and as at the same time a sharp contest had now begun at the outposts near Baccon, the 1st Brigade

marched to La Renardière. The remainder of the
Corps remained in and behind Coulmiers. The General's intention was to assume the offensive from this
point against the enemy's left flank, if, as seemed probable, the latter should attempt to push his chief
attack across the Mauve. In furtherance of this intention the cavalry of the right flank was ordered to close
in to Coulmiers.

But the superior strength of the French allowed of
their fetching a much wider compass to the left.
While General d'Aurelle with the XVth Corps de-
tained the Bavarians southward of the road from
Ouzouer to Orleans, General Chanzy advanced with
Barry's Division against their centre and directed
Jauréguiberry's Division northward against their right;
and finally the strong force of French cavalry under
General Reyau moved in the direction of Patay, thus
threatening the German communication with Paris.

This movement of the French XVIth Corps compelled General von Tann, at the very beginning of the
engagement, to despatch the 2nd Brigade, which had
constituted his reserve, to prolong his right wing
northwards towards Champs, and thus obtain touch
with the 4th Cavalry Brigade. The Bavarian Cuirassiers, retiring according to orders from St. Péravy to
the southward, about eleven o'clock encountered
Reyau's cavalry, which, however, restricted itself to a
mere cannonade.

Meanwhile, after a stout resistance, the advanced
posts of the Bavarians had been driven in by the
enemy's superior strength. The 1st Rifle Battalion,
after having retarded the advance of the French horse-
batteries through Champdry for a long time, retreated
from Baccon to La Rivière,[1] where it expected to be
received by the 2nd (Rifle Battalion). But the situa-

---

[1] According to the *Staff History*, on La Renardière and La Grande
Motte.

tion of the latter soon became very critical. Peytavin's Division closely followed up through Baccon, beset La Rivière with five batteries, and then attacked the burning village from three sides at once. After energetic reprisals the Riflemen retired in good order on the 1st Brigade in Renardière, where General Dietl had taken up a position for defence.

After the evacuation of Baccon by the Bavarians, Barry's Division had continued its advance through Champdry, and its batteries deployed opposite Coulmiers and in front of Saintry, in preparation for an assault by strong lines of tirailleurs.

The 4th Bavarian Brigade occupied the park extending to the west ; the quarries further in front were occupied by two battalions, two others were sent to the right to the farmsteads of Ormeteau and Vaurichard, so as to keep up some sort of communication with the 2nd Brigade. One battery to the south and four batteries to the north of Coulmiers were supported by the 5th Cavalry Brigade.

Thus at noon the Bavarian Corps, with only three brigades, held the ground from Renardière to the front of Gémigny, its front disproportionately extended to a length of more than four miles. But the French right wing remained quite inactive, so that the 3rd Brigade which had been sent to Préfort was recalled to Renardière.

When the French Corps had made good its foothold opposite the thin Bavarian line, it attacked in earnest at about one o'clock.

The Riflemen in Renardière had indeed repulsed the enemy's first rush, but this position was no longer tenable with only four battalions against the whole of Peytavin's Division. At about one o'clock General Dietl retired unmolested, under cover of an intermediate position, on the wood of Montpipeau, and occupied its border. Here he was joined by the 3rd Brigade, which on its retirement from Préfort had found Renardière already evacuated. The French had followed up from thence but hesitatingly, came under the fire of six batteries between the points of the forests at La Planche and Coulmiers, and made no further advance with their right wing.

In the centre Barry's Division about one o'clock had driven the Bavarian Riflemen out of the stone-quarries in front of Coulmiers. Not till three o'clock did it advance to a renewed general attack on the 4th Brigade, which was repulsed by the fire of the German guns and the repeated charges of the 5th Cavalry Brigade.

Meanwhile, d'Aries' Brigade of the XVth French Corps, after leaving Renardière, arrived southward of Coulmiers, and its batteries strengthened the fire which was being directed on that village. The Bavarian guns were compelled before the rush of the French tirailleurs to take ground further in rear, where they resumed their activity, while the infantry drove the French out of the park at the point of the bayonet.

But after four hours' fighting the resistance of this single brigade against three French brigades had become extremely arduous. Of the whole Corps only two battalions remained intact as a reserve at Bonneville, no reinforcement was to be looked for from anywhere, and on the right flank the French threatened the communications with Chartres as well as with Paris. At four in the afternoon General von der Tann gave orders to break off the fight and to retire by brigades from the left wing on Artenay.

Fresh troops of the enemy at this moment forced their way into the park of Coulmiers. Colonel Count von Ysenburg held the eastern outlets of the village, and withdrew his troops by alternate echelons through Gémigmy in good order.

It now proved of the greatest importance that the 2nd Brigade should have been able to maintain its position in front of this village, thus covering the further retreat.

At noon, General von Orff (in command of the Brigade), on approaching Champs and Cheminiers, had found these villages occupied by Deplanque's French Brigade. First he silenced its artillery, then he deployed his four battalions for action, with the 4th Cavalry Brigade on the right flank.

Reyau's Cavalry ere long came up between these two villages, after it had given up its two hours' cannonade against the Bavarian Cuirassiers and had been driven out of St. Sigismond by dismounted hussars. But this body of horse soon got out from under the fire of the Bavarian guns and moved off to the westward, it was said because it mistook Lipkow-ski's volunteers, skirmishing further to the north, for German reinforcements advancing. And when the Bavarian horse-batteries opened fire on Champs from the north-east, the French abandoned the place at about two o'clock, in great disorder.

General von Orff now brought the artillery up to within 500 paces of Cheminiers, and marched the infantry up through the intervals.

Admiral Jauréguiberry, however, arriving in person, succeeded in rallying the wavering troops, and this attack failed. The French batteries soon compelled the Bavarian horse-batteries to retire.

When, at about three o'clock, Bourdillon's Brigade and the reserve artillery of the XVIth French Corps also arrived at Champs, and news was brought of the state of the fighting at Coulmiers, General von Orff determined to refrain from all further attack, and con-fined himself to maintaining his position in front of Gémigny to the last extremity. Unshaken by the fire of the numerous hostile batteries, the weak brigade repulsed the repeated attacks of the enemy.

Thus the 4th Brigade was enabled unmolested to retire from Coulmiers by Gémigny and St. Péravy, and the 1st, from Montpipeau further eastward, on Coinces. The 2nd Brigade followed to Coinces, and finally the 3rd formed the rear-guard as far as St. Sigismond, where it halted and bivouacked. The cavalry covered the retreat on all sides.

After a short rest the retreat of the main body was continued during the night, by very bad roads. Artenay was reached by the morning. Orleans was evacuated, and the garrison which had been left there rejoined its Corps. The stores were conveyed by railway back to Toury; but one ammunition column, 150 prisoners, and the sick who could not be moved, fell into the hands of the French.

This contest of 20,000 Germans against 70,000 French cost the former about 800 in killed and wounded; the enemy's loss was nearly double.

From Artenay, on November 10th, the 2nd Brigade undertook the duty of covering the further march on Toury, where close quarters were available. Thither, too, came the 22nd Division from Chartres, and took up a position at Janville close to the Bavarians. General von der Tann had extricated himself from a difficult position with much skill and good fortune. The enemy did not attempt a pursuit. General d'Aurelle restricted himself to awaiting further reinforcements in a strong position before Orleans. The French preparations were, however, in greater activity on the Upper Loir and the Eure.

On the German side the IInd Army Corps arrived before Paris on the 5th of November; the 3rd Division was included in the investing line between the Seine and Marne; the 4th moved on to Longjumeau.

When the Guard Landwehr took possession of the peninsula of Argenteuil, a brigade of the IVth Corps became available for service on the north side of the capital. On the south side, the 17th Division at Rambouillet, the 22nd at Chartres, and the Bavarian Corps, which had moved to Ablis, with the 4th and 6th

Cavalry Divisions, were ultimately formed into a separate Army-Detachment of the IIIrd Army, under the command of the Grand Duke of Mecklenburg, and it was ordered to betake itself in the first instance to Dreux.

OPERATIONS OF THE GRAND DUKE OF MECKLENBURG.

On the 17th of November the 17th Division advanced by Maintenon.   On the left, a French detachment was driven back across the Blaise; and when a few companies of marines, who attempted to block the high-road, had been disposed of, General von Tresckow (commanding the Division) marched into Dreux that evening.   The combat had cost the Germans 50 men, the French 150 and 50 prisoners.

Prince Frederick Charles, whose forces were now at length assembled before Orleans in face of the enemy, expressed the wish that the (Grand Duke's) Detachment should advance on Tours by way of Le Mans.   The Grand Duke accordingly marched on Nogent le Rotrou, which place, being the central rendezvous of the French levies, promised to be the scene of an obstinate resistance.

After several skirmishes the Detachment approached the place, but when on the 22nd preparations were being made to storm it from three sides, it was found that the enemy had already evacuated it.   At the same time orders arrived from the supreme Head-quarter, instructing the Grand Duke to fall back at once on Beaugency to join the right wing of the IInd Army, which it was necessary should immediately be reinforced in view of the superior strength of the enemy.   " The force now massing before Orleans is to postpone all hostilities until the arrival of the Detach-ment.   The slight opposition offered by the French on the Eure and Huisne sufficiently shows that no serious danger threatens on that side; the enemy in that quarter need only be kept under observation by cavalry." The Detachment was not to be permitted even a single rest day, and its march was to be conducted with the utmost speed.

On the 23rd, the Divisions had closed up on their respective heads, and the Grand Duke on the 24th moved on Châteaudun and Vendôme; but the Bavarian Corps only got as far as Vibraye, while the two Prussian Divisions withdrew from the difficult country of the Perche, and the cavalry found the whole line of the Loir held by the enemy.

In fact, the French had sent a brigade of the troops massed behind the forest of Marchénoir by railway to Vendôme, expressly to protect the Government at Tours, while General de Sonis had advanced with the rest of the XVIIth Corps on Brou. Here on the 25th his advance met an ammunition column and bridge-train of the Bavarian Corps. At first only the 10th Cavalry Brigade could engage the enemy, but when presently two companies and eight guns had occupied the bridge over the Loir at Yèvres, the waggons were got through Brou in safety, and the enemy could not enter that place till the cavalry had continued its march.

The Bavarian Corps was meanwhile advancing on Mondoubleau and St. Calais, not certainly the shortest route to Beaugency, but, on the contrary, on the direct road to Tours. The two Divisions only reached the vicinity of Vibraye and Authon.

The appearance of a hostile force at Brou was deemed of sufficient importance to justify a détour by that place, postponing for the moment the prescribed march on the Loire. But when the 22nd Division approached Brou on the 26th, it found that the enemy had already retired during the night. The Government at Tours had ordered the whole of the XVIIth

Corps to concentrate at Vendôme for their protection. But when the German cavalry made its appearance at Cloyes and Fréteval, General Sonis considered that he could not pursue his march further along the Loir, and made a détour by Marchénoir. But two night-marches so shattered the levies for the first time collected in mass that whole swarms of .stragglers wandered about the neighbourhood all day and could only with difficulty be re-assembled at Beaugency.

To imbue the operations with unity of command, the Grand Duke was now, by instruction from the supreme Head-quarter, placed under Prince Frederick Charles's orders, and General von Stosch[1] was despatched to undertake the duties of Chief of the Staff to the Detachment. That force by the Prince's orders was to come in with all speed to Janville, whither troops of the IXth Corps would be sent to meet it by way of Orgères.

The Grand Duke therefore marched, on the 27th, with both his (Prussian) Divisions (17th and 22nd) to Bonneval, where there was already a squadron of the 2nd Cavalry Division. The Bavarian Corps, which, after finding Brou abandoned, had been directed on Courtalin, marched to Châteaudun. Having thus accomplished a junction with the IInd Army, the sorely fatigued troops of the Detachment were allowed a day's rest on the 28th, in quarters on the Loir.

SITUATION OF IIND ARMY.

(Second half of November.)

Prince Frederick Charles had hastened the advance of his army as much as possible, but it had met

---

[1] Until then Commissary-General. He succeeded Colonel von Krenski as the Grand Duke's Chief of Staff.

with many hindrances. The roads were broken up, National Guards and franctireurs stood watchful for mischief, and even the country people had taken up arms. However, by November 14th the IXth Corps with the Ist Cavalry Division reached Fontaine-bleau, whence it pursued its march to Angerville. The IIIrd Corps was following on Pithiviers. Of the Xth Corps the 40th Brigade was left at Chaumont, to make connection with the XIVth Corps; the 36th reached Montargis and Beaune la Rolande on the 21st.[1] The two brigades following in rear (37th and 39th) had a sharp encounter on the 24th at Ladon and Maizières. In this combat 170 French prisoners were taken, who belonged to a corps which, as General von Werder had already reported, was proceeding under General Crouzat's command from Chagny to Gien by railway. The order of battle was found on an officer who was among the prisoners.

That while the Grand Duke's Detachment was marching to join it, the IInd Army, only now fully concentrated, was in very close proximity to consider-able forces of the enemy, was ascertained beyond doubt by several reconnoissances.

On the 24th troops of the IXth Corps advanced along the great high-road. A few shells caused the enemy to evacuate Artenay, pursued by the cavalry as far as Croix Briquet. Early in the same day a mixed detachment of all arms from the IIIrd Corps reached Neuville aux Bois. Two detachments of the 38th Brigade marched on Bois Commun and Bellegarde, but everywhere those inquisitive reconnaissances were met by very superior numbers of the enemy.

It was ascertained that the position of the French

---

[1] There seems some confusion here. The 36th Brigade belonged, not to the Xth, but to the IXth Corps. The 38th Brigade is stated in the *Staff History* to have reached Beaune la Rolande on 23rd, the rest of the Corps (exclusive of the 40th Brigade) still behind at Montargis.

before Orleans extended for about 37 miles from the
Conie to Loing ; and the massing of troops, especially
on their (right) flank, made it highly probable that
they proposed advancing by Fontainebleau on the rear
of the besieging army. Still, this intention was not
so evident as to justify Prince Frederick Charles in
leaving the great highways from Orleans to Paris unguarded. However, to enable him to lend his left wing
timely support in case of need, he moved the 5th
Infantry Division of the IIIrd Corps and the 1st
Cavalry Division to Boynes, nearer to the Xth Corps
which was weak, and the 6th Division occupied
Pithiviers in their stead. The quarters at Bazoches
vacated by the 6th Division, were assigned to the IXth
Corps. Finally, the Grand Duke received orders to
reach Toury with his heads of columns by the 29th at
latest. These dispositions were all carried out in due
course.

Immediately after its success at Coulmiers the French
Army of the Loire seemed for the moment only to have
thought of securing itself against a counter-blow. It
retired on Orleans, threw up extensive entrenchments,
for which marine artillery was even brought up from
Cherbourg, and awaited the arrival of further reinforcements. The XXth Corps, already mentioned,
40,000 strong, joined the XVth, XVIth, and XVIIth
at Gien, in addition to one Division of the XVIIIth
newly assembled at Nevers, and finally the volunteer
bands under Cathelineau and Lipowski.

Thus the French Army round Orleans numbered
200,000 ; the German infantry opposed to this host for
the time reached a strength of not more than 45,000
men.

Gambetta soon became urgent for renewed offensive
operations. As General d'Aurelle raised objections to
an advance by Pithiviers and Malesherbes, the Dictator
himself took in hand the dispositions. In the night of
the 22nd-23rd he telegraphed orders from Tours that

the XVth Corps was at once to assemble at Chilleurs aux Bois and reach Pithiviers on the 24th; the XXth to march to Beaune la Rolande; and that then both Corps were to advance by way of Fontainebleau on Paris. The General pointed out that, according to his reckoning, 80,000 Germans must be encountered in an open country, and that it would be more advisable to await their attack in an intrenched position. Further, that this movement could be of no service in affording succour to the distressed capital, and that meanwhile there would remain unperformed the strengthening of the right wing, where on the 24th the unsteadiness of the XVIIIth and XXth Corps had caused the loss of the already mentioned fight at Ladon and Maizières.

In accordance with instructions received from Tours on the 26th, General Crouzat ordered the advance for the 28th of the two Corps he commanded—the XVIIIth by the right through Juranville, the XXth by the left through Bois Commun—for an encompassing attack on Beaune la Rolande. The XVth Corps in addition was moved up to Chambon in support, and Cathelineau's volunteers went forward to Courcelles.

As we have seen, on this same day the Grand Duke's Detachment had come up on the extreme right of the IInd German Army. On the left stood the Xth Corps with the 38th Brigade at Beaune, the 39th at Les Cotelles; the 37th, with the Corps artillery, had advanced to Marcilly between these two places.

BATTLE OF BEAUNE LA ROLANDE.

(November 28th.)

The French attack on November 28th failed because of the miscarriage of the projected combination, the two separate attempts exerting little reciprocal influence. On the right, the head of the XVIIIth Corps struck the outposts of the 39th Brigade at an early hour, in front of Juranville and Lorcy. Not until after a stout resistance were these driven in by about nine o'clock on Les Côtelles and behind the railway-embankment at Corbeilles, where they took possession of the park.

The French could now deploy in the open country in front of Juranville, and following up with strong lines of tirailleurs preceding them, they forced their way into Corbeilles and drove the garrison out to the north and west. But meanwhile, on the other side, a reinforcement from the reserve at Marcilly reached Les Côtelles, and now Colonel von Valentini passed to the attack of Juranville with the 56th Regiment. The artillery could afford no co-operation, the enemy made an obstinate resistance, and not till noon did he begin to retreat, while bitter fighting still continued round some detached houses. But when strong columns came up from Maizières and Corbeilles, the Germans were compelled to abandon the conquered village, carrying off with them 300 prisoners.

About two o'clock the greater portion of the French Corps deployed near Juranville for an attack on the position at Long Cour, into which the 39th Brigade had retired. But since the attack had not been prepared by artillery, it came to nothing under the fire of five Prussian batteries.

The first attack on Les Côtelles was also repulsed, but when it was repeated an hour later, the Germans had to abandon the place with the loss of fifty men taken prisoners. A gun, seven of the gunners of which had fallen, sank so deep in the soft ground that the few men left could not drag it out.

The XVIIIth French Corps, however, made no further way, but, as dusk came on, contented itself with an ineffective cannonade, and finally the 39th Brigade was able to maintain its position abreast of Beaune.

On the left wing of the French line of battle the attack had also from the first been of an encompassing tendency, the 2nd Division of the XXth Corps having advanced on Beaune, and the 1st on Batilly. But it was near noon before the arrival of part of its 3rd Division, which had remained in reserve, enabled the enemy to drive in the German advanced posts from Bois de la Leu to the cross-roads north-west of Beaune. And here also the 38th Brigade soon found itself under the artillery and infantry fire from Pierre Percée, the enemy continually gaining ground from the northward. The retreat had to be continued along the Cæsar road, whereon a gun, of which the men and horses had for the most part perished, fell into the enemy's hands. About the same time the 2nd French Division ascended the heights to the east of Beaune, and Colonel von Cranach was first enabled to rally the 57th Regiment further rearward, near La Rue Boussier, whereby the withdrawal of the batteries hurrying away from Marcilly was covered, and the further advance of the enemy was then arrested. Any such effort on his part entirely ceased when he was suddenly threatened on his own flank by the 1st Prussian Cavalry Division advancing from Boynes, and came under fire of its horse-batteries.

Meanwhile the 16th Regiment found itself completely isolated in Beaune, and surrounded on three sides by the enemy.

The town, which was surrounded by the remains of a high wall, and the churchyard were as far as possible prepared for defence. The enemy, after his first onset by strong swarms of riflemen had been driven back, set about bombarding the town. His shells burst through the walls of the churchyard and set a few buildings on fire, but every attempt at an assault was steadfastly repulsed.

In the meantime, General von Woyna had replenished the ammunition of his batteries, and while occupying Romainville on the right, he also took up a position opposite the copses of Pierre Percée, so that by three o'clock he was able to bring up seven companies on the east side of Beaune.

About this time assistance came with the arrival of the IIIrd Army Corps. While the 6th Division was still pressing on towards Pithiviers, the 5th had already that morning stood to arms in front of that place. The first news from Beaune had sounded so far from alarming, that the Corps-artillery retired to its quarters. Nevertheless, in consequence of the increasing cannon thunder and later information of a serious encounter, General von Alvensleben gave the word for the Corps to advance, with the 5th Division of which General von Stülpnagel had already set out of his own initiative. The 6th followed, and detached a battalion to observe owards Courcelles; wherein, however, Cathelineau's volunteers remained inactive.

Part of the 52nd Regiment, which was marching at the head of the column, turned off to the right, and, supported by artillery, began a fire-fight about 4.30 against Arconville and Batilly. Another part penetrated into the Bois de la Leu and the copses near La Pierre Percée, where it re-captured the gun which had been lost there earlier. Four batteries in position on the road from Pithiviers, behind Fosse des Prés, directed their fire on the enemy still holding his ground on the west side of Beaune, from which he was finally driven by the 12th Regiment, and pursued as far as Mont Barrois.

After dark the Xth Corps encamped about Long Cour, Beaune and Batilly, and the 5th Division in its rear; the 6th remained at Boynes, where the 1st Division of Cavalry also found accommodation.

In the battle of Beaune la Rolande General von Voigts-Rhetz had to hold his ground against the enemy with 11,000 men against 60,000, with three brigades against six Divisions, until help reached him towards evening. This action cost the Germans 900 and the

French 1300 men in killed and wounded; and 1800 unwounded prisoners fell into the hands of the Germans.

In the evening the French XXth Corps had retreated as far as Bois Commun and Bellegarde; the XVIIIth, on the contrary, had taken up its position near Vernouille and Juranville, in fact, directly in front of the Xth German Corps, on the ground which the former had won. The expectation was therefore not unnatural that the fighting would recommence on the morrow.

Prince Frederick Charles, therefore, directed the Xth and IIIrd Corps to assemble on the 29th in full preparedness. The IXth received orders to advance with two brigades towards Boynes and Bazoches, and the remaining troops were to follow as soon as the Grand Duke's Detachment should have reached the main road to Paris. Of it in the course of the day the heads arrived, the 4th Cavalry Division at Toury, the infantry at Allaines and Orgères. The 6th Cavalry Division, which was marching on the right flank, met first with opposition at Tournoisis.

Meanwhile General Crouzat had been instructed from Tours by a message which reached him on the evening of the 28th, to desist for the present from further offensive attack, and the French right wing was thereupon drawn further back. On the 30th both Corps moved leftward, in order to be again nearer to the XVth. For the purpose of disguising this lateral movement, detachments were sent in a northerly direction and met reconnoitring parties of the German Xth and IIIrd Corps, with which skirmishes took place at Maizières, St. Loup and Mont Barrois; and the movement of the French was soon detected, in the first instance on their left flank.

The Government at Tours had received news from Paris that General Ducrot would attempt on the 29th to break through the German investing lines with 100,000 men and 400 guns, and endeavour to connect with the Army of the Loire in a southerly direction. The balloon which carried this despatch had descended in Norway, whence the message had been forwarded. It was concluded from this that the General was already vigorously engaged, and that help must be no longer delayed. Commissioned by Gambetta, M. Freycinet submitted to a council of war called by General d'Aurelle, a scheme for the advance of the whole army on Pithiviers. In the event of a refusal by the Commander-in-Chief to accept the same, M. Freycinet carried an order for his supersession.

It was decided in the first place to execute a wheel to the right with the left wing, Chilleurs aux Bois forming the pivot of the movement. While a front was thus being formed against Pithiviers, the Corps of the right wing on a parallel front were to await the order to move until this was accomplished. The XXIst Corps was to be sent to Vendôme to cover the left flank.

THE ADVANCE OF THE ARMY OF THE LOIRE TO THE RELIEF OF PARIS.

As the result of those dispositions, on the 1st of December the XVIth Corps moved on Orgères, in the direction of the railway ; the XVIIth followed to Patay and St. Péravy.

Opposite to these forces, on the right wing of the IInd German Army the 17th Division of the Grand Duke's Detachment had arrived at Bazoches, the 22nd at Toury, and the Bavarian Corps reached the vicinity of Orgères. Thus the hostile shock fell first on the last body. Attacked in front by a far superior force, and threatened in flank by Michel's Cavalry Division, the 1st Bavarian Brigade was forced to retreat at three o'clock to Villepion. The 2nd Brigade approaching from Orgères, halted to the west of Nonneville, and the 4th marched up to between Villepion and Faverolles, which position the Bavarians, in spite of heavy losses, succeeded in holding for a long time. On their right wing Prince Leopold of Bavaria, with the four guns of his battery still serviceable, arrested the enemy's advance on Nonneville, but under the personal leadership of Admiral Jauréguiberry the French forced their way into Villepion. As night drew on, and the want of ammunition was becoming serious, the 1st Bavarian Brigade went to Loigny; the 2nd, however, did not retreat until five o'clock to Orgères, where also the 3rd arrived in the evening, whilst the 4th joined the 1st at Loigny.

The engagement cost both sides about 1000 men, and only the foremost Bavarian detachments were forced back for a short distance.

This measure of success, and the news from Paris, rekindled in Tours ardent hopes of victory. As will be seen further on, a sortie from Paris on 30th November had certainly so far succeeded that the village of Epinay on the northern section of the line of investment was occupied for a short time. Thereupon it was summarily concluded that this was the village of the same name which lay to the south near Longjumeau, and that there was now scarcely any obstacle to the junction of the Army of Orleans with that of Paris. Cathelineau's volunteer Corps was directed at once to occupy the forest of Fontainebleau, and the imminent annihilation of the Germans was announced to the country.

The head of the Army of Orleans, nevertheless, had barely made half a day's march in the direction of Paris, and the right wheel of the left wing remained to be accomplished. The XVIth Corps was to attempt to reach the line Allaines-Toury by the 2nd of December; the XVIIth was to follow, and the XVth, marching from

Chilleurs through Artenay, was to close to the right. The Grand Duke, on the report of the great force in which the enemy was approaching, determined to march to meet him with the whole strength of the Detachment. The requisite orders were issued at eight o'clock in the morning to the Divisions, which were already standing prepared on their respective assembling-grounds. The Bavarian Corps was directed to take up a position opposite Loigny with its left wing at Château-Goury; the 17th Division to march immediately from Santilly to Lumeau, and the 22nd from Tivernon to Baigneaux. The cavalry was to undertake the protection of both wings.

BATTLE OF LOIGNY—POUPRY.

(December 2nd.)

The Bavarian Corps was still engaged in the advance from Maladerie when the French ascended the heights to the west of Loigny. The 1st Division, therefore, marched towards Villeprévost, and the 2nd held the line Beauvilliers-Goury.

At 8 a.m. General Chanzy set out with his 2nd and 3rd Divisions from Terminiers, for Loigny and Lumeau. The 1st followed in reserve, and Michel's Cavalry Division covered the left flank. In spite of the strong fire of the defenders, the 2nd Division by nine o'clock advanced close upon Beauvilliers, but then it had to give way before the onset of the Bavarians, who now on their side attacked Loigny. When, however, at 10.30 the whole French Corps advanced, deployed on a broad front from Nonneville to Neuvilliers, they had to fall back with great losses. They, however, found a rallying point at Beauvilliers, where the fire of the Corps artillery gave pause to the advance of the enemy.

The combat surged backwards and forwards until, at 11.30, the 2nd Bavarian Brigade joined in the fray. The 4th Cavalry Division charged the left flank of the enemy ; and Michel's Division fell back on the XVIIth Corps, numerous prisoners thus falling into the hands of the German troopers. In the meantime the Bavarian infantry had marched to Ferme Morâle with intent to renew the attack, but there found itself under fire so destructive that it was forced to turn back. Thereupon the horse-batteries on the flank enfiladed the enemy's wing with such effect, that the farm was set on fire and General von Orff found himself able to take possession of it.

At Beauvilliers, meanwhile, the 2nd Division had only with great difficulty resisted the vigorous onslaughts of the French, whose rifle-swarms were already so close that the batteries were compelled to retire to positions further back. But the success of the right wing soon extended to the left. Breaking out from Beauvilliers, as well as from Château Goury, the Bavarians drove Jauréguiberry's Division back to Loigny.

Shortly after noon the firing of the French became again remarkably energetic, especially against Château Goury. The battalions of the Bavarian left wing were forced back upon the park.

During these events the two Prussian Divisions had continued their advance. The artillery of the 17th pressed on in order to engage the enemy, while the head of the infantry reached Lumeau in time to prevent its occupation by the opposing forces. Strong swarms of French riflemen fought their way up quite close to the place, but they were finally driven back by a well-directed fire of musketry and shell ; whereupon the Division assailed the right flank of the French attack.

The 22nd Division also marched through Baigneaux to Anneux, and joined in the pursuit of the retreating enemy. A number of prisoners and a battery were captured, and the enemy, after a vain attempt to make another stand near Neuvilliers, at last fled towards Terminiers in utter disorder.

After this result of the fighting about Lumeau, General von Tresckow was able to go to the assistance of the hard-pressed left wing of the Bavarians. Under cover of the fire of eight batteries the 33rd Brigade moved against the flank of the French masses which were now making a fierce attack on Château Goury. Taken by surprise, these retired upon Loigny. But there, too, the Mecklenburg battalions forced in, shoulder to shoulder with the Bavarians, and it was only in the churchyard on high ground at the west end of the village, that an obstinate resistance was made for some time longer. The French, as they retired on Villepion, suffered from a destructive fire from eighty guns massed near Loigny.

At 2.30 General von der Tann caused the whole of his 1st Division, after the replenishment of its ammunition, to advance once more ; this movement, however, was arrested by the fire of the enemy.

Michel's Division moved up to oppose the advance of the German cavalry on the right flank, but went about as soon as it came within range of the horse-batteries.

Because of the exposed condition of his right flank, General Chanzy had sent a few battalions to form a refused flank[1] near Terre-noire. Behind this a brigade of the XVIIth Corps came up near Faverolles, and to the right of Villepion the Papal Zouaves advanced against Villours.

General von Tresckow now threw in his last reserves. Two battalions of the 75th Regiment broke into the place at the first charge, and in conjunction with all the troops fighting in the vicinity, drove back the French columns to Villepion.

The approach of darkness brought the fighting here to a close.

---

[1] To the German term " Haken-stellung " there is perhaps no precisely equivalent expression in our military vocabulary. " Refused flank " is probably approximate.

While the French XVIth Corps had been fighting single-handed with great persistence all day, the XVth, according to orders, had advanced through Artenay along the Paris high-road. There it was opposed only by the 3rd Cavalry Brigade. That force was attacked about mid-day near Dambron by the 3rd French Division, which formed the left-flank column, while the other two Divisions held much further to the right.

So soon as this information came in from the cavalry, General von Wittich moved off with the whole of the 22nd Division from Anneux in the direction of Poupry. The head of the column reached that place at the double, and succeeded in driving back the enemy, who had already broken in there and occupied the forest belts to the north. Six batteries then came into action, resting on Morâle to the south. The French deployed between Dambron and Autroches, and maintained a persistent fire while their remaining Divisions came up. After an encounter with the troops from Poupry, they occupied with their right wing the small copses which lay near, in front of the forest-land to the north, placed the artillery in the intervals, and began at three o'clock an attack from thence. This, however, withered under a fire of grape-shot from the defenders, and the menace of a charge by the 3rd Cavalry Brigade, which General von Colomb had set in motion in the open country to the west of Dambron. An attack on Morâle by the left wing from Autroches likewise miscarried. But at four o'clock the French advanced along their whole front, preceded by great swarms of tirailleurs. They were repulsed at Poupry, and likewise at Morâle, at which latter place two companies of pioneers joined in the fight; on the other hand, their right wing pushed into the forest, and compelled its defenders to retreat. But Prussian battalions yet remaining in reserve, advanced from Poupry, and drove the enemy back into the copses, where he had still to defend himself against an attack by the cavalry.

The fighting was now stopped by the approach of night. The 22nd Division remained under arms till eleven o'clock in the position which it had seized, and only then withdrew to Anneux. The 3rd Cavalry Division quartered for the night in Baigneaux. The 17th Division remained in position near Lumeau, having Loigny in its front, which it occupied in concert with the Bavarians, who extended further to the right as far as Orgères.

The day had cost the French 4000 killed and wounded, and the Germans fully as many, but 2500 unwounded prisoners, eight guns, one mitrailleuse and a standard belonging to the enemy were left in possession of the latter.

On the French side, the XVth Corps retired to Artenay and received orders, under cover of a Division to be left there, to occupy the defensive position previously held on the skirt of the forest.

Thus the intended further advance of the left wing of the Army of Orleans had not succeeded. The XVIth Corps, lacking the support of the XVIIth, had indeed lost ground, but still maintained itself with its most advanced line on Villepion, Faverolles and Terminiers. General Chanzy therefore considered himself justified in making yet another effort against the German right wing on the following day.

The German strength consisted of five Corps, and stood close in front of the enemy; further reinforcements could not be immediately expected, but by the supreme Command it was judged that the moment had now come to put an end to the standing menace from the south against the investment of Paris.

At mid-day of the 2nd, the order came from the Royal Head-quarter to undertake an attack on Orleans in full strength, and in the course of that day Prince Frederick Charles gave the requisite instructions to this end.

It is here necessary to go back a little in order to see how circumstances developed events during November at various other points.

PARIS IN NOVEMBER.

The tidings, which became known on the 14th November, of the happy result of the action at Coulmiers on the 9th, had rekindled in Paris universal hope. No one doubted that the enemy would find it necessary to send large forces in the Orleans direction, which would considerably weaken the investment line, particularly in its southern section.

In order to contribute towards the hoped-for approaching relief by active co-operation, three separate armies were formed out of the garrison of Paris.

The first, under General Clément Thomas, consisted of 226 battalions of the National Guard, in round numbers 130,000 men. Its duty was the defence of the enceinte and the maintenance of quietude within the city. The second, under General Ducrot, constituted the most trustworthy element, especially the troops of the former XIIIth and XIVth Corps. This army was apportioned into three (Infantry) Corps and one Cavalry Division, and it consisted of fully 100,000 men and more than 300 guns. It was designed for active service in the field, and for making sorties on the investing forces. The third army, under General Vinoy, 70,000 strong, was made up of six Divisions of Gardes-Mobiles and one Cavalry Division; and to it also Maud'huy's Division of the line was assigned. It was to aid the more important sorties by diversions on subordinate fronts. In addition to all these details, 80,000 Gardes-Mobiles were in the forts, and 35,000 more in St. Denis under Admiral de la Ronciere.

The available military strength consequently amounted to above 400,000 men.

The garrison exhibited a lively activity in petty nocturnal enterprises. The heavy guns of the defences carried to Choisy le Roi, and even as far as Beauregard, near Versailles. On the peninsula of Gennevilliers trenchwork was energetically set about, and the task of bridge-building was undertaken. Many signs pointed to an intended effort on the part of the French to break out in a westerly direction. But since, as long as the IInd Army was still incomplete, the greatest danger threatened from the south, the supreme Command in Versailles, as already mentioned, ordered the IInd Corps into the position behind the Yvette from Villeneuve to Saclay. On the north of Paris the Guard Corps extended itself leftward as far as Aulnay, the XIIth sent one brigade across to the south bank of the Marne, and the Würtemberg Division moved into the interval between the Marne and the Seine caused by the shifting of the IInd Corps.

On November 18th the summons from Tours reached Paris, calling on the latter with all promptitude to reach the hand to the Army of the Loire ; certainly somewhat prematurely, since, as we know, that army was at the time concerning itself only in regard to defensive measures.

In Paris all preparations were actually made.for a great sortie. But as the earlier attacks on the front of the VIth Corps had shown that this section of the investment was materially strengthened by fortifications about Thiais and Chevilly, it was decided in the first instance to gain the plateau east of Joinville and from thence to bend rightward towards the south. The attention of the Germans was to be distracted by attacks in the opposite direction.

On the 18th,[1] the day on which the Army of Orleans had vainly striven to press forward to Beaune la Rolande, General Ducrot assembled the IInd Army of Paris in the neighbourhood of Vincennes, and Mont Avron was occupied on the following day by Hugues' Division of the IIIrd Army. As, however, the construction of the bridges (over the Marne) at Champigny and Bry was delayed, the battle was postponed till the 30th ; but it was left to the commanders of the

---

[1] Obvious misprint for 28th.

subordinate affairs to carry them out simultaneously with the chief enterprise or in advance of it. Accordingly, Maud'huy's Division assembled in the night of 28th-29th behind the redoubt of Hautes Bruyères, and advanced against L'Hay before daybreak.

Warned by the heavy firing from the southern forts, General von Tümpling (commanding VIth Corps) had early ordered the 12th Division to get under arms in its fighting positions, and the 11th to assemble at Fresnes.

The French, favoured by the darkness, made their way through the vineyards into L'Hay; but were successfully driven back by the Germans with the bayonet and clubbed arms.

After a prolonged fire-fight, the French renewed their onslaught at 8.30, but without success; and then the defenders, reinforced from the reserve, retaliated with a vigorous counterstroke. At ten o'clock the enemy retreated to Villejuif.

Admiral Pothuau at the same time had moved up the Seine with Marines and National Guards. An outpost at Gare aux Bœufs was surprised and captured, and Choisy le Roi was fired upon by field-guns, fortress artillery, and gunboats which appeared on the Seine. Just as the Grenadiers of the 10th (Prussian) Regiment were on the point of making an attack, General Vinoy broke off the fight.

This demonstration cost the French 1000 men and 300 uninjured prisoners; the Prussians, remaining under cover, lost only 140 men. The fortress kept up its fire till mid-day, and then the enemy was allowed a short truce, to remove his numerous wounded.

Against the front of the Vth Corps also, a strong infantry force advanced at eight o'clock upon Garches and Malmaison, and drove in part of the outposts. But it soon found itself opposed by closed battalions, and at noon retreated to Valérien.

The Attempt of the Army of Paris to Break Out.

(November 30th and December 2nd.)

On November 30th the IInd Paris Army opened the battle which was to decide the fate of the capital.

To hinder the reinforcement of the Germans towards the real point of attack, almost every section of their line of investment was again engrossed by sorties.

To the duty of pushing an attack against the southern front, General Ducrot assigned Susbielle's Division of his IInd Corps. It reached Rosny so early as three o'clock in the morning, crossed the Marne at Créteil by a field-bridge, and from thence, briskly supported by the nearest forts, opened fire on the outpost line of the Würtemberg Division, which had been pushed forward to Bonneuil and Mesly.

General von Obernitz (commanding the Division) had an extended position to maintain. His 1st Brigade was at Villiers on the peninsula of Joinville, his 2nd at Sucy en Brie, and his 3rd at Brévannes. The Division was placed under the Commander of the Army of the Meuse, who had been instructed from Versailles to reinforce it strongly by the XIIth Corps, or even by troops of the Guard Corps.

From the great accumulation of hostile forces on Mont Avron, the Saxon Corps believed itself directly threatened on the right bank of the Marne, and requested to be immediately transferred to the left; the Crown Prince of Saxony gave the order that the whole 24th Division should assemble there on the following day.

Thus for the present the only aid that could be rendered to the Würtembergers was from the wing of the IInd Corps at Villeneuve, of which the 7th Infantry Brigade moved up near Brévannes to Valenton.

The fire of its three batteries hurrying thither, first brought the advance of the French Division to a stand.

The attempt of the Würtembergers to seize Mont-Mesly failed at first; but after a strenuous artillery fire they succeeded in carrying the hill by twelve o'clock, and the Prussian battalions forced their way into Mesly. The Würtemberg horse cut in upon the enemy's retreating guns with great success. At 1.30 the reopening of the fire from the forts proclaimed the end of this sortie. It cost the Germans 350 men, and the French 1200.

During this time the front of the VIth Corps had not been at all molested. General Vinoy, who had not been informed of the advance of Susbielle's Division, when its retreat was noticed caused to be opened from Fort Ivry and the adjoining works a brisk fire, which was augmented by gunboats on the Seine and armour-plated batteries on the railway. Then Admiral Pothuau advanced against Choisy le Roi and Thiais. His Marines, after driving out the Prussian fore-posts, again settled themselves firmly in Gare aux Bœufs. But the further advance failed, and General Vinoy recalled his troops, after which the fighting at Mesly ceased, and only the thunder of artillery continued till five o'clock.

After a preliminary cannonade from Valérien the Gardes-Mobiles advanced against the front of the Vth Corps about seven o'clock. They were, however, repulsed by the outposts and supporting troops in readiness, and retired at eleven o'clock.

On the northern front of Paris there occurred also a sharp fight. At mid-day Fort de la Briche, supported by field-guns and a floating battery, opened a heavy fire on the low-lying village of Epinay on the right bank of the Seine. At two o'clock Haurion's Brigade advanced, two companies of marines pressed into the place along the bank of the river, and drove out the garrison, which consisted of only one company. A second also retired from the defence-works in a northerly direction towards Ormesson. At three o'clock in the afternoon, the village, up to some still obstinately defended farms on the further side of the mill-race, fell into the hands of the French.

Meanwhile the troops of the IVth Corps had assembled, and seven batteries came into action on the overhanging heights. The infantry rushed upon the village. from all sides with loud cheers, and about four o'clock, after a fierce street-fight, recovered possession of the posts which had been lost; and it was this transitory conquest that was to raise so great hopes in Tours. The losses on both sides amounted to 300 men.

Those affairs were all mere feints to facilitate the chief action; and whilst the investing troops were thus engaged and held fast at all points, two Corps of the IInd French Army at 6.30 in the morning crossed the bridges at Joinville and Nogent which had been completed during the night. After repulsing the German outposts they both deployed, and stretched completely across the peninsula between Champigny and Bry. The IIIrd Corps had taken the road along the north bank of the Marne, towards Neuilly, to cross the river there, thus threatening to compromise the position of the Saxon Corps, which therefore still detained the 47th Brigade on the right bank, though it had been assigned to the assistance of the Würtembergers. Consequently there were available to oppose the two French Corps on the left bank, only two German brigades extended over about four miles, the Saxon 48th about Noisy, and the Würtemberg 1st from Villiers to Chennevières.

At ten o'clock Maussion's Division advanced against the Park of Villiers. Supported by Saxon detachments from Noisy, the Würtembergers repulsed a first attack, but in following it up met with heavy losses. The French batteries of two Divisions and those of the Artillery Reserve formed line in front of the park. On their right Faron's Division, not without heavy losses, succeeded in gaining possession of Champigny,

P

and had then established itself in front of that village to defend the occupation of it.

General Ducrot's original idea had been to maintain a stationary fight on the peninsula until he should be joined at Noisy by his IIIrd Corps. But as news arrived that at eleven o'clock it was still on the northern side of the Marne, he ordered an immediate general attack by both his other Corps.

On the left the advance was checked for a considerable time by the German batteries which had been pushed forward between Noisy and Villiers, and when Colonel von Abendroth moved out from both villages with six companies of the 48th Brigade to an attack in close formation, the French fell back into the vineyards on the western slope of the plateau, leaving behind two guns, which, however, the Saxons could not carry away for want of teams.

In the centre of the line of fight, Berthaut's Division tried to push forward south of Villiers, but by the fire of five batteries in position there and at Coeuilly its ranks were so severely thinned that it gave ground before the advance of a Saxon battalion.

On the right wing, the guns which had been brought up into position in front of Champigny had at last been compelled by the German artillery to withdraw, and had sought cover further north, near the lime-kilns. A body of French infantry had advanced along the riverside to Maison Blanche, but meanwhile the 2nd Würtemberg Brigade, although itself attacked at Sucy, despatched a reinforcement of two companies and a battery to Chennevières. Advancing from the Hunting-lodge, the Würtembergers took 200 French prisoners at Maison Blanche; though, on the other hand, an attempt to carry the heights in front of Champigny with the companies assembled at Coeuilly failed with heavy loss. As the result, however, of a renewed flank-attack from the Hunting-lodge, Faron's Division, which had already been severely shaken, was obliged to retreat to Champigny.

General Ducrot decided to be content, for that day, with having established a firm footing on the left bank of the Marne, and he brought up sixteen batteries to a position in his front, to secure the wedge of ground he had gained. On the following day the attack was to be renewed by all the three Corps.

The Germans, on their part, had to congratulate themselves on having maintained their ground against greatly superior numbers. And so in the afternoon the fight gradually died away, until it broke out again in the north.

The French IIIrd Corps, marching up the right bank of the Marne, had occupied Neuilly in force, and had driven in the outposts of the Saxon 47th Brigade. Under cover of six batteries the construction of two military bridges below Neuilly was begun at ten o'clock, and finished by noon. But just at this time it happened, as we have seen, that the French were in retreat from the plateau, so the crossing did not occur until two o'clock in the afternoon. Bellemare's Division marched down the valley to Bry, where it closed on the left flank of the IInd Corps. A regiment of Zouaves, trying to ascend the plateau from Bry, lost half its men and all its officers. Notwithstanding, General Ducrot decided to employ his reinforced strength in the immediate renewal of the attack on Villiers.

Strengthened by four battalions, the Division advanced in this direction, although the artillery had not succeeded in battering down the park wall; repeated onslaughts by rifle-swarms were repulsed, and finally the French retreated into the valley. The simultaneous attacks of Berthaut's Division along the railway line and of Faron's Division on the Hunting-lodge also miscarried. Not till darkness had set in did the firing cease on both sides.

Near Chelles, on the line in which the French IIIrd Corps had been advancing in the morning, the Crown Prince of Saxony had collected the 23rd Division ; but as

soon as the enemy's real objective was penetrated, he
despatched part of the 47th Brigade and a portion of
the Corps Artillery to the threatened position held by
the Würtembergers.   Not less opportunely had General
von Obernitz, as soon as the fighting at Mesly was
over, sent three battalions to the Hunting-lodge.   In the
night orders came from the supreme Head-quarter for
the IInd and VIth Corps to send reinforcements to the
endangered points of the line of investment, and the
7th and 21st Brigades arrived at Sucy on the following
day, the 1st of December.

On the French side the attempt to break through
without help from outside was already considered as
well-nigh hopeless, and it was only the fear of popular
indignation which caused the IIIrd Army to remain
longer on the left bank of the Marne.   Instead of
attacking, the French began to intrench themselves,
and in order to clear the battlefield a truce was
arranged.   The thunder of the cannon from Mont
Avron had to serve for the present to keep up the
spirits of the Parisians.   The Germans also worked
at the strengthening of their positions, but, suffering
from the sudden and extreme cold, part at least of the
troops withdrew into quarters further rearward.

The command of the whole of the German Army
between the Marne and the Seine was assumed by
General von Fransecky (commanding IInd Corps).
The Head-quarter of the Army of the Meuse had
already given instructions that Prince George (of
Saxony) with all the available troops of the XIIth
Corps, should make surprise-attacks on Bry and Cham-
pigny in the early morning of the 2nd.

With this object, on the morning specified the 24th
Division assembled at Noisy, the 1st Würtemberg
Brigade at Villiers, and the 7th Prussian Brigade at
the Hunting-lodge.

The foremost battalions of the Saxon Division drove
back the enemy's outposts by a sudden rush, took

100 prisoners, and after storming a barricade entered Bry. Here ensued an embittered fight in the streets and houses, in which the 2nd Battalion of the 107th Regiment lost nearly all its officers. Nevertheless it maintained its hold on the northern part of the village, in spite of the heavy fire of the forts.

The Würtembergers also forced an entrance into Champigny, but soon met with fierce resistance from the enemy sheltered in the buildings. The previously occupied Bois de la Lande had to be abandoned, and General Ducrot now determined to resort to the offensive. The strong artillery line on his front came into action at about nine o'clock, and two Divisions deployed in rear of it.

Meanwhile the Fusilier battalion of the Colberg Regiment marched once more from the Hunting-lodge on Bois de la Lande, and carried it with the first onslaught. The French, firing heavily from the railway embankments, struck down the Pomeranians with clubbed rifles and at the point of the bayonet. A fierce fight was carried on at the same time at the lime-pits, where at noon 160 French laid down their arms. When six Würtemberg and nine Prussian batteries had been by degrees brought into action against Champigny, General Hartmann [1] succeeded in getting as far as the road leading to Bry. As, however, the batteries were now being masked by their own infantry, and were suffering, too, under the heavy projectiles fired from the forts, they were withdrawn into the hollow of the Hunting-lodge. At two o'clock the 1st Würtemberg and 7th Prussian Brigades established themselves firmly in the line from the churchyard of Champigny to the Bois de la Lande.

Meanwhile the French divisions of Bellemare and Susbielle had reached the battle-field from the right bank of the Marne. The two Saxon battalions in Bry, having already lost 36 officers and 638 men, were com-

[1] Commanding 3rd Infantry Division.

pelled by the approach of the enemy in very superior force, to evacuate the village and retire on Noisy, but not without taking 300 prisoners with them. The rest of the Saxon forces held Villiers, where the still available batteries also were in position.

While, at two o'clock, the French were bringing up a strong artillery mass against this point, four batteries of the IInd Corps rushed out of the hollow near the Hunting-lodge at a gallop upon their flank, and opened fire at a range of 2000 paces. In less than ten minutes the French batteries fell back and the Prussian batteries returned to their sheltered position. Several hostile battalions which, at about three o'clock, attempted a renewed assault on Villiers, were repulsed with no difficulty, and at five o'clock the fighting ceased. The French merely kept up a fire of field and fortress artillery until dark.

General Ducrot had received information in the course of the day, that the Army of the Loire was marching on Fontainebleau, and he was, therefore, very anxious to continue to maintain his position outside Paris.

During the night of December 2nd—3rd, provisions were procured, and the teams and ammunition of the batteries were made up; but the approach of support from without was in no wise confirmed.

The troops were completely exhausted by the previous disastrous fighting, and the Commander-in-Chief was justified in apprehending a repulse on the Marne by the enemy's invigorated forces. He therefore ordered a retreat, the troops being informed that the attack should be renewed as soon as their preparedness for fighting should have been re-established.

Soon after midnight the divisions were assembled behind the outposts, and the trains were sent back first. At noon the troops were able to follow over the bridges at Neuilly, Bry, and Joinville. Only one brigade remained in position to cover the passage.

The retreat was very skilfully covered by a series of small attacks on the German outposts. The French batteries had opened fire at Le Plant and Bry by daybreak, and the withdrawal of the enemy's army was completely hidden by the thick mist.

General Fransecky assembled the Saxon and the Würtemberg Divisions in a fighting position at Villiers and Cœuilly, the 7th Brigade with the Corps-Artillery of the IInd Corps and two regiments of the VIth at Chennevières, intending to wait for the expected reinforcement which the VIth Corps had agreed to furnish for the 4th. The 23rd Division also received orders from the Crown Prince of Saxony to cross to the left bank of the Marne, whilst the Guard Corps had meanwhile extended its outposts to Chelles.

So remained matters on the 3rd, with the exception of petty frays, and at four o'clock in the afternoon the troops were able to return to quarters. When early on the 4th patrols rode forward towards Bry and Champigny, they found these places vacated, and the peninsula of Joinville deserted by the enemy.

The IInd French Army, which had been severely reduced and its internal cohesion much shaken, returned to Paris ; on its own report it had lost 12,000 men. The German troops engaged had lost 6200 men, but resumed their former positions in the investing line.

This energetic attempt on the part of General Ducrot was the most serious effort that was made for the relief of Paris. It was directed towards what was at the moment the weakest point of the investment, but met with any success only at the outset.[1]

---

[1] A legend was subsequently circulated that the voice of one general in a German council of war had, in opposition to all the others, prevented the removal of the chief head-quarters from Versailles. Apart from the fact that during the whole course of the invasion no council of war was ever held, it never occurred to any member of the King's military suite to set so bad an example to the army. [Moltke.]

THE ADVANCE OF THE IST ARMY IN NOVEMBER.

The newly-formed levies in northern France were not remaining inactive. Rouen and Lille were their chief centres. In front of the latter place, the Somme with its fortified passages at Ham, Péronne, Amiens, and Abbeville afforded a line equally advantageous for attacks to the front or for secure retreat. Isolated advances had, indeed, on various occasions, been driven back by detachments of the Army of the Meuse, but these were too weak to rid themselves of the continued molestation by pursuit pushed home.

We have already seen how, after the fall of Metz, the IInd Army marched to the Loire, and the Ist into the northern departments of France.

A large portion of the Ist Army was at first detained on the Moselle by having had to undertake the transport of the numerous prisoners and the observation of the fortresses which interrupted the communications with Germany. The whole VIIth Corps was either in Metz or before Thionville and Montmédy. Of the Ist Corps, the 1st Division was detached to Rethel,[1] the 4th Brigade transported by railway through Soissons to the investment of La Fère, and the 3rd Cavalry Division sent on towards the forest of Argonnes. The remaining five brigades followed with the artillery on the 7th November.[2]

Marching on a wide front, the force reached the Oise between Compiègne and Chauny on the 20th. In front of the right wing the cavalry, supported by a battalion of Jägers, came in contact with Gardes-Mobiles at Ham and Guiscard ; in face of the infantry

---

[1] According to statement on p. 177, to Mézières.

[2] The " five brigades " mentioned in the text consisted of the 3rd of Ist Corps, and the four composing the VIIIth Corps, of which, the Ist and VIIth, the Ist Army was made up. The 1st Cavalry Division, originally belonging to the Ist Army, was transferred to the IInd Army by the reorganization following the capitulation of Metz.

columns the hostile bodies fell back on Amiens. It was learned that 15,000 men were there, and that reinforcements were continually joining.

On the 25th the 3rd Brigade reached Le Quesnel. The 15th Division of the VIIIth Corps advanced beyond Montdidier, and the 16th to Breteuil, whence it established connection with the Saxon detachments about Clermont. On the 26th the right wing closed up to Le Quesnel, the left to Moreuil and Essertaux. The cavalry scouted forward towards the Somme, the right bank of which it found occupied. The enemy's attitude indicated that he was confining himself to the defence of that position. General von Manteuffel thereupon determined to attack, without waiting for the arrival of the 1st Division, the transport of which from Rethel was extraordinarily delayed. His intention, in the first instance, was to utilize the 27th in drawing closer in his forces, which were extended along a front of some nineteen miles. But the battle was unexpectedly fought on that same day.

BATTLE OF AMIENS.

(November 17th.)

General Farre, with his 17,500 men distributed into three brigades, stood eastward of Amiens on the south bank of the Somme, about Villers Bretonneux and Longueau along the road to Péronne, holding also the villages and copses on his front. Besides these troops there were 8000 Gardes-Mobiles occupying an intrenched position about two and a half miles in front of the city.

In accordance with instructions from the Army Headquarter, General von Goeben (commanding the VIIIth Corps) had given orders for the 27th that the 15th Division should take up quarters at Fouencamps and Sains; the 16th at Rumigny and Plachy and in the villages further back; the Corps-Artillery at Gratte-panche. Consequently the VIIIth Corps was to be assembled before Amiens between the Celle and the Noye, at the distance, then, of nearly two and a half miles from the Ist Corps, and divided from it by the latter brook and the Avre. General von Bentheim (commanding the 1st Division, Ist Corps [1]) on the other hand, had sent his advanced guard, the 3rd Brigade, into quarters north of the Luce.

At an early hour that brigade seized the passages of the brook at Démuin, Hangard, and Domart. At ten o'clock it moved forward in order to occupy the appointed quarters, and as the enemy were already in possession, a fight began which gradually increased in magnitude.

The wooded heights on the north bank of the Luce were taken without any particular resistance, and maintained in spite of several counter strokes by the French. The artillery pushed forward through the intervals of the infantry. On the left the 4th Regiment seized the village of Gentelles, on the right the 44th Regiment rushed up to within 300 paces of the left flank of the French position, and by a vigorous onslaught carried by storm the earthworks at the railway cutting east of Villers Bretonneux. Soon after mid-day heavy hostile masses drew up at Bretonneux and in Cachy, directly opposite the 3rd Brigade, which was extended along a front of some four miles.

On the left wing of the Germans the 16th Division had by eleven o'clock already reached its assigned quarters, and had driven the enemy out of Hébecourt, as well as out of the woods north of that village towards Dury. The 15th Division, in compliance with the enjoined assemblage of the VIIIth Corps on the left bank of the Noye, moved westward from Moreuil through

---

[1] In effect commanding the whole Ist Corps, although nominally Manteuffel was still chief of it, as well as in command of the Ist Army.

Ailly to Dommartin, its advance guard which had been holding Hailles marching direct on Fouencamps. Thus it happened that before noon the roads from Roye and Montdidier between the two Corps were left completely uncovered by troops on the German side, while a French brigade was standing at the fork of these roads at Longueau, though, in fact, it remained absolutely inactive. This interval was at first screened only by the numerous retinue and staff escort of the Commander-in-Chief; and then it was to some extent filled by the battalion constituting the guard of the headquarter. As, however, after ten o'clock the French on their side commenced an attack on the 3rd Brigade, General von Manteuffel ordered the 15th Division to join in the fight as far as possible toward the right wing.

After a staunch defence the companies of the 4th Regiment were driven back out of the Bois de Hangard towards the declivity of the height in front of Démuin, and subsequently, having expended all their ammunition, the defenders of Gentelles were driven back to Domart.

General von Strubberg (commanding 30th Infantry Brigade, VIIIth Corps), on instructions from the scene of combat in front of the Luce, had sent four battalions in that direction, which crossed the Avre, but came under such a heavy fire from the Bois de Gentelles that their further advance was prevented, and they had to change front against the wood. Behind them, however, the other detachments of the 30th Brigade pressed forward to St. Nicolas on the right bank, and to Boves on the left, and in co-operation with the 29th Brigade drove the French from the neighbouring Ruinenberg.

Meanwhile a part of the approaching 1st Division came up behind the 3rd Brigade. The artillery positions were considerably strengthened, and the cannon fire was directed against the earthworks south of Bretonneux. As the nearest support the Crown Prince's Regiment went forward, and soon the French were again driven out of the Bois de Hangard. The East Prussians following them up, took cover in front of the earthworks; several detachments of the 4th and 44th Regiments gradually collected there from the neighbouring woods, and the enemy was then driven back from this position. Thirteen batteries now silenced the French artillery, and, after they had fired for some time on Bretonneux, the place was, at four o'clock, seized by the Prussians pouring in from all sides with drums beating. The French in its interior made only a weak defence at isolated points; for the most part they hurried over the Somme at Corbie under cover of the darkness, and with the loss of 180 unwounded prisoners.

When, somewhat later, the French General Lecointe advanced with the reserve brigade on Domart, he found that crossing point already in possession of the 1st Division, and turned back. Cachy only was held by the French till late in the evening.

The troops of the Ist Corps were distributed for the night in the hamlets to the south of the Luce; but the outposts were established on the northern bank of the Somme, and Bretonneux also remained occupied.

On the left wing of the battle-field the 16th Division had advanced to Dury, and had driven the French out of the neighbouring churchyard, but had been forced to withdraw from an attack on the enemy's extensive and strongly defended line of intrenchment. It bivouacked behind Dury.

It was night before General von Manteuffel received information which proved that the enemy had been completely defeated. Early in the morning of the 28th the patrols of the Ist Corps found the region clear of the enemy as far as the Somme, and all the bridges across the river destroyed. At noon General von Goeben entered Amiens, the citadel of which capitulated two days later with its garrison of 400 men and 30 cannon.

One peculiarity of the battle of the 27th November was the disproportionately great extent of the battle-field to the number of the troops engaged. General Farre, with 25,000 men in round numbers, covered a front of about fourteen miles from Pont de Metz south of Amiens to the east of Villers Bretonneux, and with the Somme close on his rear. The Germans attacked on approximately the same breadth of front, with the result that there was a break in the middle of their line. The danger caused by this gap was not taken advantage of during the morning through the inactivity of the enemy, and it was then nullified by the occupation of St. Nicolas.

The superiority of numbers was on the side of the Germans, for, although of the approaching 1st Division only the Crown Prince's Regiment could take part in the fighting, they were 30,000 strong. The 3rd Brigade bore the brunt of the battle, losing 630 men and 34 officers out of a total of 1300. The French also lost about 1300, besides 1000 reported missing. Part of the National Guard threw down their arms and fled to their homes. The main body of the French Corps retired on Arras.

Immediately after the battle the Ist Army was reinforced by the 4th Brigade, which had been brought from La Fère.

REDUCTION OF LA FÈRE.

(November 27th.)

This little fortress became of importance since it closed the line of railway passing through Rheims, both to Amiens and to Paris. Lying in open, wet, low ground overflowed by the Somme and its tributaries, it was difficult of approach; otherwise, the fortifica-

tions merely consisted of an isolated wall, with sundry
earthworks close in front of it, and it was entirely
seen into from heights on the east at a distance of not
more than 1500 metres.

The brigade (4th of Ist Corps) as a preliminary
measure had invested La Fère on the 15th November,
and when the siege-train arrived from Soissons with
thirty-two heavy guns, seven batteries were built and
armed during the night of the 25th on the heights
already mentioned. On the following morning these
opened fire, and on the 27th the place capitulated.
Gardes-Mobiles to the number of 2300 were taken
prisoners, and the most serviceable of the 113 guns
found were brought away to arm the citadel of Amiens.
The reinforcement of the Ist Army by the VIIth Corps
meanwhile was not yet even in prospect, since the latter
still had further work to do on the Moselle; the
greater part of the 14th Division only arrived before
Thionville on November 13th.

REDUCTION OF THIONVILLE.

(November 24th.)

This fortress, shut in on all sides by hills, was
entirely without bomb-proof protection; direct
approach from the south was, on the other hand,
rendered difficult by artificial inundations, and on
the west and north by swamps. General von Kameke
therefore decided to await the result of a heavy
bombardment before resorting to a regular attack.
Batteries were erected on both banks of the Moselle,
and on the morning of the 22nd eighty-five guns
opened fire. At first the fortress answered briskly.
In the following night the infantry detailed to the task
of throwing up the first parallel, advanced to within

600 paces of the west front, but, in consequence
of pouring rain and the condition of the ground the
work made but small progress. However, on the 24th
at mid-day the commandant proposed negotiations
for the surrender of the place. The garrison, 4000
strong, with the exception of the National Guard
belonging to the place, became prisoners and were sent
to Germany; and 199 guns, besides a considerable
amount of supplies, arms and ammunition, fell into the
hands of the conqueror.

The 14th Division was now required to lay siege to
the northern frontier fortresses, which would occupy it
for some time. The 13th Division, by orders from the
supreme Head-quarter, was assigned to the operations
in southern France.

INVESTMENT OF BELFORT IN NOVEMBER.

On the south-east section of the theatre of war Belfort
had become the centre of continual petty enterprises
on the part of French flying detachments in rear of
the XIVth Corps, which under General von Werder
stood about Vesoul.

But when the troops previously before Strasburg
had been relieved by a newly formed body from
Germany, the troops before Neu-Breisach became
available, and were set in march on Upper Alsace;
while the 1st Reserve Division reached Belfort on the
3rd November, and by the 8th had effected the preliminary investment of that place. The greater part of
the 4th Reserve Division marched to join the XIVth
Corps at Vesoul, a detachment under General von
Debschitz occupied Montbéliard, and the 67th
Regiment held Mulhouse and Delle.

Glancing back on the German successes during

November and the general military position at the end
of the month, we see the great sortie from Paris
repulsed [1]; in the north the menace to the investment
of being hemmed in done away with by General von
Manteuffel's victory at Amiens; in the east Thionville,
Breisach, Verdun, and La Fère taken, Montmédy and
Belfort surrounded; and in the south Prince Frederick
Charles ready to attack the French army before Orleans.

BATTLE OF ORLEANS.

(December 3rd and 4th.)

When soon after noon of 2nd December the telegraphed order to take the offensive against Orleans
reached the headquarter of the IInd Army, the Prince
on the same day assembled the Xth Corps at Beaune la
Rolande and Boynes, the IIIrd at Pithiviers, and the
IXth at Bazoches les Gallerandes. By evening the
collected forces had their marching orders.

The attack was to comprise two days of fighting.
The IIIrd Corps was first to advance on Loury by way
of Chilleurs aux Bois; the Xth was to follow to Chilleurs; and the IXth was to attack Artenay at half-past
nine. The 1st Cavalry Division supported by infantry
was to be on observation on the left flank towards the
Yonne; the 6th was to follow the right wing. The
Grand Duke, to whom it had been left to arrange the
details of his own march westward of the Paris main
road, ordered the 22nd Division to support the attack
on Artenay, the Bavarian Corps to advance on Lumeau,
the 17th Division to remain for the present at Anneux.

---

[1] The great sortie to the east of Paris was not repulsed until
December 2nd.

The 4th Cavalry Division was charged with the duty of scouting on the right flank.

So early as nine o'clock in the morning on the 3rd of December the IIIrd Corps met eight battalions and six batteries of the enemy at Santeau. The 12th Brigade and the artillery of the 6th Division intercalated in the columns of march in rear of the foremost battalions, thereupon deployed about La Brosse. After a few rounds a battery of the left wing had to be withdrawn from the fight which had now commenced; on the right, on the other hand, the Corps-Artillery gradually came up, and by noon seventy-eight Prussian guns were in action.

The French, yielding to strength so overwhelming, retired on Chilleurs; but, when the German batteries had advanced within 2000 paces of that place, and the right flank of the former was threatened by an assault of the Jäger battalions, they began a retreat towards the forest, and at three o'clock part of the 5th Division followed them up through the glen leading to the southward, and the 6th by the high road. As these had been obstructed in many places, it was six o'clock in the evening before the clearing by Loury was reached.

On the right, heavy musketry-firing was heard in the region of Neuville, and tidings also arrived that on the left the French had occupied Nancray.

In consequence of this, a reinforcement from the reserve remaining in Chilleurs was brought up; one regiment was thrown out fronting towards the west, a second towards the east, and under cover of the outposts extended toward the south the remainder of the troops went into bivouac and quarters at Loury.

The IXth Corps had first assembled at Château Gaillard on the main road to Paris, and then advanced along the chaussée through Dambron against Villereau. At Assas it met the enemy, who was soon driven back by its artillery, and disappeared towards Artenay. At about ten o'clock an obstinate contest was engaged in against the batteries of the 2nd French Division in

Q

position here, in which part of the Corps-Artillery presently bore part, seconded later by the batteries of the 22nd Division, which had come up to Poupry. General Martineau retreated slowly by successive detachments, his artillery leading, before the overwhelming fire of ninety guns, on La Croix Briquet and Ferme d'Arblay.

At twelve o'clock the Germans occupied Artenay, and after half an hour's rest they renewed the offensive. There occurred a long and obstinate fire-fight both of infantry and artillery, while the 22nd Division pushed forward on the enemy's left flank. At two o'clock his guns were silenced, the left-wing column of the IXth Corps seized the farm of Arblay, and the centre by hard fighting drove the enemy back along the high road through La Croix Briquet to Andeglou, where under cover of the marine artillery resistance was kept up till dark.

General Puttkamer[1] had brought up five batteries to within 800 paces of Chevilly, and the 22nd Division was advancing on the burning village, when the chief Command gave the order to halt, the Grand Duke hesitating to engage in a night attack on the intrenched village. But when, soon after, a Hussar patrol brought the information that it was already evacuated, General von Wittich ordered its occupation. The troops bivouacked in a heavy snowstorm, in and to the rear of La Croix Briquet.

About the time of the first advance the IXth Corps had sent a detachment of four Hessian battalions leftward against St. Lyé. They met with opposition at La Tour, drove the enemy back on St. Germain, but could not dislodge him from that place.

When the Xth Corps, marching round by Pithiviers unmolested, about three o'clock reached the vicinity of Chilleurs in rear of the IIIrd Corps, part of the 20th Division went on in the direction of the fighting about Neuville, the noise of which in the evening was also

---

[1] Commanding Artillery of IXth Corps.

heard at Loury. Darkness had already come on and precluded the use of artillery, but the infantry broke into the village at several points. But it found the streets barricaded, and met with obstinate resistance, so that the prosecution of the attack had to be postponed till the following day.

The XVth French Corps had sustained single-handed the onslaught of three Prussian Corps. Strong masses of the Army of Orleans, to right and to left of that Corps, made but feeble efforts in the course of the day to support it. General Chanzy alone, when at about two o'clock he heard heavy firing from Artenay, ordered forward the 2nd Division of the XVIth Corps, though he had already that morning begun his retreat on St. Péravy and Boulay. But this reinforcement encountered the Prussian 17th Division, which, coming up from Anneux, was on the point of joining in the fight at Andeglou, and with it the Bavarian Corps advancing from Lumeau. Their strong united artillery in position at Chameul and Sougy, soon forced the enemy to retire. Douzy and then Huêtre were taken, and the château of Chevilly was occupied by the 17th Division. Here too darkness put an end to the fighting. The troops of the right wing quartered at Provenchères, Chameul and rearward.

Thus the German army had made its way without very heavy fighting to within nine miles of Orleans. The French, indeed, had maintained their ground till evening in the neighbourhood of Neuville, but the forces holding on there were ordered to retire in the night. They were to gain the road from Pithiviers by Rebréchien, and make a circuit by Orleans to Chevilly. But they thus came under the fire of the IIIrd German Corps quartered in Loury, and fled in disorder back into the forest, whence they attempted to reach their destination by detachments.

It was only to be expected that the French would stoutly defend their intrenchments at Gidy and Cer-

cottes on the following day, if only to keep open their
way of retreat through Orleans. Prince Frederick
Charles therefore ordered the Grand Duke's Detachment and the IXth Corps to make an encompassing
attack on both points on the 4th. The IIIrd Corps
was to advance from Loury on Orleans, and the Xth,
again forming the reserve, was to follow to Chevilly.

General d'Aurelle had retired to Saran on the evening of the 3rd. Here he saw the 2nd Division of the
XVth Corps fleeing by in utter rout, and heard also that
the 1st had failed to make a stand at Chilleurs. The
Corps of his right wing were altogether shattered as
regarded their internal cohesion by the battle of Beaune,
and those of his left no less by the fight at Loigny.
The French General could not but dread being driven
on the Loire with undisciplined masses, and the conse-
quent block of the only passage of the river at Orleans.
He decided therefore on an eccentric retreat. Only the
XVth Corps was to retire by Orleans ; General Crouzat
was to cross the Loire at Gien, General Chanzy at
Beaugency. The reassemblage remained to be attempted behind the Sauldre. The necessary dispositions
were made during the night, and communicated to the
Government. From the Board of Green Cloth at
Tours, counter orders of course came next morning to
maintain the Orleans position, which practically was
already wrecked ; but the General adhered firmly to his
own determination.

On December 4th the IIIrd Army Corps marched
out of Loury in two columns by the high road and the
tracks through Vennecy. Both bodies reached Boigny
by noon, having met only stragglers. A detachment
was sent to the right to Neuville, which made prize
of seven derelict guns and many rifles. To the left,
another detachment occupied Chézy on the Loire.
After a short rest the main columns advanced, and by
two o'clock the 6th Division reached Vaumainbert,
which was occupied by detachments of the French

XVth Corps. Although the country was not open enough to allow of the employment of artillery, the place was taken by the Brandenburgers in spite of the stout resistance of the French Marine Infantry, and the fire of the batteries on the heights to the north of St. Loup could now be directed on the suburb of Orleans.

The 5th Division had meanwhile come up behind the 6th and took part in the fight.

The XXth French Corps, which was still at Chambon, in the eastern part of the forest opposite Beaune la Rolande, had received orders at four in the morning from Tours direct, to march on Orleans. Contrary orders had previously arrived from General d'Aurelle, but nothing subsequently came to hand. General Crouzat had, as a precaution, sent his train across the Loire by way of Jargeau, and then marched in the prescribed direction. When, at half-past two he met at Pont aux Moines the German detachment despatched to Chézy, he determined to cut his way through by force of arms; but as General von Stülpnagel reinforced his two battalions with the rest of his Division, the French general gave up that attempt and retreated across the river, making the passage at Jargeau.

On the German side the attack on St. Loup[1] was unsuccessful; and since from the locality of the fighting on the part of the other Corps no tidings reached him, and darkness was approaching, General von Alvensleben postponed any further attack on the city till the following day.

North of Orleans the IXth Army Corps advanced from La Croix Briquet on the intrenched position of Cercottes. At about one o'clock the foremost detachments of infantry entered the place. The 2nd Division of the French XVth Corps was driven back by the fire of the artillery into the vineyards in front of the city. Here the infantry alone could continue the struggle.

---

[1] The northern suburb of Orleans.

The French defended every tenable spot, and especially in the railway station close to Orleans held their own with great persistency. It and the adjacent deep road-cutting were fortified with barricades and rifle-pits, and armed with naval guns. It was not till nightfall, about half-past five, that these posts were abandoned, but the contest was continued further back. To avoid street-fighting in the dark, General von Manstein broke off the fight for the day at about seven o'clock.

The advanced guard of the 17th Division of the Grand Duke's Detachment had found Gidy intrenched and strongly occupied. But at the approach of the IXth Corps the French about eleven o'clock thought proper to abandon the position, leaving behind eight guns. The German Division, to avoid the wood, now moved in a westerly direction on Boulay, whither the 22nd and the 2nd Cavalry Division followed as a reserve.

Here the Bavarian Corps and the 4th Cavalry Division were already engaged in a fight, having previously driven the French out of Bricy and Janvry. When the artillery had for some time been in action, General von der Tann passed to the assault at about twelve o'clock. But the French did not wait for this; they beat a hasty retreat, leaving some of their guns in the defences.

The 2nd Cavalry Division took up the pursuit. The 4th Hussars of the 5th Brigade, trotting forward through Montaigu, charged a dismounted French battery and seized all its guns; another near Ormes was left to be carried off by the horse battery. From thence a strong body of French horse suddenly appeared on the left flank of the 4th Brigade as it was crossing the Châteaudun road. But the Blücher Hussars, promptly wheeling into line, drove the enemy back through the village on Ingré.

The 4th Cavalry Division was placed on observation on the right flank of the Detachment; and the Hussars of the 2nd Life Regiment here rode down 250 men forming the escort of a waggon column escaping by the road to Châteaudun, and captured the convoy.

While the Germans were thus converging on Orleans from the east and north, in the west the XVIIth French Corps and the 1st Division of the XVIth were still in the field about Patay and St. Péravy. General Chanzy had assembled the latter about Coinces, and, to protect himself against its threatened attack on his flank, General von der Tann formed front at Bricy with his 3rd Infantry Brigade, the Cuirassiers, and the artillery reserve. The 4th Cavalry Division marched on Coinces, where General von Bernhardi, clearing a wide ditch with four squadrons of Uhlans, drove a body of French horse back on St. Péravy without its having been able to do more than fire one carbine-volley. Other squadrons of the 9th Brigade rode down the French tirailleurs, and pursued the cavalry till it reached the protection of strong bodies of infantry. The 8th Brigade was in observation toward Patay, and after that place had come under the fire of a battery and been abandoned, General Chanzy gave up all further attack and retired behind the forest of Montpipeau.

The 2nd Cavalry Division now made for the Loire immediately below Orleans. Its artillery destroyed a bridge at Chapelle over which a baggage-train was passing, and compelled the French troops, which were marching towards Cléry along the further bank, to flee back to Orleans. Two military railway-trains from thence were not to be stopped by the firing, but a train coming from Tours, in which, as it happened, was Gambetta himself, returned thither with all speed.

The Bavarian Corps meanwhile was advancing by the high road, and the 22nd Division, in touch with the IXth Corps, on the old Châteaudun road; the 17th Division between the two on La Borde. This last Division at about 3.30 had to carry on its way the strongly defended village of Heurdy; and when the Bavarians from Ormes turned to the right on Ingré, it proceeded by the high road towards St. Jean de la Ruelle. Having overcome all opposition there too, the head of the Division reached the gates of Orleans at about six o'clock.

General von Tresckow entered into negotiations with the military authorities there for the orderly occupation of the town. An agreement was arrived at by ten o'clock, and shortly after midnight the Grand Duke marched in with the 17th Division, promptly followed by the 2nd Bavarian Brigade. The bridge over the Loire, which the French had not found time to blow up, was secured with all speed. The rest of the troops found quarters for the night, to the west and north of the city.

The peremptory orders from the Government to hold Orleans had shaken General d'Aurelle's original determination. When the mass of the XVth Corps arrived there in the forenoon, he was anxious to make a final stand. But the necessary orders could not be transmitted to the Corps of the right wing, nor carried out by those of the left; and by five o'clock the General in command was convinced of the futility of any further resistance. The artillery of the XVth Corps was in the first instance forwarded to La Ferté St. Aubin; the infantry followed. The XXth Corps, as we have seen, was at Jargeau; the XVIIIth recrossed the Loire at Sully; the XVIth and XVIIth moved off westward in the direction of Beaugency, but remained on the right bank of the river.

The two days' battle had cost the Germans 1700 men; the French lost 20,000, of whom 1800 were taken prisoners. Their large army lately massed before Orleans, was now split up into three separate bodies.

OFFENSIVE OPERATIONS SOUTH, EAST, AND WEST.

The troops were too much exhausted for immediate pursuit in any of these three directions.

It was ordered that only the 6th Cavalry Division, reinforced by an infantry detachment of the 18th Division, should follow up the enemy making to the southward, ascertain his whereabouts, and destroy the concentration of the railways from Bourges, Orleans and Tours at the Vierzon junction. This Cavalry was in quarters to the north of the city; the French XVth Corps had a considerable start of it, and the main body of the latter had reached Salbris, when, on December 6th, two days after the battle, General von Schmidt (commanding 14th Brigade, 6th Cavalry Division) arrived by a forced march at La Ferté St. Aubin. Here he found a detachment of the 18th Division, which had already driven the French rear-guard back on La Motte Beuvron, but was now recalled to the Loiret. Only two companies of the 36th Regiment and one of pioneers joined the further advance, and followed the cavalry partly in waggons and partly on gun-limbers.

On the 7th, under direct orders from Tours, the French Corps left the high road to the south, and made a flank march of twenty miles in an easterly direction to Aubigny Ville. The cavalry, supported to the best of their power by its artillery and the small infantry detachment, had a sharp fight with the French rear-guard at Nouan le Fuzelier, and again in the evening at Salbris, in which the French finally had the best of it. The neighbourhood being very thinly populated, the Division had to return in the night to Nouan, to find shelter from the bitter winter weather.

Long before daybreak on the 8th, the French rear-guard evacuated Salbris to avoid a further encounter with the enemy, whose strength was greatly over-estimated. After some slight skirmishes the Cavalry Division reached Vierzon that evening. The telegraph wires were cut and the railway line torn up in several places, 70 goods vans were made prize of, the direction of the enemy's retreat was ascertained, and any offensive movement on the part of the French from that side for the time was reckoned very improbable.

The Division had fulfilled its task; it was now ordered to leave one brigade in observation, and to advance in the direction of Blois with the rest. General (Count) von der Groeben (commanding 14th Cavalry Brigade) maintained his positions at Vierzon and Salbris till the 14th.

The winter marches of the 6th Cavalry Division were exceptionally arduous. It was almost impossible to travel excepting by the high roads, and they were so slippery with ice that it was often necessary to dismount and lead the horses. The inhabitants of the Sologne were extremely hostile, and troopers patrolling in advance were fired upon in every village. The French forces, on the other hand, made but a feeble resistance. Numerous prisoners and large quantities of abandoned war matériel bore witness to a hasty retreat, in many cases indicated panic-flight. Nevertheless, in spite of much desultory marching and counter-marching, the Corps on December 13th finally succeeded in joining the right wing of the Army of Orleans at Bourges. The plight in which it arrived there may be gathered from the telegraphic *Correspondance Urgente* of the Tours Government with General Bourbaki, who, when General d'Aurelle was dismissed from the command in chief, had assumed command of the three Corps.

The delegate Freycinet, who was no doubt kept well informed by the country people, assured General Bourbaki that he had only a weak force of cavalry in his front, and called upon him repeatedly, and in the most urgent terms, to advance against Blois. The General retorted that if he were to undertake that operation, not a gun, not a man of his three Corps would ever be seen again. His intention was to retreat without delay from Bourges on St. Amand, and if necessary yet further; all he dreaded was lest he should be attacked before he could accomplish this, and so be involved in overwhelming disaster.

The Minister of War himself went to Bourges, but he too renounced all idea of a serious offensive movement when he saw the disorder of the troops; " I have never seen anything so wretched." It was with difficulty that he carried his point that the Corps should not retreat, but should await events under cover of one of them pushed forward towards Vierzon.

On the day when General von Schmidt entered Vierzon, the XVth Corps was in the vicinity of Henrichemont, at about an equal distance with himself from Bourges. The XVIIIth and XXth Corps were at Aubigny Ville and Cernay, from two to three marches away. It can scarcely be doubted that if the 18th Division had followed the advance of the 6th Cavalry Division, possession would have been obtained of Bourges and of the vast military establishments there.

To the east of Orleans the IIIrd German Corps marched up the river through Châteauneuf. It met only stragglers, till on the 7th two Divisions of the XVIIIth French Corps attempted to cross to the right bank of the Loire at Gien. There came about an advanced-guard fight at Nevoy, with the result that these Divisions retreated across the bridge in the night, and continued their march on Bourges.

FIGHTING OF THE GRAND DUKE OF MECKLENBURG.

(December 7th, 8th, 9th, and 10th.)

The Grand Duke's Detachment stood westward, close to the retreating left wing of the enemy. In contrast

to the disorder of the right wing, General Chanzy, probably the most capable of all the leaders whom the
Germans had to encounter in the battle-field, had very
rapidly in so great measure restored the discipline and
spirit of his defeated troops, that they were able not
only to make a stand, but even to take the offensive.
They had, it is true, been considerably reinforced by
the newly formed XXIst Corps and by Camô's Division.
The latter formed the advanced guard at Meung; behind it were the XVIth Corps at Beaugency, the
XVIIth at Cravant, and the XXIst at St. Laurent on
the edge of the forest of Marchénoir.

On the day after the fight the troops of the Grand
Duke were given a rest-day; only the cavalry pursued the French. The 4th Cavalry Division reached
Ouzouer; the 2nd came upon considerable masses of
infantry behind Meung.

On the 7th, the Grand Duke's forces advanced on a
very wide front. The 17th Division, on the left wing,
marched on Meung, where its artillery opened a combat
with that of the enemy. The French held possession of
the narrow lanes of the village, which further westward
was pierced by the main road to Beaugency. Towards
four o'clock a Mecklenburg battalion carried Langlo-
chère by storm, but found itself threatened on both
sides by the approach of hostile columns. On the left
Foinard was presently occupied, and a gun captured
there, while on the right the 1st Bavarian Brigade
advanced on La Bourie. Here, almost at the same
moment, the 2nd Cavalry Division came up by by-roads
from Renardière, having driven the enemy out of Le
Bardon by the fire of its guns. The Bavarians had now
to march out to meet a hostile mass advancing from
Grand Chatre. Supported by the horse batteries, they
maintained till nightfall a stubborn fight, which ended
in the retreat of the French on Beaumont.

During this conflict on the left wing of the Detachment, the 1st Bavarian Division, considerably on the

right, were marching on Baccon, the 22nd on Ouzouer; and finding that the French were offering a determined resistance, the Grand Duke decided on closing in his forces to the left.

December 8th.—To this end the 22nd Division moved southward from Ouzouer through Villermain. After repulsing the swarms of tirailleurs which attacked its left flank under cover of a thick fog, General von Wittich directed his march on Cravant, to effect a junction with the right wing of the 1st Bavarian Division already engaged in a hot struggle. They had repulsed an attack of the enemy pushed forward from Villechaumont, and the 2nd (Bavarian) Division advanced by the road from Cravant to Beaugency; but when three French Divisions came on afresh, it retreated on Beaumont. Here it found support from the 1st (Bavarian Division) and 17 batteries were gradually brought up into the fighting line. Their fire and an impetuous attack from three Bavarian brigades at last forced the enemy to fall back, and the position on the high road was recovered.

The French now, on their side, brought up a strong force of artillery, and prepared to advance on Cravant with their XVIIth Corps. But the 22nd German Division having taken Beauvert and Layes by the way, had already reached Cravant at about one o'clock, and was in position there with the 4th Cavalry Division on its right and the 2nd on its left. So when, at about three o'clock, dense French columns advanced on Cravant, they were repulsed by a powerful counterstroke delivered by the 44th Brigade, in conjunction with the Bavarians, and were soon driven out of Layes, which they had entered while advancing. The five batteries nearest to Cravant had suffered so severely meanwhile that they had to be withdrawn. When finally at about four o'clock the Bavarian battalions advanced to storm the height in their front, they were met by fresh troops of the enemy, and after

losing a great part of their officers were compelled
to retreat on the artillery position at Beaumont.
Later, however, the French abandoned Villechaumont.

On the left wing of the Detachment the 17th Division pursued the retreating French through Vallées and
Villeneuve, and then at about noon made an attack
on Messas. The defence was obstinate, and it was
not till dusk that it succeeded in gaining full possession
of the place. The artillery directed its fire on dense
masses showing about Vernon, the infantry stormed the
height of Beaugency, and finally forced its way into
the town itself, where a French battery fell into its
hand. Camó's Division then retired on Tavers, and at
midnight General von Tresckow fell upon Vernon,
whence the French, taken entirely by surprise, fled to
Bonvalet.

The Headquarter of the IInd Army had determined
to set in march on Bourges the IIIrd, Xth, and IXth
Corps, from Gien, from Orleans, and also from Blois.
But the Detachment in its advance on Blois by
the right bank of the Loire had met with unexpected
resistance lasting for two days. In the supreme
Headquarter at Versailles it was regarded as indispensable that the Grand Duke should immediately be
reinforced by at least one Division. Telegraphic orders
to that effect arrived at ten o'clock on December 9th.
The IXth Corps, which was already on the march along
the left bank and had found no enemy in its front,
could not give the requisite support, since all the
bridges over the river had been blown up. The IIIrd
Corps was therefore ordered to leave only a detachment in observation at Gien, and to turn back to
Orleans. The Xth Corps was to call in its detachments standing eastward of the city and march forward
to Meung. Meanwhile on the 9th the Detachment
remained still quite unsupported while actually confronting with four Infantry Divisions, eleven French

Divisions. And early on that morning General Chanzy took the offensive.

December 9th.—The two Prussian Divisions at Beauvert and Messas stood firmly awaiting the hostile onslaught. The two Bavarian Divisions, because of their severe losses, were held in reserve at Cravant, but soon had to come up into the fighting line, when at seven o'clock strong columns of the enemy advanced on Le Mée.

Dense swarms of tirailleurs were repulsed both there and before Vernon, and were later shattered by the fire of the devoted German artillery, which silenced the French guns and then directed its fire on Villorceau. In spite of a stout defence, this village was carried and occupied about half-past ten by the Bavarian infantry. The French advance on Villechaumont in greatly superior force was also repulsed, with the assistance of three battalions and two batteries of the 22nd Division. The Thüringers[1] then stormed Cernay, where 200 French laid down their arms, and one of their batteries lost its teams and limbers.

On the right wing of the Detachment, in consequence of a misunderstanding, the Germans evacuated Layes and Beauvert, and the French occupied these villages. However, with the assistance of the 2nd Bavarian Brigade, the 44th (Brigade) drove them out again from both places. Further to the north, the 4th Cavalry Division was in observation of a French detachment approaching Villermain.

The French made renewed efforts, advancing again at mid-day on Cravant in strong columns; but this movement General Tresckow took in flank from Messas.

---

[1] In the 22nd Division of the XIth Corps—a Corps of a curiously composite character, there were three Thüringian regiments. The 43rd Brigade was wholly Thüringian, consisting as it did of the 32nd and 95th regiments (2nd and 6th Thüringers), and in the 44th Brigade was the 94th (5th Thüringers). It was the 2nd battalion of this last regiment which is referred to in the text.

He left only a weak detachment in Beaugency, and secured himself towards Tavers in the villages on his left. The main body of the 17th Division advanced on Bonvalet, reinforced the hardly-pressed Bavarians in Villorceau, and occupied itself Villemarceau in front of that place. Here the Division had to maintain a severe struggle, at about three o'clock, with close columns of the French XVIth and XVIIth Corps. The infantry rushing on the enemy with cheers succeeded, however, in repulsing him and holding its ground in spite of a hot fire. At the same time three Bavarian battalions, accompanied by cavalry and artillery, marched up from Cravant and drove the French out of Villejouan. Yet further to the right a battalion of the 32nd Regiment took possession of Ourcelle. A line from thence to Tavers defined the section of terrain laboriously wrung from the enemy.

The fight ended with the retreat of the enemy on Josnes and Dugny.

On this day the IIIrd Corps was still on the march to Orleans. The IXth from its position on the left bank, could only take part in the fighting by the fire of its artillery on Meung and Beaugency. It was not till near Blois that it met French detachments. Fifty men of one of the Hessian battalions carried the defended château of Chambord lying rightward of the line of march, and there took 200 prisoners and made prize of twelve ammunition waggons with their teams.

Of the Xth Corps only the head of its infantry reached Meung, but it sent forward a regiment of Hussars with eight batteries, which arrived at Grand Chatre by about three o'clock in the afternoon.

By order of the Headquarter of the IInd Army the Bavarian Corps was now to retire to Orleans, to recruit after its heavy losses. But even after the arrival of the Xth Corps the Grand Duke had still in his front an enemy double his strength, and instead of engaging in a pursuit he had rather to study how to maintain himself on the defensive.

December 10th.—At dawn General Chanzy renewed his attack, which even the Bavarians were presently required to join in repulsing.

At seven o'clock the French XVIIth Corps rushed in dense masses on Origny, took there 150 prisoners, and forced its way into Villejouan. This advance was met directly in front by the 43rd Brigade at Cernay, and by the 4th Bavarian Brigade with six batteries at Villechaumont; while on the right flank General von Tresckow pushed forward on Villorceau and Villemarceau. In this latter village two of his battalions, supported by four batteries, resisted every onslaught of the French from Origny and Toupenay. At noon the main body of the 17th Division advanced to the recapture of Villejouan. Here the French made an obstinate stand. An embittered and bloody fight in the streets and houses was prolonged till four o'clock, and then fresh troops of the enemy came up to recover the post the Germans still held in one detached farmstead. The artillery mass of the Prussian Division had, however, deployed to the south of Villemarceau; it was joined by two horse batteries of the Xth Corps, and the batteries of the 22nd Division also came into action from Cernay. The concentric fire of this body of artillery wrecked the subsequent attacks of the XVIIth French Corps.

Beaugency was now occupied by part of the Xth Corps. During the previous days the left flank of the German fighting position had a secure point d'appui on the Loire, but on the right such a support had been wholly lacking. The French had nevertheless hitherto made no attempt to take advantage of their superiority by a wider extension of their front. For the first time on this day did they come in on the unprotected left flank of their enemy. The greater part of the XXIst Corps deployed opposite to it, between Poisly

R

and Mézières, and at half-past ten strong columns advanced on Villermain. The Bavarians were compelled to take up with their 2nd Brigade the "hook" formation from Jouy to Coudray. Seven batteries were brought up into that line, and on its right flank the 4th Cavalry Division stood in readiness to act. By two o'clock two more horse batteries, and from Cravant four batteries of the Xth Corps arrived, which massed there with three brigades as a reserve. The fire of over a hundred German guns compelled the French to hurry their artillery out of action at three o'clock, and weak independent attacks by their infantry were repulsed without difficulty by the Germans persevering staunchly on the defence.

The French losses in this four days' battle are unknown. The Detachment lost 3400 men, of whom the larger half belonged to the two Bavarian Divisions.

The Grand Duke had succeeded in holding his own against three Corps of the enemy till the arrival of the first reinforcement, and this he owed to the bravery of all his troops, and not least to the exertions of the artillery. This arm alone lost 255 men and 356 horses. Its material was tasked to the utmost, so that finally almost all the steel guns of the light batteries of the 22nd Division, and most of the Bavarian, were rendered useless by the burning out of their vent-pieces.

The IIIrd Corps had on this day just arrived at St. Denis, and the IXth at Vienne opposite Blois; but here, too, the bridge over the Loire was found to be blown up.

On the French side, General Chanzy had learnt from the telegraphic correspondence of the Government at Tours with General Bourbaki, that nothing had come of that commander's attempt to divert part of the German IInd Army upon himself. The long delay gave General Chanzy the daily apprehension of an attack by it with its full strength; and he therefore decided on a retreat, which resulted in the removal of the Assembly from Tours to Bordeaux.

In the Grand Duke's Head-quarter the renewed offensive had been decided on for December 11th. The villages in his front remained strongly occupied, and it was only at noon of that day that the enemy's retreat became known. He was at once pursued on the left by the Xth Corps, and on the right, south of the forest of Marchénoir, by the Detachment. On the north, the 4th Cavalry Division took up the scouting.

A thaw had followed the hard frost, making the march equally difficult for friend and foe. The Germans found the roads littered with abandoned waggons and cast-away arms; the bodies of men and horses lay unburied in the fields, and in the villages were hundreds of wounded uncared for. Several thousands of stragglers were captured.

The directions [1] of the Chief of the General Staff from Versailles suggested an immediate pursuit, which should render the enemy incapable of further action for some time to come; but not to be maintained beyond Tours. The IInd Army was then to assemble at Orleans and the Detachment at Chartres, and the troops were to obtain the rest they needed. From the former point constant and strict watch could be kept on General Bourbaki's army, and to this end a connection was to be made with General von Zastrow, who with the VIIth Corps was to reach Châtillon sur Seine on the 13th. But the operations in this quarter were not to extend beyond Bourges and Nevers.

[1] The expression "Directiven" in the text cannot be succinctly translated. It was rarely, except when actually himself in the field, that the Chief of the General Staff issued actual "orders" to the higher commanders. His communications for the most part consisted of "Directiven"—messages of general suggestions as to the appropriate line of action to be pursued, leaving a wide discretion to the commanders to whom they were addressed, and refraining almost entirely from details. A collection of Moltke's "Directiven" would be perhaps the finest tribute to his military genius.

The IInd Army was accordingly in the first instance marched toward the Loir, and on the 13th reached the line Oucques—Conan—Blois, which last town was found evacuated.

On the 14th the 17th Division marched to Morée, and reached the Loir at Fréteval. A fight occurred at both these points. Though the French had yielded thus far, they seemed resolved to make a firm stand on the Loir, and had occupied Cloyes and Vendôme in great strength.

In order to attack with success, Prince Frederick Charles first proceeded to concentrate all his forces. The IIIrd Corps, which was hurrying after the army by forced marches, was in the first instance to come up into the interval between the Detachment and the Xth Corps, which was to march from Blois and Herbault on Vendôme.

But when, on the 15th, the Xth Corps was moving in the prescribed direction, its main body encountered so determined a resistance close in front of Vendôme that it could not be overcome before dark. The troops therefore retired to quarters in the rear of Ste. Anne. A left-flank detachment had found St. Amand occupied by heavy masses, and halted at Gombergean. The IIIrd Corps had advanced in the course of the day on Coulommiers, in the vicinity of Vendôme, had fought the French at Bel Essert, driven them back across the Loir and established connection with the Xth. The Grand Duke, in compliance with instructions, stood meanwhile on the defensive. The IXth Corps, after the restoration of the bridge of Blois, was at last able to follow the army, leaving a brigade in occupation of Blois.

A greatly superior force was now assembled opposite the enemy's position, and a general attack was decided on ; but to give the wearied troops some rest it was postponed till the 17th, and meanwhile, on the 16th, General Chanzy withdrew.

It had certainly been his intention to make a longer

stand in the Loir angle ; but his Generals convinced him that the condition of the troops did not permit the prolongation of active hostilities. He accordingly gave the order for the retreat of the army at daybreak by way of Montoire, St. Calais, and Vibraye to Le Mans.

Thus in the early morning (of the 17th) the Xth Corps found the French position in front of Vendôme abandoned, and it entered the city without opposition. On the French left wing only, where the marching orders had not yet arrived, General Jaurès made an attack on Fréteval, but in the evening he followed the other Corps.

INTERRUPTION OF IMPORTANT OFFENSIVE OPERATIONS IN DECEMBER.

On the 17th of December general directions were issued from Versailles to the Armies both to the north and south of Paris.

Now that General von Manteuffel was across the Somme, and Prince Frederick Charles had advanced to the Loir, the Germans held possession of almost a third of France. The enemy was everywhere driven back ; and that the German forces should not be split up, it was thought advisable that they should be concentrated into three principal groups. The Ist Army was therefore to assemble at Beauvais, the Detachment at Chartres, the IInd Army near Orleans, where the troops were to have the needful rest, and their full efficiency was to be re-established by the arrival of reservists and equipment. If the French should engage in any new enterprises, they were to be allowed to approach within striking distance, and then were to be driven back by a vigorous offensive.

For the IInd Army there was but little prospect at present of overtaking the enemy beyond the Loir ; and the reports from the Upper Loire now necessitated the bestowal of increased attention in that direction. News came from Gien that the posts left there had been driven back to Ouzouer sur Loire; and it seemed not unlikely that General Bourbaki would take the opportunity of advancing by Montargis towards Paris, or at least towards Orleans, which for the moment was occupied only by part of the Ist Bavarian Corps.

Prince Frederick Charles had got quit of his enemy probably for some considerable time, and he decided, in accordance with directions from Versailles, to assemble his forces at Orleans and maintain a waiting attitude. Only the Xth Corps was to remain behind in observation on the Loir. To secure immediate support for the Bavarian Corps in any event, the IXth Corps, on its arrival from Blois at La Chapelle Vendômoise on the 16th December, was ordered to march to Beaugency that same day, and to Orleans on the morrow. It covered nearly 52 miles in twenty-four hours, notwithstanding the badness of the weather. The IIIrd Corps followed it.

However, it was soon known that the enemy's detachment which had been seen at Gien did not form part of a large body of troops, and was intrenching itself at Briare for its own safety. So the Germans retired into comfortable rest-quarters, the Ist Bavarian Corps at Orleans, the IIIrd there and along to Beaugency, the IXth in the plain of the Loire up as far as Châteauneuf, with a strong post at Montargis.

The Bavarian Corps was later transferred to Etampes, to recover at its leisure, to recruit its numbers, and refit as to its clothing and equipment. Nor was the Grand Duke of Mecklenburg's detachment in a condition to follow General Chanzy beyond the Loir. Six weeks of daily marching and fighting had tried the troops to the utmost. The dreadful weather and the state of the roads had reduced their clothing and foot-gear to a miserable state. A reconnoissance beyond the Loir showed that the French could be overtaken by only long and rapid marches. So the Grand Duke allowed his troops a long rest, from the 18th, in the villages on the left bank of the river.

Of the IIIrd Army, General von Rheinbaben, on the other hand, occupied with the three Brigades of the 5th Cavalry Division Courtlain, Brou, and Chartres, strengthened by five battalions of Guard Landwehr and four batteries. A letter from the Chief of the General Staff at Versailles had pointed out that this cavalry might probably be employed with great success in attacking the flank and rear of the enemy's retreating columns, and the Crown Prince had already given orders that it should push forward by way of Brou in full strength on the 15th. Contrary to these orders, the Division obeyed a subsequent order which reached it on the 16th from the Grand Duke, under whose command the Division had not been placed, to take up a position on the Yères.

On this day patrols had found the roads open to Montmirail and Mondoubleau, except for French infantry in front of Cloyes, which retired after a short fray. On the left, a connection was opened with the 4th Cavalry Division. On the 17th, the 12th Cavalry Brigade entered Cloyes, already evacuated by the French ; on the 13th it advanced on Arrou, and only General von Barby (commanding the 11th Cavalry Brigade) marched on Droue with a force of all arms, where he surprised the French at their cooking, and carried off much booty.

On the 18th, the 12th Brigade did make prisoners of a few stragglers there, but the other two brigades only made a short march to the westward to La Bazoche Gouet and Arville, whence the enemy had quite disappeared. To the south of Arville a battalion of the Guard Landwehr drove the French infantry out of St. Agil.

With this the pursuit ended on the 19th. The Division retired on Nogent le Rotrou by the Grand Duke's desire, and subsequently undertook the observation of the left bank of the Seine at Vernon and Dreux.

The Grand Duke's Detachment left its quarters on the Loir on the 21st. The 22nd Division occupied Nogent le Roi, and the 17th Chatres, till the 24th. The 4th Bavarian Brigade rejoined its own Corps at Orleans.

During the remainder of December only the Xth Corps had any fighting, it having been detailed to keep watch beyond the Loir from Blois and Vendôme.

Two brigades were set on march towards Tours on the 20th. On the further side of Monnaie they met the newly-formed troops of General Ferri-Pisani, 10,000 to 15,000 strong, which were advancing from Angers and had passed through Tours.

The soaked ground made the deployment of the artillery and cavalry exceedingly difficult. The cavalry, indeed, could only pursue the retreating French in deep columns along the high roads, thus suffering severely from the enemy's fire delivered at very short range.

On the following day General von Woyna (commanding 39th Infantry Brigade) advanced unopposed with six battalions on the bridge at Tours. A light battery was brought up on the bank of the river and dispersed the rabble firing from the opposite shore, but it would have cost too many lives to storm the city, which, since the removal of the seat of Government, had ceased to be of any great importance. The detachment was withdrawn to Monnaie, and the Xth Corps went into quarters, the 19th Division at Blois, the 20th at Herbault and Vendôme.

From the latter place on the 27th, a detachment of two battalions, one squadron, and two guns marched through Montoire on Sougé on the Braye, and there met a greatly superior force. General Chanzy had in fact marched a Division of his XVIIth Corps towards Vendôme in order to draw the Prussians away from

Tours. Behind St. Quentin the weak Prussian detachment found itself hemmed in between the river and the cliff, enclosed on every side, and under heavy fire. Lieutenant-Colonel von Boltenstern succeeded, however, in cutting his way through. Without firing a shot the two Hanoverian battalions hurled themselves on the dense body of tirailleurs blocking their retreat, and fought their way out fighting hand to hand. Through the gap thus made the guns dashed after firing one round of grape-shot, and notwithstanding losses to the teams they ultimately got back safely to Montoire. The squadron also charged through two lines of riflemen and rejoined the infantry.

As a result of this incident General von Kraatz Koschlau (commanding 20th Division) brought up the remainder of his Division from Herbault, determined to clear up the situation by a fresh reconnoissance. Four battalions were to advance from Vendôme, and the 1st Cavalry Brigade from Fréteval was to scout towards Epuisay. On this same day, however, General de Jouffroy was marching with two Divisions to the attack of Vendôme.

When, at about ten o'clock, the reconnoitring force from Vendôme reached the Azay, it came under a hot fire from the further slope of the valley. Soon after six hostile battalions attacked its flank from the south, and repeated notice was brought in that considerable forces of the enemy were marching on Vendôme direct, from north of Azay by Espéreuse. General von Kraatz perceived that he would have to face a planned attack made by very superior numbers, and determined to restrict himself to the local defence of Vendôme. Under cover of a battalion firmly maintaining its position at Huchepie, he accomplished in perfect order the retreat of the detachment, which then took up a position on the railway embankment to the west of the city.

Further to the north the hostile columns, advancing over Espéreuse, had already reached Bel Air. A battalion hastening up from Vendôme re-occupied the château, but being outflanked on the right by a superior force withdrew, and likewise took up a position behind the railway. At about two o'clock the French attacked this position in dense swarms of sharpshooters, but came under the quick-fire of six batteries in position on the heights behind Vendôme, which caused their right wing to give way. A column of the enemy advanced along the left bank of the Loir from Varennes against this artillery position, but hastily retreated out of range of the fire from it.

The attacks directed against the railway from Bel Air and Tuileries were more serious; but eight companies posted there repelled them. At four o'clock the French once more advanced in strength; fortune wavered for some time, and at length, as darkness fell, they retired.

The 1st Cavalry Brigade, accompanied by two companies and a horse battery, marched on this day on Danzé. Captain Spitz, with a handful of his Westphalian Fusiliers fell on two batteries halted there, and captured two guns and three limbers. With these and fifty prisoners General von Lüderitz (commanding 1st Cavalry Brigade) returned to Fréteval by about one o'clock, after pursuing the enemy as far as Epuisay.

The attempt of the French on Vendôme had utterly failed, and they now retreated to a greater distance. General von Kraatz, however, was ordered, in the prospect of a greater enterprise to be described later, to remain meanwhile in waiting on the Loir.

THE XIVTH CORPS IN DECEMBER.

In the south-eastern theatre of war the French had at last decided on some definite action.

Garibaldi's Corps, assembled at Autun, advanced

toward Dijon on the 24th (November) ; its detachments closed up by Sombernon and St. Seine, with various skirmishes, and subjected to night surprises. Crémer's Division advanced as far as Gevrey from the south. But as soon as reinforcements reached Dijon from Gray and Is sur Tille, the enemy was driven back, and now General von Werder on his part ordered the 1st Brigade of his Corps to march on Autun. General Keller (commanding 3rd Infantry Brigade, Baden Division), arrived in front of the town on December 1st, driving the hostile detachments before him. The preparations had been made to attack on the following day, when orders came for a rapid retreat. Fresh troops had become necessary at Châtillon, to replace the posts which had been stationed to protect the railway and which had been surprised at Gray, to cope with sorties by the garrison of Besançon and also to observe Langres.

The Prussian Brigade (26th) marched on Langres, along with two cavalry regiments and three batteries, and on the 16th it met the French in the vicinity of Longeau, in number about 2000. They were repulsed, losing 200 wounded, fifty prisoners, two guns, and two ammunition waggons. General von der Goltz (commanding the Brigade) in the next few days surrounded Langres, drove the Gardes-Mobiles posted outside into the fortress, and occupied a position opposite the northern front for the protection of the railways.

In the country south of Dijon fresh assemblages of French troops had also now been observed. To disperse these General von Werder advanced on the 18th with two Baden Brigades on Nuits. In Boncourt, close to the town on the east, the advanced guard met with lively opposition, but carried the place by noon. The French, aided by their batteries posted on the heights west of Nuits, offered an obstinate defence in the deep railway cutting and at the Meuzin brook. When the main body of the Brigade came up at two o'clock, General von Glümer (commanding Baden Division) ordered a general attack. With heavy losses, especially in superior officers, the infantry now rushed across the open plain at the double against the enemy, who was under cover, and who, after maintaining a fire at short range, was driven back on Nuits so late as four o'clock in the course of a hand-to-hand struggle. At five o'clock he abandoned the place before the on-coming battalions.

The Germans had had to do with Crémer's Division, 10,000 strong, which lost 1700 men, among them 650 unwounded prisoners. The Baden Division had lost 900 men. It encamped for the night on the market-place of the town and in the villages to the eastward. Next morning the French were found to have retreated still further, but the Germans were not strong enough for pursuit. The XIVth Corps had already been obliged to spare seven battalions for the investment of Belfort. General von Werder therefore returned to Dijon, where he assembled all the forces still left to him with those of General von der Goltz from Langres, and waited to see whether the enemy would again advance against him. But the month of December ended without any further disturbance.

THE IST ARMY IN DECEMBER.

While the IInd Army was fighting on the Loire, General von Manteuffel, after the victory of Amiens, marched on Rouen.

General Farre was indeed at Arras, in the rear of this movement, but the disorder in which his troops had retired after the battle made it probable that he would do nothing, at any rate for the present. The 3rd Brigade, too, was left in Amiens, with two cavalry regiments and three batteries, to occupy the place and protect the important line of railway to Laon.

The outlook to the west was more serious than to the north, for from thence at this juncture hostile forces threatened to interfere with the investment of Paris. General Briand was at Rouen with some 20,000 men, and had advanced his leading troops up to the Epte, where at Beauvais and Gisors he came in contact with the Guard Dragoon regiment and the Saxon Cavalry Division detached from the Army of the Meuse. The detachment of infantry which accompanied the latter had lost 150 men and a gun in a night surprise.

When the Ist Army reached the Epte on December 3rd, both bodies of cavalry joined its further march, and the French retired behind the Andelles. The VIIIth Corps reached the vicinity of Rouen after petty skirmishes by the way, and found an intrenched position abandoned at Isneauville; and on December 5th General von Goeben entered the chief city of Normandy. The 29th Brigade advanced on Pont Audemer, the Ist Corps crossed the Seine higher up at Les Andelys and Pont de l'Arche. Vernon and Evreux were occupied, whence numbers of Gardes-Mobiles had retreated by railway to Liseux. On the northern bank the Guard Dragoon Regiment reconnoitred as far as Bolbec, and the Uhlan Brigade found no enemy in Dieppe.

The French had retired to Havre, and a considerable force had been conveyed in ships that were in readiness, to Honfleur on the other bank of the Seine. The 16th Division continued its march on Havre, reaching Bolbec and Lillebonne on the 11th.

The already-mentioned directions from Versailles had been communicated in advance by the Chief of the General Staff, and in accordance with them General Manteuffel now decided on leaving only the Ist Corps on the Lower Seine, and returning with the VIIIth to the Somme, where the French in Arras were now becoming active.

Besides making this evident by various small encounters, on December 9th they had attacked a company detailed to protect the reconstruction of the railway at Ham, surprising it at night, and taking most of the men prisoners; while on the 11th several French battalions advanced as far as La Fère.

To check their further progress, the Army of the Meuse had meantime sent detachments to Soissons and Compiègne. General Count von der Groeben[1] (commanding 3rd Cavalry Division) took up a position at Roye with part of the garrison of Amiens, and on the 16th met the 15th Division at Montdidier, which immediately moved up to the Somme.

Only the citadel of Amiens now remained in German occupation; but General von Manteuffel, who had not approved of the evacuation of the city, ordered its immediate reoccupation. The inhabitants had, however, remained peaceable, and on the 20th the 16th Division, which had given up the attack on Havre, arrived by way of Dieppe.

A reconnoissance fight near Querrieux made it certain that great numbers of French were drawn up on the Hallue, and General von Manteuffel now drew in the whole (VIIIth) Corps on Amiens. Reinforcements were shortly to be expected, for the 3rd Reserve Division was on the march, and had already reached St. Quentin. The 1st Corps was also ordered to send a brigade from Rouen to Amiens by railway, and the Commanding General determined to take the offensive at once with 22,600 men, all his available force at the moment.

General Faidherbe had assembled two Corps, the XXIInd and XXIIIrd. His advance on Ham and La Fère, intended to divert the Prussians from attacking Havre, had succeeded. He next turned toward Amiens, advanced to within nine miles of the city, and now stood, with 43,000 men and eighty-two guns, fronting to the west behind the Hallue. Two Divisions held the left bank of this stream for about seven miles, from

---

[1] Lieut.-General, not to be confounded with Major-General of same name commanding 14th Cavalry Brigade.

its confluence at Daours up to Contay, two standing further back, at Corbie and Fravillers. The Somme secured the left flank.

On December 23rd General von Manteuffel, with the VIIIth Corps, advanced on the road to Albert. The 3rd Brigade of the Ist Corps formed his reserve. His design was to keep the French engaged by the 15th Division on their front and left wing, and with the 16th Division to outflank their right. The unexpected extension of the French right wing prevented this, and it became a frontal battle along the whole line. The greater height of the eastern bank afforded the French a commanding artillery position, and the villages lying at the foot had in every instance to be stormed.

The French had drawn in their advanced posts to this line when at eleven o'clock the head of the 15th Division reached the grove of Querrieux, and brought up a battery. Two battalions of the 29th Brigade took the village at mid-day at the first onslaught, crossed the stream, and drove the French on the further bank out of Noyelles; but they now found themselves overwhelmed by an artillery and infantry fire from all sides. The East Prussians[1] stormed the acclivity at about four o'clock, and took two guns which were in action, but were forced to fall back into the village before the advancing French masses.

Soon after mid-day Féchencourt was won on the left, and Bussy on the right; and the enemy after a feeble resistance was driven back across the stream. On the other hand, the German Artillery could at first do nothing against the strong and well-posted batteries

---

[1] Men of the 2nd battalion 33rd Regiment (East Prussian Fusiliers), belonging to the VIIIth Corps, whose territory is the Rhine Provinces. It would be interesting to know how an East Prussian Regiment came to be incorporated into the Rhineland Corps. The Ist is the East Prussian Corps, and it was also under General v. Manteuffel, who had been the Corps Commander until the beginning of December, when its command passed to General v. Bentheim.

of the enemy. Vecquemont, however, was stormed, though stoutly defended, and a bitter street-fight lasted till the afternoon.

The 15th Division, against the intention of General Manteuffel, had become involved in fighting before the 16th, engaged further to the left, could afford it any assistance. Not till four o'clock did the 31st Brigade arrive in front of Béhencourt, when, crossing the river by flying bridges, it threw the enemy back into the village, where he maintained a stout resistance, but had ultimately to give way. The 32nd Brigade, on the extreme left, crossed the Hallue and entered Bavelincourt.

Thus all the hamlets on the river were in German possession; but the short December day was closing in, and further progress had to be postponed till the morrow. Even in the dark the French made several attempts to recover the positions they had lost, especially about Contay, where they outflanked the German position. But their attacks were repulsed both there and at Noyelles. They succeeded, indeed, in getting into Vecquemont, but were driven out again, and were lost to the Prussians now following across the stream, who even seized Daours, so that ultimately the Germans held dominion over every passage of the Hallue.

The battle was over by six o'clock. The troops moved into alarm-quarters in the captured villages, their foreposts standing close in front of the outlets.

The attack had cost the Germans 900 men; the defence had cost the French about 1000, besides 1000 unwounded prisoners who were taken into Amiens.

At daybreak on the 24th the French opened fire on General Manteuffel's position in the angle bounded by the Hallue and the Somme.

It having been ascertained that the enemy's strength was almost double that of the Germans, it was decided this day on the latter side to remain on the defensive, pending the arrival of reinforcements, and to strengthen the defence of the positions gained. The Army-Reserve was pushed forward to Corbie to threaten the left flank of the French.

But at two o'clock in the afternoon General Faidherbe took up his retreat. His insufficiently-equipped troops had suffered fearfully through the bitter winter night, and were much shaken by the unfavourable issue of the fighting of the previous day. He therefore drew them back within the area of the covering fortresses. When on the 25th the two Prussian Divisions and the cavalry pursued beyond Albert, and then close up to Arras and as far as Cambrai, they found no formed bodies at all in front of those places, and only captured some hundreds of stragglers.

When General Manteuffel had thus disposed of the enemy, he sent General von Mirus (commanding 6th Cavalry Brigade) to invest Péronne, while he himself returned to Rouen.

Since it had detached to Amiens six battalions as a reinforcement, the Ist Army Corps (at Rouen) now remained only two brigades strong. The French had 10,000 men on the right bank, and 12,000 on the left bank of the lower Seine. And these forces had come very close to Rouen; particularly on the south side within nine miles. Meanwhile, however, the Commanding-General had ordered back the 2nd Brigade from Amiens, and on its arrival the hostile bodies were once more driven back.

THE REDUCTION OF MÉZIÈRES.

(1st January, 1871.)

In the northern section of hostilities, before the end of the year, the siege of Mézières was brought to an end. After the battle of Sedan the Commandant had contributed supplies from the magazines of the fortress

S

for the maintenance of the great mass of prisoners, and it had remained, therefore, for the time exempt from attack.   Later the place precluded the use of the railroad ; still it was only kept under provisional observation till the 19th of December, when, after the fall of Montmédy, the 14th Division moved up before Mézières.

The garrison numbered only 2000 men, but it was effectively assisted by bands of volunteers outside, who displayed extraordinary activity in this broken and wooded country.   The place was not completely invested till the 25th.

Mézières stands on a mountain-spur which is surrounded on three sides by the Moselle,[1] but it is hemmed by a ring of heights.   The character of the defences, which had been strengthened by Vauban, with their numerous salient angles, was not calculated to resist modern long-range artillery.   The place exposed an isolated rampart of masonry in a circumference of from 2160 to 3250 yards, and although the long delay had been utilized in repairing the weak points by throwing up earthworks, a bombardment could not fail to be destructive to the defenders.

When Verdun had surrendered, heavy siege guns were brought by rail from Clermont to a position close in front of the southern face of the fortress.   The only hindrance to the erection of the batteries was the state of the soil, frozen to a depth of twenty inches ; and at a quarter past eight on the morning of the 31st of December 68 siege guns and 8 field-pieces opened fire. At first the fortress replied vigorously, but by the afternoon its artillery was utterly silenced, and the white flag was hoisted next day.   The garrison were taken prisoners ; considerable stores and 132 guns fell into the hands of the besiegers.   But the chief advantage gained was the opening of a new line of railway to Paris.

[1] Slip of pen for " Meuse."

PARIS IN DECEMBER.

In Paris General Ducrot had been busily employed in making good the losses sustained in the battle of Villiers. A part of the greatly reduced Ist Corps had to be consigned to the reserve; the IInd Army was re-organized. A projected sortie by way of the peninsula of Gennevillers and the heights of Franconville had not been approved by the government. There was the confident expectation of seeing the Army of Orleans appear within a short time before the capital, and steps were being taken to reach it the hand, when on the 6th December a letter from General von Moltke announced the defeat of General d'Aurelle and the occupation of Orleans. A sortie to the south would thenceforth be aimless, and after long deliberation it was at length decided to break through the enemy's lines in a northern direction by a sortie in great force.

It was true that the Morée brook afforded the besiegers some cover on that side, but only so long as the ice would not bear. And there were but three German corps of the gross strength of 81,200, extended over a front of about twenty-seven miles.[1]

By way of preparation earthworks were begun to be thrown up on the 13th, between Bondy and Courneuve, the forts of the north front were furnished with a heavier artillery equipment, and the plateau of Mont Avron was occupied by batteries. Ninety rounds of ammunition were served out to each man, with six days' rations; and four days' fodder for the horses. Packs were not to be carried, but rolled tent-pieces were to be worn as breast-protection. December 19th

[1] Viz., the section of the investment line on the northern side, from the Marne above, to the Seine below Paris, held by the Army of the Meuse, consisting of the IVth, the Guard, and XIIth (Saxon) Corps.

was the day first set for the enterprise, but there was a postponement to the 21st.

Thus, during the larger half of December the investing army had remained almost wholly undisturbed by the defenders. Regular food, warm winter clothing, and abundant supplies of comforts which the exertions of the postal service afforded, had maintained the troops in a thoroughly satisfactory condition.

The preparations which the garrison was making for a new effort did not escape the notice of the besieging forces. Deserters brought in reports of an imminent sortie. On the 20th information came from the posts of observation that large masses of troops were assembling about Merlan and Noisy le Sec; and early on the 21st the 2nd Guard Division, by order of the Commander-in-Chief of the Army of the Meuse, stood in readiness at the passages of the Morée. Part of the 1st Division remained in reserve at Gonesse; the other portion was to be relieved by the 7th Division, and made available for action. On the right wing the Guard Landwehr Division occupied the section from Chatou to Carrières St. Denis; on the left a brigade of the Saxon Corps held Sévran. The 4th Infantry Division of the IInd Corps moved to Malnoue to support, in case of need, the Würtembergers, to whom was allotted the task of holding resolutely the advanced position of Joinville opposite the French.

To divert the attention of the Germans from the true point of attack, a brisk fire was to be opened in early morning from Fort Valérien; strong bodies were to assail the right wing of the Guard Corps, General Vinoy was to lead the IIIrd Army against the Saxons, and Admiral de la Roncière was to fall upon Le Bourget with his Army Corps. This latter post, projecting as it did so prominently, it was essential to seize first of all, and not till then was General Ducrot, with the IInd Paris Army, to cross the Morée near Blanc Mesnil and Aulnay.

(COMBAT OF LE BOURGET, 21ST DECEMBER.)—Le Bourget was held by only four companies of the Queen Elizabeth Regiment, and one Guard Rifle battalion. When the mist rose at a quarter to eight, there was rained on the garrison a heavy fire from the guns of the forts and many batteries, as well as from armour-clad railway trucks. Half an hour later closed hostile columns marched on the place from east and west. In the former direction its outskirts were successfully defended for some time against seven French battalions, and on the opposite side five more were brought to a halt by the quick fire of the defenders in front of the cemetery[1]; but a detachment of marine fusiliers penetrated unhindered into the village by its northern entrance. Pressed upon on all sides by overwhelming numbers, the defenders were compelled to fall back into the southern part of the village. The garrison of the cemetery also strove to force its way thither, but part of it fell into the enemy's hands. The French advanced only step by step, suffering heavy loss in bloody street-fighting, but they did not succeed in obtaining possession of the buildings or glass-factory. Five fresh battalions of the French reserve marched up from St. Denis on the gas-works, and battered down the garden-wall with cannon-fire, but still could not crush there the steady resistance of the Germans.

At nine o'clock the latter were reinforced by one company, and at ten o'clock by seven more companies, which in a bloody hand-to-hand struggle, fought their way to the cemetery and glass-factory. By eleven the

---

[1] "Kirchhof" seems to stand in German not only for our "church-yard," but also for our "graveyard," in which latter there need be no church. In the case of Le Bourget the church stands in the village street—the reader will remember de Neuville's striking picture—and the graveyard lies outside the shabby village, and has the aspect of the modern "cemetery." That term has therefore been used.

last bodies of assailants were driven out, and Le Bourget, in expectation of a renewed attack, was occupied by fifteen companies. Two batteries of field artillery, which had been in brisk action on the Morée, were brought up to the village.

General Ducrot had meanwhile waited in vain for the signal which was to have announced the capture of Le Bourget. He had pushed forward the heads of his columns beyond Bondy and Drancy, when he was warned by the disastrous issue of the struggle on his left to abandon his intended attack on the line of the Morée.

The anticipated important enterprise lapsed into a mere cannonade, to which the German field-guns did their best to reply. In the afternoon the French retired from the field.

They had lost, by their own account, about 600 men. The troops of the Prussian Guard Corps lost 400, but 360 prisoners remained in their hands. In the evening the outposts resumed their previous positions.

The various feigned attacks of the Parisian garrison were without effect, and produced no alteration in the dispositions made on the German side. An advance from St. Denis against Stains was repulsed, and two gunboats on the Seine had to go about in consequence of the fire of four field batteries on Orgemont. The trivial sortie on Chatou was scarcely heeded. General Vinoy indeed led forward a large force along the right bank of the Marne, but that was not till the afternoon, when the fight at Le Bourget was over. The Saxon outposts retired into the fighting position near Le Chenay. One of the battalions massed there drove the enemy out of Maison Blanche that same evening, another made a grasp at Ville Evrart, where fighting went on till midnight; it lost seventy men, but brought in 600 prisoners. Next morning the French abandoned Ville Evrart, under heavy fire from the German artillery on the heights on the opposite side of the river.

Paris had now been invested for three months. The always distasteful expedient of a bombardment of a place so extensive could not of itself bring about a decisive result; and on the German side there was the full conviction that only a regular siege could accomplish the wished-for end. But the operations of the engineers had to be delayed till the artillery should be in a position to co-operate with them.

It has already been shown that the siege-artillery had been first employed against those fortified places which interrupted the rearward communications of the army. There were indeed 235 heavy pieces standing ready at Villacoublay; but it had proved impossible as yet to bring up the necessary ammunition for the attack which, once begun, must on no account be interrupted.

By the end of November, railway communication had been restored up to Chelles, but the greater part of the ammunition had meanwhile been deposited at Lagny, and from thence would now have to be carried forward by the country roads. The ordinary two-wheeled country carts proved totally unfit for the transport of shells, and only 2000 four-wheeled waggons had been collected by requisitions made over a wide area. There were brought up from Metz 960 more with horses sent from Germany, and even the teams of the IIIrd Army were taken into the service, though they were almost indispensable just then to contribute towards the efficiency of the army fighting on the Loire. Finally, all the draught horses of the pontoon columns, of the field-bridge trains, and of the trench-tool columns were brought into the ammunition-transport service. A new difficulty arose when the breaking-up of the ice necessitated the removal of the pontoon bridges over the Seine. The roads were so bad that it took the waggons nine days to get from Nanteuil to Villacoublay and back. Many broke down under their loads, and the drivers constantly took to flight. And moreover, at the instance of the

Chief of the Staff there was now laid upon the artillery yet an additional task to be carried out forthwith.

Though the besieged had not hitherto succeeded in forcing their way through the enemy's lines, they now set about widening their elbow room, with intent that by their counter-approaches the ring of investment should be further and yet further pushed back, until at last it should reach the breaking point. On the south side the French entrenchments already extended beyond Vitry and Villejuif to the Seine; and on the north, between Drancy and Fort de l'Est, there was an extensive system of trenches and batteries reaching to within 1100 yards of Le Bourget, which in part might in a manner be dignified with the title of a regular engineer-attack. The hard frost had indeed hindered the further progress of these works, but they were armed with artillery and occupied by the IInd Army. And further, a singularly favourable point of support for a sortie to the east as well as to the north, was afforded to the French in the commanding eminence of Mont Avron, which, armed with seventy heavy guns, projected into the Marne valley like a wedge between the northern and southern investing lines.

(BOMBARDMENT OF MONT AVRON, DECEMBER 27TH.) —In order to expel the French from this position fifty heavy guns from Germany, and twenty-six from before La Fère were brought up under the command of Colonel Bartsch. By the exertions of a whole battalion as a working party, two groups of battery emplacements were erected in spite of the severe frost on the western slope of the heights behind Raincy and Gagny, and on the left upland of the Marne Valley near Noisy le Grand, thus encompassing Mont Avron on two sides at a distance of from 2160 to 3250 feet.

At half-past eight on the morning of 27th December those seventy-six guns opened fire. A heavy snowstorm interfered with accurate aim, and prevented any observation of the execution done. Mont Avron and Forts Nogent and Rosny replied rapidly and heavily.

The German batteries lost two officers and twenty-five gunners, several gun-carriages broke down under their own fire, and everything pointed to the prospect that no definite result would be obtained on that day.

But the batteries had fired more effectually than had been supposed. The clear weather of the 28th allowed of greater precision; the Prussian fire proved most telling, making fearful havoc in the numerous and exposed French infantry garrison. Mont Avron was silenced, and only the forts kept up a feeble fire. General Trochu, who was present in person, ordered the abandonment of the position, which was so effectually accomplished in the night by the energetic commander, Colonel Stoffel, that only one disabled gun was left behind.

On the 29th the French fire was silent, and the hill was found deserted. The Germans had no intention of continuing to occupy the position. Their batteries now turned their fire on the forts, which suffered severely, and on the earthworks near Bondy.

By the end of the year the besiegers had succeeded in collecting the most indispensable ammunition in Villacoublay. The engineer operations were entrusted to General Kameke; the artillery was under the command of General Prince Hohenlohe.[1] The battery emplacements had long been finished, and with the dawn of the new year 100 guns of the largest calibres stood ready to open fire on the south front of Paris.

---

[1] Details as to the personnel of the artillery and engineer commands of the siege operations will be found on a later page.

THE ARMY OF THE EAST UNDER GENERAL BOURBAKI.

While the French forces were engaged in constant
fighting, in the north on the Seine and the Somme, in
the south on the Loire and the Saone, General Bourbaki's army had nowhere made itself prominent. Since
the 8th of December, when the 6th Cavalry Division
had reported its presence at Vierzon, all trace of it had
been lost. It was of course of the greatest importance to
the supreme Command that it should know the whereabouts of so large an army; only the IInd German
Army could acquire this information, and on the 22nd
it received instructions to obtain the required enlighten-
ment by means of reconnaissances.

On this errand General von Rantzau (commanding
25th Cavalry Brigade) set out from Montargis by the
right bank of the Loire towards Briare, where he found
that the French had abandoned their position on the
25th; in the course of the next few days he met them,
and was defeated.

The Hessian detachment was reinforced to a strength
of three battalions, four squadrons and six guns, but
was nevertheless driven back to Gien on the 1st of
January. The French had displayed a force of several
thousand Gardes-Mobiles, twelve guns, and a body of
marine infantry. A noticeable fact was that some of
the prisoners brought in belonged to the XVIIIth
French Corps, which formed part of the Ist Army of
the Loire.

A regiment of the 6th Cavalry Division sent out to
reconnoitre into the Sologne, returned with the report
that strong hostile columns were marching on Aubigny
Ville. On the other hand, two waggon-drivers who had
been taken prisoners declared that the French troops had
been already moved from Bourges by rail, and the newspaper reports also pointed to the same conclusion; still,
too much weight could not be attached to mere rumour
as against circumstantial intelligence. It was therefore

assumed at Versailles that the Ist Army of the Loire was still about Bourges, and that General Bourbaki, when again in a condition to fight, would act in concert with General Chanzy.

The two armies might attack the Germans at Orleans from opposite sides, or one might engage and detain them there, while the other marched to relieve the capital.

This, in fact, was what General Chanzy had in view. Since the 21st of December he had been resting in quarters in and about Le Mans, where railways from four directions facilitated the bringing up of new levies. His troops had no doubt great hardships to contend with there. In lack of shelter for such great masses part had to camp out under canvas in the snow, and suffered severely from the intense cold. The hospitals were crammed with wounded and small-pox patients. On the other hand, this close concentration was favourable to the reorganization of the details and the restoration of discipline; and the news from Paris urged the General to renewed action.

General Trochu had sent word that Paris unaided could not accomplish her freedom. Even if a sortie should prove successful, the necessary supplies for the maintenance of an army could not be carried with it, and therefore nothing but the simultaneous appearance of an army from without could meet the case. Now General Chanzy was quite ready to march on Paris, but it was indispensable that he should first know exactly what Generals Bourbaki and Faidherbe were doing.

It was clearly evident that concerted action on the part of three great Army Corps could only be devised and controlled by the chief power. The General therefore sent an officer of his Staff on the 23rd of December to Gambetta at Lyons, to express his conviction that only a combined and prompt advance could avert the fall of the capital. But the Minister believed that he

knew better. The first news of a quite different disposition of Bourbaki's army only reached General
Chanzy on the 29th, when it was already entered upon.
Nor in other respects did Gambetta's reply convey
either distinct orders or sufficient information. "You
have decimated the Mecklenburgers," wrote Gambetta,
"the Bavarians no longer exist, the rest of the German
Army is a prey to disquietude and exhaustion. Let
us persevere, and we shall drive these hordes from our
soil with empty hands." The plan of the Provisional
Government was to be the one "which would most
demoralize the German army."[1]

Under instructions so obscure from the chief authority General Chanzy, relying on his own strength,
determined to make his way to Paris without other
assistance; but he soon found himself in serious
difficulties.

On the German side there was no time to be lost in
utilizing their position between the two hostile armies,
advantageous as it was so long as those armies were
not too near. The simultaneous attacks on the 31st
December at Vendôme on the Loir, and at Briare on
the Loire, seemed to indicate that the two were already
acting on a concerted plan.

On New Year's day Prince Frederick Charles received
telegraphic instructions to re-cross the Loir without
delay, and strike at General Chanzy, as being the
nearest and most imminently dangerous enemy. With
this object the IInd Army was strengthened by the
addition of the XIIIth Corps of the Grand Duke of
Mecklenburg (17th and 22nd Divisions) and the 2nd
and 4th Divisions of Cavalry. And in addition the
5th Cavalry Division was detailed to the duty of
covering the right flank of the advance.

Only the 25th (Hessian) Division was to be left in
Orleans as a possible check on General Bourbaki,
and to maintain observation on Gien. But as a fur-

[1] "Qui démoralisera le plus l'armée Allemande."

ther provision, in case of need against a possible advance of the IInd Army of the Loire, General von Zastrow was ordered to the Armançon with the VIIth Corps;[1] and further the IInd Corps from the besieging lines was set in march to Montargis.

Prince Frederick Charles' arrangement was to have his three corps assembled on the line Vendôme—Morée by 6th January, and to order the XIIIth from Chartres on Brou.

The Advance of the IInd Army to Le Mans.

The Germans had hoped to strike the enemy in his winter quarters; but General Chanzy had provided against surprise by a cordon of strong advanced positions. Nogent le Rotrou on his left was held by Rousseau's Division, and numerous bands of volunteers; from thence strong detachments were posted through Vibraye and St. Calais up to the Braye brook, where General Jouffroy had made a halt after the last attack on Vendôme; and on the right were General Barry at La Chartre and de Curten's Division at Château Renault.

Both wings of the German army came into collision with these forces on the 5th of January.

General Baumgarth (commanding 2nd Cavalry Brigade), on the German left, had assembled at St. Amand three battalions, two cavalry regiments and two batteries. The 57th regiment stormed Villeporcher in the direction of Château Renault, evacuated it in face of an attack by four French battalions, and finally recaptured and held it. This much, at any rate, was thus ascertained, that a not inconsiderable force of the enemy was assembled in front of the left wing of the German army now marching westward. . While this movement was in prosecution General Baumgarth was

[1] In effect, with only the Corps-headquarter and the 13th Division —the 14th Division being still in the north-east.

thenceforth to undertake its protection, and with this object he was reinforced by the addition of the 6th Cavalry Division and the 1st Cavalry Brigade.

On the right wing the 44th Brigade, in its advance on Nogent le Rotrou, also had had a sharp encounter. It carried the enemy's position at La Fourche, and captured three guns, with a large number of prisoners. The main body of the Corps (the XIIIth) reached Beaumont les Autels and Brou, but the cavalry failed to penetrate the woods to the north of Nogent.

January 6th.—At six in the morning the advanced guard of General Baumgarth's detachment started on march to Prunay, but the main body could not follow, since it was attacked in force at about half-past nine. With the object of observing the enemy, the infantry had been scattered in detached posts in a wide extension from Ambloy to Villeporcher, and only a small reserve remained at La Noue. The fight soon assumed greater expansion, and the defence with difficulty maintained the line Les Haies—Pias, the turning of the German left flank being seriously threatened, upon which the 6th Cavalry Division moved up, but could only enter the fight with one horse battery. The reserve, however, moved up along the high road to Château Renault and repulsed the enemy, who had already forced his way into Les Haies. But when he renewed the attack in strong columns and developed four batteries against the place, the reserve was obliged to retire behind the Brenne.

Meanwhile the 16th Regiment, which had already reached Ambloy on its march to Vendôme, turned back to St. Amand in support, and the just assembled 38th Infantry Brigade deployed between Neuve St. Amand and St. Amand with a strong force of cavalry on its flanks. But as by some mistake St. Amand was evacuated, Duke William of Mecklenburg (commanding 6th Cavalry Division) ordered a further retreat. The infantry, however, had already come to a halt at

Huisseau and took quarters there. The advanced guard turned into Ambloy; the cavalry fell back partly on that place and partly on Villeromain.

During the engagement about St. Amand the Xth Corps itself advanced on Montoire in two columns along the left bank of the Loire, leaving on its right a battalion in front of Vendôme to secure the debouche of the IIIrd Corps through that place.

When the 20th Division reached St. Rimay at about one o'clock, it found the heights on the opposite side of the Loir occupied by General Barry's troops. The massed German batteries were brought up to the southern ridge of the valley and soon drove the French off the broad flats ; but the defile of Les Roches in the front remained quite unassailable. The broken bridge at Lavardin, lower down the stream, was therefore made practicable by the pioneers. The 19th Division having meanwhile reached that place, several battalions crossed from the south side to attack Les Roches, and easily dislodged the French. As darkness came on, preventing any further advance, the Corps found quarters in and about Montoire.

The Commander of the IIIrd Corps had intended to make a halt on this day before Vendôme, and only push forward his advanced guard as far as the Azay brook ; but this detachment soon met with so stout opposition, that the main force was compelled to advance to its assistance. General de Jouffroy, with intent to disengage General de Curten, had renewed the attack on Vendôme, and so the advanced guard of the 5th Division, approaching Villiers at about half-past one, found the 10th Jäger Battalion, which had accompanied the march of its Corps along the right bank of the Loir, engaged at that place in a sharp fight which had already lasted four hours. The advanced guard brought up its two batteries on to the plateau north of the village, and the 48th Regiment made its way forward to the slope of the lower Azay valley, the broad flat meadows of which were commanded by the French long-range rifles and completely swept by the fire of the artillery And here then the enemy came over to the attack in dense swarms of sharp-shooters.

The 8th Regiment presently came up in support, and after a short fight took possession of Le Gué du Loir on its left flank; then the further reinforcement arrived of the 10th Infantry Brigade, and by degrees the number of Prussian guns increased to thirty-six. The French artillery could not endure their fire, and within half an hour it was possible to turn it on the hostile infantry. At about half-past four the German battalions crossed the valley, made themselves masters of the vineyards and farms on the opposite heights, and finally stormed Mazange. Under cover of the darkness the French retired to Lunay.

Further to the right the advance guard of the 6th Division, having left Vendôme at eleven o'clock, found the battalion left by the Xth Corps at Courtiras fighting hard against a very superior force of the French. The 11th Brigade advanced on the Azay ravine, though not without heavy loss, and when at about half-past three the 12th also came up, and the artillery went to work vigorously, Azay was successfully stormed and the force established itself firmly on the heights beyond. Repeated counterstrokes of the enemy were repulsed in succession, and by five o'clock the fighting ended with the retirement of the French.

The IIIrd Army Corps took up quarters between the Azay stream and the Loir. A detachment occupied Danzé, higher up the river. The Corps lost thirty-nine officers and above 400 men, but captured 400 prisoners.

In the course of the day the IXth Corps crossed the upper Loir about Fréteval and St. Hilaire, without opposition, and advanced along the high road to St. Calais, as far as Busloup. The XIIIth remained at Unverre, Beaumont, and La Fourche.

Prince Frederick Charles had not been led into any change of purpose by the attack at St. Amand and the obstinate resistance at Azay. The XIIIth Corps was expected to reach Montmirail, and the XIth Epuisay, both on the 7th; the IIIrd was to continue the attack on the deep-cut channel of the Braye brook. But after the reverse experienced at St. Amand, the presence of a strong hostile force on the left flank could not be suffered to remain unregarded. Duke William had already been given verbal orders at the Head-quarter in Vendôme, to turn back forthwith to St. Amand with the 6th Cavalry Division, and in addition General von Voigts-Rhetz was ordered to support General Baumgarth if necessary with his whole Corps.

The country between the Loir and the Sarthe through which the Germans had to march, presents peculiar difficulties to an invading force, and affords marked advantages to the defence.

All the roads leading to Le Mans intersect at right angles, stream after stream flowing through broad and deeply cut meadow-valleys. Groves, villages, and châteaux with walled parks cover the highly cultivated upland; vineyards, orchards and gardens are enclosed by hedges, ditches or fences.

Hence almost the whole burthen of the impending fighting would have to be borne by the infantry; nowhere was there space for the deployment of cavalry, and the use of artillery needs must be extremely limited, since in a country so greatly enclosed guns could only singly be brought into action. The enemy's central position could be approached by only four main roads, and the communications between the marching columns, starting at the least some thirty miles apart, would be confined to the cross roads, almost impassable from the severity of the season and the hostility of the inhabitants. Any lateral mutual support was at first quite out of the question.

Under such conditions the movements could only

T

be guided by general instructions, and even the leaders of lower grades had to be left free to act at their own individual discretion. Specific orders for each day, though they would of course be issued, could not in many cases be possibly carried out. In the Army Headquarter it could not be foreseen in what situation each individual corps might find itself after a day's fighting. Reports could only come in very late at night, and the orders drawn up however early would often arrive only after the troops, because of the shortness of the day, had already set out on the march.

January 7th.—In obedience to orders from the Army Headquarter, General Voigts-Rhetz on the 7th sent the part of the 19th Division which had already reached Vendôme, back to St. Amand in reinforcement. The 38th Brigade had again entered that place early in the day, and General von Hartmann, taking over its command, advanced along the Château Renault high road, the cavalry moving on both flanks.

The column first struck the enemy near Villechauve at mid-day. A thick fog prevented the employment of the artillery, and it was at the cost of heavy loss that Villechauve, Pias, and various other farmsteads were captured. Villeporcher and the adjacent villages remained in possession of the French, who at about two o'clock advanced by the high road to the attack with several battalions. The weather had cleared, and it was soon evident that this offensive was only intended to mask the beginning of the enemy's retreat to the westward. The troops took quarters where they stood, and the reinforcements forwarded to them remained at St. Amand.

The Xth Corps, awaiting the return of the latter, remained in its quarters about La Chartre; only the 14th Cavalry Brigade went on up to La Richardière to establish connection with the IIIrd Corps. But it did not succeed in taking the village with dismounted troopers.

General von Alvensleben [1] hoped to overtake the French on the hither side of the glen of Braye, and by turning their left wing to drive them on to the Xth Corps, whose co-operation had been promised. The IIIrd Corps advanced in the direction of Epuisay, leaving one brigade to garrison Mazange, and when tidings reached it on the march that the French had evacuated Lunay and Fortan, that brigade also followed by way of the latter village.

Epuisay was found to be strongly held, and in the meantime the advanced guard of the IXth Corps, advancing from Busloup, also arrived there. But it was not till half-past one that the French were expelled from the little town, which they had strongly barricaded ; and on the hither side of the Braye they renewed their resistance in the numerous hamlets and farmsteads. A long fire fight was kept up in the thick fog; but at length, at about four o'clock, the 12th Brigade pushed forward to the edge of the valley. The 9th Brigade took possession of Savigny without meeting any serious opposition, and Sargé was stormed in the dusk.

The IIIrd Corps had lost forty-five men and had taken 200 prisoners. It found quarters behind the Braye, but threw forward outposts on its western bank. The IXth Corps found shelter in and about Epuisay, and thus, as a matter of fact, two corps were now crowded on one of the few available roads. The 2nd Cavalry Division went to the right, towards Mondoubleau, to make connection with the XIIIth Corps. The French retreated to St. Calais.

The order from the Army Head-quarter that the XIIIth Corps was to march to Montmirail, had been issued on the presumption that it would have reached Nogent le Rotrou on the 6th, whereas in fact, as has

---

[1] Lieut.-General Alvensleben II, commanding IIIrd Army Corps, not to be confounded with Infantry-General Alvensleben I, commanding IVth Corps.

been shown, it had remained at La Fourche, Beaumont, and Unverre. The Grand Duke, who expected to experience a stout resistance, did not pass to the attack of Nogent till the 7th. When the 22nd Division arrived there, it found all the villages deserted in the Upper Huisne valley and was able to enter Nogent without any fighting at two o'clock. It took up quarters there, the 4th Cavalry Division at Thirion Gardais; and only an advanced guard followed the enemy. It found the wood near Le Gibet strongly occupied, and did not succeed in forcing it till after night-fall.

The French had retired to La Ferté Bernard.

The 17th Division had at first followed in reserve. But at one o'clock, in consequence of the reports brought in, the Grand Duke detached it southward to Authon; and in order to follow the Head-quarter instructions as closely as possible he did at least push a detachment of two battalions, two cavalry regiments, and one battery towards Montmirail, under the command of General von Rauch.

January 8th.—Finding on the morning of the 8th that the enemy was not advancing to the attack of St. Amand, General von Hartmann at nine o'clocksent back the troops which had crossed the river to his support. At ten o'clock also he received instructions to join the Xth Corps; but the French still continued to hold Villeporcher and the forest lying behind it, and were also drawn up across the Château Renault high road in a very advantageous position behind the Brenne. The General recognized the necessity of making a decisive stand here, and took the best means to that end by acting himself on the offensive. Supported by the fire of his battery, and accompanied by the cavalry on either flank, six companies of the 60th Regiment marched on Villeporcher, drove back its defenders in flight into the forest of Château Renault, and took 100 prisoners. On the left the 9th Uhlans drove the Chasseurs d'Afrique before them. Not till darkness had set in did General von Hartmann proceed in the direction of Montoire.

General von Voigts-Rhetz had already set out from thence very early in the day. The night's frost had covered the roads with ice, which cruelly impeded all movements of troops. The road on the right bank of the Loir was in many places broken up. It passed through a succession of narrow defiles, and on emerging from these the advanced guard found itself face to face with a force of about 1000 Gardes-Mobiles, who had taken up a position in front of La Chartre. Their mitrailleuses were soon forced to a hasty retreat by the fire of two field-guns, but it was only after a prolonged struggle that the infantry, moving with difficulty, succeeded at 4 o'clock in entering the town, where it took up quarters. Two battalions which were sent further on the road, had to fight for their night's shelter, and all through the night were exchanging shots with the enemy at close quarters, of whom 230 were taken prisoners.

The 39th Brigade, which left Ambloy in the morning, could follow the corps only as far as Sougé.

General von Schmidt with the 14th Cavalry Brigade was sent to the right, to try to make connection with the IIIrd Corps. He was received at Vancé with a sharp fire. The leading squadron made way for the horse battery, and a volley of grape-shot from the foremost gun drove the dismounted hostile Cuirassiers behind the hedges. When two more guns were brought up into position, their shell fire dispersed in every direction a long column of cavalry.

Colonel von Alvensleben pursued the French cavalry with the 15th Uhlan Regiment till he came upon a body of infantry guarding the Etang-fort brook. The brigade halted at Vancé, after putting about 100 French *hors de combat*.

Of the IIIrd Corps the 6th Division had moved forward through St. Calais. The French tried to hold the cuttings on the greatly broken up roads; but they nowhere awaited a serious attack, and made off, for the most part in carts which were in waiting. The 5th Division, proceeding on a parallel front on the left, met with no opposition; but the state of the roads made the march extremely difficult. The corps halted on the hither side of Bouloire. The IXth Corps came up behind it into St. Calais.

The Grand Duke had moved both Divisions of the XIIIth Corps on La Ferté Bernard. On their way they came across none but stragglers, but they found the roads so utterly cut up that not till four in the afternoon did they reach the place, where they took up quarters. The French had retired to Connerré. The 4th Cavalry Division was to secure the right flank on the further advance, but could not get as far forward as Bellême; on the other hand, General von Rauch's (commanding 15th Cavalry Division) detachment despatched leftward towards Montmirail, surprised the French in Vibraye, and took possession of the bridge over the Braye.

By the evening of this day the two flank Corps of the German Army were at an equal distance from Le Mans, both on the same high road which crosses the district of the Quere from La Ferté Bernard in a southerly direction through St. Calais and La Chartre; the IIIrd Corps was further in advance, separated from each of them by the interval of a long march. A closer concentration of the forces could be attained only by a further advance along the converging highways. Prince Frederick Charles therefore issued an order at ten o'clock that evening, for the Xth Corps to march next day to Parigné l'Evêque, the IIIrd to Ardenay, and the XIIIth on to the heights of Montfort, the advanced guard of each to be pushed forward beyond these respective points. The IXth, in the centre, was to follow, while General von Hartmann was to protect Vendôme with the 38th Brigade and the 1st Division of Cavalry.

But the distances prevented the flanking corps advancing from La Chartre and La Ferté from reaching their respective destinations, and, on the 9th of January, snow-storms, ice-bound roads, and thick fog further combined to make their progress arduous beyond conception.

January 9th.—General von Hartmann marched the 38th Infantry Brigade on Château Renault, and entered the town at one o'clock, to find that Curten's French Division had started early in the morning for St. Laurent.

The incomplete Xth Corps moved this day in two columns ; the detachment of General von Woyna (commanding 39th Infantry Brigade) was to march from Pont de Braye by Vancé, the remainder of the corps from La Chartre by way of Brives to Grand Lucé.

The 20th Division had scarcely set out by this route from L'Homme, when it encountered shell and mitrailleuse-fire. Here there happened for once to be room for three batteries to advance, but in the heavy snowfall aim was out of the question. The infantry, however, by degrees drove the enemy out of sundry hamlets and farmsteads, and back across the Brives. To pursue him beyond that stream a makeshift bridge needed first to be thrown across with some loss of time, and then Chahaignes was to be seized. But in the narrow valley which had to be now traversed a vigorous resistance was to be counted on. The state of the road was such that the artillerymen and cavalry had to dismount and lead their horses. The General in command rode on a gun-carriage ; his staff went on foot. Some horses which had fallen in front presently stopped the way for the whole column ; and it therefore became necessary to send back all the Corps-artillery, which was to try next day to come on by way of Vancé.

To facilitate the march of the 20th Division, General

von Woyna had been instructed to deviate from his
direct road and attack the enemy's left. When he approached the valley the fighting had fallen silent, and
the detachment turned back to Vancé; but at Brives
at about half-past three the main column met with
fresh resistance, being received with a brisk fire from
the heights north-east of the village. Not even the infantry could move outside of the high road, so there
was no alternative to a frontal advance along it. A
closed attack by the 39th Brigade broke up and routed
the enemy. At half-past six in the evening, when quite
dark, Colonel von Valentini set out for St. Pierre with
four battalions, and took there 100 French prisoners
and a loaded train of 100 waggons. The Xth Corps
spent the night with only its advance in Brives and
Vancé, but its quarters reached back nearly to the valley
of the Loir. Nor had the 14th Brigade of Cavalry
been able to make any further headway.

Of the IIIrd Corps the 6th Division had marched
by the high road through Bouloire, with the artillery
corps; the 5th on the left along the by-roads. The
advanced guard of the 6th Division, after a lively
fire-fight, expelled the enemy from his positions
in front of Ardenay, but there at two o'clock had to
encounter a determined resistance. After General de
Jouffroy had withdrawn from St. Calais to the southward, General Chanzy pushed forward Paris' Division to
secure the high road leading from thence to Le Mans.
It had taken up a position near Ardenay, occupying the
château on the right, and on the left posting four guns
and two mitrailleuses near La Butte. To oppose
these there was only room on the road for two German
guns, which, however, in the course of half an hour
silenced the mitrailleuses, and carried on the unequal
contest with the greatest obstinacy. At about four
o'clock five companies of the 12th Brigade stormed the
château of Ardenay, while others, crossing the meadow-
land to the right, forced their way through a patch of

wood towards La Butte. As night came on the French tried to effect a general attack along the chaussée ; but this was repulsed, and the Brandenburgers [1] plunged through the heavy fire of the defenders, and without firing a shot took La Butte and Ardenay with a rush and a cheer. The French were thrown back into the valley of the Narais, losing many prisoners.

On the right a detachment of one battalion, two squadrons, and two guns, accompanied the 6th Division. It drove before it franc-tireur bodies, but at La Belle Inutile met with more serious resistance. The post was, however, carried by the 24th Regiment, which made prize of a large ammunition and provision train, and took above 100 unwounded prisoners. Count zu Lynar moved into the village for its defence.

The 5th Division met with no opposition, but the state of the roads caused extreme delay to its progress. It was not till the afternoon that its head reached the Narais at Gué de l'Aune and took up quarters there and rearward to St. Mars de Locquenay. Its advanced guard went on, however, to La Buzardière, thus forming the absolute head of the whole army. Parigné l'Évêque, on its left flank, was found to be held by the enemy.

The IXth Corps followed the IIIrd to Bouloire.

Orders from head-quarters had not yet reached La Ferté when, at nine in the morning, the Grand Duke set the XIIIth Corps in motion on Connerré. Soon after midday the 17th Division came upon the French near Sceaux, and in a struggle wherein it slowly gained ground, drove them first out of the village precincts and then off the road. The French, who

---

[1] Brandenburg is the territorial province of the IIIrd Army Corps. It was the nucleus of the Prussian monarchy, and the Hohenzollerns were Margraves and then Electors of Brandenburg for 300 years before they became Kings of Prussia. The IIIrd is unquestionably the most distinguished Corps of the Prussian line. The late Prince Frederick Charles long commanded it.

had retreated to Connerré by a forced night march, lost above 500 prisoners in this small affair. But the short day was closing in, and the advanced guard halted at dusk at Duneau. A detachment going further forward found Connerré occupied by the French, and many watch-fires blazing in the valley of the Duc. The main body of the infantry found quarters in and about Sceaux.

Rauch's detachment, ordered to rejoin the Corps, took possession of Le Croset and of the bridge over the Duc in front of that village, and also expelled the French from Thorigné.

The French stayed in Connerré only till the evening; then, leaving a company in occupation, they continued their retreat. This necessarily led from the left bank of the Huisne through the quarters taken up by the IIIrd German Corps, which was disturbed all night by wandering detachments of the enemy, even at Nuillé, where the Divisional headquarters lay.

On the extreme right the 4th Cavalry Division occupied Bellême, after driving out the French battalion which had been in occupation there.

Thus on this day the centre of the IInd Army had fought its way to within about nine miles of Le Mans; while the two wings were still some distance behind. As it was probable that the French would accept battle in a prepared position behind the Huisne, it seemed advisable to await the arrival of the Xth and XIIIth Corps; but on the other hand, this would also give the enemy time to strengthen himself. Were an immediate attack determined on, the two Divisions which had been delayed respectively at Château Renault and Le Chartre, could scarcely reach Le Mans in time, and the rest of the army would be involved everywhere in a disadvantageous contest with the hostile bodies which were being driven back concentrically on that place. Prince Frederick Charles therefore ordered the IIIrd Corps to push on through Ardenay; the Xth was to advance to Parigné, and the XIIIth on St. Mars la Bruyère, though these points could scarcely be reached from the positions actually occupied by the respective Corps this same evening (9th).

As we have seen, the French army now assembled about Le Mans had been acting on the offensive on January 6th, when General Jouffroy had advanced on Vendôme, and de Curten on St. Amand. But so early as the 7th the French found themselves reduced to the defensive along their whole front, some 50 miles in length. General Rousseau, on the left wing, had evacuated Nogent le Rotrou, and, without being pressed, began his retreat by a night march to Connerré. In the centre, the trough of the Braye was wrested from General Jouffroy; he quitted St. Calais, not rearward on Le Mans, but southward to join General Barry. On the right, General Curten had abandoned Château Renault, and set out, unpursued, on the line through Château du Loir. To effect some concert in the operations of the three Divisions of his right wing, General Chanzy placed them under the superior orders of Admiral Jauréguiberry. He pushed forward the Division Paris on Ardenay by the high road General Jouffroy had uncovered, and on the left wing he reinforced General Rousseau by stationing three Divisions more on either side of his line of retreat. General Jouffroy was to retire to Parigné l'Evêque, and a Division was sent to meet him there and at Changé.

General de Curten succeeded on the 9th in checking the progress of the German left wing for some time about Chahaignes; but the Division Paris was driven back through Ardenay, and General Rousseau, thus beset in Connerré, evacuated that village the same evening. The two Divisions of the right wing were behind as far as Jupilles and Neuillé Pont Pierre.

Under these circumstances General Chanzy ordered that on the 10th the Division Jouffroy should fall back on Parigné l'Evêque, but that the Division Paris should once more move forward on Ardenay. He sent the remaining three Divisions of the XXIst Corps to meet General Rousseau, with instructions that he was to retake Connerré and Thorigné.

The offensive movements thus planned by both sides developed into the fierce battle which, on the German side, was fought out single-handed by the IIIrd Corps.

BATTLE IN FRONT OF LE MANS.

(10th, 11th, and 12th of January.)

January 10th.—The Fighting about Parigné and Changé.—Owing to the peculiar nature of the country, deep columns could not deploy without great loss of time. General von Alvensleben therefore advanced in the centre with the 9th and 11th Infantry Brigades on Changé from Gué de l'Aune and Ardenay, moving on a broad front in comparatively small separate bodies. On the right the 12th marched by the high road to Le Mans; on the left the 10th was to start from Volnay when Parigné should be found abandoned by the French, and leaving that place on its left, was also to converge on Changé.

Parigné had, in fact, been deserted by the French, but had been reoccupied before daybreak by a brigade . of the Division Deplanque; and even before the German troops had started, the far-advanced outposts towards the forest of Loudon were smartly attacked. The greater part of the 9th Brigade had to be deployed by degrees between Blinières and the point of the forest, but only seven guns could be brought into action against the numerous French artillery. General von Stülpnagel decided to reserve his strength for the struggle at Changé, and to carry on merely a stationary fight here, which must be inevitably decided as soon as the 10th Brigade should make its appearance on the left.

That brigade, delayed by the badness of the roads, did not arrive by way of Challes till noon; but it brought two batteries to reinforce the German artillery strength, which now vigorously prepared the infantry attack on the high-lying Parigné. Half an hour later the battalions rushed on the place with shouts of "Hurrah Brandenburg!" taking a gun which the enemy had abandoned, and two mitrailleuses still in action. When the French returned to try to recover them they were again repulsed, and sacrificed another gun, two colours, and several waggons. After losing 2150 prisoners they fled to the shelter of the forest of Ruaudin. General von Stülpnagel left two battalions at Parigné to maintain observation in that quarter, and hurried on to Changé in two columns. In front of this village, at about three o'clock, the 11th Brigade met with a violent resistance at the Gué Perray brook from the other brigade of Deplanque's Division. The 2nd Battalion of the 35th Regiment lost nine officers and above 100 men in a severe struggle at Les Gars. The General in command, who was on the spot, dislodged both flanks of the enemy from his strong position, and on the left two companies succeeded in crossing the stream at La Goudrière.

These at four o'clock now fell in with the advanced guard of the 9th Brigade, which Colonel Count von der Groeben was bringing up from Parigné, having taken possession of the Château of Girardrie on the way. When the companies of the 11th Brigade sent to the right reached Auvigné simultaneously, the "General Advance" was sounded. Auvigné was stormed, the bridge north of Gué la Hart was crossed, and that village carried after a hard fight. Over 1000 prisoners more were taken from the flying French.

It was already dark, but Changé, the goal of the struggle, was not yet reached. But when a barricade outside the village had been won it was found that the 10th Brigade was already in possession. This brigade, on its way along the high road from Parigné, had met with resistance at the Châteaux Chef Raison and Paillerie. Having only two guns, it failed to silence the French artillery, but General von Stülpnagel left there only a battalion in observation, and hurried forward with part of the brigade to reinforce the fight at Gué la Hart; the other portion was directed against Changé. Here the French had already been for the most part dismissed to quarters, but they soon assembled and made a prompt and determined resistance. There ensued an embittered street-fight, which ended in about an hour's time in the surrender of the whole garrison of 800 men, who had been crowded together into the market-place.

The 12th Brigade had at last left Ardenay at eleven o'clock; it advanced along the high road without opposition as far as St. Hubert, where an abandoned commissariat train was seized. Having there aligned itself with the rest of the Corps it halted for a while, but after one o'clock was fired upon by French artillery; and the enemy again advancing along the highway, General von Buddenbrock [1] on his part passed to the attack, and drove back the enemy out of Champagné, in part across the Huisne, and in part to the heights behind the village. Two guns successfully dealt with the fire of the French artillery near Lune d'Auvours, and then the infantry expelled the French from that shelter also.

Further to the right a German battalion had taken St. Mars la Bruyère after a slight skirmish, and was subsequently joined there by General Count zu Lynar's detachment.

Fighting thus with equal skill and success the IIIrd Corps had indeed already lost 450 men; but it had brought in more than 5000 prisoners, and had won many trophies of which it had a right to be proud.

[1] Commanding 6th Division, IIIrd Corps.

The Xth Corps had started this day from Vancé and Brives, and unobstructed indeed by the enemy, but along very heavy roads, reached Grand Lucé at two o'clock. Here it took up quarters.

The IXth Corps remained at Nuillé.

Of the XIIIth Corps the 17th Division had continued its advance along the left bank of the Huisne, and found Connerré already deserted by the French. But on the further side of the river the heights of Cohernières, the railway station, and the wood to the north, were occupied by the 2nd Division of the French XXIst Corps. General von Rauch led two battalions to the attack from the south, in which shared the 22nd Division from the east, having crossed the Huisne at Sceaux and taken the direction of Beillé by the right bank. A stubborn resistance was encountered, and the fight swayed to and fro till darkness fell. The Château of Couléon, indeed, and several villages at the foot of the wooded heights were taken, but the French maintained their hold on the heights and their position at Cohernières.

The 17th Division had meanwhile continued its advance along roads frozen as smooth as glass, and reached La Belle Inutile ; the 22nd passed the night at Beillé.

This division had in the morning sent a detachment sideward to Bonnétable, whither the 4th Cavalry Division now proceeded. The 12th Cavalry Brigade followed to Bellême. Colonel von Beckedorff then continued his advance to Chanteloup, whence he drove out the French in spite of an obstinate defence.

General Chanzy had determined to risk a decisive battle in front of Le Mans. Curten's Division had not yet reached him, and only a part of Barry's had come up, but on the other hand the army from the camp of Conlie, in strength some 10,000 men, had arrived. The right wing of the French position rested its flank on the Sarthe near Arnaye[1] ; it extended for more than four

---

[1] " Arnage " on the map and in the *Staff History.*

miles along the Chemin aux Bœufs, and continued in a
slight curve leftward to the Huisne.   Barry's Division,
already weakened by previous reverses, and General
Lalande's National Guards—undisciplined and badly
armed troops—were posted on the extreme right which
was the least threatened.   Deplanque's and Roquebrune's Divisions, Desmaison's Brigade and Jouffroy's
Division, held the centre and left, the last body in the first
instance opposite to General von Alvensleben.   Behind
this line Bouëdec's Division and Colonel Marty's detachment constituted a reserve.   In all from 50,000 to 60,000
men under the command of Admiral Jauréguiberry,
with full ranks and well commanded, crowded the
entrenched front of the most important section of the
line—that between the two rivers (Sarthe and Huisne).
Five Divisions more, under the command of General
de Colomb, lined the right bank of the Huisne for a
distance of about eight and a half miles, the Division Paris was at Yvré; Gougeard's Division, also
holding the heights of Auvours on the hither side, was
northward of Champagné; then came Rousseau's Division at Montfort and Pont de Gesnes, and finally, Collin's
Division in hook-formation about Lombron.   Besides
these Villeneuve's Division, quite on the flank, fronted
toward Chanteloup.

January 11*th*.—On this day the IIIrd German
Army Corps was directly opposed to the main body
of the French forces.   It could not for the present hope for any assistance from the corps of the
flanks, and had before it the certainty of an arduous
struggle.

On the left, the Xth Corps was still this morning at
Grand Lucé, and on the right the XIIIth Corps had
been detained on the previous day by the obstinate
resistance of the French, who had held their own
between Les Cohernières and La Chapelle, and occupied
Le Chêne in their front.

The troops of the 22nd Division had necessarily lost

their formations and become mixed up in the course of the struggle in the wood, and it was not till they had been re-formed and the enemy's position had been reconnoitred by both the Divisional Commanders that the attack was renewed at about eleven o'clock.

Two battalions of the 17th Division and one battery were left in observation in front of Pont de Gesnes, on the southern bank of the Huisne; on the northern side, the Mecklenburg battalions stormed Cohernières in the afternoon after a sharp contest, and in conjunction with the Hessians forced their way westward up to the Gué and on towards Lombron about four o'clock.

Further to the right two companies of the 90th Regiment (22nd Division) meanwhile took Le Chêne by a closed attack on the obstinate defenders; the 83rd Regiment, after a sharp fire fight, stormed the farmsteads of Flouret and La Grande Métairie. Colonel von Beckedorff, on being relieved at Chanteloup by the 4th Cavalry Division, had driven the French out of St. Célerin, and he then advanced to La Chapelle-St. Rémy on the right of the Division, which occupied wide quarters behind the points it had seized.

The Mecklenburg Grenadiers had held their own for a long time at Le Gué and La Brosse against superior numbers attacking from Pont de Gesnes; but the main body of the 17th Division was retired in the evening further back to Connerré.

The more completely that General von Alvensleben had to rely solely on his own command, the more essential it was to keep the troops composing it closely concentrated. But a strong force of the enemy was now on his flank, almost indeed in his rear, on the heights of Auvours, where it was only kept at bay by his 12th Brigade, which therefore for the present was not free to advance.

And here it was that the battle first really began. The French had repossessed themselves of Champagné,

U

and had deployed artillery on the heights behind
it. When their fire had been subdued by four guns
of the brigade, two battalions advanced to an attack
on the village. It was not till after an obstinate
street-fight, that the enemy at eleven o'clock was
driven back to the heights, and the bridge over the
Huisne carried. General von Buddenbrock now let
the two battalions remain in observation, sent a third
to Lune d'Auvours, and at noon started with the rest
of the brigade to rejoin the Corps.

Meanwhile the conflict had been raging with such fury
all along the front of the latter that at twelve o'clock
Prince Frederick Charles sent orders from St. Hubert to
General Voigts-Rhetz, to hurry forward by the shortest
roads to the battle-field with the Xth Corps ; and at
the same time General von Manstein was instructed
to seize the heights of Auvours with the IXth.

It was already one o'clock when the advanced guard
of the IXth climbed up the hollow way, deep in snow,
followed by two battalions of the 12th Brigade, and
by two batteries straining every nerve. The infantry
plunged forward through the wood, strongly held as it
was by the enemy, straight on Villiers ; the skirmishers
of the Fusilier battalion of the 11th Regiment seized
three mitrailleuses in action, and when the French had
abandoned the village, turned them against the wood.

Further to the left, at about three o'clock, two
battalions of the 85th Regiment from the main body
of the 18th Division, were directed on the western
end of the ridge, supported by the Jägers and two
batteries which were brought up near Les Hêtres. To
cover them two companies moved on La Lune, and
baulked for the moment the hostile rush along the high
road. But against these movements the French opened
a heavy fire from their commanding batteries behind
Yvré. Regardless thereof the Holsteiners[1] on the

---

[1] The "Holsteiners" mentioned in the text were two battalions

left charged on a hostile battery and seized three of its guns. On the right they took possession of the neighbouring farmsteads ; and soon after five the French abandoned the whole plateau as far as its western edge.

Over it, however, a strong counter-attack was delivered in the evening, when part of Gougeard's Division charged up the slope from Yvré. Its further advance was arrested ; but the French could not be prevented from remaining there during the evening and night. Nevertheless, this offensive struggle on the part of the 18th Division had relieved the pressure on the rear and flank of the IIIrd Corps. It received the further order in the evening to secure the passage over the Huisne for use next day. Three battalions and one battery immediately crossed over to the northern bank and drove from the bridge the hostile detachments in its vicinity. The Division lost 275 men.

General von Alvensleben had delayed the advance of the IIIrd Corps till eleven o'clock, in anticipation of the arrival of the 12th Brigade.

During the night (10-11th) the French had completed their entrenchments on the skirts of the wood and had taken up their position there ; they also lined the heights on the further side of the river with numerous batteries. Thus a frontal attack must involve heavy loss, and it was impossible to out-flank lines so extensive. General von Alvensleben therefore decided on advancing at first only against the enemy's left wing, and assigned to that task the 11th Brigade. The 10th and 9th remained in reserve for the present about Changé and Gué la Hart. The 12th, released at Mont-Auvours, was indeed marching up, but on

---

of the 85th Regiment, which belonged to the 36th Brigade, 18th Division, IXth Army Corps, whose territorial region consists of Sleswig-Holstein, the Hanse towns, Mecklenburg, &c.

circuitous ways, because the high road was everywhere entirely commanded by the batteries on the
heights.

The 11th Brigade, scarcely 3000 strong, followed
the course of the Gué Perray streamlet up to the
northern end of the wood. To protect it against
the French columns threatening it from the heights,
the 35th Regiment had to form front towards the brook
and also occupied the Château of Les Arches. The
20th Regiment tried to get forward by the cattle-path,
and while holding firmly the Château of Les Noyers
and the bridge there over the Huisnes, drove back
the enemy by sheer hard fighting to Les Granges.
But he presently returned so considerably reinforced that the whole brigade had to be gradually
brought up into the fighting line. Les Granges
was lost and retaken several times with heavy loss,
particularly of officers; but the Brandenburgers
fought on staunchly.

On the left of the 11th the 10th Brigade now made
its appearance, coming up from Changé at one o'clock.
After an hour-long bloody struggle the 52nd Regiment
made itself master of the farm of Le Pavillon, of the
wooded slope in front, and the farm of Grand Anneau.
Strong columns advancing from Pontlieue were driven
back, two batteries dashed up into the Chassepôt fire
to within 800 paces of Le Tertre; yet the 12th Regiment did not succeed in getting into the farmstead till
two battalions of the 9th Brigade from Changé had
come up to its assistance. The farmstead whose possession was so obstinately disputed was taken by storm at
about five o'clock, with the co-operation of the Grenadiers of the 8th Life-Regiment.

The 52nd Regiment, having expended all its ammunition, had to retire, but the Grenadier battalions pushed
further forward on the cattle-path, where two French
guns in action were captured after a bloody mêlée;
and the enemy's repeated attempts to recover them

were steadily frustrated. A hostile battery which had been brought up westward of the wood was driven back by quick fire.

As the 35th Regiment had to be brought forward from the Gué Perray brook to support the 20th, the French had recovered possession of Les Arches. The 12th Brigade, only three battalions strong, arrived there from Auvours at two o'clock. The 64th Regiment recaptured the château after a short fight. The overwhelming artillery and musketry fire from the heights on the further side of the river prevented the German artillery from coming into action, and it was only with great difficulty and a heavy sacrifice of gunners that the pieces were brought away again ; but every attack on the château by the French from Yvré was steadily repulsed.

It was now quite dark, and only the fire of the cannon still lasted. The IIIrd Corps had taken 600 prisoners, but had also lost 500 men. It had fought its way into the heart of the French position, and its outposts were in the closest proximity to the enemy's front. And now strong, though late, reinforcements arrived.

The Xth Corps had marched from Grand Lucé to the westward in the morning, to gain the high road from Tours to Le Mans, but slippery roads again delayed its march, so that it only reached Teloche in the afternoon.

The cannon thunder heard to the northward left no doubt that General von Alvensleben was engaged in arduous fighting. The orders sent at noon from the Army Headquarter in St. Hubert sped to General Voigts-Rhetz ; but that officer rightly judged that his appearance would now have a more telling effect on the enemy's flank than on the field where the IIIrd Corps was engaged. So in spite of the exhausted state of his men, who had had no opportunity to cook on the way, he at once pushed forward without halting.

To protect himself against Curten's Division on the watch for him from Château du Loir, he despatched a battalion to Ecommoy. It was received with firing from the houses, surrounded on all sides in the darkness, and compelled to withdraw from the place ; but it then kept the road clear in the rear. of the corps.

The head of the 20th Division found Mulsanne but feebly defended, and drove the detachment back beyond the cutting of La Monnerie.

The nature of the country which here had to be traversed greatly favoured the enemy. Ditches and fences afforded his marksmen complete cover, farmsteads and copses furnished excellent defensive positions. Only eight guns could at first be brought to bear against the enemy's artillery ; but nevertheless four Westphalian and Brunswick [1] battalions steadily repelled the French, and by night-fall reached Point du Jour. The fight first became stationary on the cattle-path in front of Les Mortes Aures. Here the French swept the whole foreground with a continuous rolling fire from tiers of shelter-trenches rising one above the other.

The fight swayed to and fro for a long time, but finally the German left gained ground. The 1st Battalion of the 17th Regiment rushed on the enemy, who delivered his fire at point blank range and then made for the wood. And when now the 1st Battalion of the 56th Regiment advanced from Point du Jour, its drums beating the charge, the French carried away their mitrailleuses and evacuated Les Mortes Aures.

This battalion had received orders from the Commanding General to settle the business with the bayonet. Captain von Monbart led it on locked up close at the charging pace ; all the detachments at hand joined it, and in spite of a heavy fire from the wood

---

[1] The 17th and 92nd Regiments comprising the 46th Brigade commanded by General von Diringshofen.

La Tuilerie was reached by half-past eight; and here the 40th Brigade deployed, while the 37th stood ready to support it in front of Mulsanne. The enemy drifted away in the darkness. The constant roll of wheels, the noise of departing railway trains and the confusion of cries indicated a retreat. Yet the prisoners who were constantly being brought in, with one accord reported that a strong force was still encamped in the forest. Numerous watch-fires blazed there through the night, and instead of resting, it seemed evident that the hostile troops were preparing to engage in fresh attempts. At half-past ten the outposts reported the approach of a strong force from Pontlieue.

Hitherto it had been only the little-to-be-relied-on National Guards under General Lalande at this point with whom the German troops in this quarter of the field had had to deal; but the Admiral now sent Bouëdec's Division against La Tuilerie, and ordered General Roquebrune to support his advance.

For a full hour the Prussian battalions in first line were scourged with rifle fire in front and flank, and pelted by a hail-storm of projectiles, but no serious attack occurred.

According to French reports, the officers strove in vain to bring forward their troops; but the latter constantly hung back. A later assault made by Gardes-Mobiles was equally fruitless.

But still there was to be no rest. At two in the morning the din of fighting again made itself heard on the right. Deplanque's Division had been disturbed by a flank detachment of the 40th Brigade. This body was advancing by the road from Ruaudin to Pontlieue, to be at hand in case of need; without returning the enemy's fire, it had driven out the holders of Epinettes, and had established itself there close to the cattle-path.

January 12th.—For the impending struggle of the following day only the IIIrd and Xth Corps could be counted on. The other two Corps could only co-

operate indirectly by holding engaged a part of the
hostile forces.

Of the XIIIth Corps the 17th Division was to advance by Lombron to St. Corneille, without com-
mitting itself to a contest with the enemy still holding
the bank of the Huisne; the 22nd was ordered from
La Chapelle to Savigné. The Gué brook was to be
lightly held, and part of the artillery was to remain at
Connerré with the 7th Brigade of Cavalry.

On advancing it was found that the enemy had
already abandoned Lombron, Pont de Gesnes, and
Montfort. Arms and equipments thrown away betrayed how hurried had been the flight. Many stragglers were brought in prisoners, and it was not till
reaching the Merdereau brook at noon, that the 17th
Division met with opposition. The Château of Hyre
and St. Corneille were won about four o'clock by
an enveloping attack, and 500 French were taken
prisoners. The enemy was then driven back behind
the Parance brook, where the advanced guard halted
at dusk.

Colonel von Beckedorff's detachment of the 22nd
Division marched through Chanteloup from Sillé,
throwing back the enemy on La Croix, where a large
body of hostile troops made a stand. But when, after
a long halt, the main body of the Division came up, it
at once passed to the attack. Entire formed bodies of
French here laid down their arms, and 3000 men
with many officers became prisoners.

An attempt of the cavalry to advance across the
Sarthe to break up the railway on the further side of
the river was, however, unsuccessful.

The whole force occupying the heights of Auvours
surrendered to the IXth Corps. The 35th Brigade
marched up to Villiers, but patrols sent ahead soon
reported that the French had retired across the Huisne.
When the noise of fighting was heard at mid-
day from St. Corneille, the brigade in question was

ordered to proceed northward to support the 17th Division engaged there. The 84th Regiment, passing through La Commune, lent efficient assistance in the attack on Château Hyre. Outposts were left on the Parance for the night, but the main body of the 35th Brigade returned to Fatines, and the 36th took up quarters between Villiers and St. Mars la Bruyère.

By the battle of the previous day the position of the French before Le Mans had been forced; but they still stood firm behind the Huisnes, and as their left wing had been driven in on their centre, the latter section had been considerably strengthened. There still remained the stream to be crossed, and the steep slope to be climbed, where every row of the vineyards in terraced ascent was held by strong firing lines, and the crest of which was crowned with batteries. The passage of the Huisnes near Ivré, on the left, was covered by entrenchments with special carefulness, and the ground in front of the wood of Pontlieue had been made impassable in many places by abatis. Against such a position the artillery could be of little and the cavalry of no service, while deep snow hampered every movement of the infantry. General von Alvensleben therefore decided on standing for the present on the defensive with his right wing, while he prepared to support the advance of General von Voigts-Rhetz with his left.

The troops were roused from their short rest at six in the morning. Two French companies made their way towards the bridge at Château Les Noyers with powder-bags, but they were compelled to retreat, leaving the explosives behind them. At eight o'clock the French made a determined attack on the outposts of the 12th Regiment in the wood, and drove them in on Le Tertre. Again a combat raged furiously about this farmstead, which was almost demolished by shell fire. One by one the last battalions of the 10th Brigade were drawn into the struggle, to replace bodies which, their ammunition exhausted, had to retire.   Only four guns could be used with effect, but by eleven o'clock the enemy's fire gradually died away, and he was seen to retire on Pontlieue.   The battalions of the left wing pursued, and came out on the Parigné road in immediate touch with the Xth Corps.

General von Voigts-Rhetz had left two battalions at Mulsanne, for his protection from the direction of Ecommoy; the whole Corps, after many detachments had been unavoidably detailed from it, was assembled by about half-past seven for a further advance on Pontlieue. The main body of the 20th Division closed up by the Mulsanne road on La Tuilerie.   Three battalions of the 19th Division massed at Ruaudin to strengthen the side-ward detachments in Epinettes, while two battalions with the 14th Cavalry Brigade and the Corps' artillery, which could find no opening in the region further to the left, moved up by the roads from Parigné.

The reinforcement meanwhile arrived from Ruaudin, and General von Woyna made his way without hindrance through the forest to La Source, where he halted at one o'clock, his front parallel with that of the 20th Division.   A heavy battery of the latter had already driven away the French mitrailleuses in front of Pontlieue.   On the right a light battery of the 19th Division was brought up to La Source, and ten horse-artillery guns on to the road from Parigné.   The atmosphere was, however, so thick that their fire could only be directed by the map.

At two o'clock General von Kraatz advanced in close column on Pontlieue, whither General von Woyna was now also marching.   The southern part of the village was taken after a slight resistance ; but on the further side of the Huisne the French held the houses along the river-bank, and just as the Germans approached the bridge it was blown up.   The demolition, however, was not complete, and the foremost battalions got across over the débris to reach the enemy. Two made their way into the high street of Pontlieue, one turned left to the railway station, whence were heard signals for departing trains. Nothing interposed to hinder the railway bridge here from being blown up, and thus many prisoners were taken, besides 150 provision waggons and 1000 hundred-weight of flour.

The artillery fire was immediately directed on the town of Le Mans.

Meanwhile the detachments of the IIIrd Corps, which had become mixed up in the forest fight, had re-formed. After a ration of meat, the first for three days, had been served out to the troops, the 10th Brigade resumed its march. The Brandenburg Jäger Battalion crossed the river by the paper-mill of L'Epau, and two batteries strengthened from Château Funay the artillery fire directed on Le Mans.

When presently the infantry entered the town, a fierce struggle began in the streets, which were entirely blocked by the French trains. Entrance into individual houses had to be cleared by artillery fire; a large number of French were taken prisoners, and a vast quantity of waggons were seized. The fighting lasted till nightfall, and then the Xth Corps and half of the IIIrd took up alarm quarters in the town. The 6th Division took possession of Yvré, which the enemy had abandoned, and threw out foreposts to Les Noyers and Les Arches on the further side of the Huisne.

The actions fought by the French on this day, had been engaged in for the sole purpose of gaining time for the extrication of the army.

On learning from Admiral Jauréguiberry that every effort to get the troops to advance had failed, and that the last reserves were shattered, General Chanzy had at eight in the morning issued orders for a general retreat on Alençon, where the Minister of War had arranged for the arrival of two Divisions of the XIXth Corps from Carentan.

The advance of the IInd Army to Le Mans had been a series of seven days' incessant fighting. It was made at a season when the winter was in extremest severity. Ice and snow-drifts had rendered every movement one long struggle. Bivouacking was out of the question ; and the troops had to seek their night shelter often at a distance of some miles in rear ; their reassembling in the morning cost precious hours, and the shortness of the day then prevented their taking full advantage of their successes. Whole battalions were employed in guarding the prisoners. The roads were in such a state that the trains of the army could not be brought up ; officers and men alike marched insufficiently clothed and on scanty rations. But zeal, endurance, and discipline conquered every difficulty.

The army had sacrificed in this prolonged struggle 3200 men and 200 officers, the larger half belonging to the IIIrd Corps alone. Many companies fought under the command of non-commissioned officers.

The French estimated their losses at 6200 men, and 20,000 taken prisoners ; seventeen guns, two colours, and an abundant supply of matériel remained as trophies in the hands of the victors.

After exertions so severe the troops imperatively needed some rest. The instructions from the supreme Headquarter were that the operations were not to be extended beyond a certain limit; and it was possible that the services of the IInd Army might almost immediately be required on the Seine and the Loire. Prince Frederick Charles therefore determined to follow up the retreating enemy with only a small force.

On the French side, that each Corps might have a separate road for the retreat to Alençon, two Corps had necessarily to draw out westward in the first instance. On the evening of the last day's fight the XVIth Corps reached Chauffour on the Laval road, and the XVIIth Conlie on the road to Mayenne, each covered by its rear-guard. The XXIst was assembled at Ballon, on the left bank of the Sarthe. From these points all were to march in a northerly direction. General Chanzy still deluded himself with the hope of coming up by Evreux to the assistance of the besieged capital. He would have had thus to make a wide circuit—an arc by moving on the chord of which the Germans could easily have anticipated him; and in a country where all arms were available, his army, in the condition to which it was now reduced, must have inevitably been destroyed. Ultimately the defeated French army retired in the direction to the westward of the Sarthe.

After the distribution of rations and forage, General von Schmidt set forth at mid-day on the 13th with four battalions, eleven squadrons, and ten guns, and reached Chauffour after some skirmishing. The XIIIth Corps advanced to the Sarthe, the 17th Division sending its outposts across the river at Neuville, and the 22nd drove the French out of Ballon, whence they retired in full flight to Beaumont. The XXIst French Corps had taken up quarters this day at Sillé. The National Guards of Brittany fled wildly to Coron, and thence made homeward toward their own province. They were joined by the troops left in camp at Conlie, after the camp there had been plundered. The XVIIth Corps also went off, without halting by the Vègre as it had been ordered to do, but retreating direct on Ste. Suzanne. The XVIth withdrew on Laval, leaving Barry's Division at Chassillé as rear-guard. Numbers of abandoned waggons and cast-away arms, everywhere testified to the demoralization of the defeated forces.

On the 14th the French were driven out of Chassillé. The XVIth Corps had by this time almost entirely lost its organization; it retired during the night to St. Jean sur Erve. In the camp at Conlie were found 8000 stands of arms and 5,000,000 cartridges, as well as various other war matériel.

The Grand Duke had marched on Alençon along the right bank of the Sarthe. The French in Beaumont made a feeble resistance to the advanced guard of the 22nd Division, and lost 1400 prisoners.

On the following day General von Schmidt advanced further on the road to Laval, but found that the French had concentrated at St. Jean and posted a strong force of artillery on the heights behind the Erve. The Oldenburg Regiment [1] forced its way as far as the church of the little town, and the Brunswickers drove the enemy back on Ste. Suzanne, higher up the river, but there the pursuit ended.

Barry's and Deplanque's Divisions, according to the French estimate, had now no more than 6000 fighting men, and Curten's Division had still not yet come up, but this strength was considerably superior to that of the weak German detachment confronting it. The rest of the Xth Corps was moving up in support, but had as yet only reached Chasillé. A battalion advancing from Conlie came into conflict at Sillé with the XXIst French Corps assembled there, and sustained heavy loss. The 22nd Division of the XIIIth Corps also met with serious opposition before reaching Alençon, from the National Guards and the volunteers under Lipowski; and the attack on the town was postponed till next day.

But on the following morning the French positions in Alençon as well as in Sillé and St. Jean were abandoned. Those places were at once occupied by the Germans, and General von Schmidt marched forward, close up to Laval. Numerous stragglers from the retreating army were taken prisoners.

---

[1] The 91st Regiment, 37th Brigade, 10th Army Corps, whose recruiting ground is Hanover, Oldenburg, and Brunswick. The Hanoverian Corps consists mainly of the regiments of the old Hanoverian army of the kingdom long ruled by British sovereigns; an army whose valour, proved side by side with British troops on countless battle-fields from Minden and Dettingen to the Peninsula and Waterloo, culminated in its final battle on the glorious but luckless field of Langensalza.

Behind the Mayenne, whither now Curten's Division had arrived, the remnants of the IInd Army of the Loire re-assembled. Reduced to half its original strength, and its morale gravely shaken, it could but be unfit for service for a long time to come, and the object of the German advance on Le Mans was fully attained.

To the north of Paris, however, the French were meanwhile threatening a renewed offensive. It was necessary to draw in on the Somme the portions of the Ist Army which were still on the Lower Seine; and orders came from the supreme Head-quarter that the XIIIth Corps of the IInd Army should march on Rouen.

On the Upper Loire also French detachments had advanced against the Hessian posts about Briare, and had driven them back, on the 14th, to Ouzouer; while from the Sologne came a report of the advance of a newly-formed French Army Corps—the XXVth.

The German IXth Corps, after evacuating and destroying the camp at Conlie, was therefore sent to Orleans in support. The remainder of the IInd Army, the IIIrd and Xth Corps with the three cavalry divisions—in a strength of about 27,000 foot, 9000 horse, and 186 guns—was assembled by Prince Frederick Charles round Le Mans. The cavalry in observation on the front and flanks had several small skirmishes, but no further serious hostilities were attempted.

The 4th Cavalry Division held Alençon on the right, and on the left General von Hartmann entered Tours without any opposition.

OCCURRENCES NORTHWARD OF PARIS DURING JANUARY.

At the beginning of the New Year a considerable part of the Ist German Army was engaged in besieging

Péronne, which had afforded a safe crossing-point for the debouche of the French on the southern bank of the Somme. General Barnekow held the little place invested with the 3rd Reserve Division and the 31st Infantry Brigade. Previously it had only been kept under observation by cavalry, but circumstances had temporarily given it importance. What of the VIIIth Corps formerly on the Somme was available formed a wide curve from Amiens northward as far as Bapaume, to cover the siege.

The Ist Corps, posted at Rouen for the time, consisted only of three brigades; but the 4th was on the march thither from before Péronne, where it had been relieved. No reinforcement of the Ist Army had been effected. The 14th Division, after reducing Mézières and, soon after, Rocroy, had received fresh orders from Versailles which transferred it to another part of the theatre of war.

General Faidherbe had concentrated his troops behind the Scarpe, from their resting quarters south of Arras, and had begun his forward march on January 2nd. He advanced with the XXIInd Corps to the relief of Péronne by way of Bucquoy. The XXIIIrd followed by the high road to Bapaume. About half-past ten Derroja's Division of the former Corps obliged the 3rd Cavalry Division, as well as those battalions of the 32nd Brigade which had been attached to it, to fall back on Miraumont, followed, however, only as far as Achiet le Petit.

The other Division, under General Bessol, did not advance towards Achiet le Grand till the afternoon. There it was opposed for several hours by two companies of the 68th, a sub-division of Hussars, and two guns, which only retired in the evening on Avesnes. The French did not follow up the detachment, but threw out outposts about Bihucourt.

Payen's Division deployed on the high road at Béhagnies, and its batteries opened fire on Sapignies, where, however, General von Strubberg had posted five battalions. These repulsed the attack, and at two o'clock entered Béhagnies with a rush, took 240 prisoners, and prepared the village for defence. The enemy withdrew to Ervillers, and there once again drew out, but attempted no further attack.

The other Division of the French XXIIIrd Corps, consisting of mobilized National Guards under General Robin, moved forward on the left on Mory. There were only one battalion and a squadron of Hussars to oppose it. By extending their line on the heights of Beugnâtre, the German detachment succeeded in deceiving the enemy in regard to its weakness. The latter marched and counter-marched, and also brought up artillery, but did not attempt an attack, and remained at Mory.

The 30th German Brigade and the 3rd Cavalry Division assembled for the night in and about Bapaume. The 29th Brigade occupied the neighbouring villages on the right and the left of the Arras road.

BATTLE OF BAPAUME.—*January 3rd.*—General Faidherbe had brought his forces close up to the position which covered the investment of Péronne. His four Divisions consisted of fifty-seven battalions, which were opposed by only seventeen German battalions. He decided on the 3rd to push on in four columns to Grévillers and Biefvillers, on the high road, and to Favreuil on the east.

But General von Goeben was not inclined to give up his position at Bapaume. Under cover of a force in occupation of Favreuil, General von Kummer in the morning assembled the 30th Brigade in front of Bapaume, and behind it the 29th, of which, however, three battalions were left in the villages to left and to right. A reserve was established further to the rear at Tronsloy, whither the 8th Rifle Battalion, with two batteries, was detached; and General von Barnekow received orders to hold three battalions and the 2nd Foot Detachment in readiness at Sailly Saillisel, without raising the blockade. Finally the detachment under Prince Albrecht, jun.— three battalions, eight squadrons, and three batteries— advanced on Bertincourt, near to the subsequent battle-field. In this disposition, in bitterly cold and sullen weather, the attack of the French was awaited.

General Count von der Groeben had already sent the 7th Cavalry Brigade against the enemy's right flank, but it did not succeed in forcing its way through the villages occupied by the hostile infantry.

On the right wing the Division Robin was at Beug-nâtre met by so sharp a fire from two battalions of the 65th Regiment and two horse batteries which had joined them from Transloy, that it withdrew again on Mory. The garrison of Favreuil was reinforced by two battalions and two batteries against the approach of the Division Payen, which was marching by the high road to the eastward of that place. The first French gun moving out from Sapignies was immediately destroyed, but several batteries soon became engaged on both sides, and the French forced their way into Favreuil and St. Aubin.

The 40th Regiment advanced on these places at noon from Bertincourt, and after a lively action re-occupied them; but had to evacuate Favreuil again, and took up a position alongside of the 2nd Guard Uhlan regiment and a horse battery sideward of Frémicourt, which secured the right flank of the Division.

On the left, the Division Bessol had driven the weak garrison out of Biefvillers. The 1st Battalion of the 33rd Regiment, which moved forward to retake that place, became hotly engaged; it lost all but three of its officers, and had to retire upon Avesnes. The Division Derroja also took part in this fight. The French now brought up a strong force of artillery, and extended their firing-line to the south nearly as far as the road to Albert.

Therefore, at mid-day, General von Kummer decided to confine himself to the local defence of Bapaume. At the cost of serious loss, the artillery covered the drawing in thither of the infantry. The 1st Heavy Battery, which was the last to withdraw, lost 2 officers, 17 men, and 36 horses; its guns could only be brought out of action with the help of the infantry.

In Bapaume the 29th Brigade now prepared for an obstinate defence of the old city wall, and the 30th assembled behind the place. The French advanced leisurely as far as the suburb. Then ensued a long pause in the fighting. General Faidherbe hoped to take the town by further encompassing it, without exposing it to a bombardment followed by a storm. A brigade of the Division Derroja endeavoured to advance through Tilloy, but met there with stubborn resistance from the Rifle Battalion and two batteries which had come up from Péronne. At the same time twenty-four guns of the batteries which had retired behind Bapaume opened fire on the advancing columns, which then withdrew, at half-past three, across the road to Albert. They soon resumed the attack, and succeeded in entering Tilloy. All the neighbouring batteries now opened fire upon this village. General von Mirus, who on the advance of the 3rd Cavalry Division had been left behind in Miraumont, saw no enemy in his front there, but heard the fighting at Bapaume, and advanced from the west, as did General von Strubberg from the town, to renew the attack. The French did not await their arrival, and were driven back out of the suburb and also Avesnes. The French Divisions spent the night at Grévillers, Bihucourt, Favreuil, and Beugnâtre, thus surrounding Bapaume on three sides. The day had cost the Germans 52 officers and 698 men, and the French 53 officers and 2066 men.

But only by exerting the whole available strength of the VIIIth Corps had it been possible to withstand the preponderating attack of the enemy. It had

x 2

not yet been possible to replenish the Corps' supply of ammunition, and General von Goeben decided to immediately move back the fighting ground to behind the Somme. This movement was actually in process when the patrols brought information that the enemy was also evacuating the neighbouring villages.

The French troops, as yet unaccustomed to the vicissitudes of warfare, had suffered extremely from the previous day's fighting and the severe cold of the ensuing night. General Faidherbe could perceive that the forces before Péronne had been brought forward to Bapaume, and that the Germans thus reinforced would take the offensive. His chief object, the interruption of the siege of Péronne, had been obtained, and the General thought it best not to endanger that result by a second encounter. He led his Corps back in the direction of Arras. Of the German cavalry detachments following up the retirement the 8th Cuirassiers succeeded in breaking a French square. The 15th Division withdrew behind the Somme, immediately below Péronne, and the Saxon cavalry joined the right wing at St. Quentin.

FIGHTING ON THE LOWER SEINE.—*January 4th.*— Exactly at the same time the other Corps of the Ist Army was in conflict with the enemy on the Lower Seine. The French had not undertaken any new enterprise on the right bank of the river, but on the left bank they held the wooded heights of Bois de la Londe, which overhang the southern outlet of the Seine after its encircling the peninsula of Grand Couronne. Here General von Bentheim,[1] with a view of gaining room in this direction, had assembled half the Ist Army Corps, and advanced on the 4th of January on Les

---

[1] Who had succeeded General Manteuffel in the command of the Ist Corps, when at the beginning of December the latter found oppressive the command of a Corps along with the Command-in-Chief of the Ist Army.

Moulineaux. Before daybreak Lieut.-Colonel von Hüllessem surprised the enemy's outposts there, stormed the rock-crowned fortalice of Château Robert le Diable, and took prisoners the defenders who had sought refuge amid the ruins of the castle. The heights of Maison Brulet were then scaled under the heavy fire of the enemy, and two of his guns were taken. After a renewed resistance at St. Ouen the French withdrew on Bourgachard in the afternoon, pursued towards six in the evening by a half squadron of dragoons, two guns, and a company carried on waggons, which took from them two 12-pounders posted at the entrance of Rouge-montier, killing the gunners and capturing an ammunition waggon.

After a slight skirmish the enemy was also driven out of Bourgtheroùlde and thrown back in the direction of Brionne. The French right wing at Elbeuf during the night hastily withdrew from a position rendered precarious by the wavering of the other detachments. The affair cost 5 officers and 160 men. The loss of the French must have been equal, besides which they lost 300 prisoners and 4 guns.

General Roye posted his troops behind the Rille on the line Pont-Audemer—Brionne, but the Germans now held Bourgachard, Bourgtheroulde, and Elbeuf strongly garrisoned, with three battalions at Grand-Couronne in readiness to furnish support. The other troops returned to Rouen. An attempted advance of the French on the same day by the northern bank of the Seine had been arrested in front of Fauville, whence they again withdrew towards Harfleur.

Meanwhile it had not escaped the observation of the VIIIth Army Corps that this time the French did not seek the cover of the northern fortresses, but that they had halted south of Arras, thus betraying an intention shortly to renew the attack on the force investing Péronne.

General von Goeben therefore decided to return to
the northern bank of the Somme, to cover that operation, and there to take up a flanking position whose
front the enemy would have to cross in his advance.

On January 6th, after the troops had been permitted
one day's rest and the ammunition had been replenished,
the 30th Brigade moved to Bray, the 29th to Albert.
In close vicinity to the enemy was the 3rd Cavalry
Division at Bapaume, behind it the Guard Cavalry
Brigade. For the protection of the left flank Lieut.-
Colonel von Pestel[1] occupied Acheux, and from the
investing Corps the 3rd Reserve Division moved westward of Péronne to Feuillères. The Corps-Artillery
remained for the time on the left bank of the Somme,
since it almost seemed as if the enemy intended to direct
his attack on Amiens.

But during the next day the French did not undertake anything of importance, and on the 9th Péronne
fell.

REDUCTION OF PÉRONNE.—*January 9th.*—For fourteen
days this little place had been invested by eleven battalions, sixteen squadrons, and ten batteries. Flooded
meadows on one side, and on the other walls with
medieval towers, had secured it against a surprise;
but for the rest it was commanded on all sides by
overhanging heights.

Although the fire of fifty-eight field guns had not
done it much damage, yet in any case it must have
been very soon discontinued for want of ammunition.
A bombardment with captured French siege-artillery
remained without result. The fortress stoutly maintained its fire, and its garrison of only 3500 men even
attempted sorties.

As before mentioned, on the day of the battle of

---

[1] Commanding the 7th (Rhineland) Uhlan Regiment, the officer
who so long and so gallantly defended Saarbrücken on his own
responsibility in the earliest days of the war.

Bapaume, a portion of the besieging troops had been necessarily withdrawn to the support of the VIIIth Army Corps, and in the uncertainty as to the result of this fight it had been imperative to take precautions for the safety of the siege material. The troops that remained behind stood ready to march, and part of the heavy guns had been withdrawn. But the garrison maintained a waiting attitude.

Two days later arrived a siege-train of fifty-five heavy guns which had been brought together at La Fère. A second, of twenty-eight French siege-pieces, was on the way from Mézières. The preliminaries of a regular siege were undertaken, and when at length on the 8th of January a large ammunition-convoy arrived, the commandant was summoned to give up a defence that had now become hopeless.

On the 10th of January, General von Barnekow entered the fortress, which was found amply provided with arms, ammunition and provisions. The garrison were made prisoners.

On the 7th of January, his Majesty the King had assigned General von Manteuffel to another section of the theatre of war, and had given the supreme command of the Ist Army to General von Goeben.

Freed from concern as to Péronne, that General's only duty thenceforward was to insure the protection of the investment of Paris. For this purpose the Somme, whose passages were all in the hands of the Germans, formed a natural bulwark, behind which the attack even of a greatly superior enemy could be awaited. And some reinforcements now arrived for the VIIIth Army Corps. The peaceful condition of the Lower Seine allowed of two infantry regiments and two batteries being sent from thence to Amiens. By instructions from the supreme Head-quarter an infantry brigade of the Meuse Army was held in readiness, which in case of need was to be sent up by rail to reinforce the Ist Army.

It was still uncertain whither the enemy would direct

his stroke. General von Goeben, therefore, spread his forces behind the Somme on a prolonged extension of some forty-five miles, still holding fast the points gained in front of the river, to meet the contingency of his having to renew the offensive. In the middle of the month, the detachments of the Ist Corps under the command of General Count von der Groeben occupied Amiens, Corbie, and the line of the Hallue as a flank position. The 15th Division, holding Bray firmly, took up quarters south of that village. Next to it, on the left of Péronne, was the 3rd Reserve Division, right of it were the 16th Division and the 3rd Reserve Cavalry Brigade, holding Roisel and Vermand to the front. The 12th Cavalry Division was at St. Quentin.

The French army had already begun to advance on the Cambrai high-road, and its XXIInd Corps had pushed back the 3rd Cavalry Division first out of Bapaume and then out of Albert behind the Hallue. The XXIIIrd followed by the same road, and their objective really appears to have been Amiens. But a reconnaissance had exposed the difficulty of attacking in that direction, besides which a telegram from the War Minister announced that the Army of Paris within the next few days was to make a last supreme effort to burst the bonds of the investment, and the Army of the North was enjoined to divert, as far as possible, the enemy's forces from the capital, and draw them on itself.

In accordance with these orders General Faidherbe decided to advance without delay on St. Quentin, whither the Brigade Isnard was already marching from Cambrai. An attack on their right wing, consisting for the time solely of cavalry, directly threatened the communications of the Germans, while the vicinity of the northern forts afforded the French army shelter and also greater liberty of action.

But General von Goeben had foreseen such a leftward movement of the enemy, and concentrated all his forces to meet it.

The convalescents who were fit for service joined the ranks. Only weak detachments were left at Amiens, and because of the approach of the XIIIth Corps from the Sarthe to the Lower Seine, it was now safe to transfer the 3rd Grenadier Regiment and a heavy battery from thence to the Somme.

The departure of the French from Albert and the march of their Corps on Combles and Sailly Saillisel were soon reported by the cavalry in observation. The newly-formed Brigade Pauly occupied Bapaume, and the Brigade Isnard entered St. Quentin, whence General zur Lippe (commanding the 12th (Saxon) Cavalry Division detailed from the Army of the Meuse) retired on Ham in accordance with orders. General von Goeben now moved eastward, using the roads on both banks of the Somme so that he might the sooner reach the enemy.

January 17th.—The 12th Cavalry Brigade moved further to the right on La Fère, the 16th Division to Ham. The 3rd Reserve Division and the Guard Cavalry Brigade arrived at Nesle; the 15th Division and the Corps Artillery, at Villers Carbonnel. An Army-Reserve had been formed of the troops last brought up from Rouen, and it followed to Harbonnières. On the northern bank, the detachment under Count von der Groeben moved to the vicinity of Péronne.

The four French Divisions had so far advanced on Vermand as to be able to unite next day near St. Quentin. The XXIIIrd Corps was to move straight upon the town, the XXIInd to cross the Somme lower down, and take up a position south of St. Quentin.

January 18th.—On the German side, the 16th and the 3rd Reserve Division moved by the south bank of the Somme to Jussy and Flavy, the Army-Reserve to Ham. The 12th Cavalry Division at Vendeuil found the country east of the Oise still free from the enemy.

With the object of obtaining touch of the approaching enemy, the 15th Division was on its part to cross

the Somme at Brie, and, together with the troops of
General Count von der Groeben, to advance on Vermand
and Etreillers. General von Kummer was enjoined, in
case he found that the French had taken up a position,
merely to watch them and to follow them should they
retire northward, but should they march towards the
south, to attack them with all his force.

At half-past ten, the 29th Brigade came up on the
hither side of Tertry with the rear-guard of the XXIInd
Corps and its trains. The Hussars charged one of the
battalions guarding the latter, and drove the waggons
in the greatest disorder back on Caulaincourt, but had
to abandon prisoners and prize under the fire of the
approaching infantry. The French brigade had turned
about, and it advanced to an attack on Trescon. This
was resisted by the 65th Regiment and three batteries
until after two o'clock, when General du Bessol
reached the scene of the fight and ordered the French
brigade to resume its march on St. Quentin.

The XXIIIrd had also halted and detached a brigade
against the left flank of the 15th Division. This, however, on reaching Cauvigny Farm, came upon two
German battalions, which after a protracted fire-fight
pursued the retreating enemy and entered Caulaincourt
at half-past three, making 100 prisoners and capturing
fourteen provision-waggons.

Meanwhile Count von der Groeben had hurried
forward at the sound of firing. The General realized
that he could help most efficaciously by marching
straight on Vermand. Four batteries came into action
against Pœuilly, which was occupied by the enemy, and
when the 4th Grenadier Regiment passed to the assault
the French retreated, losing some prisoners. Many
Gardes-Mobiles were dispersed by the Uhlans. About
Vermand the whole of the XXIIIrd Corps was now in
the act of beginning to march off.

Count von der Groeben therefore posted his troops
behind the Pœuilly bottom, thereby retarding the with-

drawal of the enemy by forcing him to halt and form front against each display of pressure. The 15th Division took up quarters about Beauvois and Caulaincourt.

The sole aim of the French Generals on this day seemed to be to reach St Quentin. They neglected the opportunity of falling with their two Corps upon the single 15th Division. The XXIIIrd Corps passed the night in and westward of St. Quentin, and the XXIInd, after crossing the Somme at Sérancourt, southward of the town. A further advance either on Paris or on the German lines of communications depended now, when the latter had approached so close, on the issue of a battle; and this General Faidherbe wished to await at St. Quentin.

It was important to hold on here in case the sortie of the Paris Army should result in success. The ground offered certain advantages—the heights in front of the town gave a free range of fire and afforded a sheltered position for the reserves. It was true that the Somme divided the army in two halves, but the bridge of St. Quentin made mutual assistance possible. The enemy also occupied both sides of the river, and including the Isnard and Pauly Brigades which had come up, he finally counted 40,000 men, opposed to an enemy numerically weaker.[1] The Germans, all told, numbered exactly 32,580 combatants, of whom nearly 6000 were cavalry.

[1] Whether the author intends, in the two first sentences of this paragraph, that the advantages of the St. Quentin position should be enjoyed by Faidherbe or Goeben, appears somewhat obscure. The third sentence certainly refers to the German Army, as the succeeding one clearly shows. But this being so, there is a discrepancy between the text and the *Staff History*, as regards the side which the bridge of St. Quentin would serve in the battle. The following is quoted from that work: "Moreover, the German troops were separated by the Somme, whilst the bridges at St. Quentin enabled the French Corps to afford one another easy support."

BATTLE OF ST. QUENTIN.

(January 19th.)

General von Goeben had ordered the general attack for this day.

Covered by the occupation of Séraucourt, General von Barnekow advanced along the southern bank of the Somme, with the 16th and the 3rd Reserve Divisions from Jussy through Essigny; the 12th Cavalry Division advanced on the road leading from La Fère.

The French columns were still on the march to take up their position with its rear towards the town; and Grugies was already occupied by them. While the 32nd German Brigade advanced northward of Essigny the Reserve Division halted behind the village, and the 31st Brigade at a quarter to ten advanced on Grugies.

This attack was taken in flank on its left by the French Brigade Gislain, which had meanwhile occupied the hamlets of Contescourt and Castres. It was met in front by the Brigades Foerster and Pittié which had promptly come into action.

The fire of the German batteries was at once returned vigorously from Le Moulin de Tout Vent. At eleven o'clock the second battalion of the 69th Regiment marched in company columns across the entirely open ground against the heights on the hither side of Grugies; but the attempt, renewed four times, was frustrated by the destructive cross-fire of the enemy. The ammunition of the isolated battalion was nearly exhausted, and only when followed by six fresh companies of the 29th Regiment did it succeed in forcing the French back, after a desperate hand-to-hand fight: but the latter held their ground in front of Grugies and in the sugar-factory there.

On the right wing, the 12th Cavalry Division were advancing on the La Fère road. The French Brigade Aynes, hitherto held in reserve, rushed forward at the double to encounter it, and as Count zur Lippe had at disposition but one battalion of infantry, his advance at first was arrested at Cornet d'Or. But when at noon the Division was joined by reinforcements from Tergnier, the Saxon rifles stormed the park by the high-road, and the Schleswig-Holstein Fusiliers carried La Neuville. The French, with the loss of many prisoners, were vigorously pursued back to the suburb of St. Quentin, where first they found shelter.

Meantime, the 31st Brigade was engaged in a hot fight on both sides of the railway-line in front of Grugies; behind its right wing was the 32nd in the hollow ground on the high-road, where it suffered severely from the enemy's shell-fire; and on the left, the detachment advancing from Séraucourt did not succeed in entering Contescourt. And now the French made so determined and overwhelming an attack from Grugies, that the 16th Division had to be withdrawn as far as Essigny.

When after noon General Faidherbe joined the XXIIIrd Corps, he had reason to hope that the XXIInd Corps would be able to maintain its position. But certainly the most important result was to be looked for on the northern section of the battle-field.

Here the Division Robin had taken up a position between Fayet and Francilly. The Brigade Isnard had marched up it on its left, and the Brigade Lagrange of the Division Payen extended as far as the Somme. The Brigade Michelet remained in reserve, and the Brigade Pauly at Gricourt secured the communications rearward.

On the German left, so early as eight o'clock, General Count von der Groeben set out from Pœuilly with eight battalions and twenty-eight guns and advanced along the Roman road; the Cavalry Brigade accompanied the march on the left.

The East-Prussians [1] immediately hurled the French back from Holnon, cleared them out of Selency, and

---

[1] Companies of the Crown Prince's Grenadier Regiment (the 1st of the Prussian line), and of the East Prussian Infantry Regiment No. 44, belonging respectively to the 1st and 3rd Brigades, 1st Division, Ist Army Corps.

then advanced against Fayet and on to the heights of
Moulin Coutte.   A gun in action, ammunition-waggons,
and many prisoners were there taken from the enemy.

By degrees the twenty-eight guns were massed on
the Windmill Height and entered into a contest with
the artillery of the Division Robin.   But in the course
of half an hour the ammunition failed, since the waggons which had been sent on the previous day to the
ammunition column of the VIIIth Corps had not yet
come up with the reserve supply.   The batteries, which
were moreover suffering from infantry fire, had to
retire to Holnon, and as Francilly, immediately on the
flank and to the rear, was still occupied by the enemy,
a further advance was temporarily postponed.

On the right, General von Kummer with the 15th
Division, marching from Beauvois, had reached Etreillers at ten.   The King's Hussars cut in upon the
enemy's horse in retreat, and drove them back upon
L'Epine de Dallon, and the 29th Brigade entered Savy.
North of that place three batteries opened fire against
the artillery of the Division Payen, and then the 65th
Regiment passed to the attack of the forward-lying
copses.   The smaller one to the south was carried, but
here, as at Francilly, the Brigade Isnard maintained
itself in the larger one to the north.

At noon the Brigade Lagrange also advanced once
more on the small copse and forced its way into it for a
short time, but was again driven back by the 65th.

The 33rd Regiment was posted in readiness on the
threatened right flank of the 29th Brigade, and near it
stood in action two heavy batteries of the Corps
Artillery just arrived at Savy.   At the same time the
30th Brigade also advanced through Roupy on the right
of the 29th.

Meanwhile Colonel von Massow at one o'clock renewed
the offensive on the much more advanced left wing.
Six companies of the 44th Regiment advanced on
Fayet, and after firing into them at the shortest range,

drove the French from the place. Two batteries followed, and resumed action against the enemy's great artillery position at Moulin de Cépy.

General Paulze D'Ivoy, who saw the communications of his Corps with Cambrai in such imminent danger, had already called up the Brigade Michelet from its reserve post west of the town, and thus reinforced now advanced on Fayet. The Prussian detachments that were in the place had to be withdrawn to Moulin Coutte; but the further advance of the enemy towards these heights was arrested by a flank attack from Selency, and at the same time the farmstead of Bois des Roses was carried. The French again withdrew on Fayet.

There, at Francilly, and in the northern copses, they still held their own at half-past one, while at that hour, on the German side, all three brigades had been brought up into the fighting-line. The Army-Reserve had arrived from Ham at Roupy, but General von Goeben, who from the latter place had been watching the slow progress of the 16th Division, had already sent it at eleven o'clock through Séraucourt to the support of that Division.

Colonel von Boecking (commanding the Army-Reserve), with his three battalions, three squadrons, and two batteries, advanced from Séraucourt against Contescourt. Hastening forward with the cavalry, he brought his artillery promptly into action; and then the 41st Regiment, immediately on its arrival, passed to the attack. The battalion of the 19th Regiment which was already on the spot, joined in the fighting, and the enemy with the loss of many prisoners, was at one o'clock driven out of Contescourt and of Castres as well, towards the heights of Grugies. Against these heights the fire of the artillery, which had gradually been increased to thirty guns, was now directed.

Bent on further disputing the position, General Lecomte brought up several battalions from the brigades of Pittié and Aynès for the reinforcement of the Brigade

Gislain. The East-Prussian Regiment (41st) succeeded, nevertheless, by half-past two o'clock, in hurling the enemy by an outflanking attack from the heights into the hollow in front of Grugies. Colonel von Boecking's vigorous attack made itself felt throughout the whole front of fight.

With a view to renewing a general advance, General von Barnekow had ordered up his last reserves from Essigny, when towards three o'clock the Brigade Pittié unexpectedly pushed forward an attack along the railway line. Its right scourged by artillery fire from Castres, it found its left taken at unawares by the charge of five squadrons of reserve cavalry from the Urvilliers hollow. Simultaneously Colonel von Hartzberg advanced with the 32nd Brigade, and drove the enemy back to Moulin de Tout Vent.

The Brigade Foerster, south of Grugies, had still held out stubbornly, although now seriously threatened on the right from Giffécourt, as well as by the 12th Cavalry Division on its left flank. Its left flank now completely uncovered by the retreat of the Brigade Pittié, and its last strength exhausted by a long struggle, the brigade found itself finally forced to evacuate its long-held position. The 31st Brigade advanced along the railway-line as far as the sugar-factory, and Colonel von Boecking drove the last French detachments out of Grugies. He then prepared with his artillery the attack upon Moulin de Tout Vent. Against these heights the 41st Regiment, the battalions already ordered up from Essigny, and the 32nd Brigade advanced to a concentric attack. The French did not prolong their resistance, and indeed were already in retreat. The entire German fighting line, with the 12th Cavalry Division on its right, moved forward on the town, which was now reached by the fire of the artillery posted at Gauchy. The cavalry repeatedly broke in on the retreating hostile bodies; and the railway-station and suburb, in which was found only the rear-guard of the XXth French Corps, was occupied after a short struggle.

Whilst on the southern section of the battle-field the action took this turn, on the northern side the attacks were also being pushed.

By two o'clock the 28th Regiment advancing from Roupy by the road from Ham had carried the farmstead of l'Epine de Dallon ; and almost simultaneously Count von der Groeben's infantry came up to renew the offensive.

Whilst on the right some companies of the 4th and 44th Regiments opposed the advance of French detachments from the larger copse, Major von Elpons with six companies of the Crown Prince Grenadiers, advanced from Holnon and Selency upon Francilly, and, notwithstanding the hot fire of the defenders, forced an entrance into this very straggling village, in which many prisoners were made. As, however, the East-Prussian Regiment then advanced further south of the Roman road, it had in its turn to sustain a formidable attack.

To cover its threatened line of retreat, the Brigade Michelet once more advanced from Fayet, and the Brigade Pauly also marched from Gricourt upon Moulin Coutte. This position, which had in the meantime been strengthened by artillery, was, however, obstinately held by the 44th Regiment, and when the Grenadier companies poured in leftward towards the Roman road, the enemy's attack was here also repulsed.

Meanwhile the 29th Brigade, followed by the 30th, had already advanced in the direction of St. Quentin, the 33rd Regiment on its right and the 65th Regiment on the left. The latter regiment now took complete possession of the larger copse, and forty-eight guns were brought up on both sides of the road from Savy. The further advance of the infantry was effected in column of companies and on an extended line, because of the heavy shell fire of the French. The Brigades of Lagrange

Y

and Isnard did not await the shock, but at four o'clock retired on St. Quentin with the loss of one gun.

Their artillery once more took up a position at Rocourt, but at five o'clock had to abandon it abruptly, and the French now confined themselves to the defence of the barricaded accesses into the St. Martin suburb of St. Quentin.

Six Prussian batteries were brought up against these, and the 29th Brigade for some time maintained a stationary fire fight on the strongly held buildings and gardens; but presently several companies from Rocourt established themselves in the suburb, in which street-fighting was still continued, even after Lieutenant-Colonel von Hüllessem had succeeded in crossing the canal bridge and entering the town itself.

By four o'clock, General Faidherbe had already the conviction that the XXIIIrd Corps would probably be unable to hold its ground. In this event his choice was limited to the alternative of a night retreat, or of being shut up in St. Quentin. He had not yet formed a decision, when he met in the town General Lecointe, who reported that he had abandoned the defence of the left bank of the Somme. Thanks to the resistance still maintained by the XXIIIrd Corps on the north, the XXIInd was enabled to retire unmolested on Le Cateau.

The Commanding General now ordered General Paulze d'Ivoy to retire on that place, but the latter only received the order at six in the evening, when the brigades of the right wing—Pauly's and Miche-let's—had already started of their own accord for Cambrai. The more obstinately the two remaining brigades now defended the suburb of St. Martin, the more ominous for them must prove the result of the action. Attacked in rear by the battalions of Colonel von Boecking, the greater portion were made prisoners. The 41st Regiment alone took prisoners 54 officers and 2260 men, besides capturing 4 guns. General Faidherbe himself only escaped the same fate by the help of the inhabitants.

The action ended at half-past six in the evening, and the troops passed the night in the town and in the captured villages.

The hard-won victory had cost the Germans 96 officers and 2304 men; 3000 wounded Frenchmen were found on the battle-field, and the number of unwounded prisoners exceeded 9000.

According to theory, the pursuit should invariably clinch the victory—a postulate assented to by all, and particularly by civilians; and yet in practice it is seldom observed. Military history furnishes but few instances, such as the famous one of Belle Alliance. It requires a very strong and pitiless will to impose fresh exertions and dangers upon troops who have marched, fought and fasted for ten or twelve hours, in place of the longed-for rest and food. But even given the possession of this will, the question of pursuit will yet depend on the circumstances under which the victory has been won. It will be difficult of execution when all the bodies on the field of battle, as at König-grätz, have become so intermixed that hours are required to re-form them into tactical cohesion; or when, as at St. Quentin, all, even the troops last thrown into the action, have become so entangled that not one single tactically complete body of infantry remains at disposition. Without the support of such a body, cavalry at night will be seriously detained before every obstacle and each petty post of the enemy, and thus alone its exertions will rarely be repaid.[1]

[1] Moltke, although not quite inexperienced in the practical conduct of war on a large scale, would scarcely have ventured to express himself as above, if he had studied the teachings of *The Soldier's Pocket-Book*. The distinguished author of that profound and accurate treatise writes of pursuits in quite a different tone. "You have won a great battle," writes Lord Wolseley, "and the enemy are in full retreat; run after him; hammer him with guns; charge him with cavalry; harass him with mounted infantry; pass round

General von Goeben did not pursue the defeated enemy till the following day. His advanced cavalry ranged up to the suburb of Cambrai and the glacis of Landrecies, without meeting with any resistance, and merely brought in some hundreds of stragglers. The Infantry Divisions followed to within four miles of Cambrai. Against this fortress nothing could be undertaken through want of siege material, and there was no military advantage to be derived in extending further north. Among the news to hand it was reported that a considerable portion of the French Army of the North had retired upon Lille, Douai and Valenciennes. As fresh enterprises on its part were consequently not to be expected, General von Goeben brought his force back to the Somme, where towards the end of the month it took up rest quarters between Amiens and St. Quentin.

On the Lower Seine, the Grand Duke of Mecklenburg entered Rouen with the XIIIth Corps on the 25th, after having encountered on the march only a few franctireurs. Although General Loysel had increased his force to a strength of nearly 30,000 by reinforcements from Cherbourg, he had remained entirely inactive.

General von Goeben had in view the transfer to the Army of the Somme of that portion of the Ist Corps still about Rouen; but this was disapproved of by telegram from the supreme Head-quarter, which on political grounds ordered its continued retention there.

OCCURRENCES IN THE SOUTH-EASTERN SEAT OF WAR UP TO 17TH OF JANUARY.

SIEGE OF BELFORT.—In the south-eastern theatre of war, the forces detailed to operate against Belfort

his flanks, and keep pushing him and hitting him from morning until night. Caution is out of place when you have a beaten army before you. Wellington never delivered any crushing blow, *because he failed to pursue.*"

had been only gradually brought together under cover of the XIVth Army Corps.

The town is surrounded by a bastioned enceinte. The citadel has a wide command, built as it is on lofty rocks, which, to increase the development of fire, are encircled by successive tiers of works in terrace-formation. On the left bank of the Savoureuse, newly constructed lines of defence protected the suburb and railway station. On the high adjacent ridge to the northeast the forts of La Miotte and La Justice, with the enclosing lines connecting them with the main fortress, formed a spacious intrenched camp. Hostile occupation of the lofty eminences of the two Perches (Hautes and Basses) would certainly endanger the whole defensive position, dominating as they did even the citadel from the south at a distance of only 1100 yards, and whence the works on the left bank of the river could be brought under fire. But two forts of masonry had been constructed on the Perches before the advent of the enemy, and further to strengthen the defence the nearest copses and villages, as for instance Pérouse and Danjoutin, had been intrenched.

The fortress was by no means deficient in bomb-proof accommodation. Its armament consisted of 341 heavy guns, and it was provisioned for five months.

When immediately after the opening of the campaign, the VIIth French Corps vacated Alsace, only about 5000 Gardes-Mobiles remained in Belfort, but its garrison, increased by calling in National Guards, now exceeded 17,000.

The vigilant Commandant, Colonel Denfert, laid great stress on the maintenance in force of the environs in his front. The advanced posts were every day assigned to fresh operations, which the artillery of the fortress had to cover at extreme ranges.

On the opposite side, General von Tresckow (commanding 1st Reserve Division) had available at the outset, a force of not more than twenty weak battalions of Landwehr, five squadrons and six field-batteries, in all barely 15,000 men. He had at first to confine himself to a mere investment. The troops, intrenched in the villages round a wide circumference, had to repel many sorties.

Orders were received from the supreme Headquarter to set about the regular siege of the place. General von Mertens was charged with the direction of the engineer operations, and Lieut.-Col. Scheliha with that of the artillery attack. The difficulties of the undertaking were obvious. The rocky nature of the soil could not but increase the labour of throwing up earthworks, and the cold season was approaching. The attack could be carried on successfully only from the south against the main work—the formidable citadel. Only fifty heavy guns were available for the time, and the infantry strength was not sufficient to efficiently invest the place on all sides.

In these circumstances, there devolved on General von Tresckow the task of attempting the reduction of Belfort by a mere bombardment. Towards this purpose the attack was chiefly directed from the west, in which quarter, after the enemy's garrison had been driven out of Valdoye, the infantry occupied Essert and Bavilliers, as well as the adjacent wooded heights. On December 2nd seven batteries were constructed on the plateau between these two villages by 3000 men, under cover of two battalions. The hard-frozen ground added to the difficulties of the work; yet, notwithstanding the moonlight night, the operations would appear to have escaped the attention of the besieged. When on the following morning the sun had dispersed the fog and made visible the objects, fire was opened.

The fortress replied at first but feebly, but afterwards with increasing vigour from the entire line of works, even from Forts La Miotte and La Justice at a range of 4700 yards, and the losses in the trenches were considerable.

Four more batteries in front of Bavilliers were armed, and on the fall of La Tuilerie the infantry pressed on to within 170 yards of the enemy's most advanced trenches. The artillery fire caused a conflagration in the town ; but the ammunition was soon exhausted, whilst the lofty citadel maintained unchecked an effective fire, and repeated sorties on the part of the garrison had to be repelled. It was now clear, since no decisive result had followed the methods hitherto resorted to, that only by a regular attack could that be attained.

On the south Colonel von Ostrowski on December 13th had carried the French positions of Adelnans and the wooded heights of Le Bosmont and La Brosse. On the eastern point of the latter two batteries, and on its northern skirt four additional batteries had been thrown up, not without great difficulty arising from thaw having made the ground a swamp. On January 7th, fifty guns opened fire. The superiority of the artillery of the attack was soon manifest. Fort Bellevue suffered severely, and notably the fire from Basses Perches was entirely silenced.

But it was of grave importance that the village of Danjoutin, strongly garrisoned and intrenched by the enemy, stood in the way of a further advance. During the night of the 8th January seven companies attacked this position, and also from the northward at the same time took possession of the railway-embankment. With empty rifles the Landwehr hurled themselves against the enemy in the face of a hot fire, and charged along the village street up to the church. The supports hastening from the fortress were driven back at the railway-embankment, but the fight about the buildings in the southern quarter of the village lasted till towards noon. Of the defenders, twenty officers and 700 men were taken prisoners.

Typhus and small-pox had broken out in Belfort ; and in the besieging force also the number of the sick reached a considerable figure, caused by arduous work in inclement weather. Most of the battalions could only muster 500 men, and this weakness led General von Tresckow to devote half his force to the lighter duty of protecting the investment from without, principally towards the south.

Trustworthy intelligence estimated the French strength at Besançon at 62,000. Although hitherto entirely inactive, this force now seemed in strong earnest to press on to the relief of the hard-pressed fortress by the line of the Doubs. On this line was the fortified château of Montbéliard, held by one German battalion, and armed with heavy guns. Between the Doubs and the Swiss frontier about Delle stood General Debschitz with eight battalions, two squadrons, and two batteries, and General von Werder concentrated the XIVth Corps at Noroy, Aillevans, and Athésans, to oppose with all his strength any interruption of the siege of Belfort.

From January 5th onwards there ensued a series of engagements in front of Vesoul, as the result of which the enemy advanced from the south and west to within four miles of that town. There could be no doubt that very considerable forces were engaged in this advance. East also of the Ognon, the enemy's posts were advanced beyond Rougemont, although in lesser force. In these actions 500 prisoners were made; and it was at once evident that besides the XVIIIth, the XXIVth and XXth Corps also formed part of Bourbaki's army; a circumstance which threw a sudden light upon a totally changed phase of the war.

TRANSFER OF THE FRENCH ARMY OF THE EAST TO THE SOUTH-EASTERN SEAT OF WAR, END OF DECEMBER.—As had been expected by the supreme Headquarter at Versailles, about the beginning of January an attempt had been made to bring about combined action on the part of Generals Chanzy and Bourbaki. As we have already seen, the advance of the former had been thwarted by Prince Frederick Charles on the Loir, and Bourbaki had actually made preparations for an advance by Montargis to the relief of Paris. But he delayed its execution until the 19th December, when the IInd German Army had already returned to Orleans from its expedition to Le Mans. General Bourbaki had now to realize that the IInd Army would fall on the flank of his projected movement, and he thus the more readily concurred in another plan, devised by the Delegate de Freycinet, and approved of by the Dictator Gambetta.

This was for the XVth Corps to remain about Bourges and to cover that town in intrenched positions about Vierzon and Nevers; the XVIIIth and XXth were to proceed to Beaune by railway, and, when raised to a strength of 70,000 by an union with Garibaldi and Crémer, to occupy Dijòn. The newly-formed XXIVth Corps was also to be moved by railway from Lyons to Besançon, where, with the forces already there, a strength of 50,000 would be attained. In co-operation with the " invincibles of Dijon," it then would be easy to raise the siege of Belfort "without even striking a blow." It was expected that the mere existence of this mass of considerably above 100,000 men would avert any attacks upon the Northern fortresses ; in any case, there was the certainty of severing the enemy's various lines of communication, and the later prospect also of combined action with Faidherbe.

The railway transport of Bourbaki's army from the Loir to the Saône had already commenced by December 23rd. In the absence of all preparations, many interruptions and breaks-down in the traffic naturally occurred, and the troops suffered severely from the intense cold and from being insufficiently cared for. When Chagny and Châlons sur Saône had been reached, and it was ascertained that the Germans had already evacuated Dijon, it was decided to again entrain the troops so as to bring them nearer to Besançon ; whence arose a fresh delay, and it was only in the beginning of the new year that the Army of the East stood in readiness between Dijon and Besançon. The XVth Corps was now also ordered thither, but fourteen days were required for its transportation.

The comprehensive plan of M. Freycinet, and his sanguine expectations, were essentially favoured by the circumstance that the transfer of those great bodies of troops to a remote section of the field of war had remained concealed for a fortnight from the IInd Army, as well as from the XIVth Corps, and consequently from the chief Head-quarter. Rumours and newspaper articles had no doubt given somewhat earlier hints, but General von Werder's telegram of January 5th was the first really authentic announcement by which it was known beyond doubt that the Germans now stood face to face with an entirely altered aspect of the military situation. In Versailles the appropriate dispositions and arrangements were promptly made, and steps taken for the formation of a new Army of the South.

There was available for this purpose the IInd Corps at Montargis, and half of the VIIth under General von Zastrow at Auxerre, which during this period of uncertainty had been constantly moving to and fro between the Saône and Yonne, according as the one or the other quarter appeared to be threatened. The chief command of these two Corps, to which was afterwards added that of the XIVth, was entrusted to General von Manteuffel. General von Werder could not be immediately reinforced, and for a time the XIVth Corps was thrown upon its own resources.

Notwithstanding their superiority of strength, the French did more manœuvring than fighting. General Bourbaki aimed at outflanking the left wing of the XIVth Corps, and thus entirely cutting it off from Belfort. On January 5th the XVIIIth Corps advanced by Grandvelle, and the XXth by Echenoz le Sec, on Vesoul; but, as we have seen, they there met with opposition, and as the XXIVth Corps sent to the right to Esprels learned that Villersexel was occupied by the Germans, Bourbaki determined upon a still more easterly and circuitous route. On the 8th the two Corps of the left wing marched off to the right, the XVIIIth to Montbozon, the XXth to Rougemont; the XXIVth went back to Cuse. At the same time General Crémer received orders to move from Dijon on Vesoul. On the 9th the XXIVth and XXth Corps were at Vellechevreux and Villargent on the Arcey-Villersexel road, while the head of the XVIIIth Corps reached Villersexel and Esprels.

General von Werder had no alternative but to follow this sideward movement in all haste. He ordered the Baden Division to Athésans, the 4th Reserve Division to Aillevans, and Von der Goltz's Brigade to Noroy le Bourg. The trains were put in march to Lure.

ACTION OF VILLERSEXEL, January 9th.—Accordingly at seven in the morning the Reserve Division was sent on from Noroy to Aillevans, and began bridging the Ognon to admit of the continuation of the march. A flanking detachment of the 25th Regiment sent to the right, was fired on near Villersexel, and the attempt to carry the stone bridge at that place failed shortly after. The French with two and a half battalions occupied the town, situated on a height on the further bank of the river. Shortly afterwards reinforcements came up on the German side. Two batteries opened fire upon the place and upon the still advancing bodies of the enemy. The 25th Regiment crossed the river by the suspension bridge and broke into the walled park and into the château. At one o'clock the French were driven out of the town with the loss of many prisoners, and a pause in the fighting ensued.

The Prussian force during the fighting had been seriously threatened on its flank by the advance from Esprels of the 1st Division of the French XVIIIth Corps, with the artillery-reserve. General von der Goltz, however, opposed it by occupying the village of Moimay. He also sent to Villersexel nine companies of the 30th Regiment, to relieve the 25th Regiment there, so as to allow the latter to rejoin its own Division in the further march. His combined brigade was eventually to form the rear-guard of the whole movement.

General von Werder, who observed the considerable force in which the French were advancing on Viller-sexel from the south, concluded that there was less to be gained by forcing his own passage across the Ognon than by opposing that of the French, since the river covered his line of approach to Belfort. He therefore recalled the infantry already issuing to the southward from the town, and withdrew the batteries to the northern side of the river. Here the main body of the 4th Reserve Division took up a defensive posi-tion, and the Baden Division was called in on its march at Arpenans and Lure, as a much-needed rein-forcement to the former.

It was already evening when large columns of the French advanced on Villersexel and shelled the town.

Favoured by the darkness, they penetrated into the park and château, from which the German garrison had already been withdrawn ; and as the general condition of things did not seem to necessitate the occupation of Villersexel, the responsible officers ordered the evacua-tion of the town. Though hard pressed by the enemy, this movement had been nearly completed, when orders arrived from General von Werder to hold the town.

At once four battalions from the Reserve Division advanced to the renewed attack. The 25th Regiment turned about at the bridge over the Ognon and joined them. The Landwehr rushed into the ground floor of the straggling château, but the French defended them-selves in the upper floors and the cellars. On the staircase and in the passages of the already burning buildings there ensued a hot and changeful combat, and the fight was maintained in the streets. Not till the General in command took the matter in hand, and himself ordered it to be broken off, were dispositions made at one o'clock in the morning for a gradual retirement, which was completed by three. The Reserve Division then recrossed the bridge at Aillevans, and occupied St. Sulpice on the right.

General von der Goltz had held Moimay until evening.

Of the XIVth Corps only 15,000 had been engaged, of whom 26 officers and 553 men had fallen. The French losses amounted to 27 officers and 627 men; and they also left behind in the, hands of the Germans 700 unwounded prisoners. The French troops which chiefly took part in the operations were the XVIIIth and XXth Corps; the XXIVth Corps, on account of the fighting in its rear, had suspended its march to Arcey through Sevenans. Detachments of the gradually incoming XVth Corps advanced from southward in the direction of Belfort.

On the morning of January 10th, General von Werder massed his Corps in the vicinity of Aillevans, ready to engage the enemy should the latter attempt an advance through Villersexel. But no attack was made, and so the march could be resumed that same morning. As a matter of fact, the French with three Corps were as near to Belfort as the Germans were with three Divisions. To cover the departure the Reserve Division took up a position at Athésans, and on the following day all the forces reached and occupied the line of the Lisaine. On the right wing about Frahier and Chalonvillars stood the Baden Division; in the centre, the Reserve Brigade between Chagey and Couthenans; on the left, the Reserve Division at Héricourt and Tavey. On the south, General von Debschitz stood in observation at Delle, and Colonel von Bredow at Arcey; towards the west Colonel von Willisen was at

Lure with the detachment of eight companies, thirteen squadrons, two batteries, which had come up from Vesoul.

General von Werder had in fact, succeeded in interposing his force between the enemy and Belfort.

The French commander, under the intoxicating impression of a victory, had resigned himself to inactivity. "General Billot," he reported to the Government at Bordeaux, "has occupied Esprels and maintains himself there." We know that he was never attacked there at all, and that he did not succeed in driving away General von der Goltz from the vicinity of Moimay. "General Clinchant has carried Villersexel with extraordinary dash;" but the fight of the 9th was, as regards the Germans, maintained with only a portion of the XIVth Corps, to cover the right flank of the main body on its march. Whilst, then, this movement of the latter was prosecuted with the utmost energy, the French army remained passive for two days, ready for action and in the confident expectation that the enemy described as beaten, would come on again to fight for the supremacy. Not until the 13th did the XXIVth Corps advance on Arcey, the XXth on Saulnot, and the XVIIIth follow to Sevenans. The XVth was to support an attack on Arcey by way of Ste. Marie.

General von Werder had utilized this interval, while the troops were hastening forward, in ascertaining the eligibility of the Lisaine position and in a consultation with General von Tresckow in rear of it.

A detailed inspection showed that at Frahier the Lisaine, there but an unimportant streamlet, flows through a broad grassy hollow, and thence to Chagey through steep wooded slopes. About Héricourt the valley opens out into a wide plain, which is however commanded by the rocky heights of Mont Vaudois. Lower down the wooded heights line the river as far as Montbéliard, which with the Allaine brook forms a strong point of support and the extremity of the line.

The wooded character of the plain west of the Lisaine would necessarily increase the assailants' difficulties in the deployment of large infantry masses and a strong artillery line. It is true that during the prevailing severe cold the river was everywhere frozen over; but only two high-roads led through the forest into the valley from the direction by which the French army was advancing, one to Montbéliard, the other to Héricourt. The other accesses were narrow, hollow roads rendered difficult of use by frost.

General von Tresckow had already armed the most important points with siege guns, the castle of Montbéliard with six, and the neighbouring height of La Grange Dame with five heavy cannon. Seven were placed on Mont Vaudois and near Héricourt; besides these, twenty-one others commanded the valley of the Allaine southward as far as Delle.

All the troops that could be spared from the investing force were also withdrawn from before Belfort. Still there remained the important consideration that the available forces might not suffice to entirely cover the whole of the Lisaine line. The right wing was the locally weakest portion of the whole position, but here there was the least to be apprehended, the enemy's main attack, since the many needs of the numerous but inadequately equipped French army made the nearest possible vicinity of one of the railroads a necessity. The Vesoul line by way of Lure was broken in many places, and the Besançon line led towards the strong left wing. The country north of Chagey might therefore more weakly be held, and a reserve was formed of the largest part of the Baden Division, which was distributed in rear of the centre and left about Mandrevillars, Brévilliers and Charmont.

The respite accorded by the enemy was turned to account with the utmost zeal in the construction of rifle-pits and of battery emplacements, the establishment of telegraph and relay lines, the improvement of roads and the replenishment of supplies and ammunition.

January 13*th*.—On the morning of the 13th the advanced posts of the 3rd Reserve Division were now attacked at Arcey, Ste. Marie and Gonvillars. They were instructed to withdraw before a superior force, but to hold their own long enough to compel the deployment of the hostile columns. The combat with French artillery coming up at wide intervals was therefore prolonged for a considerable time; then, after a three hours' resistance, a new position was taken up behind the Rupt brook, and the retirement on Tavey delayed until four in the afternoon. The advanced guard of General von der Goltz, after a whole brigade had deployed against it, also took up a position at Chavanni on a parallel front with that at Couthenans.

Before the Allaine front the French did not succeed in driving General von Debschitz's advanced posts out of Dasle and Croix.

January 14*th*.—On the 14th General von Willisen with fifty dismounted Dragoons drove back the enemy advancing on Lure, and then retired with his detachment on Ronchamp.

The French army did not yet on this day undertake a serious attack. It stood with the XVth, XXIVth, and XXth Corps, closely concentrated opposite the German left and centre at a distance of scarcely four-and-a-half miles. The German right was supposed by General Bourbaki to rest upon Mont Vaudois. His plan was to cross the Lisaine in force above this point of support, and by thus turning the hostile flank to facilitate a frontal attack. The XVIIIth Army Corps and the Division Crémer were assigned to this service. A drawback to this judicious arrangement was, that the two above-mentioned bodies designed by the officer in supreme command to open the fight on the 14th, would have the longest distance to march to their task.   On this day the leading troops of the XVIIIth Army Corps barely succeeded in reaching the vicinity of Lomont through difficult hill and woodland region, and Crémer's Brigade[1] had only then begun to advance from Vesoul.   A postponement to the 15th was thereupon determined.

On the German side, a general attack by the greatly superior enemy was hourly expected, and General von Werder felt himself bound to send by telegraph to Versailles a representation of the extreme seriousness of his position.   The rivers, being frozen over, were passable, and the duty of covering Belfort deprived him of freedom of movement and endangered the existence of his corps.   He earnestly prayed that the question should be weighed, whether the investment of Belfort should continue to be maintained.

In the supreme Head-quarter it was considered that any further retirement of the XVth[2] Army Corps would have the immediate effect of raising the siege of Belfort, and causing the loss of the considerable material which had been provided therefor; that it was impossible to foresee where such further retirement would end; and that it could but delay the co-operation of the army advancing by forced marches under General von Manteuffel.   At three o'clock on the afternoon of 15th January a positive order was despatched to General von Werder to accept battle in front of Belfort.   He was, as was only fair, relieved of the moral responsibility of the consequences of a possibly disastrous issue. But before this order reached him, the General had already come to the same resolution.

---

[1] Slip of the pen for "Division."
[2] So in text; a slip of the pen, or printer's error, for the XIVth Corps, which von Werder commanded.   There was no XVth Corps in 1871.

BATTLE ON THE LISAINE.

(January 15th to 17th.)

January 15*th.*—On the morning of the 15th of January, two Divisions of the French XVth Corps, strengthened by artillery, advanced on Montbéliard; a third followed in reserve. The East-Prussian Land- wehr battalions, which had pushed forward to the Mont Chevis Farm and Ste. Suzanne, held their position for a long time, advanced on their part to the attack, and drove the heads of the enemy's columns back upon the Rupt brook. But when the latter in the afternoon deployed in greater force along the edge of the wood, the Landwehr advanced posts were at two o'clock ordered back to the left bank of the Lisaine. The town of Montbéliard, entirely commanded by the surrounding heights, was also voluntarily evacuated, only its fortified castle being held. But east of Montbéliard General von Glümer with the 1st Baden Brigade had taken up a posi- tion, and had brought up four field-batteries alongside the siege guns on the plateau of La Grange Dame.

Towards the close of the day the French, after a continuous but ineffective bombardment from eight batteries, took possession of the town, but did not make any further advance.

Neither had they prospered in their attempt to cross the Lisaine at Béthoncourt. An officer and sixty men, who had sought cover within a walled graveyard from the sharp fire of the defenders, were taken prisoners.

Further to the north the French XXIVth Corps continued to advance, but it was two o'clock before its columns were able to deploy from the wood. Four battalions did, indeed, succeed in taking possession of the village of Bussurel on the western bank of the Lisaine, but their further advance was frustrated by the fire of the defenders in cover behind the railway embankment, and by that of the Baden battalions and batteries brought up from the main reserve.

Héricourt, on the great high road from Besançon and only little more than four miles from Belfort, became a point of special importance in the German fighting line. Here in front of the Lisaine the right wing of the 4th Reserve Division struck the enemy.

The little wooded knoll of Mougnot, which forms a sort of bridge-head to the narrow gorge through which the road passes, had been fortified by the pioneers with abatis, battery emplacements and rifle-pits, the town in its rear prepared for defence, and the base of the heights on either of its sides faced with artillery. Four East-Prussian Landwehr battalions were in touch on the right with the Reserve Brigade, which held the slope of Mont Vaudois as far as Luze.

About ten o'clock the French deployed their artillery on the bare heights close to the line of approach in the vicinity of Trémoins. Upon their infantry advancing leftwards through Byans, the German detachment which till then had been left in Tavey fell back on Héricourt in reserve, and the enemy's first attack on Mougnot was shattered by the resistance of its defenders, and by the fire of sixty-one guns on the further bank of the river. The attempt was not repeated that day, and the French confined themselves to a heavy but ineffective cannonade.

According to the instructions issued by General Bourbaki, the XXth Corps was to await the result of the great outflanking movement which was to be carried out by General Billot with the XVIIIth Corps and Crémer's Division. As, however, these had not yet put in an appearance, the Army-Reserve had to be brought up leftward to Coisevaux to protect General Clinchant's flank.

The orders from the Army Head-quarter had not reached the XVIIIth Corps until midnight. It had moreover to accomplish a difficult march by deeply snowed-up woodland paths. This entailed crossings, not only between the flank columns of its 1st and 3rd Divisions, but even with the Division Crémer at Lyoffans. This Division had only by dint of the greatest exertion reached Lure during the night, and could not get further on to Béverne until nine in the morning. A fresh delay was occasioned by the order to bring up in front of the infantry the artillery—even the reserve artillery which was marching in the very rear ; and thus it happened that the XVIIIth Corps did not succeed in deploying two of its Divisions opposite Luze and Chagey till between 12 and 2 in the afternoon.

The 1st Division occupied Couthenans with one battalion, and brought up five batteries on the reverse slope of the heights to the north of that place. But the fire from the opposite bank prevented their further progress, and in a short time several of the batteries had but two guns left fit for action, although the Germans, in view of the difficulty of replenishment, used their ammunition as sparingly as possible. At three o'clock there was a pause in the artillery fight, which however was resumed energetically on the arrival of reinforcements, when the artillery of the XXIVth Corps coming from Byans took part in it. An infantry attack on a large scale was not yet attempted.

There was scarcely more vigour in the advance of the 3rd Division against Chagey, which was occupied only by a Baden battalion ; yet it was from here that the outflanking movement of the German right wing by turning Mont Vaudois was to be gone upon. The wood reached to the first houses of the village, and the only difficulty was the climb up the steep face of the height. Two French battalions suddenly burst from the gorge south of it, and drove in the Baden outposts ; the further attack was to have been supported from Couthenans on the south, but the infantry advancing from thence found itself forced to turn back by the fire from the opposite bank. Only by a renewed effort did the Zouaves succeed in entering Chagey, where a stubborn fight raged in and around the houses. Meanwhile two Baden battalions came up, who, at five o'clock, drove the enemy out of the village back into the wood. Fresh reinforcements hastened to the support of the latter from the reserve near by, the short winter's day was over, and here during the night the French attempted nothing further. The 2nd Division of the French Corps had only advanced as far as Béverne, the cavalry had not moved from Lyoffans.

The Division Crémer, despite its late arrival at Lure, had continued the march in the early morning. After the above-mentioned crossings and resultant delays the 1st Brigade advanced on Étobon, and there at noon it engaged in a fight with a Baden detachment under the command of General von Degenfeld. When the 2nd Brigade also came up, the 1st moved forward through the Bois de la Thure, with intent to cross the Lisaine above Chagey. Parts of the roads had first to be made practicable by the pioneers, involving considerable delay. The 2nd Brigade then followed in the dark, having left a detachment in observation at Étobon. A fresh collision with some Baden detachments determined General Crémer to extinguish all the watch-fires. His troops remained under arms throughout the hard winter night.

On the German side, all the troops not on guard duty found shelter in the neighbouring villages, the pioneers only being kept at work with their pickaxes. The actions had cost both sides about 600 men, without bringing about any decisive result; but every day was a gain to the defenders.

General Von Werder, on the heights north of Héricourt, had received constant reports regarding the course of the fighting from the General Staff officers sent out in various directions, by which he was able to regulate the abstraction from the reserves of reinforcements to the fighting line. The diminution of the ammunition was a cause of anxiety, since a consignment announced from Baden had not yet arrived.

General Bourbaki informed his Government that he had taken Montbéliard, it was true without the castle, had occupied the villages on the west bank of the Lisaine, and that he would attack on the 16th. He had learned from General Billot that the German right wing extended considerably beyond Mont Vaudois, whence he inferred that important reinforcements had reached the enemy, whose strength he estimated at 80,000 to 100,000 men. Nevertheless he anticipated a fortunate issue for the outflanking operation by fetching a yet wider compass to the left.

January 16th.—At half-past six on the morning of the 16th the Germans again stood to arms in the positions of the previous day.

The French again began the attack with their right wing. From the loopholed houses they fired on the Landwehr company holding the castle of Montbéliard, causing some loss among the latter as well as among the gunners. The summons to surrender was disregarded, and the fire of the fortress artillery was used to such good purpose against two batteries which showed themselves on the neighbouring height, that these were obliged to retire, leaving behind them two guns. Neither could they advance from a new position they had taken up at the farm of Mont Chevis, and where they had been reinforced by three batteries, against the fire from La Grange Dame, although the cannonade continued until dark. No attempt was made from Montbéliard to pierce the German line.

Further to the left the reinforced 1st Division of the French XVth Corps advanced on Béthoncourt. At one o'clock the fire of its artillery from Mont Chevis and Byans obliged a Baden battery to limber up, and it was then directed on the village. Large bodies had been massed in the neighbouring forest, from out which at three o'clock they advanced. General

Glümer had meantime despatched reinforcements tc the threatened front. Two determined attempts pushed close up to the village were frustrated by the destructive artillery and rifle fire of the defenders. A third attack made with a whole brigade at four o'clock, was not permitted even to approach. The losses on the French side were considerable, and the snowy field was strewn with the fallen. Some unwounded prisoners were also taken.

One Division of the XXIVth French Corps had taken up a covered position in the woods behind Byans, and as it had already occupied Bussurel on the previous day, the German defensive position here in the rear of the railway embankment appeared to be threatened from the immediate vicinity. The General in command therefore sent General Keller with two Baden Fusilier battalions and one heavy battery from Brévilliers in this direction. The latter joined the two batteries which had been engaged on the slope of the hill since morning. The fire of five of the enemy's batteries was soon silenced by the unerring projectiles from the German guns. At noon the French artillery retired from Byans, leaving there also two guns, which could only be brought away later. The infantry, one Division strong, had only threatened to pierce the line, without proceeding to carry out the attempt.

The XXth Corps brought up two Divisions against the line Héricourt—Luze. A thick fog covered the valley, and the early cannonade was at first scarcely answered by the Germans. To obtain some insight into the intentions of the enemy, two companies advanced to the height west of St. Valbert, and surprised the enemy moving up from Byans with so rapid a fire that he turned back. But soon after, at half-past nine, several battalions burst out from Tavey against the Mougnot. Two attacks were frustrated by the steady resistance of the Landwehr battalions, and a third attempt directed against the southern exit from Héricourt did not succeed. About four o'clock fresh masses of infantry again gathered against the Mougnot, but coming under fire from Mont Salamou, they shrank from further attacks, and confined themselves till evening to an ineffective cannonade.

At Chagey two Divisions of the XVIIIth Corps found themselves face to face with the Germans. They did not attempt anything.

The little spirit with which on January 16th the action along the whole front from Montbéliard to Chagey was conducted, pointed to the conclusion that the French were everywhere awaiting the issue of the scheme of out-flanking the German right wing.

This task now devolved on General Crémer. The 2nd Division of the XVIIIth Corps joined him at Etobon.

Two Divisions advanced thence on Chenebier, where General von Degenfeld stood with two battalions, two batteries, and one squadron. There could be no doubt as to the result. At eleven o'clock the Division Penhoat of the XVIIIth Corps advanced to encompass the place on the west and north, and the Division Crémer, for the purpose of barring the defenders' line of retreat on Belfort, advanced on the south, where the wood of La Thure covered his approach. The batteries of both Divisions were brought up in the afternoon on its northern edge, where they opened fire. After they had been in action for two hours, the infantry masses advanced from three sides. Under General Crémer's personal leading the Baden Fusiliers were driven from the southern to the northern part of the village, and as his encompassment therein through the wood of Montedin was practicable, General von Degenfeld, after an obstinate resistance, at three o'clock was obliged to take up his retreat in a northerly direction through Frahier. Thence he again turned south-east and took up a position in front of Chalonvillars, about the high-lying windmill of Rougeot, where, at six o'clock, he was joined by Colonel Bayer with reinforcements. The French did not pursue ; the Division Crémer, which had lost 1000 men, retired, on the contrary, into the wood of La Thure, while Penhoat's Division confined itself to the occupation of Chenebier.

Thus the German line of defence was nowhere broken on this day ; still, its extreme right wing had been driven back to within little more than three miles of Belfort.

The fortress celebrated the success of the French arms by a victory-salute, but made no serious sortie on the investing forces, weakened as they were by the despatch of reinforcements ; and the latter, on their side, quietly continued the construction of batteries.

General von Werder, anxious above all things to re-establish the fighting position on his right wing, could however only gather in as a general reserve four battalions, four squadrons, and two batteries, bringing up these from the least exposed places and even from Belfort, to Brévilliers and Mandrevillars. At eight o'clock in the evening General Keller was ordered to retake Chenebier. On this errand he left Mandrevillars with two Baden battalions, reached Moulin Rougeot at midnight, and found Frahier already occupied by Colonel Bayer.

January 17th.—On this morning eight battalions, two squadrons, and four batteries were assembled in Frahier. Three of the battalions advanced on the northern, three on the southern part of Chenebier ; the others remained in reserve at the windmill, where also three 15 cm. cannon were to be stationed.

At half-past four a.m. the first column, advancing in dead silence, surprised an outpost of the enemy's at Echevanne, but it was unavoidable that its rifle fire should make the French in Chenebier aware of the danger by which they were menaced. In the wood north of the village, the Germans met with serious resistance ; and the danger that in the darkness and the dense undergrowth the troops might fall on each other obliged their withdrawal to the outer edge of the wood.

The other column, advancing in the valley of the Lisaine, had quickened its pace from Moulin Colin as soon as the first shots were heard. The 2nd battalion of the 4th Baden Regiment rushed with cheers into the southern part of Chenebier, where a great confusion ensued. But daybreak showed that the heights on the west of the village were strongly occupied, and that columns of all arms were approach-from Etobon. At 8.30 Colonel Payen had to resolve on retirement from the half-conquered village, carrying with him 400 prisoners, and on taking up a position at the Bois de Féry, to cover the road to Belfort through Chalonvillars.

At the same time the right column, strengthened by a battalion from the reserve, renewed the attack on the wood, and after a struggle which lasted for two hours with heavy losses on both sides, at last took possession of it. But the attempt to penetrate into the barricaded and strongly-defended village was vain. A destructive fire met every attack; a single round of mitrailleuse fire, for instance, struck down twenty-one men of the Baden assailants. At three o'clock in the afternoon General Keller therefore assembled his troops at Frahier, where they were supported by four batteries.

With such inferior strength, and after failing in this attempt, it was useless to think of driving back the enemy beyond Chenebier; the only course to pursue was to hinder his further advance on Belfort. And this object was fully accomplished; the French did not pursue. Instead of out-flanking the German right, they seemed chiefly concerned for their own left. They defended Chenebier stoutly, but gave up all further offensive movements.

While awaiting the expected success of the out-flanking movement, General Bourbaki's intention seems to have been merely to occupy the enemy along his front and to hold him fast where he stood. Even during the night the Germans were alarmed at Béthoncourt and before Héricourt, while they, on their part, disturbed the French at Bussurel and in the Bois de La Thure. The infantry fire went on for hours, and numerous detachments had to spend the bitter winter's night under arms. In the morning two Divisions of the XVIIIth French Corps advanced on Chagey and Luze, but their batteries, although supported by the artillery of the Army Reserve, they could not advance against those of the Germans, and repeated attacks on those villages were unsuccessful. After one o'clock a cannonade only was maintained here. In front of Héricourt also there was an exchange of shell fire, and Bussurel, held by the French, was set on fire.

To drive the French out of Montbéliard, the town was fired on from La Grange Dame and from the Château, but ceased when the inhabitants begged forbearance on the assurance that the place was evacuated, which subsequently proved not quite true. Ten battalions of the French XVth Corps advanced from the woods in the forenoon, and tried to push on past Montbéliard, but suffered severely from the flanking fire of the heavy guns at La Grange Dame, and only a handful got into the valley of the Lisaine. The western exits from Montbéliard, and the heights immediately behind it, remained in French possession, but the offensive movements ceased at about two in the afternoon.

Further to the south, General von Debschitz's posts in front of Allaine had easily repulsed the French assailants.

On the German side there was now the conviction that no further attack would be attempted.

The condition of the French troops, not yet inured to war, was, in fact, very critical. They had been obliged to bivouac in the bitterly cold nights, sometimes under arms, and for the most part without food. Their losses

were not inconsiderable, and the superior officers whom
the commanding General assembled at three in the afternoon, in the neighbourhood of Chagey, expressed their
objections to a yet more extensive outflanking attempt
to the left, since supplies would be utterly impossible,
and the risk would be entailed of the Germans seizing
the line of the communications of the army through
Montbéliard. Then came the news that the heads of
General von Manteuffel's Corps had already reached
Fontaine-Française, and were also approaching Gray.

In these circumstances General Bourbaki considered he must resolve on a retreat. He telegraphed
to the Government that by the advice of his generals,
and to his deep regret, he had been compelled to take
up a position further in the rear, and only hoped that
the enemy might follow him. Hence this experienced
general could have felt no doubt that his army, its
attack on the Lisaine, once gone to wreck, could
only escape from a very critical position by an immediate retreat.

January 18*th.*—This morning the Germans were
under arms in their positions of the previous day, the
French still in full force before the whole front. It
was significant that they were busy in the construction
of earthworks. They had evacuated Montbéliard the
evening before in disorderly retreat, and now held
the country west of the place in strength and
entrenched.

During this day nothing occurred but a cannonade
and small skirmishes. General Keller having been
reinforced came up on the right, and as the enemy
retired to Etobon he was able to re-occupy Chenebier
in the afternoon. Further north, Colonel von Willisen again marched on Ronchamp. In the centre
Coutenans was taken possession of, and the enemy
driven out of Byans by artillery fire; but on the
other hand the Germans could not yet penetrate the
belt of forest. On the southern bank of the Allaine

General von Debschitz's detachments drove the enemy back beyond the line Exincourt-Croix.

In the three days' fighting on the Lisaine the Germans lost 1200, the French from 4000 to 5000 men.

In spite of much necessary detaching, and of the threatening proximity of the enemy, the siege-works against Belfort were uninterruptedly carried on, and as soon as the complement of the investing forces was again made up, General von Werder followed the retiring French to Etobon, Saulnot and Arcey.

THE ARTILLERY ATTACK ON PARIS.

(January, 1871.)

In the place of the IInd Corps, which had been assigned to the German Army of the South, there had come up into the Paris front the Ist Bavarian Corps, of which Gambetta had said, "The Bavarians no longer exist." It had made so good use of its time of rest in quarters south of Longjumeau that by the beginning of the New Year it was already restored to a strength of 17,500 men, with 108 guns. It was positioned on both banks of the Seine between the VIth Prussian Corps and the Würtemberg Division. The Würtembergers reached from Ormesson to the Marne, from which river the Saxons extended rightward to the Sausset brook, so as to narrow the front of the Guard Corps now that the Morée was frozen over and afforded no cover.

The duty of watching so vast a place of arms as Paris had made great demands on the endurance of the troops.

The French had gradually so extended their entrenchments outwards from Villejuif and Bruyères, that they threatened to outflank the IInd Bavarian Corps. To thwart such a flank attack the VIth Corps was obliged to keep a strong force constantly in readiness at L'Hay.

It need not be said that the supporting troops on the south front could nowhere be safe from the fire of the heavy fortress guns, nor the foreposts from that of the Chassepôts. The latter consequently often could not be relieved for several days, and the relief was usually effected at night. The less the success of the French arms in the open field, the more lavish were they in the expenditure of ammunition from their works. Mont Valérien hurled its giant shells to a distance of from four to five miles, but this incessant cannonade, to the din of which the ear was soon accustomed, did little damage.

THE ARTILLERY ATTACK ON THE SOUTHERN FRONT. —Till Mont Avron was taken, the Germans had only been able to oppose field guns to French fortress artillery. But early in January their preparations were at last so far forward that seventeen batteries, long since completed, could be armed with heavy guns against the south front of Paris. A battery stood apart on the left flank in the park of St. Cloud to the north of Sèvres; four were close together on the steep slope of the height west of the Château Meudon; five on the edge of the plateau of Moulin de la Tour, where the mill, serving to guide the aim of the enemy, had been blown up. Four more batteries occupied a lower position between Fontenay and Bagneux. Two, between Chevilly and La Rue, served as protection against a flank movement from Villejuif, with the field artillery of the IInd Bavarian and VIth Corps. Dressing-stations were prepared, and intermediate depôts were supplied with reserve ammunition from the great magazines at Villacoublay.

Under Generals von Kameke [1] and Prince Hohenlohe [2]

---

[1] Previously commanding the XIVth Infantry Division.
[2] Previously commanding the artillery of the Guard Corps, the well-

Colonels von Rieff and von Ramm conducted the artillery attack, General Schulz commanded the engineer . attack. The men served twenty-four hours in the batteries, and then had two days' rest. The officers had but one day's rest.

The heavy guns were brought up on January 3rd, by day, into the batteries which lay covered, without any interference ; into all the others during the night, after the enemy's outposts had been driven in. Thus on the morning of the 4th 98 guns were ready to open fire: of these 28 were directed on Issy, 28 on Vanves, and 18 on Montrouge, 10 against the emplacements between the first two forts. But a thick fog hid every object, and it was not till January 5th at 8.30 in the morning, that the signal shot was given for opening fire.

January 5th.—The enemy promptly replied. There were in Fort Valérien 106 guns, in Issy 90, in Vannes 84, and in Montrouge 52; there were about 70 in the sectors of the enceinte concerned and at Villejuif, 16-cm. guns for the most part ; so the attack at first was heavily taxed. But when at about noon all its batteries came into action, the situation gradually improved and the greater accuracy of the German fire . told. Fort Issy had almost entirely ceased firing by two o'clock, nine guns were dismounted in Vanves, and its garrison had lost thirty men ; only Montrouge still replied with vigour. The fire was now taken up by the guns of the enceinte, but the forts never again gained

known military author, best known in England as "Prince Kraft." The slight ambiguity in the text may be removed by the more specific statement that General von Kameke was Chief Director of the Engineer attack, Prince Kraft Chief Director of the Artillery attack on Paris as a whole. On the south front Colonel von Rieff commanded the siege artillery, Major-General Schulz was Engineer-in-chief. On the north and east fronts within the Army of the Meuse Colonels Bartsch and Oppermann had the corresponding commands. Colonel von Ramm is nowhere mentioned in the official distribution of the respective staffs.

the upper hand of the attack. Some gunboats appearing about Point du Jour very soon had to retire. The field artillery of the IInd Bavarian and VIth Corps also co-operated so energetically that no attack was attempted from the works at Villejuif, nor was a single shot fired on the batteries at Bagneux. A number of wall-pieces and long-range Chassepôts taken from the enemy did such good service that the French abandoned more and more of their rayon. The German outposts took possession of the trenches of Clamart, and in the course of the night reversed them against the defence.

Only a couple of 15-cm. shells were thrown into the city itself as a serious warning ; the first thing to be done was to batter down the outworks, and for some few days the firing was exclusively directed on these. A stubborn return fire came from Montrouge and from a mortar-battery in a very advantageous position behind the high railway embankment to the east of Issy ; and especially from the south front of the enceinte, nearly four and a half miles long in a straight line. Foggy weather on some days necessitated the suspension or entire cessation of firing. But meanwhile the foreposts had advanced to within 815 and 490 yards of Forts Issy and Vanves respectively. New batteries were constructed further forward, and armed with thirty-six guns from those evacuated in rear.

January 10th.—The French garrison meanwhile was again displaying great activity. On January 10th it succeeded in the dark hours in surprising the weakly-held post of Clamart. Three battalions were now posted in the place, and a shelter-trench some 1300 yards long was dug connecting Clamart with Châtillon.[1]

---

[1] A casual reader might perhaps infer from these curt sentences, that the French, having possessed themselves by surprise of the weak German post of Clamart, placed in it a garrison of three battalions. The facts were, that the French battalion was

January 13*th.*—The IInd Army of Paris was still outside the city on the east and north fronts from Nogent to Aubervillers. After some small alarms, on the evening of the 13th strong bodies advanced from Courneuve and Drancy against Le Bourget under cover of a heavy fire from the forts. But the troops in occupation there were on the alert, and being soon reinforced by several companies, repulsed the attempts of the French to storm it, repeated as they were until two o'clock in the morning.

January 14*th.*—On this day the French made a renewed sortie on Clamart with 500 marine infantry and several battalions of National Guards. These last assembled at the adjacent railway-station with a great deal of noise, and their approach was reported about midnight. The fight lasted a full hour, and ended with the retreat, or rather flight, of the assailants. Patrols followed them close up to the trenches of Issy.

The ranges were so great that hitherto the fire from the enceinte was not yet subdued. Battery No. 1, lying isolated in the Park of St. Cloud, suffered most, being fired upon from two bastions of the enceinte, from Point du Jour, and from Mont Valérien. The steep cliff behind the battery facilitated the aim of the enemy. Its parapet was repeatedly shattered, and it was only the most zealous devotion which enabled the struggle to be continued at this point. The enemy also concentrated a heavy fire on batteries Nos. 19 and 21, pushed forward into a position specially threatening to Fort Vanves. The long-range fire from the

scarcely in possession of Clamart when it abandoned village and redoubt; whereupon, to guard against any future attempt on the place on the part of the French, the Germans occupied the village with three battalions and the redoubt with two companies; and further to ensure the security of the position, since it was one of some importance, connected it with Châtillon in the manner described.

A a

enceinte dropped from a high angle close behind the
parapet, breaking through the platforms, and inflicting
serious injuries on a great many gunners. The powder-
magazines blew up in two of the batteries, and both
the battery commanders and several other superior
officers were wounded.

On the east front of Paris, the fifty-eight German
guns remaining there after the reduction of Mont
Avron were opposed by 151 of the enemy. The
former nevertheless soon proved their superiority; the
forts only occasionally came into action; the
French withdrew their outposts up to the works, and
altogether vacated the peninsula of St. Maur. By
degrees the heavy siege-guns could be removed from
their previous positions to the Morée brook.

The forts on the south front had meanwhile suffered
severely. The ruin in Issy was visible to the naked
eye; fires broke out there repeatedly, and the powder-
magazine had to be cleared out at great risk in the
night of January 16th. Fort Vanves had lost seventy
men; it opened fire usually every morning, but soon
became silent. Montrouge, on the contrary, on some
days still fired over 500 rounds from eighteen guns.
But here, too, the casemates no longer afforded
any shelter, and one of the bastions lay a heap of
ruins.

In spite of the steady fire from the enceinte, a
part of Paris itself was disturbed by the 15-cm. shells.
An elevation of 30 degrees, obtained by a special con-
trivance, sent the projectiles into the heart of the city.
From 300 to 400 shells were fired daily.

Under the pressure of "public opinion" the Government, after repeated deliberations, decided once more
on a new enterprise in force, to be directed this time
against the German batteries about Châtillon. The collective superior commanders agreed, indeed, that sorties
could promise no success without the co-operation of
a relieving army from the outside; but, on the 8th,

Gambetta had announced the " victory " of the Army of the North at Bapaume, and further had promised that both the Armies of the Loire should advance. Hereupon General Trochu advised that at least the moment should be awaited when the investing army before Paris should be weakened by having to detach anew part of its strength ; but he was opposed by the other members of the Government, especially by Monsieur Jules Favre. That gentleman declared that the Maires of Paris were indignant at the bombardment, that the representatives of the city must be allowed some insight into the military situation, and, above all, that negotiations ought long since to have been entered into.

Finally, on January 15th, it was determined that the German lines should be broken through at Montretout, Garches, and Buzanval.

While confusion and dissensions thus prevailed in Paris, the unity of the German nation, under the Emperor William, was solemnly proclaimed at Versailles.

BATTLE OF MONT VALÉRIEN.

(January 19th.)

The sortie was planned to take place on January 19th. On that day, as we have seen, General Faidherbe advanced as far as St. Quentin on the way to Paris, and the army which was to make the sortie stood on the eastern and northern fronts of the capital. The attempt to break through was, however, made in the opposite direction. But in fact, the peninsula of Gennevilliers was now the only ground on which large masses of troops could still be deployed without being exposed for hours while they were being assembled, to the fire of the German artillery.

A a 2

Two days previously the mobilized National Guards had already relieved the three Divisions of the sortie-Army from the positions they had held; and those Divisions, collectively 90,000 strong, were to move to the attack in three columns simultaneously. General Vinoy on the left, supported by the fire from the enceinte, was to carry the height of Montretout; General Bellemare in the centre was to push forward through Garches; General Ducrot on the right by way of the Château of Buzanval.

The attack was set to begin at six in the morning, but blocks occurred at the bridges of Asnières and Neuilly, as no specific orders had been issued for regulating the crossing. When at seven o'clock the signal to advance was made from Mont Valérien, only the advance of General Vinoy's force was ready, the other columns had not yet deployed, and the last detachments tailed back as far as Courbevoix. Before they had reached their rendezvous-points the left wing was already marching on St. Cloud with fifteen battalions.

These at first met only isolated posts and patrols, eighty-nine men in all, who rushed into the open gorge of the redoubt of Montretout, and there made a stand for some time; they then fought their way out with great bravery, but some of them were taken prisoners. There, and in the northern part of St. Cloud, the French promptly prepared for defence.

The centre column under General Bellemare also took possession without difficulty of the height of Maison du Curé.

Not till now, at nearly nine o'clock, did the first supports of the German forepost line appear on the scene. Till within a short time the observatories had been able to report nothing but "thick fog;" but reports from the right and left wings announced that a serious attack was threatened on the whole front from St. Cloud to Bougival. The Vth Corps was now alarmed, and General von Kirchbach betook himself to the 9th

Division. On the German right, in the park of St. Cloud, stood the 17th Brigade ; on the left, behind the Porte de Longboyau, the 20th ; the other troops of the Corps marched from their quarters in Versailles and the villages to its north, to Jardy and Beauregard. The Crown Prince ordered six battalions of the Guard Landwehr and a Bavarian Brigade to Versailles, and himself rode to the Hospice of Brezin ; the King went to Marly.

The French meanwhile had seized the foremost houses of Garches, and made their eastward way here and there through the breaches in the wall into the park of the Château of Buzanval. The 5th Jäger Battalion, supported by single companies of the 58th and 59th Regiments, hurried forward and drove the enemy back out of Garches, occupied the cemetery on its north, and still reached the advanced post of La Bergerie just at the right time. The other bodies under General von Bothmer (commanding 17th Brigade, 9th Division, Vth Corps), by order from the commanding General, maintained a stationary fight on the skirts of the park of St. Cloud, to gain time. About half-past nine they repulsed an attack by Bellemare's column, arrested the advance of the enemy along the Rue Impériale of St. Cloud, and themselves took the offensive from the Grille d'Orleans and the Porte Jaune. Five French battalions unsuccessfully assaulted La Bergerie. A section of Engineers tried with great devotion to demolish the wall surrounding the court, but the frozen dynamite did not explode, and the Jägers held the position steadfastly throughout the day.

The attacks of the French had hitherto been undertaken without assistance from their artillery. The batteries of General Vinoy's advance had been seriously delayed by crossing with the centre column, and were now detained at Briqueterie to meet the contingency of a repulse. General Bellemare's batteries tried to get up the slope of the height of Garches, but the exhaustion of the teams made it necessary to take up a position at Fouilleuse. Meanwhile the batteries of the German 9th Division came up by degrees, and by noon thirty-six guns had opened fire. In St. Cloud a hot street-fight was going on.

Only General Ducrot on the French right wing had opened the battle with his strong force of artillery, which came into position on both sides of Rueil. The tirailleurs then advanced and made their way through the park of Buzanval to its western boundary-wall, but were driven back by the 50th Fusilier Regiment which had hastened forward.

At half-past ten the chief attack ensued at this point, supported by part of the central column. It found only an under-officer's post at Malmaison, but at the eastern exit from Bougival near La Jouchère and Porte de Longboyau, it encountered the already re-inforced line of posts of the 20th Infantry Brigade. General von Schmidt (commanding 10th Infantry Division) still held back at Beauregard the reserve of the 10th Division. A murderous fire from the well-covered German infantry broke the onset of the French, and converted it by mid-day into a stationary fire fight, in which the German artillery also took part with great effect. Two batteries of the 10th Division at St. Michel were reinforced by two Guard batteries brought up from St. Germain to Louvenciennes; a third came into action near Chatou and forced an armour-plated train halted at the railway station north of Rueil to retire rapidly to Nanterre. Four batteries of the IVth Corps finally opened fire from Carrières, heedless of the fire of Valérien, and shelled the dense masses of hostile infantry halted in rear of Rueil.

At two o'clock the French decided on renewing the attack. When two of their batteries had shelled Porte de Longboyau a brigade marched on that point, and a second on the western wall of the park of the Château Buzanval; a third followed in support. Not less bold

than unsuccessful was the attempt of a section of
Engineers, one officer and ten men, to blow up part of
the wall; they all fell together. The attacking
columns had advanced to within 200 paces, when
thirteen German companies at the moment met them,
broke and stopped their rush by pouring fire into them
at short range, and presently routed the hostile columns
in disorder, in spite of the devoted exertions of the
officers.

The French, however, still found a strong protection
in the park-wall, which had been prepared for defence
with great skill and with the utmost rapidity; and
the advance of several companies from Brezin and La
Bergerie on this wall was repulsed with heavy loss.

But the strength of the French attack was already
broken. So early as three o'clock a movement of
retreat was observable in their left wing, and as dusk
fell the French centre began to withdraw from the
heights of Maison du Curé. When Colonel von Köthen
pursued, with a small force, several battalions indeed
fronted, and even threatened a sharp counter-attack;
but timely support arrived from La Bergerie, Garches,
and Porte Jaune, and, backed by the fire of the batteries, the pursuit was followed up. The King's Grenadiers drove back the enemy to the vicinity of
Fouilleuse.

The Germans, however, had not yet succeeded in
repossessing themselves of the Montretout redoubt.
The chief hindrance arose from their having been
unable to advance through the town of St. Cloud. As,
however, the possession of this position was indispensable for the protection of the right wing, General von
Kirchbach gave orders that it was to be retaken either
that evening or early next morning.

General von Sandrart (commanding 9th Infantry
Division) decided on immediate action, and at eight
that evening five battalions went forward on this duty.
Only a few French were found in the redoubt and were

taken prisoners; but in the town the struggle was severe. Finally the Germans had to restrict themselves to blockading the houses held temporarily by the enemy. The French also clung to the outer park-wall of Buzanval throughout the night. The Guard Landwehr and the Bavarian Brigade were therefore assigned quarters in Versailles, to form a strong reserve at hand in case of need on the following day. The remainder of the troops withdrew into their former quarters.

At half-past five General Trochu had issued the order for a retreat. He perceived that the prolongation of the struggle could afford no success, especially as the National Guards were becoming insubordinate. The brave defenders of St. Cloud were forgotten in these directions. They did not surrender till the day after, when artillery was brought against the houses they occupied. And the park-wall was not relinquished till the following morning.

The French attack of January 19th was wrecked even before it had reached the main position of the defenders. The reserves in readiness on the German side had not needed to be brought into action. The Vth Corps alone had driven back an enemy of four times its own strength. It lost 40 officers and 570 men; the loss of the French in killed and wounded was 145 officers and 3423 men, besides 44 officers and 458 men taken prisoners.

When the fog lifted at about eleven o'clock on the morning of the 20th, their long columns were seen retreating on Paris across the peninsula of Gennevilliers.

PROSECUTION OF THE ARTILLERY ATTACK ON PARIS
UP TO THE ARMISTICE.

After the repulse of this last struggle for release on the part of the garrison, the extension of the artillery attack to the north front of the defensive position was now determined on. The siege guns no longer needed against the minor French fortresses and on the Marne had been parked for this object at Villiers le Bel. The Army of the Meuse had prepared abundant material for the construction of batteries, and had collected a waggon park of above 600 vehicles. Twelve batteries had already been built in the lines between Le Bourget and the Lake of Enghien, the arming of which followed, for the most part, under cover of night. On January 21st eighty-one heavy guns were ready for action, and Colonel Bartsch opened fire at nine that morning on Forts La Briche, Double Couronne, and de l'Est.

The forts, which opposed the attack with 143 heavy guns, replied vigorously, and on the following day the thick weather prevented the German batteries from resuming their fire till the afternoon. But the ground in front was abandoned by the French, and the outposts of the Guards and IVth Corps took possession of Ville-taneuse and Temps Perdu. During the nights the fire was directed on St. Denis, with every endeavour to spare the Cathedral, and many conflagrations occurred. By the 23rd the vigorous prosecution of the cannonade had materially subdued the fire of the defence. La Briche was wholly silenced, and the other forts only fired occasional salvos. During the night of the 25th four batteries were advanced to within 1300 and 950 yards respectively of the enemy's main works. The engineer attack also could now be undertaken, and a series of new batteries was constructed, which, however, were never used.

The effect of this bombardment of only six days' duration was decisive. The forts had suffered extraordinarily. In contrast to those of the south front they were destitute of the powerful backing of the enceinte, and they lacked, too, bomb-proof shelter. The provisional bomb-proofs were pierced by shells, the powder-magazines were in the greatest danger, and the garrisons had nowhere any more cover. The inhabitants of St. Denis fled to Paris in crowds, and the impaired immunity from storm of the sorely battered works was an insuperable obstacle to a longer maintenance of the defence. This northern attack cost the Germans one officer and 25 men; the French stated their loss at 180.

The fire of the forts on the east front was kept under, and the Würtemberg Field Artillery sufficed to prevent the enemy from renewing his foothold on the peninsula of St. Maur.

The south front meanwhile suffered more and more from the steady bombardment. The enceinte and the sunken mortar batteries behind the ceinture railway were still active, but in the forts the barracks were reduced to ruins, partly battered in and partly burnt down, and the garrisons had to take shelter in the emptied powder-magazines. The covered ways could no longer be traversed safely, the parapets afforded no protection. In Vanves the embrasures were filled up with sand-bags; in the southern curtain of Issy five blocks of casemates had been pierced by shells penetrating the shielding walls. Even the detached gorge-walls of Vanves and Montrouge were destroyed, forty guns were dismounted, and seventy gun carriages wrecked.

The whole condition of France, political and military, and above all the situation in Paris, was such as to cause the Government the gravest anxiety.

Since the return of Monsieur Thiers from his diplomatic tour, it was certain that no mediatory interposition by any foreign power could be expected. The distress of the capital had become more and more severe. Scarcity and high prices had long borne heavily on its population; provisions were exhausted, and even the stores of the garrison had been seriously encroached on. Fuel was lacking in the lasting cold, and petroleum was an inefficient substitute for gas. When the long-deferred bombardment of the south side of Paris was had recourse to, the people took refuge in the cellars or fled to the remoter quarters of the city; and when it was also begun on the northern side the inhabitants of St. Denis crowded into the capital.

The great sortie of the 19th had proved a total failure, and no relief was to be hoped for from outside since Gambetta had sent news of the disaster at Le Mans. The Paris Army, of whose inactivity he complained, was reduced to a third of its original strength by cold, sickness, and desertion, and the heart taken out of it by repeated miscarriages. Its horses had to be slaughtered to provide meat for the inhabitants, and General Trochu declared any further offensive movements to be quite hopeless; the means even of passive resistance were exhausted.

Hitherto the Government had been able to keep the populace in good humour by highly-coloured reports, but now the disastrous state of affairs could no longer be concealed. All its projects were now denounced.

There was a large class of people in Paris who were but little affected by the general distress. Numbers of civilians had been armed for the defence of their country and were fed and well paid by the authorities, without having too much to do in return. They were joined by all the dubious social elements, which found their reckoning in the disorganized situation. These had been quite satisfied with the condition which the 4th of September had created, and a little later they displayed themselves in the hideous form of the Commune. Already some popular gatherings had been dispersed only by force of arms, and even a part of the National Guard were not free from mutinous tendencies. The revolutionary clubs, too, supported by the press, clamoured for further enterprises, even a sortie *en masse* of all the inhabitants of Paris. Thus the feeble Government, dependent as it was on popular favour alone, was under pressure from the impossible demands of an ignorant mob on the one hand, and, on the other, the inexorable force of actual facts.

There was absolutely no expedient possible but the capitulation of the capital; every delay intensified the necessity, and enforced the acceptance of harder terms. Unless all the railways were at once thrown open for the transport of supplies from a very wide area, the horrors of famine would inevitably fall on a population of more than two million souls; and later it might not be practicable to cope with the emergency. Yet no one dared utter the fatal word " capitulation," no one would undertake the responsibility for the inevitable.

A great council of war was held on the 21st. In it all the elder Generals pronounced any further offensive measures to be quite impossible. It was proposed that a council of the younger officers should also be held, but no decision was arrived at. As, however, some one must be made answerable for every misfortune, General Trochu, originally the most popular member of the Government, was dismissed from his position as Governor, and the chief military command was entrusted to General Vinoy. General Ducrot resigned his command.

All this did nothing to improve the situation, so on the 23rd, Monsieur Jules Favre made his appearance at Versailles to negotiate in the first instance for an armistice.

On the German side there was readiness to meet this request; but of course some guarantee had to be forthcoming that the capital, after having been reprovisioned, would not renew its resistance. The surrender of the forts, inclusive of Mont Valérien and the town of St. Denis, as well as the disarmament of the enceinte was demanded and acceded to.

Hostilities were to be suspended on the evening of the 26th, so far as Paris was concerned, and all supplies to be freely given. A general armistice of twenty-one days was then to come in force on the 31st of January, exclusive, however, of the departments of Doubs, Jura, and Côte d'or, and the fortress of Belfort, where for the time operations were still being carried on, in which both sides were hopeful of success.

This armistice gave the Government of National Defence the time necessary for assembling a freely-elected National Assembly at Bordeaux, which should decide whether the war should be continued, or on what conditions peace should be concluded. The election of the deputies was unimpeded and uninfluenced even in the parts of the country occupied by the Germans.

The regular forces of the Paris garrison, troops of the line, marines, and Gardes-Mobiles, had to lay down their arms at once; only 12,000 men and the National Guard were allowed to retain them for the preservation of order inside the city. The troops of the garrison were interned there during the armistice; on its expiry they were to be regarded as prisoners. As to their subsequent transfer to Germany, where every available place was already overflowing with prisoners, the question was postponed in expectation of a probable peace.

The forts were occupied on the 29th without opposition.

There were taken over from the Field Army of Paris 602 guns, 1,770,000 stand of arms, and above 1000 ammunition waggons; from the fortress 1362 heavy guns, 1680 gun-carriages, 860 limbers, 3,500,000 cartridges, 4000 hundred-weight of powder, 200,000 shells, and 100,000 bombs.

The blockade of Paris, which had lasted 132 days, was over, and the greater part of the German forces which had so long stood fast under its walls, was released to end the war in the open field.

THE OPERATIONS OF THE ARMY OF THE SOUTH UNDER GENERAL VON MANTEUFFEL.

The two Army Corps under General von Manteuffel consisted altogether of fifty-six battalions, twenty squadrons, and 168 guns. When it arrived at Châtillon sur Seine on January 12th, the IInd Corps was on the right, and the VIIth on the left on an extension from Noyers Montigny of about forty-five miles. One brigade, under General von Dannenberg, which had already several times been in contact with portions of the French Army of the Vosges, was pushed forward to Vilaines and was charged with the duty of covering the right flank.

Several good roads led from the quarters specified in the direction of Dijon; to Vesoul, on the contrary, there were only bad tracks deep in snow over the southern slope of the wild plateau of Langres. The Commander-in-Chief, nevertheless, chose this direction, that he might as soon as possible afford General von Werder at least indirect assistance by approaching in the rear of the enemy threatening his brother-officer.

The march had to pass midway between the towns of Dijon and Langres, both points strongly occupied by the French. Wooded heights and deep ravines separated the columns and precluded mutual support; each body had to provide for its individual safety in every direction. The troops had previously undergone severe fatigues, and badly as they needed rest not one halt-day could be granted, nor could the evil plight of their boots and the horses' shoes be in any way remedied. On January 14th the march was begun in a thick fog and bitter cold, along roads frozen as smooth as glass.

The maintenance of supplies required special attention, and at first the 8th Brigade had to be left behind to secure the all-important railway-line Tonnerre—Nuits—Châtillon, until connections could be established by way of Epinal.

On the very first day's march the advanced guard of the VIIth Corps had a fight before Langres. A force from the garrison of 15,000 men was driven in on the fortress with the loss of a flag, and a detachment had to be left behind in observation of the place. Under cover of it the VIIth Corps marched past the fortress next day, while the IInd advanced to the Ignon Brook.

The weather changed during the night of the 15th. As a change from fourteen degrees of frost there came storm and rain. The water lay on the frozen roads, and it was with the greatest difficulty that the VIIth Corps reached Prauthoy, and the IInd Moloy, closing in to the left.

On the 18th the left wing advanced South-East on Frettes and Champlitte, the right assembled at Is sur Tille, and its advanced guard, after a march of thirty-one miles, reached the bridges at Gray. On the flank and rear of the Corps there had been some trivial fighting, but the cruel march across the mountains had been accomplished, and the cultivated valley of the Saône was reached.

General von Manteuffel had already received news of the satisfactory course of the first day's fighting on the Lisaine. Later telegrams from General von Werder reported that the French Army of the East would probably be obliged to retire under difficulties, and the German commander at once determined to cut off its retreat by advancing to the Doubs below Besançon.

The defeated French army was still numerically greatly superior to the German force. The troops 'had to be again called upon for severe exertions. They were required once more to cross a thinly-populated mountainous region, where it would be a matter of great difficulty to procure food and the shelter needful during the bitter winter nights. Strong hostile forces had to be left in the rear at Langres, Dijon, and Auxonne, and that under very insufficient observation. However, in spite of every obstacle the advance in this new direction was begun on the 19th.

The first difficulty would have been the crossing of the Saône, here very deep and about sixty-six yards wide, and full of drifting ice, had not the advanced guard of the IInd Corps found Gray abandoned by the French and both the bridges uninjured; whereupon it occupied the town. The head of the VIIth Corps crossed the river by the intact railway-bridge at Savaycux, and by a pontoon bridge thrown across by the pioneers higher up.

On the following day both Corps advanced in a southerly direction, the VIIth to Gy, the IInd to Pesmes. Here the latter also now crossed the Ognon after driving off by artillery fire a French detachment which tried to oppose the construction of the bridges.

On the 21st, at half past two, the advanced guard of the IInd Corps found Dôle occupied by the enemy. General von Koblinski (commanding 5th Infantry Brigade) attacked at once. In spite of a violent street-fight in which the townspeople took part, the Grenadiers of the 2nd Regiment made their way through the town and on the further side seized a train of 230 waggons of provisions and military necessaries, intended for Besançon and left standing in the railway-station.

While the Doubs was thus crossed by the IInd Corps at this point, so the VIIth Corps opened itself a passage across the Ognon at Marmay and Pin.

General von Werder had been instructed to follow close on the heels of the retreating enemy, and while the latter still maintained his position on the front of the XIVth Corps, the 2nd Baden Brigade on the right wing had advanced to Etobon, while Colonel von Willisen with his twelve squadrons had moved out beyond Lure. On the left, Colonel von Zimmermann with the East-Prussian Landwehr had driven the French out of Ste. Marie. These detachments everywhere found cast-away arms and portions of equipment, and hundreds willingly gave themselves up as prisoners.

During the next few days General von Werder effected a general left-wheel to the south. The right wing held Villersexel, and it was the left wing only that met the enemy in great masses at L'Isle sur le Doubs, and afterwards at Clerval and Baume les Dames.

General Bourbaki had withdrawn from the Lisaine on the 18th. The XXIVth Corps only was left on the left bank of the Doubs, with orders to defend toward the north the defiles in the steep mountain-paths of the Lomont range eastward of Clerval ; all the other troops withdrew between the Doubs and the Ognon, with the Division Crémer as rearguard. The Ognon might have formed a natural protection for the right flank of the French army, and orders had been given for the destruction of all the bridges over it ; but we have seen how little they had been obeyed.

On the 21st the XVth and XXth Corps arrived in the neighbourhood of Baume les Dames, the XVIIIth at Marchaux ; and here, having the stronghold of Besançon close at his back, General Bourbaki desired to await for the present the further movements of the enemy. In order that his forces should still muster in full strength, the commandant of Besançon was instructed to send forward to Blamont all the battalions of Mobiles-Guards he could spare so as to relieve the

XXIVth Corps. Nine battalions of mobilized National
Guards had actually previously reached Besançon, which
might have been substituted as desired, but they came
armed with Enfield rifles, for which there was no
ammunition in the fortress. Thus they would there
only have added to the mouths to be filled, and General
Rolland had simply sent them back again. The Intendant-General declared it impossible any longer to bring
up the supplies ordered by him for the maintenance
of the army ; but what proved decisive was the news
received this day that not only was the line of the Ognon
lost, but that the Germans had already crossed the
Doubs.

Under these circumstances the French Commander-
in-Chief determined to continue his retreat on Besançon
and there cross to the southern bank of the Doubs, so as
not to be compelled to give battle with the river in his
rear. The trains were sent off during the night, but
above all things the XVth Corps was ordered at
once to occupy Quingey with a whole division,
and defend that position to extremity, in order to
keep open the communications of the Corps with the
interior. All the other Corps were to concentrate
round Besançon, even the XXIVth, which consequently
gave up the defence of the Lomont passes.

General Bourbaki reported his situation to the
Minister of War, who held out hopes of supporting him
with the portion of the XVth Corps still remaining on
the Loire. Assistance could have been more quickly
and effectually given from Dijon.

The Government had assembled there a very considerable force to replace the Division Crémer gone to
join the Army of the East, for the defence of the ancient
capital of Burgundy and to constitute a point of support
to the operations of General Bourbaki. A Corps of
20,000 men was assigned to the local defence; a very
inappropriately-named Army of the Vosges, more than
40,000 strong, was to do duty in the field. But this was

of little effect in hindering the toilsome advance of the Germans over the mountains. The detachments in observation allowed themselves to be driven in by General von Kettler (commanding 8th Infantry Brigade), who followed the movement of both Corps on the right flank ; and they retired on Dijon. Colonel Bombonnel, stationed at Gray,, urgently begged for reinforcements to enable him to defend the passages of the Saône; his applications were refused because Dijon was in too great peril, and it was not till the Prussians had already crossed the river that "General" Garibaldi began to move.

He set out on the 19th in three columns in the direction of Is sur Tille, where there still remained only part of the (German) 4th Infantry Division. But he advanced little more than four miles. Garibaldi subsequently confined himself to watching reconnoitring parties which advanced to meet him from the heights of Messigny, and he then retired on Dijon with his troops marching to the strains of the Marseillaise.

Nevertheless, the enemy was held in too small estimation in General Manteuffel's headquarter, when General von Kettler was simply ordered to go and take Dijon.

The greatest care had been bestowed in strengthening the place. Numerous earthworks, and other erections specially constructed for defence protected it to the northward ; more especially had Talant and Fontaine les Dijon been transformed into two detached forts and armed with heavy guns which commanded all the approaches on that side. The whole constituted a position which could be held against a much larger force than the five and a half battalions of the 8th Brigade with which General Kettler advanced to the attack.

FIGHTING AT DIJON, JANUARY 21ST AND 22ND.— This force had reached Turcey and St. Seine, and on the 21st advanced in two columns from the west on Dijon, still distant some fourteen miles. Major von

Conta from Is sur Tille on the north was approaching with a small reinforcement. The "Franctireurs de la Mort," the "Compagnie de la Revanche," and other volunteer bands as well as Mobiles-Guards were without much difficulty driven out of the villages on the way, and beyond the deep ravine of the Suzon; the village of Plombieres on the right, which was defended with spirit, was stormed, and Daix was carried on the left; but in front of the fortified position of the French, and within reach of the fire of their heavy batteries, the bold advance was forced to come to a stand. Major von Conta had also pushed on with continuous fighting, but failed to effect a junction with the brigade before dark. General von Kettler, recognizing the overwhelming superiority of the French, finally restricted himself to repulsing their sorties.

The French lost seven officers and 430 men in prisoners alone; but the fighting also cost the brigade nineteen officers and 322 men. The troops had performed a severe march in bad weather along heavy roads, and had not been able to cook either before or after the fight; the ammunition could only be replenished from a convoy which was expected next day. Nevertheless General von Kettler did not hesitate to remain for the night in the positions he had gained immediately in front of the enemy, and then to seek shelter-quarters in the nearest villages.

The French allowed him to do so without any serious opposition. Inactivity so utter caused General von Kettler the suspicion that the main body of the enemy had probably withdrawn by Auxonne to the support of the Army of the East, and he determined to bring it back on Dijon by a renewed attack.

On the 23rd at eleven o'clock, by a flank march along the enemy's front, after his advanced guard had routed a detachment of Gardes-Mobiles, he reached the farm of Valmy on the Langres road, and advanced with his two batteries against the walled and strongly-held village of Pouilly. Here, as was almost always the case when engaged in the defence of buildings, the French made a stout resistance. The 61st Regiment had to storm each house in turn, and it was not till the château was in flames that the strong body of defenders who had taken refuge in the upper floors, surrendered.

Beyond this place the enemy were found deployed in an entrenched position between Talant, which had been converted into a fort, and a large factory-building on the high-road. Here the advance was checked till the remainder of the regiment came up from Valmy, and the defenders at various points were driven back on the suburb.

It was evident that the French were still at Dijon in full force, and the object of the undertaking had therefore been attained. But now unfortunately a tragic episode occurred, for the storming of the factory was absolutely insisted on—a great building, almost impregnable against infantry unaided. When all the senior officers had been killed, a first-lieutenant, whose horse had been shot and he himself wounded, took the command of the 2nd battalion. No sooner had the 5th company, only forty strong, advanced from the neighbouring quarry, than it came under a hot fire from all sides. The leader was at once wounded, and the sergeant who carried the colour fell dead after a few steps; so did the second-lieutenant and the battalion adjutant, who had again raised the standard. It was passed from hand to hand, carried first by the officers then by the men; every bearer fell. The brave Pomeranians [1] nevertheless rushed on the building, but there was no entrance anywhere on that side, and at last the under-officer retreated on the quarry with the remnant of the

---

[1] Men of the 2nd Battalion, 61st Regiment, 8th Brigade, 4th Division, IInd Corps, which Corps consisted exclusively of Pomeranians.

little band. Here, for the first time, the colour was missed. Volunteers went out again in the darkness to search for it, but only one man returned unwounded. It was not till afterwards that the French found the banner, shot to ribbons, in a pool of blood under the dead. This was the only German colour lost throughout the war, and only thus was this one lost.

The enemy took prisoners eight officers and 150 men, and the brigade sustained a fresh loss of sixteen officers and 362 men. It mustered at Pouilly, and remained under arms till eight o'clock to meet possible pursuit; only then were quarters taken in the neighbouring villages.

OPERATIONS OF THE ARMY OF THE SOUTH.—The commission to take Dijon could not be executed; but the bold advance of this weak brigade cowed the hostile army into inactivity, so that General von Manteuffel was able to pursue his march unopposed.

He had given to both his corps as their objective the enemy's line of retreat south of Besançon.

From this fortress there were but few roads to the south of France available for troops, through the riven and rugged regions of the western Jura. The most direct connection was by the road and railway to Lons le Saulnier, on which Quingey and Byans were the most important barriers. Further to the east, but by a wide détour, a road runs by Ornans, Salins and Champagnole to St. Laurent and Morez. Several ways, however, radiate from Besançon and converge in Pontarlier, by using the passes peculiar to this range, called "Cluses," which pierce transversely the mountain chains and afford the valleys intercommunication. From Pontarlier one road only runs past Mouthe, and along the Swiss frontier in awkward proximity thereto.

January 22nd.—On this day the advanced guard of the 13th Division marched from Audeux to St. Vit, and after breaking up the railway and plundering a number of loaded waggons, down the riverside to Dampierre. On the way four bridges over the Doubs were found uninjured and were taken possession of. The advanced guard of the 14th Division moved from Emagny to observe Besançon. The IInd Corps closed on Dôle and pushed reconnoitring parties across the river.

January 23rd.—The concentric movement of all the bodies of the German army was continued.

General Debschitz, approaching from the north, in passing Roches found only the abandoned camping ground of the French XXIVth Corps. The 4th Reserve Division occupied L'Isle without opposition, and met no resistance till it reached Clerval and Baume.

On the Ognon the Baden Division drove the French out of Montbozon.

In the centre of the army the VIIth Corps pushed the advanced guard of the 14th Division forward on Dannemarie, near Besançon. A fight ensued there in the form only of a cannonade which lasted till night. The 13th Division, again, which had crossed the Doubs at Dampierre, advanced on Quingey.

For want of rolling stock it had been possible to forward only one French brigade by railway, and the last trains were received at the Byans station with Prussian shells. These troops were in so bad case that they were unable even to place outposts. They abandoned Quingey almost without a struggle, and their hurried retreat on Besançon and beyond the Loue, stopped the advance of reinforcements already on the way. Thus 800 prisoners and a train of 400 convalescents fell into the hands of the Prussian advanced guard, who at once broke up the railway at Abbans-dessous.

On the right wing, the head of the IInd Corps advanced by the valley of the Loue on the southern bank. Several cuttings on this road had been prepared for defence, but were found undefended. It was at Villers Farlay that it first encountered a strong body of the enemy.

On the evening of this day, of the French forces the XXth Corps was on the north and the XVIIIth on the west of Besançon, at the distance of about four miles. Cavalry, artillery and the train were passing through the town or encamped on the glacis of the fortress. The XXIVth Corps was on the march thither, and the 2nd and 3rd Divisions of the XVth were in possession of the southern bank of the Doubs about Baume and Larnod; but the 1st Division had not suc-ceeded in holding Quingey. Thus the most direct and important line of communications of the French army was cut, and its position, by this fresh mischance, seriously compromised. Impracticable projects and counsels from Bordeaux poured in freely, but did not mend matters; and on the 24th General Bourbaki summoned the superior officers to a council of war.

January 24th.—The Generals declared that they had scarcely more than half their men under arms, and these were more inclined to fly than to fight. General Pallu alone thought he might answer for the men of the army reserve. The Intendant-General reported that, without trenching on the magazines of the place, the supplies in hand would last for four days at most. General Billot was in favour of attempting to fight a way through to Auxonne, but he declined to take the com-mand in chief which was offered him. The exhaustion of the troops and their evidently increasing insubordi-nation gave little hope of the success of offensive operations. So there was no alternative but to retire on Pontarlier, as the Commander-in-Chief had pro-posed.

This recourse, even, was seriously threatened. To relieve himself from pressure on the north, General Bourbaki ordered the XXIVth Corps to advance once more and hold the Lomont passes. On the south the XVth was to defend the deep mountain-ravine of the Loue, and General Crémer was more especially to cover the retreat of the army on the right flank, which was most seriously threatened. For this difficult task, in addition to his own Division, a Division of the XXth Corps and the army reserve as the most trustworthy troops were placed under his command. The XVIIIth and the remainder of the XXth were to await marching-orders at Besançon.

In the German Head-quarter, where of course the plans of the French could not be known, various possibilities had to be reckoned with.

If the French remained at Besançon there would be no need to attack them there ; the place was not suited for the accommodation of a large army, and its supplies could not long hold out. That they would again attempt to advance northwards was scarcely likely ; by doing so they would be cutting loose from all their resources, and must encounter the larger part of the XIVth German Corps on the Ognon.

An attempt to break through to Dijon seemed more possible. But this would be opposed at St. Vit by the 13th Division, at Pesmes by Colonel von Willisen's detachment, and finally by General von Kettler.

Thus a retreat on Pontarlier seemed the most likely course ; and to hinder their further march from that place would in the first instance be the duty of the IInd Corps, while in the meantime the VIIth was observing the enemy massed in Besançon, and opposing his sorties on both sides of the river.

The Commander-in-Chief therefore confined himself to giving general directions to his Generals, expressly authorizing them to act on their own judgment in eventualities which could not be foreseen.

General von Werder was instructed to advance by Marnay, and to place the 14th Division in touch with the Baden Division and Von der Goltz's Brigade, and then to distribute these bodies along the right bank of the Doubs. The 4th Reserve Division restored the bridges at L'Isle and Baume, and crossed over to the left bank. Colonel von Willisen was to join the VIIth

Corps to supply its lack of cavalry. The IInd Corps was assembled behind Villers Farlay.

January 25th.—Reconnaissances on a large scale were arranged for next day. The reconnaissance of the VIIth Corps resulted in a sharp fight at Vorges. The head of the IInd Corps met the enemy in front of Salins and at Arbois, but found that the latter had not yet reached Poligny.

January 26th.—The advanced guard of the IInd Corps advanced on Salins. The fronts of the high-perched forts of St. André and Belin near the town, looked toward Switzerland, but their fire commanded also on flank and rear the plain to the south and west on the enemy's line of march. Salins constituted a strong barrier on the road to St. Laurent, and as long as it was held would cover the line of retreat of columns marching from Besançon to Pontarlier.

The two field-batteries of the advanced guard could, of course, do little against the heavy guns of the forts; but the Fusiliers of the 2nd Regiment advanced in rushes of small detachments up the narrow ravine, scaled its rugged faces, and, supported by the two Grenadier battalions, forced their way, about half-past two, into the railway-station and suburb of St. Pierre; but with the loss of 3 officers and 109 men.

Soon after General von Koblinski arrived by way of St. Thiébaud with the 42nd Regiment. As in consequence of the representations of the Mayor the commandant refrained from bombarding the town, the advanced guard was able to take up its quarters therein; the main body of the 3rd Division retreated from under the fire of the forts on Mouchard, and the defile remained closed again to further penetration. It was necessary to turn it by the south.

In that direction the 4th Division had already marched to Arbois, its head further forward up to Pont d'Héry; it found Poligny and Champagnole on the right still unoccupied.

The VIIth Corps reconnoitred both banks of the Doubs, and found the enemy in strong positions at Busy and at Vorges.

The 4th Reserve Division advanced along the southern bank as far as St. Juan d'Adam, near Besançon; the remainder of the XIVth Corps marched on Etuz' and Marnay.

General von Kettler's report of the fighting on the 21st and 23rd determined General von Manteuffel to make a renewed attempt on Dijon. He detailed to this duty General Hann von Weyhern (commanding 4th Infantry Division, IInd Corps), placing him in command of the 8th Brigade, with Colonel von Willisen's troops and Degenfeld's Baden Brigade.

On the French side, General Bressoles had started on the 24th, in obedience to orders, to take renewed possession of the passages of the Doubs and the Lomont defiles. He had, in the first instance, turned against Baume with d'Aries' Division; but as he did not succeed even in driving the German outposts out of Pont les Moulins, he retired to Vercel. In consequence of this, on the morning of the 26th, Carré's Division, which had found the passes of the Lomont unoccupied, also moved to Pierre Fontaine. Comagny's Division had already retreated to Morteau, and was making its way unmolested to Pontarlier.

General Bourbaki was greatly disturbed by this failure of his right wing; more perhaps than was needful, since, in fact, only one German division stood north of him, which at most could drive his rearguard on Pontarlier, while the main force of the enemy threatened him far more seriously on the west. He nevertheless ordered a renewed advance, on the 26th, of the XXIVth Corps, which was now to be supported by the XVIIIth. But the march through Besançon of the latter, through streets covered with ice, took up the whole of the day which should have been devoted to the attack, so that nothing came of the scheme.

The Army Reserve had reached Ornans, and stood there in readiness. The two other Divisions advanced on the road to Salins, but heard while on the march that the Germans had just carried that place. They then occupied in Déservillers and Villeneuve d'Amont, the roads leading from thence to Pontarlier.

The War Minister, meanwhile, had decisively refused permission for the general retreat of the army, without any regard to the imperative necessities of the case.

The military dilettanteism which fancied it could direct the movements of the army from Bordeaux is characterized in a telegram of the afternoon of the 25th. Monsieur de Freycinet gives it as his " firm conviction "[1] that General Bourbaki, if he would concentrate his troops, and, if necessary come to an understanding with Garibaldi, would be strong enough to fight his way out, " either by Dôle, or by Mouchard, or by Gray, or by Pontailler" (north of Auxonne). The choice was left to him.

Still more amazing was the further suggestion that if indeed the state of the army prohibited a long march, it should be embarked on the railway at Chagey, under the eye, no doubt, of the pursuing enemy.

Such communications could only avail to shatter the brave commander's self-confidence. The disastrous reports which poured in from all sides, and the state of the troops which he had seen for himself as the XVIIIth Corps marched through the town, crushed his last hope and led him to attempt his own life.

The Commander had of course to bear the blame of the total failure of a campaign planned by Freycinet; his dismissal from the command was already on its way. General Clinchant was appointed in his stead, and under these disastrous circumstances took the command of the army.

All the Generals were, no doubt, extremely reluctant

---

[1] " Conviction bien arrêtée."

to bring their weary and dispirited troops into serious contact with the enemy. Every line of retreat was closely threatened, excepting only that on Pontarlier. The new Commander-in-Chief had no choice but to carry out the plans of his predecessor. He at once ordered the further march. He himself proceeded to Pontarlier. In that strong position he hoped to be able at least to give the troops a short rest. No large bodies of the Germans had been met with so far, the ammunition columns had got safely through, and if the defiles of Vaux, Les Planches, and St. Laurent could be reached and held in advance of the enemy there was still a possibility of escape to the southwards.

On the evening of the 27th, the Division Poullet was at Levier, nearest to the Germans; the two other Divisions under General Crémer, with the XVth and XXth Corps, were écheloned on the road from Ornans to Sombacourt; the XVIIIth Corps alone was on the eastern road through Nods. The XXIVth, in a miserable condition, had reached Montbenoît with its head at Pontarlier; two Divisions were still in Besançon.

On this same day General von Fransecky collected the main body of the IInd Corps at Arbois, and rein-forced General du Trossel's posts at Pont d'Héry.

The XIVth Corps relieved the 14th Division of the VIIth Corps at St. Vit; the latter advanced to the right of the 13th Division into the Loue angle, which the French had already abandoned.

On the north, General von Debschitz held Blamont and Pont du Roide, while General von Schmeling watched Besançon from St. Juan, and General von der Goltz marched on Arbois to form a reserve.

January 28th.—Suspecting that the French were already on the march by Champagnole on St. Laurent, General Fransecky, to cut off from them that line of retreat, advanced on the following day in a southerly direction with the IInd Corps.

General du Trossel reached Champagnole without

opposition, and thence sent his cavalry along the road to Pontarlier. Lieutenant-Colonel von Guretzky arrived at Nozeroy with a squadron of the 11th Dragoons, and found the place occupied; but he made prize of fifty-six provision-waggons and the military-chest, taking the escort prisoners.

The 5th and 6th Brigades advanced on Poligny and Pont du Navoy.

The 13th Division of the VIIth Corps, having been relieved at Quingey by the Baden troops, assembled at La Chapelle, while the 14th advanced on Déservillers. Its head found no enemy in Bolandoz, although his camp-fires were still smouldering; so that the main hostile army was not overtaken on that day.

General Clinchant had in fact moved his Corps closer on Pontarlier. But it soon became evident that supplies were not procurable for any long stay there. General Crémer received orders that night to move forward at once to Les Planches and St. Laurent with three cavalry regiments standing already on the road to Mouthe. The mountain-roads were deep in snow, but by forced marching he reached the points designated on the following afternoon. The XXIVth Corps and a brigade of the Division Poullett followed next day, and the latter also occupied with two battalions the village of Bonneveaux at the entrance to the defiles of Vaux. On the evening of the 28th the rest of the French army stood as follows: the XVIIIth Corps was behind the Drugeon at Houtaud close before Pontarlier; the 1st Division of the XVth had advanced over the brook to Sombacourt, the 3rd Division was in the town. On the left the 2nd and 3rd Divisions of the XXth Corps held the villages from Chaffois to Frasne, and on the right the army reserve occupied Byans.

General von Manteuffel had ordered for the 29th a general advance on Pontarlier, where at last the French must certainly be found.

January 29th.—Of the IInd Corps General Koblinsky

had set out from Poligny in the night. When he reached Champagnole and had assembled the whole of the 5th Brigade he moved forward therefrom at about seven o'clock. General du Trossel with the 7th Brigade also reached Censeau without finding the enemy.

On the right Colonel von Wedell marched from Pont du Navoy on Les Planches with four battalions of the 6th Brigade. He found only dismounted troopers, posts probably left by General Crémer which were easily dispersed by the Jägers. Detachments were then sent out in different directions, and everywhere met with scattered troops; but at Foncine le Bas the head of the XXIVth Corps was found, and Colonel von Wedell now blocked the last line of retreat which had remained to the French.

With the rest of the IInd Corps General von Hartmann marched unopposed on Nozeroy.

The 14th Division of the VIIth Corps had not received the order to advance on Pontarlier till somewhat late; it did not start from Déservillers until noon, and only reached Levier at three o'clock, where, at the same hour, the head of the 13th Division also arrived from Villeneuve d'Amont, the state of the roads having greatly delayed its march.

The advanced guard of three battalions, half a squadron, and one battery, had met only stragglers on the way, and General von Zastrow commanded it to push forward to the Drugeon brook. In the forest on the left of the road closed detachments of the enemy were retiring on Sombacourt, and Major von Brederlow with the 1st battalion of the 77th Regiment turned off to attack that village lying on the flank. The 2nd company under Captain von Vietinghof dashed into it through Sept Fontaines with loud cheers, and was at once closely surrounded by strong bodies of the enemy; but the other companies soon came to its assistance. The first Division of the XVth French Corps was here completely routed without the Army Reserve

close at hand in Byans having come to its support.
Fifty officers, including two generals, and 2700 men
were taken prisoners; ten guns, seven mitrailleuses,
forty-eight waggons, 319 horses and 3500 stand of arms
fell into the hands of the Hanoverian battalion [1] which
was left in occupation of Sombacourt.

The rest of the advanced guard had meanwhile approached Chaffois, where the road opens out from the
mountains into the wide valley of the Drugeon. That
village, as we have seen, was occupied by the 2nd
Division of the XXth Corps.

Colonel von Cosel passed at once to the attack.
Three companies of the 53rd Regiment surprised the
French field-posts and took possession of the first houses
of the village, but then the whole mass of the French
XVIIIth Corps barred his further progress. By degrees all the available forces had to join in the
fighting, and also reinforcements had to be brought up
from the main body of the 14th Division. The fight
lasted with great obstinacy for an hour and a half, when
suddenly the French ceased firing and laid down their
arms. They claimed that an armistice had already
been agreed on.

Monsieur Jules Favre had, in fact, telegraphed to
Bordeaux at a quarter-past eleven on the night of the
28th, that an armistice of twenty-one days had been
concluded, without adding, however, that, with his consent, the three eastern departments had been excluded
from its operations. The information, in this imperfect
form, was transmitted to the civil authorities by the
Delegation at 12.15 of the 29th; but Monsieur Freycinet
did not forward it to the military authorities, whom
the matter principally concerned, till 3.30 in the
afternoon.

Thus could General Clinchant in all good faith trans-

---

[1] The 77th Hanoverian Fusilier Regiment, of which this was the
2nd battalion, belonged to the 25th Brigade, 13th Division, VIIth
(Westphalian) Army Corps.

mit to General Thornton, in command of the Divisions at Chaffois, a message which, as regarded the Army of the East, was altogether incorrect. The latter at once sent his staff officer to the Prussian advanced guard, which was still in action, who demanded the cessation of the firing in recognition of the official communication.

General von Manteuffel had received in Arbois at five in the morning, full particulars from the supreme Head-quarter of the terms of the armistice, according to which the army of the South was to prosecute its operations to a final issue. An army order announcing this to all the troops was at once sent out, but did not reach the VIIth Corps till evening.

Nothing was known there of any armistice; however, the tidings might be on the way, and General von Zastrow granted the temporary cessation of hostilities, and even sanctioned the release of his prisoners, but without their arms.

Chaffois, with the exception of a couple of farmsteads, remained in possession of the 14th Division, which found such quarters there as might be; the 13th occupied the villages from Sept Fontaines back to Déservillers.

January 30th.—In full confidence in the news from the seat of Government, General Clinchant, on the 30th, suspended the movements of his army. The newly-appointed Commander of the XXIVth Corps, General Comagny, also gave up his intended attempt to cut his way with 10,000 men at Foncine through Colonel von Wedell's weak brigade. The other Corps, after the unfortunate course of the fighting on the previous evening, had drawn in close on Pontarlier; but detachments of cavalry were sent out on the roads to Besançon and St. Laurent, to establish a line of demarcation and also to keep up communications with the fortress and with Southern France.

On receiving the army order at about eleven o'clock, General Zastrow gave notice to the enemy in his front of the resumption of hostilities, but restricted his immediate demands to the complete evacuation of Chaffois, which was complied with. Otherwise the Corps remained inactive where it was.

Of the IInd Corps General du Trossel had set out very early from Censeau, but the appearance of a French flag of truce, and his fear of offending against the law of nations, here too occasioned considerable hesitation. The forest of Frasne was not clear of the French till evening. Lieutenant-Colonel von Guretzky made his way into the village with quite a small force, and took prisoners twelve officers and 1500 men who held it, with two colours. The 5th Brigade then also moved up into Frasne; the rest of the Corps occupied the same quarters as on the previous day.

A flag of truce had presented itself at Les Planches, but Colonel von Wedell had simply dismissed the bearer. The outposts of the XIVth Corps did the same.

On the north of Pontarlier, General von Schmeling advanced to Pierre Fontaine, General von Debschitz to Maiche.

January 31*st.*—Early in the morning of this day the French Colonel Varaigne made his appearance at General von Manteuffel's head-quarters at Villeneuve, with the proposal that a cessation of hostilities for thirty-six hours should be agreed upon, till the existing condition of uncertainty should be removed; but this proposal was refused, as on the German side there were no doubts whatsoever. Permission was granted for the despatch of an application to Versailles, but it was at the same time explained that the movements of the Army of the South would not be suspended pending the arrival of the answer.

On this day, however, the IInd Army Corps marched only to Dompierre on a parallel front with the VIIth, its advanced guard pushing forward on the Drugeon to Ste. Colombe and La Rivière. Thence, in the evening, a company of the Colberg Grenadiers crossed the steep mountain ridge and descended on La'Planée, where it took 500 prisoners. A right-flank detachment of two battalions and one battery under Lieutenant-Colonel Liebe marched unopposed up the long pass of Bonne-vaux to Vaux, and took prisoners 2 officers and 688 men. The enemy then abandoned the defile of Granges Ste. Marie and retired to St. Antoine in the mountains.

The Corps had found every road strewn with cast-away arms and camp utensils, and had taken in all 4000 prisoners.

Of the VIIth Corps, as soon as the enemy had been informed of the resumption of hostilities, the 14th Division bent leftward on the Drugeon and up to La Vrine, whence a connection was effected with the 4th Reserve Division of the XIVth Corps in St. Gorgon. The 13th Division advanced to Sept Fontaines. Pontarlier was now completely surrounded, and General von Manteuffel fixed February 1st for the general attack thereon. The IInd Corps was to advance from the south-west, the VIIth from the north-west ; General von der Goltz was to establish himself in front of Levier in reserve.

Meanwhile the French Commander-in-Chief had conceived doubts whether everything was quite right with the communications from his Government. All the mountain-passes leading to the south were now lost, and an escape in that direction was no longer to be hoped for. General Clinchant had already sent rearward the baggage and ammunition columns, the sick and worn-out men, through La Cluse under shelter of the forts of Joux and Neuv. And when in the afternoon a message from Bordeaux brought the intelligence that in fact the Army of the East had been excluded from the armistice, the Commander-in-Chief summoned his generals to a council of war. Every General present declared that he could no longer answer for his troops. General Clinchant himself therefore went out the same evening to Les Verrières, to conclude negotiations he had already opened, in virtue of which on the following day,

February 1st, the army was to cross the Swiss frontier by three roads.

To cover this retreat, the Army Reserve was to hold Pontarlier till all the baggage-trains should have passed La Cluse, while the XVIIIth Corps was to take up a covering position between the two forts. Defensive works there were at once set about. What of the XVth Corps on the way by Morez had failed in getting through with the cavalry was to try to cross into Switzerland at any available point.

February 1st.—When the advanced guard of the IInd Corps now advanced on Pontarlier from Ste. Colombe, it met with but slight resistance at the railway station. The Colberg Grenadiers took possession of the town without a struggle, and captured many prisoners, but then found the road on the further side entirely blocked by guns and waggons. They could pass beyond on either side of the road only with difficulty through deep snow. Just in front of La Cluse the road winds between high rocky precipices into the wide basin of the Doubs, completely commanded by the isolated fortalice of Joux perched on the solid rock. On debouching into the open the foremost companies were received by a hot fire. Four guns, dragged up thither with the greatest exertions, could make no head against the heavy guns of the fort, and the French themselves here passed to the attack.

The Colberg Fusiliers had meanwhile climbed the heights to the left, followed by the 2nd Battalion of the Regiment and a battalion of the 49th Regiment, which drove the French out of the farmsteads on the rifted upland. The steep cliff on the right was also scaled, several rifle sub-divisions of the 49th climbed the acclivity up to La Cluse, and the Colberg Grenadiers advanced to the foot of Fort Neuv.

To take the strong fortalices by storm was obviously impossible, and furthermore because of the nature of the ground the fugitive enemy could scarcely be overtaken in force. Of the French, 23 officers and 1600 men were taken prisoners, with 400 loaded waggons ; of the Germans, 19 officers and 365 men had fallen, mostly of the Colberg Regiment. The troops spent the night on the field of the fighting

As no large force could come into action at La Cluse, General von Fransecky had ordered the main body of the Corps to march further southward to Ste. Marie. To avoid the necessity of crossing the steep chain of the Jura, General von Hartmann first betook himself to Pontarlier to avail himself of the better roads from thence, but his progress was stopped, the fight at La Cluse having assumed unexpected proportions. The VIIth Corps and the 4th Reserve Division, which had reached the Doubs at noon, were equally unable to get at the enemy.

During the whole day the French columns were crossing the Swiss frontier. The Army Reserve in Pontarlier was at the beginning swept away by the tide of baggage-waggons and drivers, and only joined the XVIIIth Corps on reaching La Cluse. During the night they both followed the general line of retreat. Only the cavalry and the 1st Division of the XXIVth Corps reached the neighbouring department of l'Ain to the southward, the latter force reduced to a few hundred men. There crossed the frontier on to Swiss soil some 80,000 Frenchmen.

General Manteuffel had transferred his headquarters to Pontarlier. There, in the course of the night, he first heard through Berlin of the convention arranged between General Clinchant and Colonel Herzog of the Swiss Confederation.

General von Manteuffel had achieved the important success of his three weeks' campaign by hard marching and constant fighting, although there had been no pitched battle since that of the Lisaine. These marches, indeed, had been such as none but well-seasoned troops could have accomplished under bold and skilful leadership, under every form of fatigue and hardship, in the worst season and through a difficult country.

Thus two French armies were now prisoners in Germany, a third interned in the capital, and the fourth disarmed on foreign soil.

GENERAL HANN VON WEYHERN'S MARCH ON DIJON.

It only remains to cast a backward glance on the advance on Dijon, with the conduct of which General Hann von Weyhern was charged on January 26th.

On that same day Garibaldi received instructions there to take energetic measures against Dôle and Mouchard.

To support him, the Government, indefatigable in the evolution of new forces, was to put in march 15,000 Gardes-Mobiles under General Crouzat from Lyons to Lons le Saulnier, and a XXVIth Corps in course of formation at Châtellerault was to be sent from thence to Beaune. As it was beyond doubt that General von Manteuffel had moved with a strong force on the communications of the Army of the East, the specific order was transmitted on the 27th to the Commander of the Army of the Vosges, to leave only from 8000 to 10,000 men in Dijon and to advance at once with his main force beyond Dôle.

But the General was always greatly concerned for the safety of Dijon ; he occupied the principal positions on the slopes of the Côte d'Ôr and detached a small force to St. Jean de Losne, behind the canal of Bourgogne. Of 700 volunteers who had marched on Dôle, no trace was ever found there.

Langres had shown more energy ; several and often successful attacks on small outpost companies and etappen troops had been made from it from time to time.

General Hann von Weyhern's purpose of attacking Dijon from the south had to be abandoned, because the bridge over the Saône at St. Jean de Losne had been destroyed. He therefore on the 29th crossed the river at Apremont, and on the 31st assembled his detachments at Arc sur Tille. Here again General Bordone, the Chief of the general staff of the Army of the Vosges, vainly insisted that an armistice was in force. On the 31st General von Kettler marched with an advanced guard on Varois. To cut off the enemy's communications with Auxonne a left-flank detachment made itself master of the bridge over the Ouche at Fauverney. The first shells drove the French back on their intrenched position on the line St. Apollinaire— Mirande.

When the attempt to establish an armistice failed, General Bordone determined to evacuate Dijon in the course of the night and retire upon assured neutral ground. Thus, on February 1st, the head of the advanced guard found the position in front of the city abandoned, and General von Kettler marched in without encountering any opposition, just as the last train of French troops moved out of the railway-station. Sombernon and Nuits were also occupied on the 2nd.

OCCUPATION OF THE DEPARTMENTS OF THE DOUBS, JURA, AND CÔTE D'OR.

Nothing now remained for General von Manteuffel but to establish the military occupation of the three Departments which he had won, and to guard them from without.

General Pelissier was still in the open field within their bounds, having reached Lons le Saulnier with the

15,000 Gardes-Mobiles who had come up from Lyons
and had been joined by the battalions sent back
from Besançon by General Rolland, by no means an
insignificant force numerically, but practically of no
great efficiency.   The commanders were recommended
to retire and avoid further bloodshed ; and they did so,
as soon as some detachments of the IInd German Corps
advanced on Lons le Saulnier and St. Laurent.   Others
occupied Mouthe and Les Allemands, where were
found twenty-eight field-guns which had been abandoned by the French.   As a measure of precaution,
the Swiss frontier was watched by eight battalions.
The fortalices of Salins, the little fortress of Auxonne,
and Besançon, were kept under observation from the
eastward.   Although the Department of Haute-Marne
was included in the armistice, the commandant of
Langres had refused to recognize the authority of his
Government.   So this place had to be invested, and
probably besieged.   General von der Goltz was
promptly ordered to advance once more on it, and
General von Krenski was already on the march thither
with seven battalions, two squadrons and two batteries,
and a siege train from Longwy, which he had brought
to capitulate on January 25th, after a bombardment of
six days' duration.   But it was not called into requi-
sition at Langres.   General von Manteuffel aimed at
no further tactical results ; he was anxious to save his
troops from further losses, and to afford them all possible relief after their exceptional exertions.   Not
till now were the baggage-waggons brought up, even
those of the superior staff officers having been necessarily left behind during the advance into the Jura.
The troops were distributed for the sake of comfort
in roomy quarters, but in readiness for action at any
moment, the IInd Corps in the Jura, the VIIth in the
Côte d'Or, the XIVth in the department of the Doubs.
But the siege of Belfort was still to be vigorously
carried on.

PROSECUTION OF THE SIEGE OF BELFORT.

Immediately after the battle on the Lisaine the forces investing Belfort were increased to 27 battalions, 6 squadrons, 6 field batteries, 24 companies of fortress artillery, and 6 companies of fortress pioneers; 17,602 infantry, 4699 artillerymen, and 1166 pioneers, in all 23,467 men, with 707 horses and 34 field-guns.

The place was invested on the north and west by only a few battalions, and the main force was assembled to the south and east.

On January 20th the eastern batteries opened a heavy fire on Pérouse. Colonel Denfert concluded that an attack was imminent, and placed four battalions of his most trusted troops in the village, which had been prepared for an obstinate defence.

At about midnight, two battalions of the 67th Regiment advanced from Chêvremont on the Haut Taillis wood without firing a shot. Once inside it there was a determined struggle, but the French were driven back on the village, and the pioneers immediately intrenched the skirt of the wood towards Pérouse under a heavy fire from the forts. Half an hour later two Landwehr battalions advanced from Bessoncourt to the copse on the north of the village. They were received with a heavy fire, but made their way onward over abatis, pits and wire-entanglements, driving the enemy back into the quarries. A stationary fight now ensued, but the 67th presently renewed the attack, and without allowing themselves to be checked by the earthworks forced their way into Pérouse. They took possession of the eastern half of the straggling village at about half-past two, and the detachment defending the quarries, finding itself threatened, retreated. At five o'clock, Colonel Denfert abandoned the western part of the village, which was now completely occupied by the Germans. The losses on the German side were 8 officers and 178 men ; the French left 5 officers and 93 men prisoners.

January 21st to 27th.—The next day the construction of the first parallel was undertaken, extending about 2000 yards from Donjoutin to Haut Taillis. Five battalions and two companies of Sappers were employed in this work, and were undisturbed by the French ; but the rocky soil prevented its being constructed of the prescribed width.

General von Tresckow considered that he might thus early succeed in carrying both the Perches forts by a determined assault. Two half redoubts with ditches more than three yards deep cut perpendicularly in the solid rock, casemated traverses and bomb-proof block-houses in the gorge, afforded protection to the defenders. Each work was armed with seven 12-cm. cannon, and they were connected by trenches, behind which reserves were in readiness. On the right flank this position was protected by a battalion and a sortie-battery in Le Fourneau ; on the left the adjacent wood was cleared, cut down to a distance of 650 yards, and wire-entanglements between the stumps formed an almost impenetrable obstacle. In front the gentle slope of the ridge was under the cross-fire of the two forts.

When on the previous evening of the 26th the construction of the parallel was sufficiently advanced to allow of its being occupied by larger detachments, the assault was fixed for the 27th. Two columns, each of one battalion, one company of Sappers, and two guns, passed to the attack at daybreak on that morning. Two companies of Schneidemühl's Landwehr Battalion advanced against the front of Basses Perches and threw themselves on the ground within from 65 to 110 yards of the work. A sub-division of sharp-shooters and a few pioneers reached the ditch and unhesitatingly leaped in ; the two other (Landwehr) companies, going round the fort by the left, got into its rear, and here too the men jumped into the ditch of the gorge. But the

French who had been driven out of their shelter-trenches were now assembled, and the battalion from Le Fourneau came up. All the forts of the place opened fire on the bare and unprotected space in front of the parallel, and an attempt of reinforcements to cross it failed. The 7th Company of the Landwehr Battalion was surrounded by greatly superior numbers, and after a brave struggle was for the most part made captive. Most of the men in the ditch were still able to escape.

The advance of the right column against Hautes-Perches also failed. It had to cross 1100 yards of open ground. The encompassment of the fort was attempted, but it was impossible to force through the abatis and other obstacles under the destructive fire of the enemy.

This abortive attempt cost 10 officers and 427 men; and the slower process of an engineer attack had to be resumed.

January 28th to February 15th.—As the approaches to the forts progressed the flying sap could be carried forward about 330 yards every night unopposed by the enemy. In spite of all the difficulties caused by the nature of the soil, on February 1st the second parallel was thrown up at half distance from the Perches.

As the Fort of la Justice was a special hindrance to the operations, two new batteries had to be constructed to the east of Pérouse against it. Four mortar-batteries on the flanks of the parallel now directed their fire on the Perches at very short range. Three batteries were also constructed in the Bois des Perches to fire on the citadel, and one on the skirt of the wood near Bavilliers against the defences of the city. Henceforward 1500 shells a day were fired on the fortress and its outworks.

But further the prosecution of the attack became more and more difficult. The withdrawal of General Debschitz had seriously reduced the working strength of the besieging force. There were only nine battalions for the exhausting service in the trenches. Specially serious was the heavy loss in pioneers, and two fresh companies had to be brought up from Strasburg. The bright moonlight illuminating the fields of snow far and wide made it impossible to proceed with the flying saps. Sap-rollers had to be used; the heads of the saps had to be protected by sandbags and the sides by gabions, while the earth for filling had often to be brought from a long distance in the rear.

On the head of all this, on February 3rd, a thaw set in, and the water from the heights filled the trenches, so that all communication had to be carried on across the open ground. Torrents of rain damaged the finished works; the parapet of the first parallel gave way altogether in places, and the banquette was washed away. The bottomless tracks made the arming of the batteries unspeakably difficult, and the teams of the columns and field artillery had to be employed in bringing up the ammunition. Many guns had become useless by overheating, while the enemy understood, by rapidly running out their guns, firing, and then running them back again, how to interrupt the work. Not merely was it necessary to continue the shelling of the Perches during the night, but a brisk rifle fire had to be kept up against them. Only now and then did the batteries newly placed in the parallels succeed in entirely silencing the guns of Hautes Perches. Epaulments had to be erected against Fort Bellevue and the defences of the railway-station, and Fort des Barres resumed activity. That under such exertions and the abominable weather the health of the troops suffered severely, need not be said; the battalions could often only muster 300 men for duty.

Meanwhile, however, the artillery of the attack had unquestionably become very much superior to that of the defence, and, in spite of every obstacle, the saps were pushed on to the edge of the ditch of Les Perches.

On February 8th, at one in the afternoon, Captain Roese had gabions flung into the ditch of Hautes Perches, sprang into it with five sappers, and rapidly scaled the parapet by the steps hewn in the scarp. He was immediately followed by the trench guard, but only a few of the French were surprised in the casemated traverses. The situation of the garrison of the forts had in fact become extremely difficult. Ammunition had to be brought up under the enemy's fire, water could only be had from the pond at Vernier, and cooking could only be done inside the works. Colonel Denfert had already given orders to bury the material. Unseen by the besiegers the guns of which the carriages could still be moved had been withdrawn, and only one company left in each fort, which in case of a surprise was to fire and fly. Nothing was to be found in the abandoned work but wrecked gun-carriages and four damaged guns. This fort was at once reversed so that its front faced the fortress, but at three o'clock the latter opened so heavy a fire on the lost positions that the working parties had to take shelter in the ditches.

The garrison in Basses Perches attempted some resistance, but under cover of a reserve it soon retired to Le Fourneau, leaving five guns and much shattered material. Here also the fire of the place at first compelled the working parties to break off, but four 15-cm. mortars were at length brought into the fort, and two 9-cm. guns were placed on the spur of the hill to the westward, which directed their fire on Le Fourneau and Bellevue. During the night of the 9th the two works were connected by a shelter-trench 680 yards long, and thus the third parallel was established.

The position was now such that the attack could immediately be directed on the citadel, and on it the batteries in the Bois des Perches and presently those in the second parallel opened fire. Moitte, Justice, and Bellevue were shelled simultaneously. General von Debschitz had returned, so that the investing corps was thus again brought up to its full strength, and all the conditions were improved by the return of the frost. By the 13th ninety-seven guns were ready in the third parallel.

The town had suffered terribly from the prolonged bombardment. Nearly all the buildings were damaged, fifteen completely burnt down, and in the adjoining villages 164 houses had been destroyed by the defenders themselves. The fortifications showed not less visible indications of serious damage, particularly the citadel. The hewn-stone facing of its front-wall had crumbled into the ditch. Half of the mantleted embrasures had been shattered, the expense powder magazines had been blown up, and a number of casemated traverses pierced. The guns in the upper batteries could only be reached by ladders. The garrison, of its original strength of 372 officers and 17,322 men, had lost 32 officers and 4713 men, besides 336 citizens. The place was no longer tenable; besides there now came the news that the army from which alone relief was to be expected, had laid down its arms.

Under these circumstances General von Tresckow summoned the commandant after a defence so brave to surrender the fortress, with free withdrawal for the garrison, this concession having the sanction of his Majesty. The French Government itself authorized the commandant to accept these terms. Colonel Denfert, however, insisted that he must be given a more direct order. To procure this an officer was sent to Basle, pending whose return there was a provisional armistice.

On the 15th a convention was signed at Versailles, which extended the armistice to the three departments which till then had been excluded from it, and also to Belfort; but the 1st article demanded the surrender of that place.

After the conclusion of the definitive treaty, the garrison, in the course of the 17th and 18th, with its arms and trains, left the precincts of the fortress and withdrew by way of L'Isle sur Doubs and St. Hippolyte into the country occupied by French troops. The march was effected in detachments of 1000 men at intervals of 5 km., the last of which Colonel Denfert accompanied. The supplies which remained in the fortress were conveyed in rear of the departing troops in 150 Prussian proviant waggons. At 3 o'clock in the afternoon of February 18th Lieutenant-General von Tresckow entered the place at the head of detachments from all the troops of the investing corps.

There were found 341 guns, of which 56 were useless, 356 gun-carriages, of which 119 were shot to pieces, and 22,000 stand of arms, besides considerable supplies of ammunition and provisions.

The siege had cost the Germans 88 officers and 2049 men, 245 of whom were released from imprisonment by the capitulation. Immediately was set about the work of restoring and arming the fortress, and of the levelling of the siege works.

THE ARMISTICE.

On the basis of the agreement of January 28th a line of demarcation was drawn, from which both parties were to withdraw their outposts to a distance of 10 km. The line ran south from the mouth of the Seine as far as the Sarthe, crossed the Loire at Saumur, followed the Creuse, turned eastward past Vierzon, Clamécy and

Chagny, and then met the Swiss frontier, after bending to the north of Châlons sur Saône and south of Lons le Saulnier and St. Laurent. The two departments of Pas de Calais and du Nord, as well as the promontory of Havre, were particularly excluded.

The fortresses still held by French troops in the districts occupied by the Germans were assigned a rayon in proportion to their importance.

In carrying out the details of the agreement a liberal interpretation was in most instances allowed. The arrangements had the sanction of those members of the Government of National Defence who were in Paris; while the delegates at Bordeaux, who had hitherto conducted the war, at first held aloof, and indeed, as yet had not been made acquainted with the detailed conditions. Gambetta, it is true, allowed the suspension of operations, but could not give the commanders more precise instructions.

General Faidherbe was thus without orders with regard to the evacuation of Dieppe and Abbeville. General von Goeben, however, refrained from taking immediate possession of these places. On the west of the Seine, the Grand Duke was forced to proclaim that the non-recognition of the line of demarcation would be followed by an immediate recommencement of hostilities.

The commandant of the garrison at Langres also raised difficulties, and only withdrew within his rayon on February 7th, as did General Rolland later at Besançon. Auxonne was at first unwilling to give up control of the railway. Bitsch, which had not been worth the trouble of a serious attack, repudiated the convention; the investment had therefore to be strengthened, and only in March, when threatened with a determined attack, did the garrison abandon its peak of rock.

Nor did the volunteers acquiesce at once, and there were collisions with them at various points. But after the conditions were finally settled, no more serious quarrels occurred between the inhabitants and the German troops during the whole course of the armistice.

All the German corps before Paris occupied the forts lying in their front, more specifically the Vth took over Mont Valérien, and the IVth the town of St. Denis. Between the forts and the enceinte there lay a neutral zone, which civilians were allowed to cross only by specified roads placed under control of German examining troops.

Apprehensive as it was of the indignation of the populace, the French Government had hesitated so long to utter the word " capitulation," that now, even with the resumption of free communication, Paris was threatened with an outbreak of actual famine. The superfluous stores in the German magazines were therefore placed at the disposal of its authorities. The respective chief-Commands, the local Governments-General, and the Etappen-Inspections received instructions to place no difficulties in the way of the repair of the railways and roads in their districts, and the French authorities were even allowed to make use, under German supervision, of the repaired railroads which the invaders used to supply their own army. Nevertheless, the first provision-train only arrived in Paris on February 3rd, and it was the middle of the month before the French had succeeded in remedying the prevalent distress in the capital.

The German prisoners were at once given up. The surrender of arms and war-material followed by degrees, also the payment of the 200 million francs war-contribution imposed on the city.

But it was still doubtful if the party of " war to the bitter end " in Bordeaux would fall in with the arrangements made by the Paris Government, and whether the National Assembly about to be convened would finally ratify the conditions of peace imposed by the conquerors. The necessary measures in case of the resumption of

D d

hostilities were therefore taken on the French as well as
on the German side.

The distribution of the French forces at the establishment of the armistice was not favourable.

By General Faidherbe's advice the Army of the
North was wholly disbanded, as being too weak to face
the strength opposing it. After the XXIInd Corps
had been transported by sea to Cherbourg, the Army
of Brittany under General de Colomb was composed of
it, the XXVIIth and part of the XIXth Corps, and,
including Lipowski's volunteers, Cathelineau's and other
details, its strength was some 150,000 men. General
Loysel with 30,000 ill-armed and raw Gardes-Mobiles
remained in the trenches of Havre.

General Chanzy, after his retreat on Mayenne, had
made a movement to the left, preparatory to a new
operation with the IInd Army of the Loire from the
Caen base, which, however, was never carried out.
The XVIIIth, XXIst, XVIth, and XXVIth Corps stood
between the lower Loire and the Cher from Angers to
Châteauroux, in a strength of about 160,000 men strong,
the XXVth under General Pourcet was at Bourges,
and General de Pointe's Corps at Nevers. The Army
of the Vosges had withdrawn southward of Châlons sur
Saône, and the remains of the Army of the East
assembled under General Crémer at Chambéry as the
XXIVth Corps.

The total of all the field-troops amounted to 534,452
men. The volunteers, even those most to be relied on,
were dismissed, and the National Guard was designated
as for the present "incapable of rendering any military
service." In the depôts, the camps of instruction, and
in Algiers there were still 354,000 men, and 132,000
recruits were on the lists as the contingent for 1871,
but had not yet been called up.

In case the war should be persisted in, a plan for
limiting it to the defensive in the south-east of France
was under consideration, for which, however, according

to the report sent on February 8th by the Committee of Inquiry to the National Assembly, scarcely more than 252,000 men in fighting condition were available. The fleet, besides, had given up so considerable a number of its men and guns for service on land, that it was no longer able for any great undertaking at sea.

On the German side the first consideration was to reinforce the troops to their full war-strength, and replenish the magazines.

The forts round Paris were at once armed on their fronts facing the enceinte. In and between these were 680 guns, 145 of which were captured French pieces; more than enough to keep the restless population under control. A part of the forces previously occupied in the siege, being no longer required, were removed, in order that the remaining troops should have better accommodation. Besides, it seemed desirable to strengthen the IInd Army, which had in its front the enemy's principal force. In consequence the IVth Corps marched to Nogent le Rotrou, the Vth to Orleans, and the IXth, relieved there, to Vendôme; so that now the quarters of this army extended from Alençon to Tours, and up the Loire as far as Gien and Auxerre.

The Ist Army was in the north with the VIIIth Corps on the Somme, and the Ist on both sides of the Lower Seine; in the south the Army of the South occupied the line of demarcation from Baume to Switzerland, and the country in the rear.

At the end of February the German field-army on French soil consisted of:—

Infantry . 464,221 men with 1674 guns.
Cavalry . 55,562 horses.

Troops in garrison:—

Infantry . 105,272 men with 68 guns.
Cavalry . 5681 horses.

Total . 630,736 men and 1742 guns.

Reserve forces remaining in Germany :—

3288 officers.

204,684 men.

26,603 horses.

Arrangements were so made, that in case of a recommencement of hostilities, the strongest resistance could be made at all points. The armistice had nearly reached its end, and the troops had already been more closely collected to be ready to take the initiative of the offensive towards the south, when the Chancellor of the Confederation announced the extension of the armistice to the 24th, which was again prolonged to midnight on the 26th.

Considerable difficulties had arisen from the differences of opinion with regard to the election of the National Assembly, between the Government in Paris and the Delegation at Bordeaux. The Germans wished to see carried out the choice, not of a party, but of the whole nation, expressed by a free suffrage. But Gambetta had ruled, in violation of the conditions of the armistice, that all who after December 2nd, 1851, had held any position in the Imperial Government should be ineligible to vote. It was not till the Parisian Government had obtained a majority by sending several of its members to Bordeaux, and after the dictator had resigned on February 6th, that the elections proceeded quickly and unhindered.

The deputies duly assembled in Bordeaux by the 12th, the appointed day. M. Thiers was elected chief of the executive, and went to Paris on the 19th with Jules Favre, determined to end the aimless war at any cost.

Negotiations for peace were opened, and after five days' vigorous discussion, when at last on the German side the concession to restore Belfort was made, the preliminaries were signed on the afternoon of the 26th.

France bound herself to give up in favour of Germany a part of Lorraine, and the province of Alsace with the

exception of Belfort, and also to pay a war indemnity
of five milliards of francs.

The evacuation of the districts in occupation of the
German armies was to begin immediately on the ratification of the treaty, and be continued by degrees in
proportion as the money was paid. While the German
troops remained on French soil they were to be maintained at the charge of the country. On the other
hand all requisitioning on the part of the Germans was
to cease. Immediately on the first instalment of
evacuation the French forces were to retire behind the
Loire, with the exception of 20,000 men in Paris and
the necessary garrisons in the fortresses.

After the ratification of these preliminaries, further
terms were to be discussed in Brussels, and the return
of the French prisoners would begin. The armistice
was prolonged to March 12th ; but it was in the option
of either of the belligerent powers to end it after March
3rd by giving three days' notice.

Finally, it was stipulated that the German Army
should have the satisfaction of marching into Paris, and
remaining there till the ratification of the treaty ; but
would be restricted to the section of the city from Point
du Jour to the Rue du Faubourg St. Honoré. The
entry was made on March 1st, after a parade at Long-
champs before his Majesty of 30,000 men, consisting
of 11,000 of the VIth, 11,000 of the IInd Bavarian,
and 8000 of the XIth Army Corps. On the 3rd and
5th of March this force was to have been relieved by
successive bodies of the same strength, but M. Thiers
succeeded by March 1st in getting the National
Assembly at Bordeaux to accept the treaty, after the
deposition of the Napoleonic dynasty had been decreed.
The exchange of ratifications took place in the afternoon
of the 2nd, and on the 3rd the first instalment of troops
of occupation marched out of Paris back into its
quarters.

THE HOMEWARD MARCH OF THE GERMAN ARMY.

By the IIIrd Article, the whole territory between the Seine and the Loire, excepting Paris, was to be evacuated with as little delay as possible by the troops of both sides; the right bank of the former river, on the other hand, was only to be cleared on the conclusion of the definitive treaty of peace. Even then the six eastern departments were still to remain in German possession as a pledge for the last three milliards; not, however, to be occupied by more than 50,000 men.

The marching directions were drawn up in the supreme Headquarter, with a view as well to the comfort of the troops as to the reconstitution of the original order of battle, and the possibility of rapid assembly in case of need.

The forces detailed for permanent occupation of the ceded provinces marched thither at once.

The Reserve and Landwehr troops at home were to be disbanded, as well as the Baden Division, which, however, for the present was to remain there as a mobilized force. The Governments-General in Lorraine, Rheims, and Versailles were to be done away with, and their powers taken over by the local Commanding-Generals. In the maintenance of order in the rear of the army, the VIth and XIIth Corps, as well as the Würtemberg Field Division, were placed at the direct disposition of the supreme Headquarter.

By March 31st the Army had taken full possession of the new territory assigned to it, bounded on the west by the course of the Seine from its source to its mouth.

The Ist Army was in the departments of Seine-Inférieure and Somme, the IInd in front of Paris in the departments of Oise and Seine et Marne, the IIIrd in the departments of Aube and Haute Marne, the Army of the South in the districts most lately hostile. The forts of Paris on the left bank were given up to the French authorities; the siege park and the captured war material had been removed. In consideration of the desire of the French Government that the National Assembly might be allowed as early as possible to sit at Versailles, the supreme Head-quarter was removed to Ferrières, even sooner than had been agreed. On March 15th his Majesty left Nancy for Berlin.

All the troops that were left before Paris were placed under the command of the Crown Prince of Saxony, and General von Manteuffel was nominated Commander of the Army of Occupation.

At the moment when France had freed herself by a heavy sacrifice, an enemy of the most dangerous character appeared from within, in the Commune of Paris.

The 40,000 men left there proved themselves unequal to the task of keeping the rebellious agitation under control; which even during the siege had on several occasions betrayed its existence, and now actually broke out in open civil war. Large masses of people, fraternizing with the National and Mobile Guards, possessed themselves of the guns and set themselves in armed resistance to the Government. M. Thiers had already, by March 18th, summoned to Versailles such regiments as could still be trusted, to withdraw them from the disquieting influence of party impulses, and for the protection of the National Assembly there. The French capital was a prey to revolution, and now became an object of pillage by French troops.

The Germans could easily have put a speedy end to the matter, but what Government could allow its rights to be vindicated by foreign bayonets? The German Commanders consequently limited themselves to forbidding at least within their own districts any movement of disturbance, and to preventing all further ingress into Paris from outside. The disarmament operations which had commenced were interrupted; the troops of the IIIrd Army were drawn closer to the forts, and the outposts were replaced along the line of demarcation, whereon 200,000 men could now be collected within two days. The authorities in Paris were also warned that any attempt to arm the fronts facing the Germans would be followed by the immediate bombardment of the city. The insurgents however, were fully occupied in destroying and burning, and in executing their commanders in the interior of Paris. They did not turn against their foreign enemy, but against the Government chosen by the nation, and prepared for an attack on Versailles.

The high officers of State there, bound by the conditions of the armistice treaty, were almost defence-less; meanwhile the Germans were prepared and willing to allow a reinforcement of 80,000 French troops to be moved up from Besançon, Auxerre and Cambrai, the transport of whom would be furthered by the German troops in occupation of the districts through which they would have to pass.

The release of the prisoners on the other hand was temporarily restricted. These were, for the most part, disciplined regulars; but they might not improbably join the hostile party, so in the first instance only 20,000 troops of the line were set free.

On April 4th General MacMahon advanced with the Government troops against Paris, and entered the city on the 21st. As he was then engaged for eight days in barricade fighting, and as great bands of fugitives threatened to break through the German lines, the IIIrd Army was ordered to take closer order. The outposts advanced almost to the gates of the city, and barred all communication through them until, at the end of the month, Paris was again in the control of the French Government.

In the meantime, the negotiations commenced in Brussels and continued in Frankfort were making rapid progress, and on May 10th the definitive treaty of peace based on the preliminaries was signed. The

mutual ratification followed within the appointed time
of ten days.

Thus a war, carried on with such a vast expenditure
of force on both sides, was brought to an end by
incessant and restless energy in the short period of
seven months.

Even in the first four weeks eight battles were
fought, under which the French Empire crumbled, and
the French Army was swept from the field.

Fresh forces, numerous but incompetent, equalized
the original numerical superiority of the Germans,
and twelve more battles needed to be fought, to safeguard the decisive siege of the enemy's capital.

Twenty fortified places were taken, and not a single
day passed on which there was not fighting somewhere,
on a larger or smaller scale.

The war cost the Germans heavy sacrifice ; they
lost 6247 officers, 123,453 men, 1 colour, 6 guns.

The total losses of the French were incalculable ; in
prisoners only they amounted to :—

In Germany	. .	11,860 officers,	371,981 men.
In Paris	. . .	7,456 „	241,686 „
Disarmed in Switzer-land	. . .	2,192 „	88,381 „
		21,508 officers,	702,048 men.

There were captured 107 colours and eagles, 1915
field-guns, 5526 fortress guns.

Strasburg and Metz, which had been alienated from
the Fatherland in a time of weakness, were recovered,
and the German Empire had risen anew.

THE END.

APPENDIX.

APPENDIX.

IN the accounts of historical events, as they are handed down to posterity, mistakes assume the form of legends which it is not always easy subsequently to disprove.

Among others is the fable which ascribes, with particular zest and as a matter of regular custom, the great decisions taken in the course of our latest campaigns, to the deliberations of a council of war previously convened.

For instance, the battle of Königgrätz.

I can relate in a few lines the circumstances under which an event of such far-reaching importance had birth.

Feldzeugmeister Benedek had, in his advance to the northward, to secure himself against the IInd Prussian Army marching on the east over the mountains of Silesia. To this end four of his Corps had one after another been pushed forward on his right flank, and had all been beaten within three days. They now joined the main body of the Austrian Army, which had meanwhile reached the vicinity of Dubenetz.

Here, then, on June 30th, almost the whole of the Austrian forces were standing actually inside the line of operations between the two Prussian armies; of which the Ist was already fighting its way to Gitschin, designated from Berlin as the common point of concentration, and the IInd had also advanced close on the Upper Elbe; thus they were both so near that the enemy could not attack the one without the other falling on his rear. The strategic advantage was nullified by the tactical disadvantage.

In these circumstances, and having already lost 40,000 men in previous battles, General Benedek gave up the advance, and during the night of June 30th began his retreat on Königgrätz.

The movement of six Army Corps and four Cavalry Divisions, marching in only four columns, which were necessarily very deep, could not be accomplished in the course of a single day. They halted very closely concentrated between Trotina and Lipa; but when on July 2nd they still remained there, it was owing to the extreme fatigue of the troops, and the difficulty, nay, impossibility, of withdrawing so large a body of men beyond the Elbe, under the eyes of an active enemy and by a limited number of passages. In fact, the Austrian general could no longer manœuvre; he had no alternative but to fight.

It is a noteworthy fact that neither his advance on Dubenetz nor his retreat on Lipa was known to the Prussians. These movements were concealed from the IInd Army by the Elbe, and the cavalry of the Ist was a mass of more than 8000 horse collected in one unwieldy Corps. The four squadrons attached to each Infantry Division were of course not able to undertake reconnoissances, as subsequently was later done in 1870 by a more advantageous plan of formation.

Thus in the Royal head-quarters at Gitschin nothing certain was known. It was supposed that the main body of the hostile army was still advancing, and that it would take up a position with the Elbe in its front and its flanks resting on the fortresses of Josephstadt and Königgrätz. There were, then, these alternatives—either to turn this extremely strong position, or attack it in front.

By the adoption of the first the communications of the Austrian Army with Pardubitz would be so seriously threatened that it might probably be compelled to retreat. But to secure the safety of such a movement our IInd Army must relieve our Ist and cross over to the right bank of the Elbe. And in this· case the flank march of the latter close past the enemy's front might easily be interfered with, if passages enough across the river had been prepared by him.

In the second case, success could only be hoped for if an advance of the IInd Army on the right flank of the enemy's position could be combined with the attack in front. For this it must be kept on the left bank.

The separation of the two armies, which was for the present intentionally maintained, allowed of either plan being followed; but mine was the serious responsibility of advising his Majesty which should be chosen.

To keep both alternatives open for the present, General von Herwarth was ordered to occupy Pardubitz, and the Crown Prince to remain on the left bank of the Elbe, to reconnoitre that river as well as the Aupa and the Metau, and to remove all obstacles which might oppose a crossing in one or the other direction. At length, on July 2ud, Prince Frederick Charles was ordered, in the event of his finding a large force in front of the Elbe, to attack it at once. But, on the evening of that day, it came to the knowledge of the Prince that the whole Austrian Army had marched to and was in position on the Bistritz; and in obedience to instructions received, he at once ordered the Ist Army and the Army of the Elbe to assemble close in front of the enemy by daybreak next morning.

General von Voigts-Rhetz brought the news at eleven o'clock in the evening to the King at Gitschin, and his Majesty sent him over to me.

This information dispelled all doubts and lifted a weight from my heart. With a "Thank God!" I sprang out of bed, and hastened across to the King, who was lodged on the other side of the Market Place.

His Majesty also had gone to rest in his little camp-bed. After a brief explanation on my part, he said he fully understood the situation, decided on giving battle next day with all three armies in co-operation, and desired me to transmit the necessary orders to the Crown Prince, who was at once to cross the Elbe.

The whole interview with his Majesty lasted barely ten minutes. No one else was present.

This was the "Council of War" before Königgrätz.

General von Podbielski and Major Count Wartensleben shared my quarters. The orders to the IInd Army were drawn up forthwith and despatched in duplicate by two different routes by midnight. One, carried by General von Voigts-Rhetz, informed Prince Frederick Charles of all the dispositions; the other was sent direct to Koniginhof.

In the course of his night-ride of above twenty-eight miles, Lieutenant-Colonel Count Finckenstein had to pass the rayon of the Ist Army Corps, which was furthest to the rear. He handed to the officer on duty a special letter to be forwarded immediately to the general in command, ordering an immediate assemblage of his troops and an independent advance, even before orders should reach him from Königinhof.

The position of the Austrians on July 3rd had a front of not more than 4½ miles. Our three armies advanced on it in an encompassing arc of about twenty-four miles in extent. But while in the centre the Ist and IInd Corps of the Ist Army stood before daylight close in front of the enemy, on the right wing General von Herwath had to advance on the Bistritz from Smidar in the dark, by very bad roads, above nine miles; and on the left, the orders from the Royal head-quarter could not even reach the Crown Prince before four in the morning. It was therefore decided that the centre would have to maintain a detaining engagement for several hours. Above all, a possible offensive on the part of the enemy must here be met, and for this the whole IIIrd Corps and the cavalry corps stood ready; but the battle could only be decided by the double flank attack by both the flanking armies.[1]

I had ridden out early to the heights in front of Sadowa with my officers, and at eight o'clock the King also arrived there.

It was a dull morning, and from time to time a shower fell. The horizon was dim, yet on the right the white clouds of smoke showed that the heads of the 1st Army were already fighting some way off, in front of the villages on the Bistritz. On the left, in the woods of Swip, brisk rifle-firing was audible. Behind the King, besides his staff, were his royal guests, with their numerous suites of adjutants, equerries, and led horses, in number as many as two squadrons. An Austrian battery seemed to have selected them to aim at, and compelled him to move away with a smaller following.

Soon afterwards, with Count Wartensleben, I rode through the village of Sadowa, which the enemy had already abandoned. The advanced guard of the 8th Division had massed its guns behind the wood under cover of the sharpshooters who had been sent forward, but many shells fell there from a large battery in front of the exits from the copses. As we rode further along the road we admired the coolness of a huge ox, which went on its way, heedless of the shot, and seemed determined to charge the enemy's position.

The formidable array of the IIIrd and Xth Austrian Corps' Artillery opposite the wood prevented any attempt to break through it, and I was in time to countermand an order which had been given to do so.

Meanwhile, further to the left, General von Fransecky had vigorously passed to the offensive. After a sharp struggle he had driven the enemy out of the Swip woods, and come through to the further side. Against him he had the IVth Austrian Corps; but now the IInd and part of the IIIrd Austrian Corps turned on the 7th Division; 57 battalions against 14. In the thick brushwood all the bodies had become mixed, personal command was impossible, and, in spite of our obstinate resistance, isolated detachments were taken prisoners, and others were dispersed.

Such a rabble rushed out of the wood at the very moment when the King and his staff rode up; his Majesty looked on with some displeasure,[2] but the wounded officer, who was trying to keep his little band together, at once led it back into the fight. In spite of heavy losses the division got firm possession of the northern side of the wood. It had drawn on itself very considerable forces of the enemy, which were subsequently missing from the positions which it was their duty to have defended.

It was now eleven o'clock. The heads of the 1st Army had crossed the Bistritz, and taken most of the villages on its further bank; but these were only the enemy's advanced posts, which he had no intention of obstinately holding. His Corps held a position behind, whence their 250 guns commanded the open plain which had to be crossed for the delivery of a further attack. On the right, General von Herwarth had reached the Bistritz, but on the left nothing was yet to be seen of the Crown Prince.

---

[1] viz. The IInd Army, commanded by the Crown Prince of Prussia, which was to strike the Austrian right flank and right rear; and the Army of the Elbe, commanded by General Herwarth von Bittenfeld, which was to strike the Austrian left flank.

[2] I have a history of the war, published at Tokio, in the Japanese language, with very original illustrations. One of these has for its title, ".The King scolding the Army." [MOLTKE.]

The battle had come to a standstill. In the centre the 1st Army was still fighting about the villages on the Bistritz; the cavalry could, not get forward, and the artillery found no good position to occupy. The troops had been for five hours under the enemy's lively fire, without food, to prepare which there had been no time.

Some doubt as to the issue of the battle existed probably in many minds; perhaps in that of Count Bismarck, as he offered me his cigar case. As I was subsequently informed, he took it for a good sign that of two cigars I coolly selected the better one.

The King asked me at about this time what I thought of the prospects of the battle. I replied, " Your Majesty to-day will not only win the battle, but decide the war."

It could not be otherwise.

We had the advantage in numbers,[1] which in war is never to be despised; and it was certain that our IInd Army must finally appear on the flank and rear of the Austrians.

At about 1.30 a white cloud was seen on the height, crowned with trees, and visible from afar, on which our field-glasses had been centred. It was indeed not yet the IInd Army, but the smoke of the fire which, directed thereon, announced its near approach. The joyful shout, "The Crown Prince is coming!" ran through the ranks. I sent the wished-for news to General von Herwarth, who meanwhile had carried Problus, in spite of the heroic defence of the Saxons.

The IInd Army had started at 7.30 in the morning; only the 1st Corps had delayed till about 9·15. The advance by bad roads, in part across the fields, had taken much time. The hill-road stretching from Horenowes to Trotina, if efficiently held, could not but be a serious obstacle. But in its eager pressure on Fransecky's Division the enemy's right wing had made a wheel to the left, so that it lay open to some extent to the attack on its rear now impending.

The Crown Prince's progress was not yet visible to us, but at about half-past three the King ordered the advance of the 1st Army also.

As we emerged from the wood of Sadowa into the open we found still a part of the great battery which had so long prevented us from debouching here, but the teams and gunners lay stretched by the wrecked guns. There was nothing else to be seen of the enemy over a wide distance.

The Austrian retreat from the position grasped by us on two sides, had become inevitable, and had, in fact, been effected some time before. Their admirable artillery, firing on to the last moment, had screened their retreat and given the infantry a long start. The crossing of the Bistritz seriously

---

[1] During a long peace the sphere of action of the War Minister's department and the General Staff were not distinctly defined. The providing for the troops in peace was the function of the former, and in war time a number of official duties which could be superintended by the central authorities at home. Thus the place of the Minister of War was not at head-quarters, but at Berlin. The Chief of the General Staff, on the other hand, from the moment when the mobilization is ordered, assumes the whole responsibility for the marching and transport already prepared for during peace, both for the first assembling of the forces, and for their subsequent employment, for which he has only to ask the consent of the Commander-in-Chief—always, with us, the King.

How necessary this disjunction of the two authorities is, I had to experience in June, 1866. Without my knowledge the order had been given for the VIIth Corps to remain on the Rhine. It was only by my representations that the 16th Division was moved up into Bohemia, and our numerical superiority thus brought up to a decisive strength. [MOLTKE.]

delayed the advance, especially of the cavalry, so that only isolated detachments of it yet came up with the enemy.

We rode at a smart gallop across the wide field of battle, without looking much about us on the scene of horror. Finally, we found our three armies which had at last pushed on into a circumscribed space from their several directions, and had got much mixed. It took twenty-four hours to remedy the confusion and re-form the bodies; an immediate pursuit was impossible, but the victory was complete.

The exhausted men now sought resting-places in the villages or the open field as best they might. Anything that came to hand by way of food was of course taken; my wandering ox probably among the rest. The death-cries of pigs and geese were heard; but necessity knows no law, and the baggage-waggons were naturally not on the spot.

The King, too, remained at a hamlet on the field. Only I and my two officers had to journey some twenty-four miles back to Gitschin, where the bureaux were.

We had set out thence at four in the morning, and had been fourteen hours in the saddle. In the hurry of departure no one had thought of providing himself with food. An Uhlan of the 2nd Regiment had bestowed on me a slice of sausage, bread he had none himself. On our way back we met the endless train of provision and ammunition waggons, often extending all across the road. We did not reach our quarters till midnight. There was nothing to eat even here at this hour, but I was so exhausted that I threw myself on my bed in great-coat and sash, and fell asleep instantly. Next morning new orders had to be prepared and laid before his Majesty at Horitz.

The Great King [1] had needed to struggle for seven years to reduce the might of Austria, which his more fortunate and also more powerful grandson [2] had achieved in as many weeks. The campaign had proved decisive in the first eight days from June 27th to July 3rd.

The war of 1866 was entered on not as a defensive measure to meet a threat against the existence of Prussia, nor in obedience to public opinion and the voice of the people: it was a struggle, long foreseen and calmly prepared for, recognized as a necessity by the Cabinet, not for territorial aggrandizement or material advantage, but for an ideal end—the establishment of power. Not a foot of land was exacted from defeated Austria, but she had to renounce all part in the hegemony of Germany.

The Princes of the Reich had themselves to blame that the old Empire had now for centuries allowed domestic politics to override German national politics. Austria had exhausted her strength in conquests south of the Alps while she left the western German provinces unprotected, instead of following the road pointed out by the course of the Danube. Her centre of gravity lay outside of Germany; Prussia's lay within it. Prussia felt her strength, and that it behoved her to assume the leadership of the German races. The regrettable but unavoidable exclusion of one of them from the new Reich could only be to a small extent remedied by a subsequent alliance. But Germany has become immeasurably greater without Austria, than it was before with Austria.

But all this has nothing to do with the legends of which I am telling. One of these has been sung in verse, and in fine verse too.

The scene is Versailles. The French are making a sortie from Paris, and the generals, instead of betaking themselves to their fighting troops, are assembled to consider whether head-quarters may safely remain any longer

---

[1] Frederick the Great.

[2] Wilhelm was not the grandson, but the great-grand-nephew of Frederick the Great. The term is very rarely used in the wider sense of "descendant;" but Frederick was childless.

E e

at Versailles. Opinions are divided, no one dares speak out. The Chief of the General Staff, who is above all called on to express his views, remains silent. The perplexity seems to be great. Only the War Minister rises and protests with the greatest emphasis against a measure so injurious from a political and military point of view as a removal. He is warmly thanked by the King as being the only man who has the courage to speak the truth freely and fearlessly.

The truth is that while the King and his whole escort had ridden out to the Vth Army Corps, the Marshal of the household, in his over-anxiety, had the horses put to the royal carriages, and this became known in the town; and indeed may have excited all sorts of hopes in the sanguine inhabitants.

Versailles was protected by four Army Corps. It never entered anybody's head to think of evacuating the town.

I can positively assert no Council of War was ever held either in 1866 or 1870-71.

Excepting on the march and on days of battle, an audience was regularly held by his Majesty at ten o'clock, at which I, accompanied by the Quartermaster-General, laid the latest reports and information before him, and made our suggestions on that basis. The Chief of the Military Cabinet and the Minister of War were also present, and while the head-quarters of the IIIrd Army were at Versailles, the Crown Prince also; but all merely as listeners. The King occasionally required them to give him information on one point or another; but I do not remember that he ever asked for advice concerning the operations in the field or the suggestions I made.

These, which I always discussed beforehand with my staff officers, were, on the contrary, generally maturely weighed by his Majesty himself. He always pointed out with a military eye and an invariably correct estimate of the situation, all the objections that might be raised to their execution; but as in war every step is beset with danger, the plans laid before him were invariably adopted.

ORDERS OF BATTLE

OF THE

FRENCH AND GERMAN ARMIES IN THE FIRST PERIOD OF THE FRANCO-GERMAN WAR.

———◆———

ORDER OF BATTLE OF THE FRENCH ARMIES.

———

ORDER OF BATTLE OF THE "ARMY OF THE RHINE."

Commander-in-Chief: The Emperor Napoleon III.
Major-General: Marshal Le Bœuf.
Aide-Major-General: General Dejean.
Chiefs of Staff: Generals Jarras and Lebrun.
Commanding Artillery: General Soleille.
Commanding Engineer: General Coffinières de Nordeck.
Aides-de-camp to the Emperor: Generals Prince do la Moscawa, do Castlenau, Count Reille, Viscount Pajol.

THE IMPERIAL GUARD.

General Bourbaki.
Chief of Staff: General d'Auvergne.
Commanding Artillery: General Pé-de-Arros.

1st *Infantry Division:* General Deligny.

1st Brigade: General Brincourt.
    Chasseurs of the Guard.
    1st and 2nd Voltigeurs of the Guard.
2nd Brigade: General Garnier.
    3rd and 4th Voltigeurs of the Guard.
Division-Artillery.
    Two 4-pounder batteries, one mitrailleuse battery.

2nd *Infantry Division:* General Picard.

1st Brigade: General Jeanningros.
    Zouaves of the Guard (two battalions).
1st Grenadiers of the Guard.
2nd Brigade: General Poitevin de la Croix.
    2nd and 3rd Grenadiers of the Guard.
Division-Artillery.
    Two 4-pounder batteries, one mitrailleuse battery.

E e 2

Cavalry Division : General Desvaux.
1st Brigade : General Halma du Frétay.
   Guides.
   Chasseurs of the Guard.
2nd Brigade : General de France.
   Lancers of the Guard.
   Dragoons of the Guard.
3rd Brigade : General du Preuil.
   Cuirassiers of the Guard.
   Carabiniers of the Guard.

Reserve Artillery : Colonel Clappier
Four horse-artillery batteries.

1st Corps.

Marshal MacMahon, afterwards General Ducrot.
Chief of Staff : General Colson.
Commanding Artillery : General Forgeot.

1st Infantry Division : General Ducrot.

1st Brigade : General Moreno.
   13th Chasseur battalion.
   18th and 96th Line regiments.
2nd Brigade : General de Postis du Houlbec.
   45th and 74th Line regiments.
Division-Artillery.
   Two 4-pounder batteries and one mitrailleuse battery.

2nd Infantry Division : General Abel Douay, afterwards General Pellé.

1st Brigade : General Pelletier de Montmarie.
   16th Chasseur battalion.
   50th and 78th Line regiments.
2nd Brigade : General Pellé.
   1st regiment of Zouaves.
   1st regiment of Turcos.
Division-Artillery.
   Two 4-pounder batteries, one mitrailleuse battery.

3rd Infantry Division : General Raoult.

1st Brigade : General L'Heriller.
   8th Chasseur battalion.
   2nd Zouave regiment.
   36th Line regiment.
2nd Brigade : General Lefèvre.
   2nd regiment of Turcos.
   48th Line regiment.
Division-Artillery.
   Two 4-pounder batteries, one mitrailleuse battery.

4th Infantry Division : General de Lartigue.

1st Brigade : General Fraboulet de Kerléadec.
   1st battalion of Chasseurs.
   3rd Zouave regiment.
   56th Line regiment.

2nd Brigade : General Lacretelle.
   3rd regiment of Turcos.
   87th Line regiment.
Division-Artillery.
   Two 4-pounder batteries, one mitrailleuse battery.

Cavalry Division : General Duhesme.

1st Brigade : General de Septeuil.
   3rd Hussar regiment.
   11th Chasseur regiment.
2nd Brigade : General de Nansouty.
   2nd and 6th Lancer regiments.
   10th Dragoon regiment.
3rd Brigade : General Michel.
   8th and 9th Cuirassier regiments.

Reserve Artillery : Colonel de Vassart.

Two 4-pounder batteries.
Two 12-pounder batteries.
Four horse-artillery batteries.

2ND CORPS.

General Frossard.
Chief of Staff : General Saget.
Commanding Artillery : General Gagnoux.

1st Infantry Division : General Vergé

1st Brigade : General Letellier-Valazé.
   3rd battalion of Chasseurs.
   32nd and 55th Line regiments.
2nd Brigade : General Jobivet.
   76th and 77th Line regiments.
Division-Artillery.
   Two 4-pounder, one mitrailleuse battery.

2nd Infantry Division : General Bataille.

1st Brigade : General Pouget.
   12th battalion of Chasseurs.
   8th and 23rd Line regiments.
2nd Brigade : General Fauvart-Bastoul.
   66th and 67th Line regiments.
Division-Artillery.
   Two 4-pounder, one mitrailleuse battery.

3rd Infantry Division : General Laveaucoupet.

1st Brigade : General Doens.
   10th battalion of Chasseurs.
   2nd and 63rd Line regiments.
2nd Brigade : General Michelet.
   24th and 40th Line regiments.
Division-Artillery.
   Two 4-pounder, one mitrailleuse battery.

Cavalry Division : General Lichtlin.

1st Brigade : General de Valabrèque.
   4th and 5th regiments of Chasseurs.

2nd Brigade : General Bachelier.
7th and 12th regiments of Dragoons.

Reserve-Artillery : Colonel Baudouin.

Two 4-pounder batteries.
Two 12-pounder batteries.
Two mitrailleuse batteries.

3RD CORPS.

Marshal Bazaine, afterwards General Decaen.
Chief of Staff : General Manèque.
Commanding Artillery : General de Rochebouet.

1st Infantry Division : General Montaudon.

1st Brigade : General Aymard.
18th Chasseur battalion.
51st and 62nd Line regiments.
2nd Brigade : General Clinchant.
81st and 95th Line regiments.
Division-Artillery.
Two 4-pounder, one mitrailleuse battery.

2nd Infantry Division : General de Castagny.

1st Brigade : General Cambriels.
15th Chasseur battalion.
19th and 41st Line regiments.
2nd Brigade : General Duplessis.
69th and 90th Line regiments.
Division-Artillery.
Two 4-pounder, one mitrailleuse battery.

3rd Infantry Division : General Metman.

1st Brigade : General de Potier.
7th Chasseur battalion.
7th and 29th Line regiments.
2nd Brigade : General Arnaudeau.
59th and 71st Line regiments.
Division-Artillery.
Two 4-pounder, one mitrailleuse battery.

4th Infantry Division : General Decaen.

1st Brigade : General de Brauer.
11th Chasseur battalion.
44th and 60th Line regiments.
2nd Brigade : General Sanglé-Ferrières.
80th and 85th Line regiments.
Division-Artillery.
Two 4-pounder, one mitrailleuse battery.

Cavalry Division : General de Clérembault.

1st Brigade : General de Bruchard.
2nd, 3rd, and 10th Chasseur regiments.
2nd Brigade : General de Maubranches.
2nd and 4th Dragoon regiments.
3rd Brigade : General de Juniac.
5th and 8th Dragoon regiments.

Reserve Artillery : Colonel de Lajaille.

Two 4-pounder batteries.
Two 12-pounder batteries.
Four horse-artillery batteries.

4TH CORPS.

General de Ladmirault.
Chief of Staff : General Desaint de Martille.
Commanding Artillery : General Laffaile.

1st Infantry Division : General de Cissey.

1st Brigade : General Count Brayer.
  20th Chasseur battalion.
  1st and 6th Line regiments.
2nd Brigade : General de Golberg.
  57th and 73rd Line regiments.
Division-Artillery.
  Two 4-pounder, one mitrailleuse battery.

2nd Infantry Division : General Rose.

1st Brigade : General Bellecourt.
  5th Chasseur battalion.
  13th and 43rd Line Regiments.
2nd Brigade : General Pradier.
  64th and 98th Line regiments.
Division-Artillery.
  Two 4-pounder, one mitrailleuse battery.

3rd Infantry Division : General de Lorencez.

1st Brigade : General Pajol.
  2nd Chasseur battalion.
  15th and 33rd Line regiments.
2nd Brigade : General Berger.
  54th and 65th Line regiments.
Division-Artillery.
  Two 4-pounder, one mitrailleuse battery.

Cavalry Division : General Legrand.

1st Brigade : General de Montaigu.
  2nd and 7th Hussar regiments.
2nd Brigade : General de Gondrecourt.
  3rd and 11th Dragoon regiments.

Reserve-Artillery : Colonel Soleille.

Two 4-pounder batteries.
Two 12-pounder batteries.
Two horse-artillery batteries.

5TH CORPS.

General de Failly.
Chief of Staff: General Besson.
Commanding Artillery : General Liédot.

1st Infantry Division : General Goze.

1st Brigade : General Grenier.
   4th Chasseur battalion.
   11th and 46th Line regiments.
2nd Brigade : General Nicolas.
   61st and 86th Line regiments.
Division-Artillery.
   Two 4-pounder, one mitrailleuse battery.

2nd Infantry Division : General de l'Abadie d'Aydroin.

1st Brigade : General Lapasset.
   14th Chasseur battalion.
   49th and 84th Line regiments.
2nd Brigade : General de Maussiou.
   88th and 97th Line regiments.
Division-Artillery.
   Two 4-pounder, one mitrailleuse battery.

3rd Infantry Division : General Guyot de Lespart.

1st Brigade : General Abbatucci.
   19th Chasseur battalion.
   17th and 27th Line regiments.
2nd Brigade : General de Fontanges de Couzan.
   30th and 68th Line regiments.
Division-Artillery.
   Two 4-pounder, one mitrailleuse battery.

Cavalry Division : General Brahaut.

1st Brigade : General Pierre de Bernis.
   5th and 12th Chasseur regiments.
2nd Brigade : General de la Mortière.
   3rd and 5th Lancer regiments.
Division-Artillery.
   One battery of horse-artillery.

Reserve-Artillery : Colonel de Salignac-Fénelon.

   Two 4-pounder batteries.
   Two 12-pounder batteries.
   Two horse-artillery batteries.

6TH CORPS.

Marshal Canrobert.
Chief of Staff: General Henri.
Commanding Artillery : General de Berkheim.

1st Infantry Division : General Tixier.

1st Brigade : General Péchot.
   9th Chasseur battalion.
   4th and 10th Line regiments.
2nd Brigade : General Le Roy de Dais.
   12th and 100th Line regiments.
Division-Artillery.
   Two 4-pounder, one mitrailleuse battery.

2nd Infantry Division : General Bisson.

1st Brigade : General Noël.
    9th and 14th Line regiments.
2nd Brigade : General Maurice.
    20th and 30th Line regiments.
Division-Artillery.
    Two 4-pounder, one mitrailleuse battery.

3rd Infantry Division : General La Font de Villiers.

1st Brigade : General Becquet de Sonnay.
    75th and 91st Line regiments.
2nd Brigade : General Colin.
    93rd Line regiment.
Division-Artillery.
    Two 4-pounder, one mitrailleuse battery.

4th Infantry Division : General Levassor-Sorval.

1st Brigade : General de Marguenat.
    25th and 26th Line regiments.
2nd Brigade : General de Chanaleilles.
    28th and 70th Line regiments.
Division-Artillery.
    Two 4-pounder, one mitrailleuse battery.

Cavalry Division : General de Salignac-Fénelon.

1st Brigade : General Tilliard.
    1st Hussar regiment.
    6th Chasseur regiment.
2nd Brigade : General Savaresse.
    1st and 7th Lancer regiments.
3rd Brigade : General de Béville.
    5th and 6th Cuirassier regiments.
Division-Artillery.
    Two batteries of horse-artillery.

Reserve-Artillery : Colonel de Montluisant.

Two 4-pounder batteries.
Two 12-pounder batteries.
Four batteries of horse-artillery.

7TH CORPS.

General Felix Douay.
Chief of Staff : General Renson.
Commanding Artillery : General Liègard.

1st Infantry Division : General Conseil-Dumesnil.

1st Brigade : General Le Norman de Bretteville.
    17th Chasseur battalion.
    3rd and 21st Line regiments.
2nd Brigade : General Maire.
    47th and 99th Line regiments.
Division-Artillery.
    Two 4-pounder, two mitrailleuse batteries.

2nd Infantry Division : General Liébert.

1st Brigade : General Guiomar.
  6th Chasseur battalion.
  5th and 37th Line regiments.
2nd Brigade : General de la Bastide.
  53rd and 89th Line regiments.
Division-Artillery.
  Two 4-pounder, one mitrailleuse battery.

3rd Infantry Division : General Dumont.

1st Brigade : General Bordas.
  52nd and 72nd Line regiments.
2nd Brigade : General Bittard des Portes.
  82nd and 83rd Line regiments.
Division-Artillery.
  Two 4-pounder, one mitrailleuse battery.

Cavalry Division : General Ameil.

1st Brigade : General Cambriel.
  4th Hussar regiments
  4th and 8th Lancer regiments.
2nd Brigade : General Jolif du Coulombier.
  6th Hussar regiment.
  6th Dragoon regiment.
Division-Artillery.
  One battery of horse-artillery.

Reserve Artillery.

Two 4-pounder batteries.
Two 12-pounder batteries.
Two batteries horse-artillery.

RESERVE CAVALRY.

1st Division : General du Barrail.

1st Brigade : General Margueritte.
  1st and 3rd regiments Chasseurs d'Afrique.
2nd Brigade : General de Lajaille.
  2nd and 4th regiments Chasseurs d'Afrique.
Division-Artillery.
  Two batteries of horse-artillery.

2nd Division : General de Bonnemains.

1st Brigade : General Girard.
  1st and 2nd Cuirassier regiments.
2nd Brigade : . . . .
  3rd and 4th Cuirassier regiments.
Division-Artillery.
  Two batteries of horse-artillery.

3rd Division : General Marquis de Forton.

1st Brigade : General Prince J. Murat.
  1st and 9th Dragoon regiments.
2nd Brigade : General de Grammont.
  7th and 10th Cuirassier regiments.
Division-Artillery.
  Two batteries of horse-artillery.

General Cann.
Chief of Staff: Colonel Laffont do Ladébat.
13th Field-Artillery regiment.
 Eight 12-pounder batteries.
18th Field-Artillery regiment.
 Eight batteries of horse-artillery.
Three mountain batteries.

Note.—The 6th Corps (Canrobert), when ordered to Metz from Châlons, left there three line regiments, its cavalry division, and reserve artillery.

The battle of Wörth divided the original Army of the Rhine into two parts, one of which is generally known as "The Army of Metz," and the other, with additions, became "The Army of Châlons." Their respective "Orders of Battle" follow:—

ORDER OF BATTLE OF THE ARMY OF CHÂLONS.

Commander-in-Chief: Marshal MacMahon, Duke of Magenta, afterwards General de Wimpfen.
Chief of Staff: General Faure.
Commanding Artillery: General Forgeot.
Commanding Engineer: General Dejean.
Intendant-General: Rousillon.

1st Corps.

General Ducrot.
Chief of Staff: Colonel Robert.
Commanding Artillery: General Frigola.

1st *Infantry Division*: General Wolff.

1st Brigade: General Moreno.
 13th Chasseur battalion.
 18th and 96th Line regiments.
2nd Brigade: General de Postis du Houlbec.
 45th Line regiment.
 1st Zouave regiment.
Division-Artillery.
 Two 4-pounder, one mitrailleuse battery.

2nd *Infantry Division:* General Pellé.

1st Brigade: General Pelletier de Montmarie.
 16th Chasseur battalion.
 50th and 74th Line regiments.
2nd Brigade: General Gandil.
 78th Line regiment.
 1st regiment of Turcos.
 1st "marching" regiment.
Division-Artillery.
 Two 4-pounder, one mitrailleuse battery.

3rd Infantry Division : General L'Heriller.

1st Brigade : General Carteret-Trécourt.
    8th Chasseur battalion.
    2nd Zouave regiment.
    36th Line regiment.
2nd Brigade : General Lefébvre.
    2nd regiment of Turcos.
    48th Line regiment.
    1st battalion of Franc-tireurs of Paris.
Division-Artillery.
    Two 4 pounder, one mitrailleuse battery.

4th Infantry Division : General de Lartigue.

1st Brigade : General Fraboulet de Kerléadec.
    1st Chasseur battalion.
    3rd regiment of Tirailleurs (Turcos).
    56th Line regiment.
2nd Brigade : General de Bellemare.
    3rd Zouave regiment.
    2nd "marching" regiment.
Division-Artillery.
    Two 4-pounder, one mitrailleuse battery.

Cavalry Division : General Duhesme ; after August 25, General Michel.

1st Brigade : General de Septeuil.
    3rd Hussar regiment.
    11th Chasseur regiment.
2nd Brigade : General de Nansouty.
    2nd and 6th Lancer regiments.
    10th Dragoon regiment.
3rd Brigade : General Michel.
    8th and 9th Cuirassier regiments.

Reserve Artillery : Colonel Grouvell.

Two 4-pounder batteries.
Two 12-pounder batteries.
Four batteries of horse-artillery.

5TH CORPS.

General de Failly.
Chief of Staff : General Besson.
Commanding Artillery, General Liédot.

1st Infantry Division : General Goze.

1st Brigade : General Grenier, later General Saurin.
    4th Chasseur battalion.
    11th and 46th Line regiments.
2nd Brigade : General Baron Nicolas-Nicolas.
    61st and 86th Line regiments.
Division-Artillery.
    Two 4-pounder, one mitrailleuse battery.

2nd Infantry Division : General de l'Abadie d'Aydrein.

1st Brigade : General Lapasset.
(With the army of Metz.)
2nd Brigade : General de Maussion.
88th and 97th Line regiments.
Division-Artillery.
Two 4-pounder, one mitrailleuse battery.

3rd Infantry Division : General Guyot de l'Lespart.

1st Brigade : General Abbatucci.
19th Chasseur battalion.
17th and 27th Line regiments.
2nd Brigade : General de Fontanges de Couzan.
30th and 68th Line regiments.
Division-Artillery.
Two 4-pounder, one mitrailleuse battery.

Cavalry Division : General Brahaut.

1st Brigade : General Viscount Pierre de Bernis.
5th and 6th Chasseur regiments.
2nd Brigade : General de la Mortière.
3rd and 5th Lancer regiments.
Division-Artillery.
One battery of horse-artillery.

Reserve Artillery : Colonel de Salignac-Fénelon.

Two 4-pounder batteries.
Two 12-pounder batteries.
Two batteries of horse-artillery.

7th CORPS.

General Felix Douay.
Chief of Staff : General Renson.
Commanding Artillery : General Liègard.

1st Infantry Division : General Conseil-Dumesnil.

1st Brigade : General Morand, afterwards General la Brettevillois.
17th Chasseur battalion.
3rd and 21st Line regiments.
2nd Brigade : General St. Hilaire.
47th and 99th Line regiments.
Division-Artillery.
Two 4-pounder, two mitrailleuse batteries.

2nd Infantry Division : General Liébert.

1st Brigade : General Guiomar.
6th Chasseur battalion.
5th and 37th Line regiments.
2nd Brigade : General de la Bastide.
53rd and 89th Line regiments.
Division-Artillery.
Two 4-pounder, one mitrailleuse battery.

3rd Infantry Division : General Dumont.

1st Brigade : General Bordas.
    52nd and 72nd Line regiments.
2nd Brigade : General Bittard des Portes.
    82nd and 83rd Line regiments.
Division-Artillery.
    Two 4-pounder, one mitrailleuse battery.

Cavalry Brigade : General Ameil.

1st Brigade : General Cambriel.
    4th Hussar regiment.
    4th and 8th Lancer regiments.
2nd Brigade : General du Coulombier (appointed).
Division-Artillery.
    One battery of horse-artillery.

Reserve-Artillery : Colonel Aubac.

Two 4-pounder batteries.
Two 12-pounder batteries.
Two batteries of horse-artillery.

12TH CORPS.

General Lebrun.
Chief of Staff: General Gresley.
Commanding Artillery : General d'Ouvrier de Villègly.

1st Infantry Division : General Grandchamp.

1st Brigade : General Cambriels.
    1 Chasseur marching battalion.
    22nd and 34th Line regiments.
2nd Brigade : General de Villeneuve.
    58th and 72nd Line regiments.
Division-Artillery.
    Two 4-pounder, one mitrailleuse battery.

2nd Infantry Division : General Lacretelle.

1st Brigade : General Bernier Maligny.
    14th, 20th, and 30th Line regiments.
2nd Brigade : General Marquisan.
    3rd and 4th marching regiments.
Division-Artillery.
    Two 4-pounder, two mitrailleuse batteries.

3rd Infantry Division : General de Vassoigne.

1st Brigade : General Reboul.
    1st and 2nd regiments of marine infantry.
2nd Brigade : General Martin de Paillières.
    3rd and 4th regiments of marine infantry.
Division-Artillery.
    Two 4-pounder, one mitrailleuse battery.

Cavalry Division : General de Salignac-Fénelon.

1st Brigade: General Savaresse.
1st and 7th Lancer regiments.
2nd Brigade : General de Béville.
5th and 6th Cuirassier regiments.
3rd Brigade : General Leforestier de Vendeune.
7th and 8th Chasseurs.

Reserve Artillery : Colonel Brisac.

Two 4-pounder batteries.
Two 12-pounder batteries.
Two batteries of horse-artillery.

RESERVE CAVALRY.

1st Reserve Cavalry Division : General Margueritte.

1st Brigade : General Tillard.
1st and 2nd Chasseurs regiments.
2nd Brigade : General de Galiffet.
1st, 3rd and 4th Chasseurs d'Afrique.
Division-Artillery.
Two batteries of horse-artillery.

2nd Reserve Cavalry Division : General de Bonnemains.

1st Brigade : General Girard.
1st Hussar regiment.
47th Chasseur regiment.
2nd Brigade : General de Brauer.
2nd and 3rd Cuirassiers.

ORDER OF BATTLE OF THE ARMY OF METZ.

Commander-in-Chief : Marshal Bazaine.
Chief of Staff : General Jarras.
Commanding Artillery : General Soleille.
Commanding Engineer : General Viala.

THE IMPERIAL GUARD.

General Bourbaki (afterwards General Desvaux).
Chief of Staff : General d'Auvergne.
Commanding Artillery : General Pé-de-Arros.
(Detail as above.)

2ND CORPS.

General Frossard.
(Detail as above with the exception of the 3rd Division (Laveaucoupet's) detached to garrison duty.)

3RD CORPS.

General Decaen, afterwards Marshal Le Bœuf.
(Detail as above.)

4TH CORPS.

General de Ladmirault.

(Detail as above.)

6TH CORPS.

Marshal Canrobert.
(Detail as above, with the exception that the Corps when ordered up to
Metz, left behind at Châlons three infantry regiments, its cavalry divi-
sion, its reserve artillery, and division artillery of the 2nd Division.

LAPASSET'S BRIGADE (from attached 5th Corps).
General Lapasset.
    14th Chasseur battalion.
    49th and 84th Line regiments.

RESERVE CAVALRY.

1st Reserve Cavalry Division : General du Barrail.

1st Brigade : General Margueritte.
    (Vide Army of Châlons.)
2nd Brigade : General de Lajaille.
    2nd Regiment of Chasseurs d'Afrique.
    (The 4th regiment of Chasseurs d'Afrique remained at Châlons.)
Division-Artillery.
    Two batteries of horse-artillery.

2nd Reserve Cavalry Division : General de Forton.

1st Brigade : General Prince J. Murat.
    1st and 9th Dragoon regiments.
2nd Brigade : General de Grammont.
    7th and 10th Cuirassier regiments.

GREAT ARTILLERY RESERVE.

(As above, less six batteries detached to the 6th Corps.)

ORDER OF BATTLE OF THE GERMAN ARMIES
ON 1st AUGUST, 1870.

Commander-in-Chief : H.M. the King of Prussia.
King's aides-de-camp : General von Boyen ; Lieut.-General von Treskow ;
    Major-General von Steinäcker ; Colonel Count Lehndorff ; Lieut.-
    Colonel Prince Radziwill ; Lieut.-Colonel Count Waldersee ; Major
    von Alten.
Chief of Staff : General Baron von Moltke.
Quarter-Master General : Lieut.-General von Podbielski.
Divisional Chiefs of Staff : Lieut.-Colonel Bronsart von Schellendorf ;
    Lieut.-Colonel von Verdy du Vernois ; Lieut.-Colonel von Branden-
    stein.
Inspector-General of Artillery : General von Hindersin.
Inspector-General of Engineers : Lieut.-General von Kleist.
Commissary-General : Lieut.-General von Stosch.

I. ARMY.

Commander-in-Chief: General von Steinmetz, afterwards General von Manteuffel.
Chief of Staff: Major-General von Sperling.
Quartermaster-General: Colonel Count von Wartensleben.
Commanding Artillery: Lieut.-General Schwartz.
Commanding Engineer: Major-General Biehler.

7TH CORPS—WESTPHALIA.

Infantry-General von Zastrow.
Chief of Staff: Colonel von Unger.
Commanding Artillery: Major-General von Zimmermann.
Commanding Engineer: Major Treumann.

13th Infantry Division: Lieut.-General von Glümer.

25th Brigade: Major-General Baron v. d. Osten Sacken.
  1st Westphalian Infantry regiment, No. 13.
  Hanoverian Fusilier regiment, No. 73.
26th Brigade: Major-General Baron v. d. Goltz.
  2nd Westphalian Infantry regiment, No. 15.
  6th Westphalian Infantry regiment, No. 55.
Attached to Division:
  7th Westphalian Jäger battalion.
  1st Westphalian Hussar regiment, No. 8.
  Five batteries (two heavy, two light, and one horse-artillery) of the 7th field-artillery regiment.
2nd Field-pioneer company, 7th corps, with entrenching tool-column.
3rd Field-pioneer company, 7th corps.

14th Infantry Division: Lieut.-General von Kamecke.

27th Brigade: Major-General von François.
  Lower Rhine Fusilier regiment, No. 39.
  1st Hanoverian Infantry regiment, No. 74.
28th Brigade; Major-General von Woyna.
  5th Westphalian Infantry regiment, No. 53.
  2nd Hanoverian Infantry regiment, No. 77.
Attached to Division:
  Four batteries (two heavy and two light) of the 7th Westphalian field-artillery regiment.
  Hanoverian Hussar regiment, No. 15.
  1st Field-pioneer company, 7th corps, with light bridging-train.

Corps-Artillery: Colonel von Helden-Sarnowski.

Two Horse artillery, two light, and two heavy field-batteries of the 7th Field-artillery regiment.
Artillery Ammunition columns.
Infantry   „   „
    „   Pontoon   „
The 7th Westphalian train-battalion.

8TH CORPS—RHINE PROVINCES.

Infantry-General von Goeben.
Chief of Staff: Colonel von Witzendorff.
Commanding Artillery: Colonel von Kamecke.
Commanding Engineer: Lieut.-Colonel Schulz.

F f

15th Infantry Division : Lieut.-General von Weltzien.

29th Brigade : Major-General von Wedell.
　East Prussian Fusilier regiment, No. 33.
　7th Brandenburg Infantry regiment, No. 60.
30th Brigade : Major-General von Strubberg.
　2nd Rhine Province Infantry regiment, No. 28.
　4th Magdeburg Infantry regiment, No. 67.
Attached to Division :
　8th Rhine Province Jäger battalion.
　King's Hussar regiment (1st Rhine), No. 7.
　Four batteries (two heavy, two light) of 8th Field-Artillery regiment.
　2nd Field-pioneer company, 8th corps, with entrenching tool-
　column.

16th Infantry Division : Lieut.-General von Barnekow.

31st Brigade : Major-General Count Neidhardt v. Gneisenau.
　3rd Rhine Province Infantry regiment, No. 29.
　7th Rhine Province Infantry regiment, No. 69.
32nd Brigade : Colonel von Rex.
　Hohenzollern Fusilier regiment, No. 40.
　4th Thuringian Infantry regiment, No. 72.
Attached to Division :
　2nd Rhine Hussar regiment, No. 9.
　Four batteries (two heavy, two light) of 8th Field-artillery regiment.
　1st Field-pioneer company, 8th corps, with light bridging-train.
　3rd Field-pioneer company, 8th corps.

Corps Artillery : Colonel von Broecker.

Two batteries of horse-artillery, two heavy and two light field batteries,
　of the 8th Field-artillery regiment.
Artillery, Infantry, and pontoon columns belonging to the 8th Field-
　artillery regiment.
The 8th, Rhenish, train-battalion.

3RD CAVALRY DIVISION.

Lieut.-General Count v. d. Gröben.

6th Cavalry Brigade : Major-General von Mirus.
　Rhine Prov. Cuirassier regiment, No. 8.
　　,,　　,, Uhlan regiment, No. 7.
7th Cavalry Brigade : Major-General Count zu Dohna.
　Westphalian Uhlan regiment, No. 5.
　2nd Hanoverian Uhlan regiment, No. 14.
One battery of horse-artillery of the 7th Westphalian Field-artillery
　regiment.

1ST CORPS—EAST PRUSSIA.

Cavalry-General Baron von Manteuffel.
Chief of Staff : Lieut.-Colonel v. d. Burg.
Commanding Artillery : Major-General von Bergmann.
Commanding Engineer : Major Fahland.

1st Infantry Division : Lieut.-General von Bentheim.

1st Brigade : Major-General von Gayl.
　Crown Prince's Grenadier regiment (1st East Prussian), No. 1.
　5th East Prussian Infantry regiment, No. 41.

2nd Brigade : Major-General von Falkenstein.
　2nd East Prussian Grenadier regiment, No. 3.
　6th　　,,　　　,,　　Infantry regiment, No. 43.
Attached to Division :
　East Prussian Jäger battalion, No. 1.
　Lithuanian Dragoon regiment, No. 1.
　Four batteries (two heavy, two light) of 1st East Prussian Field-
　　artillery regiment.
　2nd Field-pioneer company, 1st corps, with entrenching tool-column.
　3rd Field-pioneer company, 1st corps.

2nd Infantry Division : Major-General von Pritzelwitz.

3rd Brigade : Major-General von Memerty.
　3rd East Prussian Grenadier regiment, No. 4.
　7th　,,　　　,,　　Infantry regiment, No. 44.
4th Brigade : Major-General von Zzlinitzki.
　4th East Prussian Grenadier regiment, No. 5.
　8th　,,　　　,,　　Infantry regiment, No. 45.
Attached to Division :
　East Prussian Dragoon regiment, No. 10.
　Four batteries (two heavy, two light) of 1st, East Prussian, Field-
　　artillery regiment.
　1st Field-pioneer company, 1st corps, with light bridging-train.

Corps-Artillery : Colonel Jungé.

Two batteries of horse-artillery ⎫
Two light field-batteries　　　　⎬ of 1st, East Prussian,
Two heavy　,,　　　　,,　　　　 ⎭　Field-artillery regiment.
Artillery and Infantry ammunition, and pontoon columns belonging to 1st
　Field-artillery regiment.
The 1st East Prussian train-battalion.

1st Cavalry Division.

Lieut.-General von Hartmann.

1st Cavalry Brigade : Major-General von Lüderitz.
　Queen's Cuirassier regiment (Pomeranian), No. 2.
　1st Pomeranian Uhlan regiment, No. 4.
　2nd　　,,　　　　,,　　　　No. 9.
2nd Cavalry Brigade : Major-General Baumgarth.
　East Prussian Cuirassier regiment, No. 3.
　　,,　　　,,　　Uhlan regiment, No. 8.
　Lithuanian　　,,　　　,,　　No. 12.
One battery of horse-artillery of the 1st, East Prussian, Field-artillery
　regiment.

II. ARMY.

Commander-in-Chief : Cavalry-General H.R.H. Prince Frederic Charles
　of Prussia.
Chief of Staff : Major-General von Stiehle.
Quartermaster-General : Colonel von Hertzberg.
Commanding Artillery : Lieut.-General von Colomier.
Commanding Engineer : Colonel Leuthaus.

GUARD CORPS—GENERAL.

Cavalry-General H.R.H. Prince August of Würtemberg.
Chief of Staff : Major-General von Dannenberg.
Commanding Artillery: Major-General Prince Kraft of Hohenloh
 Ingelsingen.
Commanding Engineer : Lieut.-Colonel Bogun vou Wangenheim.

1st Guard-Infantry Division : Major-General von Pape.

1st Brigade : Major-General von Kessel.
 1st regiment of Foot Guards.
 3rd　　,,　　　　,,
2nd Brigade : Major-General Baron von Medem.
 2nd regiment of Foot Guards.
 Guard Fusilier regiment.
 4th regiment of Foot Guards.
Attached to Division :
 Guard Jäger battalion.
 　,,　Hussar regiment.
 Four batteries (two heavy, two light) of Guard field-artillery regiment.
 1st Field-pioneer company of the Guard with light bridging-train.

2nd Guard-Infantry Division ; Lieut.-General von Budritzki.

3rd Brigade : Colonel Knappe von Knappstaedt.
 1st Guard Grenadier regiment (Emperor Alexander's).
 3rd　　,,　　　　,,　　　　,,　(Queen Elizabeth's).
4th Brigade : Major-General von Berger.
 2nd Guard Grenadier regiment (Emperor Francis').
 4th　　,,　　　　,,　　　　,,　(Queen's).
Attached to Division :
 Guard Rifle battalion.
 2nd Guard Uhlan regiment.
 Four batteries (two heavy, two light) of Guard field-artillery regiment.
 2nd Field-pioneer company of the Guard with entrenching tool-
  column.
 3rd Field-pioneer company of the Guard.

Guard-Cavalry Division : Lieut.-General Count v. d. Goltz.

1st Brigade : Major-General Count von Brandenburg I.
 Regiment of the Guard du Corps.
 Guard Cuirassier regiment.
2nd Brigade : Major-General H.R.H. Prince Albert of Prussia.
 1st Guard Uhlan regiment.
 3rd　　,,　　　　,,　　　　,,
3rd Brigade : Major-General Count von Brandenburg II.
 1st Guard Dragoon regiment.
 2nd　,,　　　　,,　　　　,,

Corps-Artillery : Colonel von Scherbening.

 Three batteries of horse-artillery ⎱ of the Guard field-artillery
 Two light field-batteries　　　 ⎰ regiment.
 Two heavy　,,
Artillery ammunition, Infantry ammunition, and pontoon columns of the
 Guard field-artillery regiment.
Guard train-battalion.

3RD CORPS—BRANDENBURG.

Lieut.-General von Alvensleben II.
Chief of Staff: Colonel von Voigts-Rhetz.
Commanding Artillery: Major-General von Bülow.
Commanding Engineer: Major Sabarth.

5th Infantry Division: Lieut.-General von Stülpnagel.

9th Brigade: Major-General von Döring.
    Leib.-Grenadier regiment (1st Brandenburg), No. 8.
    5th Brandenburg Infantry regiment, No. 48.
10th Brigade: Major-General von Schwerin.
    2nd Brandenburg Grenadier regiment, No. 12.
    6th Brandenburg Infantry regiment, No. 52.
Attached to Division:
    Brandenburg Jäger battalion, No. 3.
    2nd Brandenburg Dragoon regiment, No. 12.
    Four batteries (two heavy, two light) of the Brandenburg Field-artillery regiment, No. 3.
    3rd Field-pioneer company, 3rd corps.

6th Infantry Division: Lieut.-General Baron von Buddenbrock.

11th Brigade: Major-General von Rothmaler.
    3rd Brandenburg Infantry regiment, No. 20.
    Brandenburg Fusilier regiment, No. 35.
12th Brigade: Colonel von Bismarck.
    4th Brandenburg Infantry regiment, No. 24.
    8th Brandenburg Infantry regiment, No. 64.
Attached to Division:
    1st Brandenburg Dragoon regiment, No. 2.
    Four batteries (two heavy, two light) of the Brandenburg field-artillery regiment, No. 3.
    2nd Field-pioneer company, 3rd corps, with entrenching tool-column.

Corps-Artillery: Colonel von Dresky.

Two batteries of horse-artillery ⎫
Two heavy field-batteries   ⎬ of the Brandenburg field-
Two light „   „   ⎭ artillery regiment, No. 3.
    1st Field-pioneer company, 3rd corps, with light bridging-train.
Artillery ammunition, Infantry ammunition, and pontoon columns of the Brandenburg field-artillery regiment, No. 3.
Brandenburg train battalion.

4TH CORPS—SAXON PROVINCES AND ANHALT.

Infantry-General von Alvensleben I.
Chief of Staff: Colonel von Thile.
Commanding Artillery: Major-General von Scherbening.
Commanding Engineer: Lieut-Colonel von Eltester.

7th Infantry Division: Lieut.-General von Grosz von Schwarzhoff.

13th Brigade: Major-General von Vorries.
    1st Magdeburg Infantry regiment, No. 26.
    3rd Magdeburg Infantry regiment, No. 66.
14th Brigade: Major-General von Zychlinski.
    2nd Magdeburg Infantry regiment, No. 27.
    Anhalt Infantry regiment, No. 93.

Attached to Division :
  Magdeburg Jäger battalion, No. 4.
  Westphalian Dragoon regiment, No. 7.
  Four batteries (two heavy, two light) of the Magdeburg field-artillery
    regiment.
  2nd Field-pioneer company, 4th corps, with entrenching tool-column.
  3rd Field-pioneer company, 4th corps.

8th Infantry Division : Lieut.-General von Schöler.

15th Brigade : Major-General von Kessler.
  1st Thuringian Infantry regiment, No. 31.
  3rd   „   „   „   No. 71.
16th Brigade : Colonel von Scheffler.
  Schleswig-Holstein Fusilier regiment, No. 86.
  7th Thuringian Infantry regiment, No. 96.
Attached to Division :
  Thuringian Hussar regiment, No. 12.
  Four batteries (two heavy, two light) of the Magdeburg field-artillery
    regiment, No. 4.
  1st Field-pioneer company, 4th corps, with light bridge-train.

Corps-Artillery : Colonel Crusius.

Two batteries of horse-artillery ⎫ of the Magdeburg field-artillery
Two light field-batteries   ⎬ regiment, No. 4.
Two heavy „   „   ⎭
Artillery ammunition, infantry ammunition, and pontoon columns belong-
ing to Magdeburg field-artillery regiment, No. 4.
Magdeburg train-battalion, No. 4.

9TH CORPS—SCHLESWIG-HOLSTEIN AND HESSE.

Infantry-General von Manstein.
Chief of Staff: Major Bronsart von Schellendorf.
Commanding Artillery : Major-General Baron von Puttkammer.
Commanding Engineer : Major Hutier.

18th Infantry Division : Lieut.-General Baron von Wrangel.

35th Brigade : Major-General von Blumenthal.
  Magdeburg Fusilier regiment, No. 36.
  Schleswig Infantry regiment, No. 84.
36th Brigade : Major-General von Below.
  2nd Silesian Grenadier regiment, No. 11.
  Holstein Infantry regiment, No. 85.
Attached to Division :
  Lauenburg Jäger battalion, No. 9.
  Magdeburg Dragoon regiment, No. 6.
  Four batteries (two heavy, two light) of Schleswig-Holstein field-
    artillery regiment, No. 9.
  2nd Field-pioneer company, 9th corps, with entrenching tool-column.
  3rd Field-pioneer company, 9th corps.

Hessian Division (25th) : Lieut.-General Prince Louis of Hesse.

49th Brigade : Major-General von Wittich.
  1st Infantry regiment (Body Guard).
  2nd   „   „   (Grand Duke's).
  1st (Guard) Jäger battalion.

50th Brigade : Colonel von Lynker.
   3rd Infantry regiment.
   4th   „   „
   2nd Jäger battalion.
(25th) Cavalry Brigade : Major-General Baron von Schlotheim.
   1st Reiter regiment (Guard Chevauxlegers).
   2nd „   „ (Leib Chevauxlegers).
   One battery of horse-artillery.
   Five field-batteries (two heavy, three light).
   Pioneer company with light field bridge-train.

Corps-Artillery : Colonel von Jagemann.

One battery of horse-artillery ⎫
Two light field-batteries   ⎬ of the Schleswig-Holstein field-
Two heavy „   „   ⎭ artillery regiment, No. 9.

10TH CORPS—HANOVER, OLDENBURG, AND BRUNSWICK.

Infantry-General von Voigts-Rhetz.
Chief of Staff : Lieut.-Colonel von Caprivi.
Commanding Artillery : Colonel Baron v. d. Becke.
Commanding Engineer : Lieut.-Colonel Cramer.

19th Infantry Division : Lieut.-General von Schwartzkoppen.
37th Brigade : Colonel Lehmann.
   East Frisian Infantry regiment, No. 78.
   Oldenburg Infantry regiment, No. 91.
38th Brigade : Major-General von Wedell.
   3rd Westphalian Infantry regiment, No. 16.
   8th   „   „   „   No. 57.
Attached to Division :
   1st Hanoverian Dragoon regiment, No. 9.
   Four batteries (two heavy, two light) of Hanoverian field-artillery
      regiment, No. 10.
   2nd Field-pioneer company, 10th corps, with entrenching tool-
      column.
   3rd Field-pioneer company, 10th corps.

20th Infantry Division : Major-General von Kraatz-Koschlau.
39th Brigade : Major-General von Woyna.
   7th Westphalian Infantry regiment, No. 56.
   3rd Hanoverian Infantry regiment, No. 79.
40th Brigade : Major-General von Diringshofen.
   4th Westphalian Infantry regiment, No. 17.
   Brunswick Infantry regiment, No. 92.
Attached to Division :
   Hanoverian Jäger battalion, No. 10.
   2nd Hanoverian Dragoon regiment, No. 16.
   Four batteries (two heavy, two light) of Hanoverian field-artillery
      regiment, No. 10.
   1st Field-pioneer company, 10th corps, with light bridge-train.

Corps-Artillery : Colonel Baron v. d. Goltz.

Two batteries of horse-artillery ⎫
Two heavy field-batteries   ⎬ of Hanoverian field-artillery
Two light „   „   ⎭ regiment, No. 10.
Artillery and Infantry ammunition columns belonging to Hanoverian
   field-artillery regiment, No. 10.
Hanoverian train-battalion, No. 10.

12TH CORPS—KINGDOM OF SAXONY.

Infantry-General H.R.H. the Crown Prince of Saxony, afterwards Prince George.
Chief of Staff: Lieut.-Colonel von Zeschwitz.
Commanding Artillery: Major-General Köhler.
Commanding Engineer: Major Klemna.

1st *Infantry Division*, No. 23: Lieut.-General H.R.H. Prince George of Saxony, afterwards Major-General von Montbé.

1st Brigade, No. 45: Major-General von Craushaar.
    1st (Leib) Grenadier regiment, No. 100.
    2nd (King William of Prussia) Grenadier regiment, No. 101.
    Rifle (Fusilier) regiment, No. 108.
2nd Brigade, No. 46: Colonel von Montbé.
    3rd Infantry regiment (Crown Prince's), No. 102.
    4th   ,,   ,,   No. 103.
Attached to Division:
    1st Reiter regiment (Crown Prince's).
    Four batteries (two heavy, two light) of 12th field-artillery regiment.
    2nd company of 12th Pioneer battalion with entrenching tool-column.
    4th company of 12th Pioneer battalion.

2nd *Infantry Division*, No. 24: Major-General Nehrhoff von Holderberg.

3rd Brigade, No. 47: Major-General Tauscher.
    5th Infantry regiment (Prince Frederic August's), No. 104.
    6th Infantry regiment, No. 105.
    1st Jäger battalion (Crown Prince's), No. 12.
4th Brigade, No. 48: Colonel von Schulz.
    7th Infantry regiment (Prince George's), No. 106.
    8th   ,,   ,,   No. 107.
    2nd Jäger battalion, No. 13.
Attached to Division:
    2nd Reiter regiment.
    Four batteries (two heavy, two light) of 12th field-artillery regiment.
    3rd company of 12th Pioneer battalion with light bridge-train.

Cavalry Division, No. 12: Major-General Count Lippe.

1st Cavalry Brigade, No. 23: Major-General Krug von Nidda.
    Guard Reiter regiment.
    1st Uhlan regiment, No. 17.
2nd Cavalry Brigade, No. 24: Major-General Senfft von Pilsach.
    3rd Reiter regiment.
    2nd Uhlan regiment, No. 18.
Attached to Division:
    One battery of horse-artillery of 12th field-artillery regiment.

Corps-Artillery: Colonel Funcke.

One battery of horse-artillery ⎫
Three light field-batteries ⎬ of the 12th field-artillery regiment.
Three heavy ,,   ,, ⎭
Artillery and infantry ammunition, and pontoon columns of the 12th field-artillery regiment.
12th train-battalion.

5TH CAVALRY DIVISION.

Lieut.-General Baron von Rheinbaben.

11th Cavalry Brigade : Major-General von Barby.
Westphalian Cuirassier regiment, No. 4.
1st Hanoverian Uhlan regiment. No. 13.
Oldenburg Dragoon regiment, No. 19.
12th Cavalry Brigade : Major-General von Bredow.
Magdeburg Cuirassier regiment, No. 7.
Altmark Uhlan regiment, No. 16.
Schleswig-Holstein Dragoon regiment, No. 13.
13th Cavalry Brigade : Major-General von Redern.
Magdeburg Hussar regiment, No. 10.
2nd Westphalian Hussar regiment, No. 11.
Brunswick Hussar regiment, No. 17.
Attached to Division :
Two batteries horse-artillery.

6TH CAVALRY DIVISION.

Lieut.-General H.S.H. Duke William of Mecklenburg-Schwerin.
14th Cavalry Brigade : Major-General Baron von Diepenbroick-Grüter.
Brandenburg Cuirassier regiment, No. 6 (Emp. Nicholas I. of Russia).
1st Brandenburg Uhlan regiment, No. 3 (Emperor of Russia).
Schleswig-Holstein Uhlan regiment, No. 15.
15th Cavalry Brigade : Major-General von Rauch.
Brandenburg Hussar regiment, No. 3 (Zieten's Hussars).
Schleswig-Holstein Hussar regiment, No. 16.
Attached to Division :
One battery of horse-artillery.

2ND CORPS—POMERANIA.

Infantry-General von Fransecky.
Chief of Staff: Colonel von Wichmann.
Commanding Artillery : Major-General von Kleist.
Commanding Engineer : Major Sandkuhl.

3rd Infantry Division: Major-General von Hartmann.

5th Brigade : Major-General von Koblinski.
Grenadier regiment : King Frederic William IV. (1st Pomeranian),
No. 2.
5th Pomeranian Infantry regiment, No. 42.
6th Brigade : Colonel v. d. Decken.
3rd Pomeranian Infantry Regiment, No. 14.
7th Pomeranian Infantry regiment, No. 54.
Attached to Division :
Pomeranian Jäger battalion, No. 2.
Neumark Dragoon regiment, No. 3.
Four batteries (two heavy, two light) of the 2nd Pomeranian field-
artillery regiment.
1st Field-pioneer company, 2nd corps, with light bridge-train.

4th Infantry Division: Lieut.-General Hann von Weyhern.

7th Brigade : Major-General du Trossel.
Colberg Grenadier regiment (2nd Pomeranian), No. 9.
6th Pomeranian Infantry regiment, No. 49.

8th Brigade: Major-General von Kettler.
    4th Pomeranian Infantry regiment, No. 21.
    8th Pomeranian Infantry regiment, No. 61.
Attached to Division:
    Pomeranian Dragoon regiment, No. 11.
    Four batteries (two heavy, two light) of Pomeranian field-artillery
      regiment, No. 2.
    2nd Field-pioneer company, 2nd corps, with entrenching tool-column.
    3rd Field-pioneer company, 2nd corps.

Corps-Artillery: Colonel Petzel.

Two batteries of horse-artillery } of the Pomeranian field-artillery
Two light field-batteries   } regiment, No. 2.
Two heavy „   „   }
Artillery and infantry ammunition and pontoon columns of Pomeranian
field-artillery regiment, No. 2.
Pomeranian train-battalion, No. 2.

III. ARMY.

Commander-in-Chief: Infantry-General H.R.H. the Crown Prince of
    Prussia.
Chief of Staff: Lieut.-General von Blumenthal.
Quartermaster-General: Colonel von Gottberg.
Commanding Artillery: Lieut.-General Herkt.
Commanding Engineer: Major-General Schulz.

5TH CORPS—POSEN AND LIEGNITZ.

Lieutenant-General von Kirchbach.
Chief of Staff: Colonel v. d. Esch.
Commanding Artillery: Colonel Gaede.
Commanding Engineer: Major Owstein.

9th Infantry Division: Major-General von Sandrart.

17th Brigade: Colonel von Bothmer.
    3rd Posen Infantry regiment, No. 58.
    4th   „   „   „   No. 59.
18th Brigade: Major-General von Voigts-Rhetz.
    King's Grenadier regiment (2nd West Prussian), No. 7.
    2nd Lower Silesian Infantry regiment, No. 47.
Attached to Division:
    1st Silesian Jäger battalion, No. 5.
    1st Silesian Dragoon regiment, No 4.
    Four batteries (two heavy, two light) of the Lower Silesian field-
      artillery regiment, No. 5.
    1st Field-pioneer company, 5th corps, with light bridge-train.

10th Infantry Division: Lieut.-General von Schmidt.

19th Brigade: Colonel von Henning auf Schönhoff.
    1st West Prussian Grenadier regiment, No. 6.
    1st Lower Silesian Infantry regiment, No. 46.
20th Brigade: Major-General Walther von Montbary.
    Westphalian Fusilier regiment, No. 37.
    3rd Lower Silesian Infantry regiment, No. 50.

Attached to Division :
  Kurmark Dragoon regiment, No. 14.
  Four batteries (two heavy, two light) of field-artillery regiment, No. 5.
  2nd Field-pioneer company, 5th corps, with entrenching tool-column.
  3rd   „   „   „   „

· *Corps-Artillery :* Lieut.-Colonel Köhler.

Two batteries of horse-artillery ⎫
Two light field-batteries   ⎬ of the Lower Silesian field-
Two heavy „   „   ⎭ artillery regiment, No. 5.

Artillery and infantry ammunition, and pontoon columns of field-artillery regiment, No. 5.
Lower Silesian train-battalion, No. 5.

11TH CORPS—HESSE, NASSAU, SAXE-WEIMAR, &c.

Lieut.-General von Bose.
Chief of Staff: Major-General Stein von Kaminski.
Commanding Artillery : Major-General Hausmann.
Commanding Engineer : Major Crüger.

21st Infantry Division : Lieut.-General von Schachtmeyer.

41st Brigade : Colonel von Koblinski.
  Hessian Fusilier regiment, No. 80.
  1st Nassau Infantry regiment, No. 87.
42nd Brigade : Major-General von Thiele.
  2nd Hessian Infantry regiment, No. 82.
  2nd Nassau Infantry regiment, No. 88.
Attached to Division :
  Hessian Jäger battalion, No. 11.
  2nd Hessian Hussar regiment, No. 14.
  Four batteries (two heavy, two light) of Hessian field-artillery regiment, No. 11.
  1st Field-pioneer company, 11th corps, with light bridge-train.

22nd Infantry Division : Lieut.-General von Gersdorff.

43rd Brigade : Colonel von Kontzki.
  2nd Thüringian Infantry regiment, No. 32.
  6th   „   „   „ No. 95.
44th Brigade : Major-General von Schkopp.
  3rd Hessian Infantry regiment, No. 83.
  5th Thüringian „   „   No. 94.
Attached to Division :
  1st Hessian Hussar regiment, No. 13.
  Four batteries (two heavy, two light) of Hessian field-artillery regiment.
  2nd Field-pioneer company, 11th corps, with entrenching tool-column.
  3rd Field-pioneer company, 11th corps.

Corps-Artillery : Colonel von Oppeln-Bronikowski.

Two batteries of horse-artillery ⎫
Two light field-batteries   ⎬ of Hessian field-artillery
Two heavy „   „   ⎭ regiment, No. 11.

Artillery and Infantry ammunition, and pontoon columns of 11th field-artillery regiment.
Hessian train-battalion, No. 11.

1st BAVARIAN CORPS.

Infantry-General Baron von der Tann-Rathsamhausen.
Chief of Staff: Lieut.-Colonel von Heinleth.
Director of Field-Artillery: Major-General von Malaisé.
Director of Engineers: Lieut.-Colonel Riem.

1st Infantry Division : Lieut.-General von Stephan.

1st Brigade: Major-General Dietl.
    Infantry body-guard regiment.
    Two battalions of 1st Infantry regiment (King's).
    2nd Jäger battalion.
2nd Brigade: Major-General von Orff.
    2nd Infantry regiment (Crown Prince's).
    Two battalions of 11th Infantry regiment (v. d. Tann).
    4th Jäger battalion.
Attached to Division :
    9th Jäger battalion.
    3rd Chevauxlegers regiment (Duke Maximilian's).
    Two 4-pounder and two 6-pounder batteries.

2nd Infantry Division : Lieut.-General Count Papponheim.

3rd Brigade : Major-General Schumacher.
    3rd Infantry regiment (Prince Charles of Bavaria).
    Two battalions of 12th Infantry regiment (Queen Amalie of Greece).
    1st Jäger battalion.
4th Brigade: Major-General Baron von der Tann.
    10th Infantry regiment (Prince Louis).
    Two battalions of 13th Infantry regiment (Emperor Francis Joseph of Austria).
    7th Jäger battalion.
Attached to Division :
    4th Chevauxlegers regiment (King's).
    Two 4-pounder and two 6-pounder batteries.
Cuirassier Brigade : Major-General von Tausch.
    1st Cuirassier regiment (Prince Charles of Bavaria).
    2nd   ,,   ,,   (Prince Adalbert).
    6th Chevauxlegers regiment (Grand Duke Constantine Nicolaju-sitch).
    One battery of horse-artillery.

Brigade of Reserve-Artillery : Colonel Bronzetti.

1st Division. Two 6-pounder, one 4-pounder battery.⎫
2nd   ,,   Two 6-pounder batteries.   ⎬ 42 guns.
3rd   ,,   Two 6-pounder batteries.   ⎭
1st Field-Engineer Division.

2ND BAVARIAN CORPS.

Infantry-General von Hartmann.
Chief of Staff: Colonel Baron von Horn.
Director of Field-Artillery: Major-General Lutz.
Director of Field-Engineering : Lieut.-Colonel Fogt.

3rd Infantry Division : Lieut.-General von Walther.

5th Brigade : Major-General von Schleich.
    6th Infantry regiment (King William of Prussia).
    Two battalions of 7th Infantry regiment (Hohenhausen).
    8th Jäger battalion.

6th Brigade : Colonel Borries von Wissell.
Two battalions of 14th Infantry regiment (Hartmann).
15th Infantry regiment (King John of Saxony).
3rd Jäger battalion.
Attached to Division :
1st Chevauxlegers regiment (Emperor Alexander of Russia).
Two 4-pounder and two 6-pounder batteries.

4th Infantry Division: Lieut.-General Count von Bothmer.
7th Brigade : Major-General von Thiereck.
Two battalions of 5th Infantry regiments (Grand Duke of Hesse).
9th Infantry regiment (Werde).
6th Jäger battalion.
8th Brigade : Major-General Maillinger.
3rd battalion of 1st Infantry regiment.

3rd	,,	,, 5th	,,	,,
1st	,,	,, 7th	,,	,,
3rd	,,	,, 11th	,,	,,
3rd	,,	,, 14th	,,	,,

5th Jäger battalion.
Attached to Division :
10th Jäger battalion.
2nd Chevauxlegers regiment.
Two 4-pounder and two 6-pounder batteries.
Uhlan Brigade : Major-General Baron von Mulzer.
1st Uhlan regiment (Archduke Nicholas of Russia).
2nd Uhlan regiment (King's).
5th Chevauxlegers regiment (Prince Otto's).
One battery of horse-artillery.
Brigade of Reserve Artillery : Colonel von Pillement.
1st Division :
One 4-pounder horse-artillery battery.
Two 6-pounder field batteries.
2nd Division :
Two 6-pounder field batteries.
3rd Division :
Two 6-pounder field batteries.
2nd Field-Engineer Division.

WÜRTEMBERG DIVISION.
Lieut.-General von Obernitz.

Chief of Staff : Colonel von Friebig.
1st Brigade : Major-General von Reitzenstein.
1st Infantry regiment (Queen Olga) (two battalions).
7th ,, ,, (two battalions).
2nd Jäger battalion.
2nd Brigade : Major-General von Strakloff.
2nd Infantry regiment (two battalions).
5th ,, ,, (King Charles's battalion).
3rd Jäger battalion.
3rd Brigade : Major-General Baron von Hügel.
3rd Infantry regiment (two battalions).
8th ,, ,, ,,
1st Jäger battalion.
Cavalry Brigade : Major-General Count von Schéler.
1st Reiter regiment (King Charles) (four squadrons).
2nd ,, ,, (King William) (two ,,).
4th ,, ,, (Queen Olga) (four ,,).

Artillery.

1st Field-artillery Division :
   Two 4-pounder and one 6-pounder batteries.
2nd Field-artillery Division :
   Two 4-pounder and one 6-pounder batteries.
3rd Field-artillery Division :
   Two 4-pounder and one 6-pounder batteries.

BADEN DIVISION. [1]

Lieut.-General von Beyer.

Chief of Staff : Lieut.-Colonel von Lesxczynski.
1st Brigade : Lieut.-General du Jarrys Baron La Roche.
   1st Leib Grenadier regiment.
   Fusilier battalion of 4th Infantry regiment.
   2nd Grenadier regiment (King of Prussia).
Combined (3rd) Brigade : Major-General Keller.
   3rd Infantry regiment.
   5th   „   „
Attached to Division :
   3rd Dragoon regiment (Prince Charles).
   Four batteries (two heavy, two light).
   Company of pontooners with light bridge-train and entrenching tool-
       column.
Cavalry Brigade : Major-General Baron La Roche-Starkenfels.
   1st Leib Dragoon regiment.
   2nd Dragoon regiment (Margrave Maximilian).
   One battery of horse-artillery.

Corps-Artillery.

Two heavy and two light field batteries.

4TH CAVALRY DIVISION.

Cavalry-General H.R.H. Prince Albert of Prussia.

8th Cavalry Brigade : Major-General von Hontheim.
   West Prussian Cuirassier regiment, No. 5.
   Posen Uhlan regiment, No. 10.
9th Cavalry Brigade : Major-General von Bernhardi.
   West Prussian Uhlan regiment, No. 1.
   Thuringian Uhlan regiment, No. 6.
10th Cavalry Brigade : Major-General von Krosigk.
   2nd Leib Hussar regiment, No. 2.
   Rhine Province Dragoon regiment, No. 5.
Two batteries of horse-artillery.

6TH ARMY CORPS—SILESIA.

Cavalry-General von Tümpling.
Chief of Staff: Colonel von Salviati.
Commanding Artillery : Colonel von Ramm.
Commanding Engineer : Major Albrecht.

---

[1] Subsequently many changes in the commands.

11th Infantry Division : Lieut.-General von Gordon.

21st Brigade : Major-General von Malachowski.
  1st Silesian Grenadier regiment, No. 10.
  1st Posen Infantry regiment, No. 18.
22nd Brigade : Major-General von Eckartsberg.
  Silesian Fusilier regiment, No. 38.
  4th Lower Silesian Infantry regiment, No. 51.
Attached to Division :
  2nd Silesian Jäger battalion, No. 6.
  2nd Silesian Dragoon regiment, No. 8.
  Four batteries (two heavy, two light) of the Silesian field-artillery regiment, No. 6.
  3rd Field-pioneer company, 6th corps.

12th Infantry Division : Lieut.-General von Hoffmann.

23rd Brigade : Major-General Gündell.
  1st Upper Silesian Infantry regiment, No. 22.
  3rd   ,,   ,,   ,,   ,,   No. 62.
24th Brigade : Major-General von Fabeck.
  2nd Upper Silesian Infantry regiment, No. 23.
  4th   ,,   ,,   ,,   ,,   No. 63.
Attached to Division :
  3rd Silesian Dragoon regiment, No. 15.
  Four batteries (two heavy, two light) of the Silesian field-artillery regiment, No. 6.
  1st Field-pioneer company, 6th corps, with light bridge-train.
  2nd Field-pioneer company, 6th corps, with entrenching tool-column.

Corps-Artillery : Colonel Arnold.

Two batteries of horse-artillery ⎫
Two light field-batteries   ⎬ of the Silesian field-artillery
Two heavy ,,   ,,   ⎭ regiment, No. 6.
Artillery and Infantry ammunition, and pontoon columns of Silesian field-artillery regiment.
Silesian train battalion, No. 6.

2ND CAVALRY DIVISION.

Lieut.-General Count Stolberg-Wernigerode.

3rd Cavalry Brigade : Major-General von Colomb.
  Silesian Leib Cuirassier regiment, No. 1.
  Silesian Uhlan regiment, No. 2.
4th Cavalry Brigade : Major-General Baron von Barnekow.
  1st Leib Hussar regiment, No. 1.
  Pomeranian Hussar regiment (Blucher's Hussars), No. 5.
5th Cavalry Brigade : Major-General von Baumbach.
  1st Silesian Hussar regiment, No. 4.
  2nd   ,,   ,,   ,,   No. 6.
Two batteries of horse-artillery.

THE END.